# STRATEGIC
# CORPORATE
# SOCIAL
# RESPONSIBILITY

*Thea C. Werther,*
*who understands the idea of*
*responsibility in all its dimensions.*
*and*
*Taiko Chandler*
♥ Δ ☺ ∞ ▱ ⇨ ⑤

# STRATEGIC
# CORPORATE
# SOCIAL
# RESPONSIBILITY

*Stakeholders in a Global Environment*

WILLIAM B. WERTHER, JR. ● DAVID CHANDLER

*University of Miami*

**SAGE** Publications
Thousand Oaks ■ London ■ New Delhi

*For information:*

Sage Publications, Inc.
2455 Teller Road
Thousand Oaks, California 91320
E-mail: order@sagepub.com

Sage Publications Ltd.
1 Oliver's Yard
55 City Road
London EC1Y 1SP
United Kingdom

Sage Publications India Pvt. Ltd.
B-42, Panchsheel Enclave
Post Box 4109
New Delhi 110 017  India

Printed in the United States of America

*Library of Congress Cataloging-in-Publication Data*

Werther, William B.
Strategic corporate social responsibility: Stakeholders in a global environment /
William B. Werther, Jr. and David B. Chandler.
    p. cm.
Includes bibliographical references and index.
ISBN 978-1-4129-1372-0 (cloth) — ISBN 978-1-4129-1373-7 (pbk.)
    1. Social responsibility of business. 2. Social responsibility of business—Case studies.
I. Chandler, David B. II. Title.
HD60.W46 2006
658.4′08—dc22                                                    2005019006

This book is printed on acid-free paper.

09   8   7   6   5   4   3

| | |
|---|---|
| *Acquisitions Editor:* | Al Bruckner |
| *Editorial Assistant:* | MaryAnn Vail |
| *Production Editor:* | Diane S. Foster |
| *Developmental Editor:* | Katja Fried |
| *Copy Editor:* | Robert Holm |
| *Typesetter:* | C&M Digitals (P) Ltd. |
| *Proofreader:* | Libby Larson |
| *Indexer:* | Molly Hall |
| *Cover Designer:* | Candice Harman |

# CONTENTS

# LIST OF FIGURES

# FOREWORD

**W**hat is the busy business leader to make of this phenomenon known as corporate social responsibility (CSR)? In many places, it has become defined by the process of giving money away, and yet people talk about there being a business case. It focuses on meeting the demands of stakeholders, and yet stakeholders are capricious. They change their minds. They can punish you today for doing precisely what they demanded of you yesterday. And then there are other voices that will seek to persuade you that the entire CSR movement is a cunning antibusiness plot—a Trojan horse driven by campaign groups (NGOs) to force businesses to act against their own interests. At best, it is a movement full of jargon and incomprehensible to all but the most seasoned of commentators. In short, it is surely a lot easier to get back onto the hamster wheel of meeting the next quarter's results and leave such arcane matters to someone else.

Increasing numbers of businesses have begun to discover that this is simply not an option. They have found themselves faced with enormous dilemmas that go to the heart of their business model. CSR is no longer defined—if it ever really was—by the process of how much money a business gives away but by how that business makes its money in the first place. It is not only about the programs to reduce emissions or to invest in a local school, it is about how the company resolves the dilemmas around its core product or service, how that product is produced, and how and to whom it is marketed.

For instance, the food industry has found itself under attack for being part of the problem of growing levels of obesity. There is discussion about whether marketing to children should be allowed at all. The pharmaceuticals, which have a business model that uses profit to fuel constant innovation in new drugs and treatments, have found themselves attacked for daring to make that profit from lifesaving medicines that people cannot afford. Every industry has its issues—live and emerging—which potentially affect a business's license to operate.

CSR is therefore about sustainable wealth creation. It is about making products and services in a way that can be sustained socially and environmentally and which will be supported by broader society. Resolving dilemmas among the competing interests of stakeholders means that difficult, often very strategic, decisions need to be taken.

*Strategic Corporate Social Responsibility* goes a long way toward clearing away the fog. William Werther and David Chandler help us to realize that once you see CSR in terms of its strategic implications for the core business you realize that well-understood business principles apply.

It is a sign of the immaturity of the CSR movement overall that anyone should think otherwise. We fully accept that marketing campaigns, for example, will achieve their objectives only if the message is right, if the product positioning meets a mood or a real need. And so it is that skill in execution is an important part of how CSR principles are applied. There is no automatic lever to be pulled, resulting in a surge of goodwill and cash to the bottom line. CSR is about managing the relationships that are central to the future success of the business, and initiatives taken in its name can go disastrously wrong if badly performed. William Werther and David Chandler provide a valuable list of case studies that, unusually for these sorts of works, provides a real focus on those that did badly and those that have struggled against the odds, not just the (often self-proclaimed) examples of best practice.

The important thing is that expectations in this area can be managed. The qualities that make for good leadership in any conventionally understood sense will serve the business well in how it develops key relationships. Proactive engagement in emerging issues is the most successful approach. The establishment of understanding and trust during the easy times makes it a lot more likely that people will support you when the inevitable problem occurs.

Good management, however, is not enough. Strategic CSR demands that the company must take stock of the real fundamentals, what it is in business to achieve. There is no reason to be defensive about a core imperative to make a profit. Millions of ordinary citizens depend on company profits through savings and pension funds, and the wealth that businesses create through goods and services, leading to jobs in the community, makes a real contribution to the societies where they operate. Many business leaders become deeply frustrated when the argument is advanced for more philanthropic activities on the basis that business should "put something back." They see business putting a lot in rather than taking out.

The starting point for any responsible business must be to be profitable. Programs run in the name of CSR that damage profits, leading to business failure, job losses, and worse, are the very opposite of responsible business practice.

But the act of creating profits is not the full story. It is perfectly possible to create short-term profits while eroding the resource base on which they ultimately depend or by abusing trust and being careless to the consequences. There are changing expectations on businesses: that they will manage their overall impact on society, that they will aim to maximize the positive contributions and minimize the negative, and in addition, that they will act as genuine corporate citizens, using their skills, resources, and other assets to help to resolve common problems. This is the case whether those problems are global issues like climate change or local ones like crime or poor education. And companies should respond to these expectations, because ultimately it is good for business if these problems can be tackled. As Gandhi said, they are common problems, and there will either be common solutions or no solutions.

That is why the anticorporate movement is just plain wrong. Environmental sustainability and poverty eradication will not be achieved by the forces of good somehow "defeating" the corporations. In many aspects, the leadership companies are ahead of the politicians and even the NGOs in framing the opportunities inherent in the need to find solutions to problems. Where CSR is healthiest, it is because it has been led by business—with business leaders coming together in partnership with others to make a difference.

But businesses are still more often seen as part of the problem rather than part of the solution, and CSR is still more often seen as a nice-to-do add-on. It takes real leadership to take CSR to the strategic level—to frame the purpose of the business as being to create profit by doing good business in every sense of the word. This timely book comes as a welcome boost for all of those who see this as the real challenge of CSR.

*—Mallen Baker*
Development Director, Business in the Community
Editor, *Business Respect*

# PREFACE

## WHY CORPORATE SOCIAL RESPONSIBILITY MATTERS

Corporate social responsibility (CSR) represents nothing less than an attempt to define the future of our society. Corporate citizenship, as CSR is also called, matters because it influences all aspects of business. And businesses matter because they create much of the wealth and well-being in society. As such, CSR is increasingly crucial to both business and societal success.

Central to the concept of CSR is deciding where companies fit within the social fabric. By addressing business ethics, corporate governance, environmental concerns, and other issues, society creates a dynamic context in which firms operate. The context is *dynamic* because the ideal mix of business goals and societal expectations evolve over time. Along the way, complex questions arise: Why does a business exist? Is the goal simply to maximize profits? Or do for-profits serve other goals? Who defines the boundaries between private profits and the public good? What obligations do businesses have to the societies in which they operate? To whom are companies ultimately accountable? Restated, should businesses focus on shareholders alone, or are there other stakeholders who matter? Can the interests of firms, owners, and other stakeholders be aligned, or are they inherently in conflict?

Businesses are largely responsible for creating wealth and driving progress within society; however, they do not act alone. Governments are crucial because they set the rules and parameters within which society and businesses operate. In addition, nonprofit or nongovernmental organizations (NGOs) exist to do social good without seeking profit or fulfilling the duties of a government organization, reaching where politics and profit do not. Nevertheless, without the innovations capitalism inspires, social and economic progress declines. Without the great wealth-producing engines of business, the taxes and charity needed to run government and nonprofits would fade away, in time reducing our standard of living to some primitive level. A simple example "thought experiment" underscores these points: Look around and subtract everything produced by businesses. What is left? Or another example: What is the difference between the poorest and wealthiest nations? Is it not primarily the productivity and innovations of businesses set in a societal-defined context?

Businesses produce much of what is good in our society. At the same time, businesses can also cause great harm, as pollution, layoffs, industrial accidents, and other consequences amply demonstrate. When these toxic by-products become onerous to society, nonprofits may emerge to ameliorate the harm; however, their dependence on external funding often limits these organizations. Alternatively, governments react by regulating business operations. But, as legislation to address social ills indicates, the reach of government is often slow and not always effective. Only after public consensus is reached does political will follow. Yet a successful alignment of dynamic business self-interest and general social benefit creates a win-win situation, as when a new lifesaving drug emerges from the profit motive.

Between the great good and terrible harm businesses produce lies concern about the proper role of corporations in society, particularly as globalization, technological innovation, and other changes expand their reach and potential. Moreover, this concern has gained renewed attention after the high-level accounting and other scandals that emerged in the early years of the new century. Three events illustrate a conscious determination to reassert the importance of socially responsible behavior and ethics in business: (a) the passage of Sarbanes-Oxley (2002), which has added stringent and costly requirements to final reporting by publicly traded firms; (b) requirements by the Securities and Exchange Commission (2003) that companies disclose whether or not they have implemented a code of ethics; and (c) revised federal sentencing guidelines in the United States (2004), which "require companies to make stronger commitments to ethical standards and prove they are living up to those commitments."[1] The impact of these changes is reflected in the growth of the Ethics Officers Association (http://www. eoa.org/), a professional association for those responsible for ethics within organizations, which has grown to more than 1,200 members since being founded in 1992.[2] And, although ethics has become a prominent concern within business, it is but one element of the broad scope associated with CSR.

At one narrow extreme, the Nobel Prize–winning economist Milton Friedman argues, "Few trends could so thoroughly undermine the very foundations of our free society as the acceptance by corporate officials of a social responsibility other than to make as much money for their stockholders as possible."[3] At the other end of the spectrum, corporations are increasingly expected to act with a multiple-constituency approach—embracing the needs and concerns of employees, shareholders, lenders, suppliers, customers, communities, and the wider environment in which they operate. Which perspective is ideal? Which is right? Are the two positions necessarily mutually exclusive? Perhaps, more accurately, what is the best mix of the two that produces a sustainable society, which maximizes the benefit and welfare for all?

*Strategic Corporate Social Responsibility* provides a framework within which readers can explore and answer these questions for themselves. This book identifies the key issues of CSR, models them around conceptual frameworks, and provides both the means and the (re)sources for exploring this ever changing topic of importance. As your journey of exploration will reveal, even simple answers are colored by honest debate, wherein reasonable, honorable, and well-intentioned people disagree and, sometimes, disagree vehemently.

What makes this exploration exciting is that CSR is as topical as this morning's headlines. Jobs and job losses, corruption and scientific breakthroughs, pollution and technological innovations, personal greed and corporate charity, all spring from the relentless drive for innovation in pursuit of profit that we call "business." CSR is also as fluid as the news, with companies faring well regarding some aspects of CSR, while falling foul in other areas. For the purposes of this book, however, failure in one area of CSR does not preclude a company from being studied in those areas in which it excels.

CSR brings you to the cutting edge, where corporate competencies mold the business strategies that enable firms to compete with each other. And, when they compete in the marketplace, CSR offers a sustainable path between unbridled capitalism, with its mixed consequences, and rigidly regulated economies plagued with artificial and stifling limitations. CSR helps businesses optimize both the *ends* of profit and the *means* of execution. And, as we will argue further, forces are afoot that heighten the importance of optimizing this balance *today,* which will make CSR considerations even more important *tomorrow.*

Still, the question remains: What issues matter under the broad heading of corporate social responsibility? The answer, we believe, depends on the for-profit's industry and its strategy, or *how* it delivers value to its customers. But, since these both vary widely, the appropriate mix of issues will differ from firm to firm and change as firms adapt their strategy and execution to their specific business context. The result? It is impossible to prescribe the exact CSR mix to deal with the landscape any single firm is likely to face. Instead, we argue that a strategic lens offers the best viewpoint through which to study CSR and a firm's increasingly turbulent business environment.

Hence, we view *strategic CSR* from a stakeholder perspective that embraces an external environment made up of many constituent groups, all of whom have a stake in the business's profit-seeking activity. Who are the stakeholders in each situation? Which claims are legitimate? Who decides legitimacy? We believe these and other issues force business thinkers to understand CSR from a stakeholder vantage point that is set against the backdrop of each firm's industry and strategy.

A *stakeholder perspective,* viewed through a strategic lens, conveys the complexity of balancing competing interests in forming company policy, regardless of whether CSR is taught as a separate course or as a supplement to a capstone corporate strategy or public policy course. Still, two additional constraints remain:

- How to cover the broad range of topics that fall under the CSR banner without being encyclopedic?
- How to organize a book that maximizes learning and interest for today's computer-literate reader?

What makes *Strategic Corporate Social Responsibility* a unique roadmap for this journey is our approach and underlying thesis: Exploration is the best form of learning. We focus on the technological innovation that makes CSR more relevant today than ever before: the Internet. In these pages, you will find scores of issues, case studies, and Internet-based resources. We believe, rather than laying out each issue in detail, computer-literate readers will prefer the original sources. By seeking out the Web sites and documentation (online), readers will become more engaged and better placed to construct their own informed opinions. If you are one who likes to form your own opinions, then *Strategic Corporate Social Responsibility* is a guide to help you on your way. It intends first to provoke you and then present you with a roadmap of questions, examples, case studies, and signposts to guide your Internet-based search for solutions and examples.

In our own search, we have found that there are no simple answers and few absolutes regarding the questions that arise in these pages. Where simple solutions are prescribed, unintended consequences usually arise. Many answers are relative to a specific industry and to the specific situation in which each company finds itself. And even when answers exist, they inevitably are a result of tradeoffs among competing stakeholder freedoms with few parties emerging completely satisfied. Few solutions are applicable across the board.

An ancient Chinese proverb:

> Give a hungry man a fish,
> And he eats today;
> Teach him to fish,
> And he eats today and tomorrow.

In that spirit, this book does not seek solutions to the pressing CSR problems of today. Undoubtedly, such solutions would be generalizations of limited use, quickly outdated by changing societal expectations. Rather, we present a stakeholder perspective as the most effective means of understanding the bigger picture of strategic CSR. If we have been successful in our task, we believe this sensitivity to external claimants and an analysis of their claims is the CSR equivalent of teaching to fish for today and tomorrow.

Understanding the issues at hand and the past mistakes made by companies, as well as possessing a structural framework that allows an overall perspective, is crucial for your avoiding these same mistakes in the future. Likewise, companies that are successful in addressing CSR today will provide guidance on how best to deal with issues yet to arise.

The journey you are about to undertake will help equip you for a business world that is changing at an accelerating rate. It will increase your understanding and sophistication as a thinker, as a businessperson, and as an informed citizen.

*William B. Werther Jr.*
*David Chandler*

---

If you have any questions or comments concerning the content of this publication, please feel free to contact William B. Werther Jr. at werther@miami.edu

---

## Disclaimer

An important feature of this book is its many Internet-based resources. Relying on such resources, however, presents two specific issues: First, due to the dynamic nature of the Internet, some of the URLs provided will change or disappear over time. One resource for tracking down missing Web sites is the digital library being created by Internet Archive (http://www.archive.org/). Second, in order to present a balanced and varied selection of resources for further investigation, we have provided links to many organizations in this book. It is not our intention to endorse these organizations or validate their messages in any way but rather to present their voice as part of the ongoing debate relating to each particular issue.

## NOTES

1.    Newsdesk, 'Ethics officers—a growing breed?,' *Ethical Corporation Magazine,* February 7, 2005, http://www.ethicalcorp.com/content.asp?ContentID=3466
2.    Ibid.
3.    Friedman, Milton, 'Capitalism and Freedom,' University of Chicago Press, 1962, p. 133.

# PLAN OF THE BOOK

*S*trategic Corporate Social Responsibility is organized into three parts. Part I of the book highlights the scope of corporate social responsibility (CSR). Chapter 1 discusses different viewpoints about CSR, outlining the reasons for and against. It identifies why CSR is a growing concern to students and leaders of business. Though businesses are economic entities that exist to meet needs in society and further the financial interests of their owners, we argue that the most effective way to achieve this today is by considering the needs and values of key stakeholder groups. These other *nonowner* stakeholders are vital because they can affect the success, even the survival, of the business. Most important, this chapter defines CSR in light of the global, Internet, and communications-driven environment that corporations operate within today.

Chapter 2 looks at the anti-CSR argument by asking the question, Do stakeholders care about CSR? The economic argument for CSR presupposes an economic advantage for a company that is a net contributor to society, or at least a belief that there is economic disadvantage for any company that negatively affects key stakeholder groups. Managers, as suggested by advertising campaigns and philanthropic activities, already understand the benefits for businesses that are perceived as making a positive contribution. Although many people say they want responsible companies, however, there are limits to what societies and consumers are willing to pay for the privilege. This willingness to pay for social responsibility is arguable and central to the CSR debate. Without sufficient stakeholder interest in CSR behavior, corporations have less incentive to embrace CSR.

Chapter 3 places CSR within a strategic context, arguing that CSR exists, or should exist, within the strategic framework of the organization. As the firm matches its capabilities with the opportunities in its competitive environment, it pursues its mission in order to move the firm toward its aspirations, or vision. CSR is an integral part of this strategic process because it serves to filter how businesses interact with their environments and implement their ideas. Whereas strategy seeks competitive success, CSR acts as a screen that helps ensure profit motives do not harm the firm's long-term viability. Planetwide trends of increased affluence, globalization, the Internet, massive media conglomeration, and branding combine to heighten the strategic importance of CSR today. Moreover, these trends increase the importance of CSR in the future.

Chapter 4 concludes Part I by exploring the challenges of integrating CSR into the firm's competitive strategies and its organizational culture. Here our intent is to identify the factors that strengthen or impede the creation of a strategic CSR orientation at the firm level. Central to this integration process is the commitment of senior management. Strategic direction, mission statements, and day-to-day operating policies must all reinforce this commitment to attaining CSR goals. Ultimately, in order to integrate CSR into the firm's strategies and its culture, leaders must start an ongoing dialog within the organization and with key stakeholders about the strategic and operational importance of CSR. This chapter provides a framework for implementing an effective CSR policy throughout the organization.

Part II begins with a list of issues that define CSR in practice, each broken down into one of the three stakeholder groups: organizational, economic, or societal stakeholders. Chapter 5 contains issues primarily involving organizational stakeholders; Chapter 6, economic stakeholders; and Chapter 7, societal stakeholders. Each issue is illustrated with a real-life mini–case study and supporting sources. Differing viewpoints are also available via the Web sites provided.

Part II also reveals the unique nature of the book. We believe that the scope of CSR is a mosaic of issues. Which issues are most important today or tomorrow evolve with changes in society and the competitive environment. Moreover, given individual student and faculty interests, our approach in Part II is to introduce issues briefly and then provide Internet-accessible source material as a link to further investigation.

Chapter 8 completes Part II, offering a number of additional corporate examples of CSR in action. These brief examples are broken down into four sections highlighting companies that are (a) implementing CSR effectively, (b) being criticized for their CSR efforts, (c) trying to do CSR right but ultimately failing, and (d) persevering with CSR against all the odds.

Part III of the book is a value-added appendix that makes this publication an appropriate addition to any professional or business library. It offers a variety of information sources focused on the specific subject of CSR, divided into three sections: (a) a directory of CSR-focused organizations with Web site references, (b) online CSR news and information sources, and (c) a more traditional bibliography of published sources (journal articles and books) about CSR.

Part III is intended as an additional resource for the reader interested in information beyond the case study references and URLs provided throughout the book. In such a rapidly evolving field, however, it is foolhardy to attempt to present exhaustive accounts. The lists in the appendix are not presented as complete but intended as stepping stones to help the eager reader delve farther into this complex subject.

# ACKNOWLEDGMENTS

This book was produced with the cooperation and support of the University of Miami Ethics Programs (http://www.miami.edu/ethics/).

Though we remain ultimately responsible for the structure, concepts, and methodology of *Strategic Corporate Social Responsibility*, the project would not have been possible without the help of many others. Begun by one of the authors as a project for the University of Miami's Ethics Programs, this research has morphed into the book before you.

Crucial to the development of this publication has been the support of the School of Business Administration at the University of Miami and, in particular, the role played by Dean Paul Sugrue. We also extend our thanks to Dr. Linda Neider, Chair of the Management Department, and to Dr. Rene Sacasas, Chair of the Business Law Department. Without the Business School's support, the classroom laboratory where these ideas were tested, and the encouragement of colleagues, *Strategic Corporate Social Responsibility* would not have been possible.

We would like also to express our sincere gratitude to Professors Ken Goodman and Anita Cava, Codirectors of the University of Miami Ethics Programs, for creating the opportunity and environment that helped germinate many of the ideas contained within this book. We would particularly like to thank Anita Cava of the University of Miami's Business Law Department for doing so much to make this project possible.

We are especially appreciative of the support of the Provost's Office at the University of Miami and the willingness to grant the authors copyright permission to use these materials. Without Provost Luis Glaser's authorization, this book would not have happened.

Professor William Frederick of the Joseph M. Katz Business School at the University of Pittsburgh provided valuable and objective support as many of these ideas took shape. As one of the founders of the CSR/business and society field, his input was of particular value to the authors.

Others who reviewed drafts of the book and offered beneficial advice are Dr. Jennifer Bremer of the University of North Carolina at Chapel Hill; Dr. Linda Clarke of Florida International University; David Grayson, coauthor of *Corporate Social Opportunity!*; Dr. Michael Hopkins, Chair and CEO of MHC International Ltd; and Marjorie Kelly, editor of *Business Ethics* magazine. This publication is a better product because of their insights and involvement.

Al Bruckner, MaryAnn Vail, and Katja Fried at Sage Publications were incredibly supportive of this project from the beginning and greatly assisted in ensuring it came to fruition. Diane Foster and Robert Holm formed the wonderful editing team that converted our computer files into this finished book. The professionalism and efficiency of all involved helped make the process as painless as possible, while guiding us toward the finish line.

Many thanks to Reid Cushman, also of the University of Miami Ethics Programs, who early on pushed for a distinction between a moral and an economic argument for CSR and for both to be equally convincing. The research assistance of Adrienne Englert and Michael Karavolos was extremely helpful.

Our gratitude also extends to Dean James Foley, Jeanne Batridge, and the Office of Undergraduate Academic Services in the School of Business Administration at the University of Miami for their support and friendship, and for their subscription to the *Wall Street Journal*!

We would like to express our continued appreciation and admiration for Daniella Levine and Barbara Garrett and the work they do through the Human Services Coalition of Miami-Dade County (http://www.hscdade.org/), the Greater Miami Prosperity Campaign (http://www.prosperitycampaign.com/), and Community Prosperity Initiative (http://www.prosperitycampaign.com/cpi.htm). Their tireless progress and constant innovation are building an environment in Miami where many of the ideas expressed in this book are becoming reality.

Finally, we would like to thank Leonard Turkel—mentor, *social entrepreneur,* and Codirector of the Center for Nonprofit Management at the University of Miami (http://nonprofit.miami.edu/)—who ceaselessly finds ways of bettering both his community and the people around him. We deeply appreciate his catalytic role in this project and in our lives.

# Part I

# WHAT IS CORPORATE SOCIAL RESPONSIBILITY?

**P**art I of *Strategic Corporate Social Responsibility* highlights the scope of corporate social responsibility (CSR). Chapter 1 identifies the different viewpoints of CSR and then shows why CSR is of growing concern to business students and leaders. Though businesses are economic entities that exist to further the financial interests of their owners, it is not their sole concern. Without the balance of a multistakeholder approach, firms can become exploitive, antisocial, and corrupt, losing legitimacy and their ability to pursue the economic goals of the owners over the long term.

Chapter 2 explores some of the arguments *against* business involvement with CSR. Expectations about CSR appear in different ways in different cultures and play out on a firm-by-firm, industry-by-industry basis. Businesses that embrace CSR can be a source of pride, retention, and invigoration for members inside the firm and are also more likely to engender the support of external stakeholders.

Chapter 3 places CSR in a strategic context. Pursuit of the firm's mission must strike a balance between economic ends and socially acceptable means. Restated, strategy seeks competitive success, whereas CSR acts as a filter that helps ensure profit-directed actions do not harm stakeholders and the firm's viability over the long term.

Chapter 4 presents a plan to integrate CSR into the firm's competitive strategies and organizational culture. Central to that integration process is strong senior management commitment. Ultimately, if CSR is to be an integral part of the firm's culture and strategies, leaders must start an ongoing dialog within the organization and with its key stakeholders about the strategic and operational importance of CSR.

# Chapter 1

## TOWARD A RESPONSIBLE SOCIETY

**P**eople create organizations to leverage their collective resources in pursuit of common goals. As organizations pursue these goals, they interact with others inside a larger context called society. Based on their purpose, organizations can be classified as for-profits, governments, or nonprofits. At a minimum, *for-profits* seek gain for their owners; *governments* exist to define the rules and structures of society within which all organizations must operate; and *nonprofits* (sometimes called NGOs—nongovernmental organizations) emerge to achieve social good when the political will or the profit motive is insufficient to address society's needs. For example, more than 477,000 social workers are employed largely outside the public sector in the United States—many in the nonprofit community and medical organizations—filling needs not met by government or the private sector.[1]

Whether called corporations, companies, businesses, proprietorships, or firms, for-profit organizations also interact with society, affecting government, nonprofits, and other stakeholders. As R. Edward Freeman defined them, a firm's stakeholders include those who effect or are affected by the firm's goals.[2] Simply put, they include those groups that have a stake in the firm's operations (see Figure 1.1).

As the impact of business on society has grown, the range of stakeholders whose concerns a company needs to address has fluctuated from the narrow view of owners to a broader range of constituents (including employees and customers) and back again, at the end of the 20th century, to a disproportionate focus on shareholders. Today, companies once again are beginning to adopt a broader stakeholder outlook, extending their perspective to include constituents such as the communities in which they operate.

Just because an individual or organization meets this definition of an "interested constituent," however, does not compel a firm (either legally or logically) to comply with every stakeholder demand. Nevertheless, affected parties ignored long enough may take action, such as product boycotts, against the firm or turn to government for redress. In democratic societies, laws (such as antidiscrimination statutes), rulings by government agencies (such as the Internal Revenue Service's tax exempt regulations for nonprofits), and judicial interpretations (such as court rulings on the liabilities of board members) cumulatively provide a minimal framework for business operations that reflects a rough consensus of the governed. Because government cannot anticipate every possible interaction, however, legal action takes

**Figure 1.1** A Firm's Stakeholders

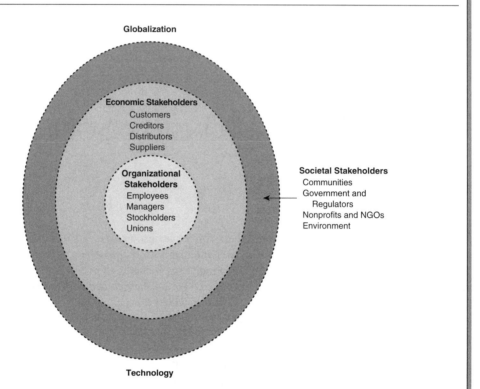

A firm has three kinds of stakeholders: organizational stakeholders (internal to the firm) and economic and societal stakeholders (external to the firm).

Together, the three kinds of stakeholders form a concentric set of circles with the firm's organizational stakeholders at the center within a larger circle signifying the firm's economic stakeholders. Both of these circles sit within the largest outside circle, which represents society and the firm's societal stakeholders. Therefore, a firm's employees are, first and foremost, organizational stakeholders. They are also, however, occasional customers of the company, as well as members of the society within which the firm operates. The government that regulates the firm's industry, however, is only a societal stakeholder and has no economic relationship with the company, nor is it any formal part of the organization.

The firm's economic stakeholders represent the interface between the organizational and societal stakeholders. Therefore, a firm's customers are, first and foremost, economic stakeholders of the firm. They are not organizational (internal) stakeholders, but they are part of the society within which the firm operates. They are also one of the primary means by which the firm delivers its product and interacts with its society.

Without the economic interface, an organization loses its mechanism of accountability and, therefore, its legitimacy over the long term. This is true regardless of whether the organization is a business, government, or nonprofit.

The three layers of a firm's stakeholders all sit within the larger context of a globalizing business environment, driven by revolutionary technology that is raising the importance of CSR for businesses today.

time, and a general consensus is often slow to form; regulatory powers often lag behind the need for action. This is particularly so in areas of rapid change, such as information technology and medical research. Thus, we arrive at the discretionary area of decision making that businesses face on a day-to-day basis and two questions from which the study of corporate social responsibility (CSR) springs:

- What is the relationship between a business and the societies within which it operates?
- What responsibilities do businesses owe society to self-regulate their actions in pursuit of profit?

CSR is both critical and controversial. It is critical because the for-profit sector is the largest and most innovative part of any free society's economy: It drives social progress and affluence. Companies intertwine with the societies in which they operate in mutually beneficial ways. The term *company* comes from a combination of the Latin words *cum* and *panis,* the literal translation of which originally meant "breaking bread together."[3] Today, the meaning of a company implies a far greater degree of complexity. Companies create most of the jobs, wealth, and innovations that enable the larger society to prosper. They are the primary delivery system for food, housing, medicines, medical care, and other necessities of life. Without modern day corporations, the jobs, taxes, donations, and other resources that support governments and nonprofits would dramatically decline, significantly affecting the wealth and well-being of society as a whole. Businesses are the engines of society that propel us toward a better future.

In growing recognition of this mutually beneficial interdependence, corporate and academic alliances are being formed, in addition to professional associations and investment research, that underscore the importance of CSR. For example:

The European Academy of Business in Society (EABIS)—an alliance of leading companies and business schools working together on corporate responsibility—[in 2005] launched a 1 million euro, 3 year partnership. . . . The launch comes at a time when corporate responsibility is rapidly moving up the management education agenda in business schools and companies are increasingly stressing the need to develop new knowledge and skills for current and future leaders on this topic.[4]

At the same time, however, controversy remains. People who have thought deeply about "Why does a business exist?" or "What is the purpose of business within society?" do not agree on the answers. Do companies have obligations beyond the benefits their economic success already provides? Although the Nobel Prize–winning economist Milton Friedman argued against CSR in the 1960s because it distracted leaders from economic goals, a more balanced view comes from Dave Packard, a cofounder of Hewlett-Packard:

I think many people assume, wrongly, that a company exists simply to make money. While this is an important result of a company's existence, we have to go deeper and find the real reasons for our being. As we investigate this, we inevitably conclude that a group of people get together and exist as an institution that we call a company so that they are able to accomplish something collectively that they could not accomplish separately—they make a contribution to society, a phrase which sounds trite but is fundamental.[5]

## WHAT IS CSR?

The entirety of CSR can be discerned from the three words this phrase contains: *corporate, social,* and *responsibility.* CSR covers the relationship between corporations (or other large organizations) and the societies with which they interact. CSR also includes the responsibilities that are inherent on both sides of these relationships. CSR defines *society* in its widest sense, and on many levels, to include all stakeholder and constituent groups that maintain an ongoing interest in the organization's operations. Figure 1.2 provides an elaboration of the related theories and terminology surrounding CSR.

---

**Figure 1.2**   CSR—Terminology, Concepts, and Definitions[6]

---

Consistent definitions, labels, and vocabulary have yet to be solidly established in the field of CSR, although these issues are increasingly being addressed as the problem becomes more widely recognized. The range of competing terminology that is used is a source of confusion and disagreement. In our research, we have seen CSR referred to in many ways:

- "Corporate responsibility" or "business responsibility"
- "Corporate citizenship" or "global business citizenship"
- "Corporate community engagement"
- "Community relations"
- "Corporate stewardship"
- "Social responsibility"

Brief definitions of the key CSR concepts, as well as other CSR-related labels, are detailed below in an attempt to provide the reader with the language applied within the field. These concepts and terms are widely discussed in the CSR literature and referred to throughout this book:

*Advocacy advertising:* Efforts by firms to communicate their political, social, or business arguments with the intent of positioning the company favorably in the eyes of the public or to sway the public toward their point of view.

*Business citizenship:* Societal-oriented actions by firms seeking to be seen by their stakeholders as constructive members of society.

*Business ethics:* The application of ethics and ethical theory to the decisions of business.

*Cause-related marketing:* Efforts to gain customers by tying purchases of the firm's goods or services to a benefit provided by the firm to a nonprofit organization or charity as, for example, when a proportion of sales are donated to an identified cause.

*Civic engagement:* Efforts by employees to improve communities in which the firm operates.

*Coalitions:* Collections of firms, stakeholders, or individuals collaborating to achieve common goals.

*Community advocacy panels (CAPS):* Formal or informal groups of citizens who advise organizations about areas of common interest. Topics range widely but can be collectively defined as matters in which the organization's existence affects the local community.

*Consumerism:* Efforts by actual or potential customers to be represented in organizational decision making. The overarching collection of consumer activism is also referred to as the "consumer movement," which has given rise to consumer rights and laws.

*Corporate citizenship:* See *Business citizenship.*

*Corporate governance:* The structure and systems that officially allocate power within organizations and manage the relationships between the owners and managers of a business.[7]

*Corporate philanthropy:* Contributions by firms that benefit stakeholders and the community, usually through financial or in-kind donations to nonprofit organizations.

*Corporate responsibility:* A term similar in meaning to *corporate social responsibility* but preferred by some companies.

*Corporate social responsibility (CSR):* The broad concept that businesses are more than just profit-seeking entities and, therefore, also have an obligation to benefit society (see *Strategic corporate social responsibility*).

*Corporate sustainability:* Business operations that can be continued over the long term without degrading the ecological environment.

*Enlightened self-interest:* Without forsaking economic goals leading to financial success, businesses can operate in a socially conscious manner.

*Ethics:* A guide to moral behavior based on culturally embedded definitions of right and wrong.

*Globalization:* The process by which organizations transcend nation boundaries in their communication and operations.

*Iron law of social responsibility:* The axiom that suggests that those who use power in ways society deems to be abusive will eventually lose their freedom or power to continue acting in that way.

*Nongovernmental organizations (NGOs):* Organizations that pursue social good exclusively rather than profits or the political requirements of government, although many of the activities conducted by an NGO might be government programs or receive government funding. For example, an NGO might help feed the poor after a disaster, although this activity may be seen as a governmental task in other societies or under other conditions (see *Nonprofits*).

*Nonprofits:* Organizations that exist to meet societal needs rather than seek profits for their owners or the political concerns of government. Nonprofits often differ from NGOs by having a domestic, rather than international, focus.

*Public policy:* Government decisions aimed at establishing rules and guidelines for action with the intent of providing benefit (or preventing harm) to society.

*Stakeholders:* Those who have an effect on, or are affected by, a firm's actions.

*Strategic corporate social responsibility:* The idea that CSR should be integrated into the firm's strategic perspective and operations because of the long-term benefit this brings to the organization.

*Strategic planning:* The process (often annual) whereby firms create or reformulate plans for future time periods.

*Sweatshops:* Operations that employ children or apply working standards deemed to be unsafe, unfair, or harsh—often as viewed from the perspective of more affluent societies.

*Transparency:* The extent to which organizational decisions and operating procedures are open or visible to outsiders.

*Triple bottom line:* An evaluation of businesses by comprehensively assessing their financial, environmental, and social performance.

*Values:* Beliefs about appropriate goals, actions, and conditions.

*Whistleblower:* An insider who alleges organizational misconduct and communicates those allegations of wrongdoing outside the firm to the media, prosecutors, or others.

Stakeholder groups range from clearly defined consumers, employees, suppliers, creditors, and regulating authorities to other more amorphous constituents such as local communities and even the environment. For the firm, tradeoffs must be made among these competing interests. Issues of legitimacy and accountability exist, with many nonprofit organizations, for example, claiming expertise and demanding representative status, even when it is unclear exactly how many people support their vision or claims. Ultimately, however, each firm must identify those stakeholders that constitute its operating environment and then prioritize their strategic importance to the organization. Increasingly, firms need to incorporate the concerns of stakeholder groups within the organization's strategic outlook or risk losing societal legitimacy. CSR helps firms embrace these decisions and adjust the internal strategic planning process to maximize the long-term viability of the organization. Consider some different viewpoints:

> The notion of companies looking beyond profits to their role in society is generally termed corporate social responsibility (CSR). . . . It refers to a company linking itself with ethical values, transparency, employee relations, compliance with legal requirements and overall respect for the communities in which they operate. It goes beyond the occasional community service action, however, as CSR is a corporate philosophy that drives strategic decision-making, partner selection, hiring practices and, ultimately, brand development. (*South China Morning Post,* 2002)[8]

> CSR is about businesses and other organizations going beyond the legal obligations to manage the impact they have on the environment and society. In particular, this could include how organizations interact with their employees, suppliers, customers and the communities in which they operate, as well as the extent they attempt to protect the environment. (*The Institute of Directors,* UK, 2002)[9]

> The social responsibility of business encompasses the economic, legal, ethical, and discretionary expectations that society has of organizations at a given point in time. (Archie B. Carroll, 1979)[10]

Figure 1.3 elaborates on Archie Carroll's conceptual framework. This useful typology is not rigid, however; issues can, and do, evolve over time.

CSR is, therefore, a fluid concept. Importantly, it is both a means and an end. It is an integral element of the firm's strategy: the way the firm goes about delivering its products or services to markets (*means*). It is also a way of maintaining the legitimacy of its actions in the larger society by bringing stakeholder concerns to the foreground (*end*). The success of a firm's CSR reflects how well it has been able to navigate stakeholder concerns while implementing its business model. CSR means valuing the interdependent relationships that exist among businesses, their stakeholder groups, the economic system, and the communities within which they exist. CSR is a vehicle for discussing the obligations a business has to its immediate society, a way of proposing policy ideas on how those obligations can be met, as well as a tool by which the mutual benefits for meeting those obligations can be identified. Simply put, CSR addresses a company's relationships with its stakeholders.

CSR covers an uneven blend of issues that rise and fall in importance from firm to firm over time. Recently, ethics and corporate governance, for example, have been of growing concern to students and practitioners of CSR. This is a result of the lack of board oversight that led to a variety of accounting-related scandals being exposed during the first decade of this century. The corporate response to this heightened concern is evidenced by the rapid growth of the Ethics Officers Association, which since its founding in 1992, has grown to more than 1,200 members (http://www.eoa.org/)—much of that expansion occurring since 2000. As a result of this fluctuating blend, both as an academic study and as a managerial practice, CSR is complex and still

---

Corporate Social Responsibility Hierarchy

---

Archie Carroll, University of Georgia, was one of the first academics to make a distinction between different kinds of organizational responsibilities. He referred to this distinction as a firm's "pyramid of corporate social responsibility"[11] (adapted in Figure 1.3).

Fundamentally, a firm's responsibility is to produce an acceptable return on its owners' investment. An important component of this, within a law-based society, is a duty to act within the legal framework drawn up by the government and judiciary. Taken one step further, a firm has an ethical responsibility to *do no harm* to its stakeholders and within its operating environment. Finally, firms have a discretionary responsibility, which represents more proactive, strategic behaviors that can benefit the firm and society, or both.

One of the central theses of this book is that what was ethical, or even discretionary in Carroll's model, is becoming increasingly necessary today due to the changing environment within which businesses operate. As such, ethical responsibilities are more likely to stand on a par with economic and legal responsibilities as foundational for business success. In order to fulfill its fundamental economic obligations to owners in today's globalizing and wired world, a firm should incorporate a broader and broader stakeholder perspective within its strategic outlook. As societal expectations of the firm rise, so the penalties imposed by stakeholders for perceived CSR lapses will become prohibitive.

**Figure 1.3**   The Hierarchy of Corporate Social Responsibility

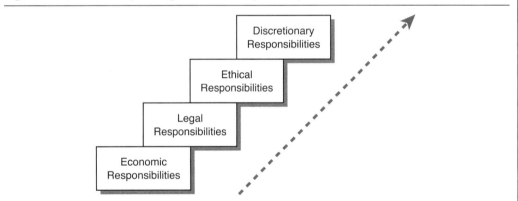

SOURCE: Archie B. Carroll, 'The Pyramid of Corporate Social Responsibility: Toward the Moral Management of Organizational Stakeholders,' *Business Horizons*, July-August, 1991.

---

evolving. It is a much broader concept than business ethics, for example (see Figure 1.2). And, because these issues affect all aspects of strategy, as well as form a key element of day-to-day operating activities, CSR's cutting edge can be controversial, especially among those stakeholders whose interests are not considered primary by decision makers.

## CORPORATE STRATEGY AND CSR

CSR is a key element of business strategy. Strategy strives to provide the business with a source of sustainable competitive advantage. For any competitive advantage to be sustainable, however, the strategy must be acceptable to the wider environment in which the firm competes. CSR done incorrectly—or worse completely ignored—may threaten whatever comparative advantage the firm holds within its industry. One hundred years ago, for example, Standard Oil Trust pressured industry suppliers to treat Standard Oil's competitors unfairly in the eyes of society. The result was a series of antitrust laws introduced by government that eventually forced Standard Oil to break into separate companies. Today, Greenpeace and other activist groups highlight corporate actions they deem to be socially irresponsible, sometimes leading to voluntary corrective action on the part of companies (such as Shell's change of course regarding the breakup of the *Brent Spar* oil platform[12]) and other times leading to legislative changes (as with the current restrictions on hunting certain whale species).[13]

## WHAT CSR IS AND IS NOT

CSR embraces the range of economic, legal, ethical, and discretionary actions that affect the economic performance of the firm (see Figure 1.3). A significant part of a firm's CSR, there-fore, is complying with the legal or regulatory requirements faced in day-to-day operations. To break these regulations is to break the law, which is not socially responsible. Clearly, adhering to the law is an important component of any ethical organization. But, legal com-pliance is merely a minimum condition of CSR.[14] *Strategic CSR* focuses more on the ethical and discretionary concerns that are less precisely defined and for which there is often no clear societal consensus.

Ideally, leaders should address stakeholder concerns in ways that carry strategic benefits for the firm. CSR is not about saving the whales or ending poverty or other worthwhile goals that are unrelated to a firm's operations and are better left to government or nonprofits. Instead, CSR is about the economic, legal, ethical, and discretionary issues stakeholders view as affecting the firm's plans and actions. The solutions to these issues, the overlap where eco-nomic benefit and social benefit meet, is at the heart of any successful CSR policy. Michael Porter and Mark Kramer outline this approach in defining "strategic corporate philanthropy," but the same approach can be applied to the wider issue of CSR:

> The acid test of good corporate philanthropy is whether the desired social change is so ben-eficial to the company that the organization would pursue the change even if no one ever knew about it.[15]

Beyond the desired changes are the *approaches* employed to achieve those changes. Too often, the end (shareholder wealth, for example) has been used to justify the means (pollut-ing the environment). Strategic CSR is concerned with both the ends of economic viability *and* the means of being socially responsible.

The connection between these two concepts is an important focus for strategic CSR, which sets it apart from other social responsibility areas. This distinction becomes apparent when discussing an issue such as ethics, which is concerned about the honesty, judgment, and integrity with which various stakeholders are treated. There is no debate: Ethical behavior is a prerequisite assumption for strategic CSR. It is hard to see how a firm's actions could be both socially responsible and unethical. Ethics, however, is not the central focus for strategic CSR, except insofar as constituents are affected or the larger society defines the firm's approaches as unethical, thus harming the firm's societal legitimacy and profit potential. Likewise, a rich body of other socially important issues also exists outside the direct focus of strategic CSR. Concerns over domestic and international income disparity, gender issues, discrimination, human rights, spirituality and workplace religiosity, technological impacts on indigenous populations, and other issues all affect societal well-being. Unless firms take actions directly affecting stakeholders in these areas, however, the study of these topics might better fall under ethics, public policy, sociology, or developmental economics courses, which are better suited to explore these complex and socially important topics in greater depth.

## THE EVOLUTION OF CSR

The need for social responsibility among businesses is not a new concept. Ancient Chinese, Egyptian, and Sumerian writings often delineated rules for commerce to facilitate trade and ensure that the wider public's interests were considered. Ever since, public concern about the interaction between business and society has grown in proportion to the growth of corporate activity:

> Concerns about the excesses of the East India Company were commonly expressed in the seventeenth century. There has been a tradition of benevolent capitalism in the UK for over 150 years. Quakers, such as Barclays and Cadbury, as well as socialists, such as Engels and Morris, experimented with socially responsible and values-based forms of business. And Victorian philanthropy could be said to be responsible for considerable portions of the urban landscape of older town centres today.[16]

Evidence of social activism in response to organizational actions also stretches back across the centuries, mirroring the legal and commercial development of companies as they established themselves as the driving force of market-based societies:

> The first large-scale consumer boycott? England in the 1790s over slave-harvested sugar. (It succeeded in forcing the importer to switch to free-labor sources.) In 1612, English jurist Edward Coke complained that corporations "cannot commit treason, nor be outlawed or excommunicated, for they have no souls."[17]

Although wealthy industrialists have long sought to balance the actions of their firms with personal or corporate philanthropy as a response to social activism or complaints, CSR ultimately originates with leaders who view their role as stewards of resources owned by others (e.g., shareholders, the environment). These leaders face a balancing act that addresses the tradeoffs between the owners (shareholders) that employ them and the society that enables their firms to prosper. When society (or even elements of society) views leaders and their firms as not meeting societal needs, activism results, whether in 18th century England or today.

Current examples of social activism in response to a perceived lack of CSR by organizations are in this morning's newspapers and TV news. Whether civil disobedience in Seattle, Turin, or Cancun protesting the impact of global corporations on developing societies, consumer boycotts of specific products deemed to have been produced in a manner counter to the public good, or NGO-led unfavorable publicity about sweatshop conditions or other unsavory operating activities permitted by branded-clothing firms, CSR has become an increasingly relevant topic in recent decades in corporate boardrooms, business school classrooms, and family living rooms.

In addition to public relations fiascos that damage a firm's sales and image, the direct financial impact of CSR failures in a litigious society is never far behind. Widespread, long-term industry practices, which may have previously been deemed discretionary or ethical concerns, can be deemed illegal or socially unacceptable under aggressive legal prosecution or novel social activism. Such violations are less likely in firms with a strong commitment to CSR. For example, the sustained campaign by New York Attorney General Eliot Spitzer against Wall Street and the financial industry in the early years of this century indicates the dangers of assuming that yesterday's accepted business practices will necessarily be acceptable to others today. Businesses operate against an ever changing background of what is considered socially responsible. CSR is not a stagnant concept. It continues to evolve as cultural expectations change, both here and abroad.

On the one hand, these ever changing standards and expectations compound the complexity faced by corporate decision makers. Worse, those standards vary from society to society, even among cultures within a given society. Faced with a kaleidoscopic background of evolving standards, business decision makers must consider a variety of factors on the way to implementation. For example, in the early history of the United States, the Alien Tort Claims Act "was originally intended to reassure Europe that the fledgling U.S. wouldn't harbor pirates or assassins. It permits foreigners to sue in U.S. courts for violations of the law of 'nations.'"[18]

Today, this 1789 law is being used to try and hold U.S. firms accountable for their actions overseas, as well as the actions of their partners (whether other businesses or governments). Thus, what may be legal, even encouraged, in one country may bring legal repercussions in another. And, this is not just an isolated example. Firms such as Citibank, Coca-Cola, IBM, JCPenny, Levi Strauss, Pfizer, Gap, Limited, Texaco, and Unocal have all faced possible suits under this same law, which may extend to hundreds of other national and international firms.[19] Unocal, the company in this list whose case had advanced the furthest in U.S. courts, announced in December 2004, on the eve of having its case heard on appeal, that it would settle for an undisclosed sum:[20]

> Lawsuits filed by 15 villagers from Myanmar . . . said the company "turned a blind eye" to atrocities allegedly committed by soldiers guarding a natural gas pipeline built by the company and its partners in the 1990s. . . . A joint statement by the two sides said Unocal would pay the plaintiffs an unspecified sum and fund programmes to improve living conditions for people living near the pipeline.[21]

Nike, more commonly, reacted to stakeholder criticism by demanding that its suppliers provide their employees with wages and working conditions that meet the expectations of consumers in developed societies—consumers who might boycott Nike products if they see the company acting unfairly to workers in poor countries by permitting low wages or poor working conditions among suppliers. Today, media and NGO activists are more likely to criticize the poor treatment of workers in developing economies by holding corporations to standards found in their home markets, especially the United States and the European Union (EU). The result is increased complexity and risk that can harm economic outcomes when CSR is lacking.

On the other hand, it is important to reinforce that the pursuit of economic gain remains an absolute necessity. CSR does not repeal the laws of economics under which for-profit organizations must operate (to society's benefit). For example, manufacturing offshore in a low-cost environment remains a valid strategic decision, particularly in an increasingly globalizing business world. Where CSR considerations play a major role is in how such decisions are made and implemented.

As societies rethink the balance between societal needs and economic progress, CSR will continue to evolve in importance and complexity. And, although this complexity muddies the wealth-creating waters, an awareness of these evolving expectations holds the potential for increased competitive advantage. The examples above indicate, however, that a sense of the cultural context within which CSR has developed is crucial.

## THE CULTURAL AND CONTEXTUAL ASSUMPTIONS

As already discussed, firms operate within the broader context of society. The resulting interaction requires a CSR perspective for firms to maintain their social legitimacy. Yet, societies differ, and so, therefore, does what they consider acceptable. Though differences range from the anthropological and sociological to the historical and demographic, two dimensions consistently influence the role of CSR: democracy and economics.

Different societies define the relationship between business and society in different ways. Unique expectations spring from many factors, with wealthy societies having greater resources and, perhaps, more demanding expectations that emerge from the greater options wealth brings. The reasoning is straightforward: In poor democracies, the general social well-being is focused on the necessities of life: food, shelter, transportation, education, medicine, social order, jobs, and the like. Governmental or self-imposed CSR restrictions add costs that poor societies can ill afford. As societies advance, however, expectations change and the *general social well-being* is redefined. This ongoing redefinition and evolution of societal expectations causes the CSR response also to evolve.

Differences in CSR expectations among rich and poor societies are a matter of priorities. For example, the need for transportation evolves into a need for nonpolluting forms of transportation as society becomes more affluent. Though poor societies value clean air just as advanced ones do, there are other competing needs that may take priority, one of which will be the need for low-cost transportation. As a society prospers economically, new expectations compel producers to make vehicles that pollute less—a shift in emphasis. In time, these expectations may evolve from a discretionary to a mandatory (legal) requirement.

---

An example: In the 1980s, air pollution in downtown Santiago, Chile, was an important issue, just as it was in Los Angeles, California. The problem, however, was addressed differently in relation to the level of economic development found in these two pollution-retaining basins. Stringent laws went into effect in the Los Angeles basin during the 1980s. At the same time in Chile, necessities (including low-cost transportation) got a higher priority because of widespread poverty. After more than a decade of robust economic growth, however, Chileans eventually used democratic processes to put limitations on the number of cars entering Santiago. This shift in priorities reflected their changing societal needs and expectations.

   This example reinforces the idea that it is in any organization's best interest (for-profit, nonprofit, or governmental) to anticipate, reflect, and strive to meet the changing needs of its stakeholders in order to remain successful. In the case of for-profits, the primary stakeholder groups are its owners (its shareholders), consumers, and employees, without which the business fails. Other constituents, however, from suppliers to the local community, also matter. Therefore, businesses must satisfy key groups among these constituents if they hope to remain viable over the long term. When the expectations of different stakeholders conflict, CSR enters a gray area and management has to balance competing interests. An example of such conflicts exists among different classes of investors in the firm, as elaborated on in Figure 1.4. We do not seek to prescribe solutions here, but merely raise key issues worth considering.

---

**Figure 1.4**   The Shareholder Shift—From Investor to Speculator

The evolving role of shareholders has greatly influenced the CSR debate and strengthened the case for adopting a broader stakeholder approach to a business's strategic outlook.

   The role of ownership has narrowed considerably over time. Shares today are less and less perceived as a long-term investment in a company and more and more as a stand-alone, short-term investment for personal benefit. A distinction can be drawn, therefore, between *investors,* who *invest* in companies with a share price that reflects sound economic fundamentals (e.g., a reasonable price-earnings (p/e) ratio, profitability, long-term planning), and *speculators,* who *gamble* on shares based on whether they think the share price will rise, irrespective of whether it deserves to go up or whether it is valued at a fair price:

> It starts with the fact that the average holding period for stocks has dropped from five years in the mid-1970s to six months today. People aren't investing in your company; they're investing in your stock. That's a huge difference.[22]

This trend was taken to an extreme during the Internet boom when share trading was driven purely by speculation and the desire to maximize investment returns. There was little attempt to establish a company's business worth or potential:

> Amazon's entire float changes hands twice a week. . . . It would take average annual profits of over $1 billion to make sense of Amazon's current $20 billion-odd market value. Yet Amazon's total sales in 1998 were only $600 million. . . . Today's appetite for equities rests on an erroneous belief that they are a one-way bet: that, in the long run, they always pay higher returns than other assets.[23]

   In these instances, is it true to say that shareholders actually *own* the company in which they are investing—in the sense that an owner wants to protect the item being held? Perhaps driven by the preponderance of institutional (versus individual) investors, there is an increasing tendency today to register indifference to the overall health of an organization and seek merely to protect the dollar investment:

> Anglo-Saxon Inc. no longer has any real owners, just a bunch of punters holding betting slips that happen to have its name on them. . . . [Shareholders] have stopped behaving like owners. This is partly because so many shares are now held by institutions, which see their job as managing money, not owning companies. . . . The trick, for success at any size, is to ensure that a company makes the best investment decisions. That is usually done when the deciders are also the owners.[24]

This changing nature of investment in companies and the evolving relationship between company and owners has seen the importance of shareholders rise to a position that is distracting for businesses. Managers now have to concentrate a disproportionate amount of their time on the short-term considerations of quarterly results, dividend levels, and share price in order to keep demanding shareholders happy, particularly in English-speaking-dominated economies. This short-term perspective often comes at the cost of long-term strategic considerations of the company and its business interests. Many observers see this development as a corruption of the fundamental purpose of a company issuing shares, as well as how those shares are later traded on the stock market. In investment and loyalty terms, the link between shareholder and company has largely disappeared, with a shrinking number of institutional and individual investors today taking the long view.

This transitory element of equity trading is taken to the extreme by the rise of day trading, a phenomenon that emerged in the United States at the height of the Internet boom,[25] but also found its way to other countries such as the UK.[26] Day trading became possible because of the rise in personal Internet access and developing communications technology. It is often conducted by "quick-triggered amateurs,"[27] with little or no expertise. It can be defined as speculation, "where investors buy shares with the express intent of selling for a quick profit, often within 24 hours."[28] Day trading presents additional compelling evidence that any link the investor has with the long-term interests of the company in which they are investing has been largely severed.[29] Short-term profit is the only goal, and the consequences for not delivering that short-term profit can be severe. As Bill George, the retired CEO of Medtronic, observed,

> They want to know why you didn't make the numbers. . . . You tell them, we're investing in our research programs for the long term. But that doesn't fly. . . . When you [miss stated targets] your stock gets inordinately punished. . . . If your earnings are up 15 percent, but they expected 20 percent, then your stock will go down—not 5 percent, but 25 percent. Then you're vulnerable to a takeover.[30]

Businesses still have a duty to provide a return for investors. It is central to their economic mission; but the idea that shareholders have the best interests of the firm at heart no longer necessarily holds true. In today's business environment, a broader stakeholder perspective will provide the stability necessary for managers to chart the best course for the company so that it remains a viable entity over the medium to long term. This is in the interests of a company's *investors* rather than those of its *speculators*.

CSR represents an argument for a firm's economic interests, where satisfying stakeholder needs becomes central to retaining societal legitimacy (and, therefore, financial viability) over the long term. Much debate (and criticism) in CSR springs from well-meaning parties arguing the same "facts" from different perspectives, breaking down along partisan and ideological lines. A brief introduction to the underlying moral, rational, and economic arguments within the CSR field follows.

## A MORAL ARGUMENT FOR CSR

Although recognizing that profits are necessary for any business to survive, it is also important to note that for-profit organizations are only able to obtain those profits because of the society in which they operate. CSR emerges from this interaction and the interdependent relationship between for-profits and society. It is shaped by individual and societal standards of morality, ethics, and values that define contemporary views of human rights and social justice.

Thus, to what extent does a business have an obligation to repay the debt it owes society for its continued business success? That is, what responsibilities do businesses face in return for the benefits society grants? And also, to what extent do the profits the business generates, the jobs it provides, and the taxes it pays already meet those obligations? As an academic study, CSR represents an organized approach to answering these questions. As an applied discipline, it represents the extent to which businesses need to deliver on their societal obligations as defined by society.

---

### A Moral Argument for CSR

CSR broadly represents the relationship between a company and the principles expected by the wider society within which it operates. It assumes businesses recognize that for-profit entities do not exist in a vacuum and that a large part of their success comes as much from actions that are congruent with societal values as from factors internal to the company.

---

Charles Handy makes a convincing moral argument for businesses going beyond the goals of maximizing profit and satisfying shareholders above all other stakeholders:

> The purpose of a business . . . is not to make a profit, full stop. It is to make a profit so that the business can do something more or better. That "something" becomes the real justification for the business. . . . It is a moral issue. To mistake the means for the end is to be turned in on oneself, which Saint Augustine called one of the greatest sins. . . . It is salutary to ask about any organization, "If it did not exist, would we invent it?" "Only if it could do something better or more useful than anyone else" would have to be the answer, and profit would be the means to that larger end.[31]

At one level, the moral argument for CSR reflects a give-and-take approach, based on a meshing of the firm's values and those of society. Society makes business possible and provides it directly or indirectly with what for-profits need to succeed, ranging from education and healthy workers to a safe and stable physical and legal infrastructure, not to mention a consumer market for their products. Because society's contributions make businesses possible, those businesses have an obligation to society to operate in ways that are deemed socially responsible and beneficial. And, because businesses operate within the larger context of society, society has the right and the power to define expectations for those who operate within its boundaries:

> Conservatives and Republicans may like to portray "wealth-producing" businesses as precarious affairs that bestow their gifts independently of the society in which they trade. The opposite is the case. The intellectual, human and physical infrastructure that creates successful companies, alongside their markets, is a social product and that, in turn, is shaped by the character of that society's public conversation and the capacity to build effective social institutions and processes.[32]

At a deeper level, societies rest upon a cultural heritage that grows out of a confluence of religion, mores, and folkways. This heritage gives rise to a belief system that defines the boundaries of socially and morally acceptable behaviors by people and organizations. Though not always codified into dogma or laws, the cultural heritage leads to an evolving definition of social justice, human rights, and environmental stewardship, the violation of which is deemed morally wrong and socially irresponsible. To violate these implicit moral boundaries can lead to a loss of legitimacy.

## A RATIONAL ARGUMENT FOR CSR

The loss of societal legitimacy can lead to the countervailing power of social activism, restrictive legislation, or other constraints on the firm's freedom to pursue its economic and other interests. Violations of ethical and discretionary standards are not just inappropriate; they present a rational argument for CSR.

Because societal sanctions, such as laws, fines, prohibitions, boycotts, or social activism, affect the firm's strategic goals, efforts to comply with societal expectations are rational, regardless of moral arguments. When compliance with moral expectations is based on highly subjective values, the rational argument rests on sanction avoidance: It may be more cost-effective, for example, to address issues voluntarily rather than wait for a mandatory requirement based on some government or judicial approach. Archie Carroll argues that businesses can wait for the legally mandated requirements and then react to them.[33] This reactive approach may permit for-profits to ignore their moral obligations and concentrate on maximizing profits or other business goals; however, it also inevitably leads to strictures being imposed that not only force mandatory compliance but often force compliance in ways that are neither preferable nor efficient from the firm's viewpoint. By ignoring the opportunity to shape and influence the debate in the short term through proactive behaviors, an organization is more likely to find its business operations and strategy hampered over the long term.

An example: One need only consider the course of affirmative action in the United States. Prior to the 1960s, businesses could discriminate against current or potential employees on the basis of race, sex, religion, age, national origin, veteran's status, pregnancy, disability, sexual preference, and other nonmeritorious criteria. Putting aside the moral concerns, doing so was a discretionary right that was legal, if far from ethical. Social activism moved these ethical and discretionary decisions into the arena of public debate and, in time, into legal prohibitions. The result for many businesses guilty of past or present discrimination meant affirmative action plans to redress racial or other imbalances in their workforce. Those organizations that lagged quickly found themselves the test case in litigation focused on institutionalizing the new legislation.

We are not suggesting firms should have been proactive to ensure discrimination remained legal. That would be a moral or ethical lapse and would have involved fighting the evolving societal consensus. Instead, the rational argument advocates self-interest in avoiding the inevitable confrontation. By not adopting a proactive (or at least accommodative) approach to fair treatment, many businesses found their behavior suddenly (and expensively) curtailed through legislation, judicial and agency interpretations, and penalties because of a failure to interpret correctly the evolving social and business environment.

---

**A Rational Argument for CSR**

CSR is a rational argument for businesses seeking to maximize their performance by minimizing restrictions on operations. In today's globalizing world, where individuals and activist organizations feel empowered to enact change, CSR represents a means of anticipating and reflecting societal concerns to minimize operational and financial limitations on business.

---

The rational argument for CSR is summarized by the *iron law of social responsibility,* which states that in a free society discretionary abuse of societal responsibilities leads, eventually, to mandated solutions.[34] Restated, in a democratic society, power is taken away from those who abuse it. The history of uprisings—from Cromwell in England, to the American and French Revolutions to the overthrow of the Shah of Iran or Saddam Hussein in Iraq— underscores the conclusion that abusers seed their own destruction.

Parallels exist in the business arena. Financial scandals centering on Enron, WorldCom, Adelphia, HealthSouth, and other U.S. businesses caused discretion-limiting laws and rulings that move previously discretionary and ethical issues into the legal arena. It has been reported that already, "Citigroup's total bill for bubble-related litigation has reached $9 billion," a figure that could go higher.[35] Perhaps most revealing is the estimate that if the bank had not settled various litigation efforts, the firm's actions could have cost as much as $54 billion.[36] Acting proactively in a socially responsible manner is a rational business response—particularly so in light of the overwhelming anecdotal evidence that discretionary abuses lead to a loss of decision-making freedoms and financial repercussions for for-profit organizations.

## AN ECONOMIC ARGUMENT FOR CSR

Summing the moral and rational arguments for CSR leads to an economic argument. To incorporate CSR into operations offers a potential point of differentiation and competitive market advantage upon which future success can be built, besides avoiding moral, legal, and other sanctions.

---

**An Economic Argument for CSR**

CSR is an argument of economic self-interest for business. CSR adds value because it allows companies to reflect the needs and concerns of their various stakeholder groups. By doing so, a company is more likely to retain its societal legitimacy, and maximize its financial viability, over the long term. Simply put, CSR is a way of matching corporate operations with societal values at a time when these parameters can change rapidly.

---

CSR influences all aspects of a business's day-to-day operations. Everything an organization does interacts with one or more of its stakeholder groups. Companies today need to build a watertight image with respect to all stakeholders. Whether as an employer, producer, buyer, supplier, or as an investment, increasingly the attractiveness and success of a company today is linked to the strength of its image and its brand(s). Concerning investments, for example, about 10% of all investment in the United States is classified as a "socially responsible investment,"[37] a phenomenon that is spreading throughout the developed world.[38] Certainly, even for those who believe that the only purpose of a business is to increase the wealth of the owners, to be perceived as socially irresponsible risks losing access to an already significant (and growing) segment of investors and their capital. CSR affects operations within a corporation because of the need to consider constituent groups. Each area builds on all the others to create a composite of the corporation in the eyes of its stakeholders.

*Strategic Corporate Social Responsibility* expounds the economic argument in favor of CSR. We believe it is the clearest of the three (moral, rational, and economic) arguments supporting CSR and emphasizes the importance of CSR for businesses today.

## WHY IS CSR IMPORTANT?

CSR is important because it influences all aspects of a company's operations. Increasingly, consumers want to buy products from companies they trust; suppliers want to form business partnerships with companies they can rely on; employees want to work for companies they respect; large investment funds want to support firms that they see as socially responsible; and nonprofits and NGOs want to work together with companies seeking practical solutions to common goals. Satisfying each of these stakeholder groups (and others) allows companies to maximize their commitment to their owners (their ultimate stakeholders), who benefit most when all of these groups' needs are being met. As Carly Fiorina, former chair and chief executive officer of Hewlett-Packard, noted,

> I honestly believe that the winning companies of this century will be those who prove with their actions that they can be profitable and increase social value—companies that both do well and do good. . . . Increasingly, shareowners, customers, partners and employees are going to vote with their feet—rewarding those companies that fuel social change through business. This is simply the new reality of business—one that we should and must embrace.[39]

CSR is increasingly crucial to success because it gives companies a mission and strategy around which multiple constituents can rally. The businesses most likely to succeed in today's rapidly evolving global environment will be those best able to balance the often conflicting interests of their multiple stakeholders. Lifestyle brand firms, in particular, need to live the ideals they convey to their consumers.

## WHY IS CSR RELEVANT TODAY?

CSR as an element of strategy is becoming increasingly relevant for businesses today because of four identifiable trends—trends that seem likely to continue and grow in importance throughout the 21st century:

### Increasing Affluence

Affluent consumers can afford to choose the products they buy and are more likely to pay a premium for a brand they trust. A poorer society, in need of work and inward investment, is less likely to enforce strict regulations and penalize organizations that might otherwise take their business and money elsewhere. Affluence matters. Increasing affluence on a global basis will make CSR matter more in the future.

## Changing Social Expectations

Consumers in developed societies expect more from the companies whose products they buy. This sense has increased in the wake of the corporate scandals at the turn of this century that reduced public trust in corporations and public confidence in the ability of regulatory agencies to control corporate excess.

## Globalization and the Free Flow of Information

The growing influence of global media conglomerates makes sure that any CSR lapses by companies are brought rapidly to the attention of the public—often instantaneously— worldwide. Scandal is news, and yesterday's eyewitnesses are today armed with pocket-size video cameras or pictures taken by mobile phones that provide all the evidence necessary to convict by TV. In addition, the Internet fuels communication among activist groups and like-minded individuals, empowering them to spread their message while giving them the means to coordinate collective action.

## Ecological Sustainability

When the Alaskan pipeline was built in the 1970s, crews could drive on the hardened permafrost 200 days a year. Today, climatic changes leave the permafrost solid for only 100 days each year. Increasing raw materials prices, rising mutation rates among amphibian populations, and other growing anecdotal evidence all suggest that the Earth has ecological limits. Whether these limits are fast approaching is a complicated issue on which the experts do not agree; however, firms that are seen as indifferent to their environmental responsibilities are likely to be criticized and penalized: by court-imposed fines (*Exxon Valdez*[40]), negative publicity (Monsanto's genetically modified foods[41]), or confrontations by activist groups (Friends of the Earth[42]).

# BEYOND TRENDS TO CONTEXT

Beyond the trends in CSR that we identify in this chapter, CSR must also work in practice. It must allow firms to prosper and also act as a conduit for stakeholder concerns. But does CSR matter to stakeholders? Are stakeholders willing to enter the debate and impose their views on corporations? Arguments *against* CSR (and the often unintended implications of progressive CSR applications) exist and will be explored in Chapter 2. Chapter 3 puts CSR into strategic perspective and expands on the growing importance of CSR and its impact on corporate strategy. Issues that influence the implementation of CSR within a strategic decision-making framework provide the basis for Chapter 4, which will conclude Part I of *Strategic Corporate Social Responsibility*.

## QUESTIONS FOR DISCUSSION AND REVIEW

1. Why do firms exist? What value do businesses serve for society?

2. Define *corporate social responsibility*. What arguments in favor of CSR seem most important to you?

3. Name the four responsibilities of a firm outlined in Archie Carroll's "Pyramid of CSR" model. Illustrate your definitions of each level with corporate examples.

4. Milton Friedman argued, "Few trends could so thoroughly undermine the very foundations of our free society as the acceptance by corporate officials of a social responsibility other than to make as much money for their stockholders as possible." Give two arguments in support of his assertion and two against.

5. Using a real-life example, list a firm's stakeholders and attempt to prioritize their importance. What criteria should be used in deciding between competing stakeholder interests?

6. Discuss briefly the primary moral, rational, and economic arguments for CSR?

7. What four factors make CSR more relevant today?

## NOTES

1. U.S. Department of Labor, Bureau of Labor Statistics, May 2005, http://stats.bls.gov/oco/ocos060.htm#emply

2. R. Edward Freeman, 'Strategic Management: A Stakeholder Approach,' Pitman, 1984, p46.

3. John Micklethwait & Adrian Wooldridge, 'The Company: A Short History of a Revolutionary Idea,' Modern Library, 2003, p8.

4. *CSRWire,* April 13, 2005, http://www.csrwire.com/article.cgi/3773.html

5. Charles Handy, 'What's a Business For?' *Harvard Business Review,* December 2002, p54.

6. For a comprehensive review of the evolution of CSR as an academic discipline see Archie B. Carroll, 'Corporate Social Responsibility: Evolution of a Definitional Construct,' *Business and Society,* Vol. 38, No. 3, September 1999, pp 268–295. Also, traditional textbooks elaborate on these issues: see James E. Post et al, 'Business and Society: Corporate Strategy, Public Policy, Ethics,' 10th edition, McGraw-Hill, 2002.

7. Corporate governance has risen to prominence within the CSR field because of high-profile corporate scandals following the Internet bubble around the turn of this century. Much of the legislative response was an attempt to redress the balance of power between management and stockholders, represented by the board of directors. This issue revisits the fundamental conflict between principals (owners) and their agents (managers), an issue that has plagued limited liability joint stock companies ever since they were established in the UK by the Companies Act of 1862 (see John Micklethwait & Adrian Woolridge, 'The Company: A Short History of a Revolutionary Idea,' Modern Library, 2003, pp xvi & xviii).

8. Michael McComb, 'Profit to Be Found in Companies That Care,' *South China Morning Post,* April 14, 2002, p5.

9. Ruth Lea, 'Corporate Social Responsibility: IoD Member Opinion Survey,' *The Institute of Directors,* UK, November, 2002, p10.

10.  Archie B. Carroll, 'A Three-Dimensional Conceptual Model of Corporate Performance,' *Academy of Management Review,* 1979, Vol. 4, No. 4, p500.

11.  Archie B. Carroll, 'The Pyramid of Corporate Social Responsibility: Toward the Moral Management of Organizational Stakeholders,' *Business Horizons,* July–August, 1991.

12.  http://archive.greenpeace.org/comms/brent/brent.html

13.  http://whales.greenpeace.org/GP_and_whales/index.html

14.  It is worth noting here, however, that actions that appear to be legally permissible may still result in lawsuits filed against firms, under obscure treaties and statutes, by innovative activists seeking to right actual or perceived wrongs. In the words of Anita Cava, law professor at the University of Miami, "It only takes a plaintiff!"

15.  Michael Porter & Mark Kramer, 'The Competitive Advantage of Corporate Philanthropy,' *Harvard Business Review,* Vol. 80, Issue 12, December 2002, p67.

16.  Adrian Henriques, 'Ten things you always wanted to know about CSR (but were afraid to ask); Part One: A Brief History of Corporate Social Responsibility (CSR),' *Ethical Corporation Magazine,* May 26, 2003, http://www.ethicalcorp.com/content.asp?ContentID=594

17.  Michael Arndt, 'An Ode to 'The Money-Spinner,' *BusinessWeek,* March 24, 2003, pp 22–23; review of 'The Company: A Short History of a Revolutionary Idea,' by John Micklethwait & Adrian Wooldridge, Modern Library, 2003.

18.  Paul Magnusson, 'Making a Federal Case Out of Overseas Abuses,' *BusinessWeek,* November 25, 2002, p78.

19.  Ibid.

20.  William Baue, 'Unocal Alien Tort Claims Act Case Settlement Boosts Corporate Accountability,' *CSRWire,* December 16, 2004, http://www.csrwire.com/sfarticle.cgi?id=1591

21.  Lisa Roner, 'Unocal settles landmark human rights suits,' *Ethical Corporation Magazine,* December 20, 2004, http://www.ethicalcorp.com/content.asp?ContentID=3312

22.  Bill George, retired CEO of Medtronic, speaking to Marjorie Kelly, 'Conversations with the Masters,' *Business Ethics,* Spring 2004, pp 4–5.

23.  *The Economist,* Editorial, January 30, 1999, pp 17–18.

24.  'Punters or Proprietors? A Survey of Capitalism,' *The Economist,* May 5–11, 1990, pp 21–23.

25.  The numbers of day traders "swelled to more than 100,000 in the late 1990s." Ianthe Jeanne Dugan, 'For Day Traders, German Index Is Overnight Sensation,' *Wall Street Journal,* October 19, 2004, pA1.

26.  At the height of the Internet boom in 1999, there were estimated to be 40,000 online share-trading accounts in the UK. This figure was expected to "grow to 700,000 within four years," according to Fletcher Research. 'Day Trading: Gambling on the Edge,' *The Independent,* July 31, 1999, p21.

27.  *Wall Street Journal,* October 19, 2004, op. cit.

28.  *The Independent,* July 31, 1999, op. cit.

29.  In a legislative reaction to the presence of growing numbers of day traders, "new Federal rules in 2001 required that people trading stocks more than four times a week keep $25,000 in their accounts at all times." *Wall Street Journal,* October 19, 2004, op. cit.

30.  *Business Ethics,* Spring 2004, pp 4–5, op. cit.

31.  Handy, op. cit.

32.  Will Hutton, 'The Body Politic Lies Bleeding,' *The Observer*, May 13, 2001, http://observer.guardian.co.uk/2001election/story/0,490038,00.html

33.  Carroll, 1979, op. cit.

34.  Keith Davis & Robert Blomstrom, 'Business and Its Environment,' McGraw-Hill, 1966.

35.  'Citi Still Has a Few Tabs to Settle Up,' *Fortune,* May 31, 2004, p38.

36.  'Rainy Day,' *The Economist,* May 15, 2004, p73.

37.  Ritchie Lowry, 'Capitalism with a Conscience: About Socially Responsible Investing,' http://www
.goodmoney.com/qna.htm

38.  'Your Guide to Socially Responsible Investing: Facts & Figures,' *SRI Compass,* http://www
.sricompass.org/trends/Factsandfigures/#number_of_funds

39.  'Corporate Social Responsibility,' http://www.hp.com/hpinfo/globalcitizenship/csr/

40.  'Images From the Exxon Valdez Oil Spill,' National Oceanic and Atmospheric Administration,
March 7, 2001, http://response.restoration.noaa.gov/photos/exxon/exxon.html

41.  'Farmers & Consumers Protest at Monsanto's Headquarters in St. Louis,' Organic Consumers
Association, August 19, 2000, http://www.organicconsumers.org/corp/monprotest.cfm

42.  'Campaigns: Corporates,' http://www.foe.co.uk/campaigns/corporates/index.html

# Chapter 2

# CSR: Do Stakeholders Care?

**W**hether stakeholders care, there are compelling reasons for firms to support CSR from a strategic perspective, as we suggested in Chapter 1. Nevertheless, unprincipled behavior, even outright disregard for CSR, does not always have a direct and immediate impact on each and every firm. Sometimes stakeholders are willing to overlook socially irresponsible behavior because other issues are more pressing. For example, an employer with terrible employment practices that are despised by employees or nearby town folk may not reap the negative consequences of its actions for many years because the jobs are vital to the well-being of the employees and their community. Just because stakeholders (employees and the local community in this example) do not react immediately does not mean that CSR is unimportant. Socially irresponsible behavior without immediate consequences does not mean that behavior is or should be condoned. It just means that other issues take precedence—for now. As circumstances or societal expectations evolve, the lack of CSR may radically change the prospects for the firm that ignores CSR. In an attempt to provide a balanced perspective, in this chapter we examine why stakeholders may not always care or, even when they do care, why they may not evidence that concern with action. We propose that not only does CSR matter in its own right but that the failure to be socially responsible from the perspective of stakeholders will at some point carry economic repercussions for any firm.

## DO STAKEHOLDERS CARE?

The argument in favor of CSR presupposes that there are benefits for a company being perceived as a net contributor to the society in which it is based. At the very least, there are economic disadvantages for firms that act contrary to the expectations of key stakeholders. Managers already understand the benefits of being perceived as an important and positive influence within a local community, as suggested by existing advertising campaign strategies and corporate philanthropy. The extent to which that perceived image differs from societal expectations measures the CSR deficit.

Although many people say they want responsible companies, however, in reality there is a limit to how much society and stakeholders are willing to impose their views and affect corporate actions. How many and how much stakeholders are willing or able to pay for socially responsible behavior is debatable. For example, consider consumers as one stakeholder group. Although it appears that the numbers of socially concerned are growing—the Co-op Bank estimated "that 2002 'ethical' consumption in the U.K. reached £19.9 billion (US$ 34.4 billion)"[1]— a large component of consumer-driven economic pressure still demands that companies compete in terms of price or other more traditional characteristics, such as quality. To what extent are investors, suppliers, and other stakeholders willing to give up benefits in the name of CSR? Are employees, creditors, regulators, and other key stakeholders always willing to exert influence when they enjoy some degree of leverage?

Many CSR advocates have relied on the moral argument for their cause, which boils down to the notion that businesses *should* act in a socially responsible manner because it is the *right* thing to do; however, values, such as judgments of right and wrong, are subjective, and can be subordinated within organizations to profit, sales, or other bottom-line considerations. Companies may wish or intend to act in a socially responsible manner for a variety of reasons, but they are more likely to commit consistently and wholeheartedly to CSR business practices if they are convinced of the rational or economic benefits of doing so. Stakeholder needs and concerns become more evident and measurable for firms when key groups are willing to support their words with actions.

## STAKEHOLDER ADVOCACY

Stakeholders best encourage CSR behavior when they represent rational or economic motives for the firm. Although this advocacy often comes from customers, investors, or other external activists, internal advocates (including founders, leaders, and employees) can also push a CSR agenda. Proponents of an economic argument for CSR believe that the most efficient means of maximizing profits is to ensure that companies meet the needs and values of the widest possible range of these stakeholders. Though firms have motives to respond to stakeholder concerns, however, stakeholders also carry a responsibility to educate themselves about a firm's activities and respond appropriately. Do stakeholders care *enough* to push their own agenda and be the fuel that drives corporations to become increasingly responsive in the 21st century?

If stakeholders do care, then firms need to ensure their actions do not run counter to the prevailing consensus; otherwise, they run the risk of negatively affecting the bottom line. If stakeholders do not care, then there is little economic incentive for firms to incorporate a CSR perspective within the organization *today* (though, admittedly, there may be moral or rational reasons for doing so).

The revolution in communications technology, which fueled the growth of the Internet and global media industry, has presented stakeholders with the opportunity to effectively mobilize and convey their collective message to corporations. They now have previously unimaginable abilities to monitor corporate operations and widely and quickly disseminate any actions or information they feel do not represent their best interests. In this manner, the communications revolution has been a great leveler of corporate power.

**Figure 2.1**   The Two Phases of Globalization

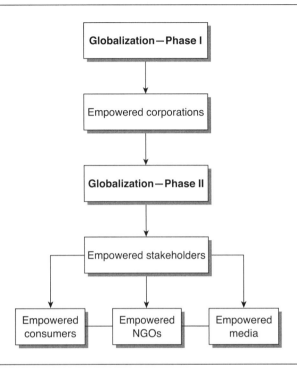

As Figure 2.1 illustrates, globalization has facilitated a great expansion in corporate influence. Today, global companies span nation boundaries, outsourcing large elements of operations off-shore, incorporating supply chain efficiencies, cutting costs, and growing their brands into cultural icons that span the globe: Think of Coke, Nike, or McDonald's, as examples. Phase two of globalization has been marked by countervailing pressures from stakeholders with access to increased sources of information about firms and to increased means of acting on that information. Thomas Friedman, with greater historical perspective, refers to this as the

> era of "Globalization 3.0," following Globalization 1.0, which ran from 1492 until 1800 and was driven by countries' sheer brawn, and Globalization 2.0, in which the "key agent of change, the dynamic force of driving global integration, was multinational companies" driven to look abroad for markets and labor. . . . That epoch ended around 2000, replaced by one in which individuals are the main agents doing the globalizing, pushed by . . . software [and a] global fiber-optic network that has made us all next-door neighbors."[2]

Globalization presents powerful tools that stakeholders can use to represent their best interests—that is, if they are willing to take advantage of the opportunity and if they really care.

## WHAT DO STAKEHOLDERS THINK?

To the extent that they indicate which issues are on the minds of stakeholders, opinion surveys can serve as a useful tool, although the message polls send may not always be clear. On one hand, in 2002,

> Only 17 percent of Americans rate business executives' ethics as high or very high, down from 25 percent a year ago, according to a Gallup poll sponsored by CNN and *USA TODAY.*[3]

On the other, a survey of 1,100 students on 27 university campuses in the United States by the nonprofit organization SIFE (Students in Free Enterprise, http://www.sife.org/), which aims to teach ethical business practices to students, reveals that ethical concerns and applications can easily diverge:

> Some 59% [of college students polled] admit cheating on a test (66% of men, 54% of women). And only 19% say they would report a classmate who cheated (23% of men, but 15% of women).[4]

An indicator of hope for a future in which CSR becomes more prominent, therefore, is the degree to which individual and corporate responsibility is being integrated within the education of future business leaders. To what extent are ethics and CSR classes entering the business school curriculum?

The *Beyond Grey Pinstripes* (http://www.beyondgreypinstripes.org/) annual reports measure progress in this area by identifying "the most innovative MBA programs and faculty infusing environmental and social impact management into the business school curriculum." In the organization's 2003 report, more than "1,000 courses, 800 extracurricular activities, 150 institutes and 700 articles from academic journals" were identified as meeting this criteria within the top 100 MBA programs.

Net Impact (http://www.net-impact.org/) is another example of progress. The organization, originally founded as Students for Responsible Business in 1993, boasts a growing membership of "emerging business leaders" and MBA graduates. The group's goal is to build a network of "new leaders for better business" and advance the case for the power and influence of business to be used in a way that positively influences society as a whole:

> The impact of business on our world is unequaled by that of any other institution. Today's business leaders are in a unique position to influence what happens in society for years to come. With this power comes monumental responsibility. We can choose to ignore this responsibility. . . . Or, as business leaders, we can realize our potential to create lasting social change. Net Impact exists for this purpose—to harness the power of business to create a better world.[5]

A growing awareness and acceptance of CSR and related ethical issues is significant. The extent to which future business leaders are aware of the importance of this issue will increase the likelihood of its acceptance in a corporate setting. More important from a corporate perspective, however, is the extent to which a growing awareness of CSR affects the business bottom line. If the market rewards CSR-sensitive companies and CSR-insensitive companies are punished, that will provide the greatest incentives for leaders to begin integrating CSR policies into their strategic perspective and day-to-day operations.

Public opinion, expressed through surveys, is one way to measure a society's attitudes towards CSR.[6] To what extent, however, do people tell pollsters their true feelings rather than merely what they think they should say or what they think the pollster wants to hear? Consider the issue of SUVs, for example. Many people realize that they consume disproportionate resources, pollute the environment, and have other negative consequences for society. Yet, they have been a mainstay of profitability for their producers. Should producers stop making SUVs in the name of CSR? If they did, would others merely step in and replace them? And, what about shareholders—the investors and risk takers? Do Ford and other manufacturers have an obligation to these stakeholders, too?

Undoubtedly, most people would agree that some degree of responsibility is a desirable trait; however, does self-interest outweigh one's sense of responsibility to society? Will customers, for example, continue buying the cheapest product on the shelf while failing to ask the necessary questions to determine whether or not a company is socially responsible? Will other stakeholders question whether pronouncements of social responsibility are merely superficial public relations attempts to raise the company's profile?

To examine the perspectives of multiple stakeholders, two extended case studies are presented that question the notion that CSR is poised to become a widespread and integral component of business strategic planning. The first of these case studies is Wal-Mart. Besides being the largest firm on Earth, Wal-Mart embodies the full range of domestic and international CSR concerns as it expands globally, appearing to sweep before it all in its path. Following that, a narrower case study, Martha Stewart, examines the strength of brand image when put to a CSR test in full view of multiple stakeholders. We rely on these extended examples to illustrate the interconnections among corporate actions and consequences, from the perspective of customers, communities, shareholders, and other stakeholders. It is hoped these two extended examples will create greater awareness that CSR-related actions can release a cascade of effects, all of which are tempered by economic, cultural, and other realities. Our intent is not to praise or condemn, merely to highlight the scope of CSR, as seen through these two firms.

## THE WAL-MART CONUNDRUM

Wal-Mart, the world's largest company, is a test case for CSR:

> [Wal-Mart] is three times the size of the No. 2 retailer, France's Carrefour. Every week, 138 million shoppers visit Wal-Mart's 4,750 stores; [in 2002] 82% of American households made at least one purchase at Wal-Mart.[7]

Wal-Mart—whose total annual revenue represents "a sum greater than the economies of all but 30 of the world's nations,"[8] and is growing faster than any of them—is an extremely successful and influential company. At the foundation of the company's success, however, is its strategy of minimizing costs, which relies on many policies that affect stakeholders in different ways.

The argument *against* CSR offers up Wal-Mart as its main case in point. Wal-Mart has suffered considerable criticism about its alleged insensitivity to local communities, employees, and other constituents. Yet, if stakeholders really cared about CSR, Wal-Mart would not be nearly as successful as it is. The result is a mixed picture. Why is it that whenever the company enters a new market, some greet it like a liberating force and others see it as a conquering imperialist? As one headline read,

Wal-Mart Invades, and Mexico Gladly Surrenders.[9]

A brief survey of article headlines indicates the negative feelings the company generates and concerns about its long-term influence:

Is Wal-Mart Too Powerful?[10]

The Wal-Martization of America[11]

Will Wal-Mart Steal Christmas?[12]

Wal-Mart: Cruising for a Bruising?[13]

Is Wal-Mart Good for America?[14]

The paradox that surrounds Wal-Mart and the controversy generated by its success is why the company is a case study in so many different business disciplines. Overall, does the company provide a net positive or net negative impact on the societies in which it is based? As one writer observed, "Wal-Mart might well be both America's most admired and most hated company."[15] And does the fact that consumers continue to shop at the store (20 million customers pass through Wal-Mart's doors every day[16]) critically undermine the economic argument for CSR?

## IS WAL-MART GOOD FOR SOCIETY?

Is it healthy for an economy to have companies with the size and power of Wal-Mart? As *Fortune* observed, "Wal-Mart CEO Lee Scott rules the commercial strip the way Julius Caesar once ruled the Roman republic."[17] For Wal-Mart, "Everyday low prices" has become its all-encompassing mantra and the means to the company's success: "It is the fundamental tenet of a cult masquerading as a company."[18]

Proponents of the pro–Wal-Mart case credit the company with directly saving U.S. consumers $20 billion, because of the downward pressure it exerts on prices, and another $80 billion due to the price reductions it forces on competitors, on an annual basis.[19] It gives consumers what they indicate (with their shopping practices) they want—low prices. Yet the methods by which Wal-Mart achieves these cost savings and low prices are also having a lasting impact, often negative, in the eyes of other stakeholders:

"It's become a social phenomenon that people resent and fear."[20]

The Wal-Mart conundrum is magnified when the long-term impact of the company's policies are followed through. We suspect that the same people who are complaining today about the number of U.S. jobs being exported overseas, particularly manufacturing jobs, also form a significant percentage of Wal-Mart consumers, to whom the company's low prices are so attractive:

"Wal-Mart is a double-edged sword, and both edges are quite sharp," Bernstein of the Economic Policy Institute said. "On the price side, consumers wouldn't flood Wal-Mart if there wasn't something there they liked, the low prices. On the other hand, by sticking solidly to the low-wage path, they create tons of low-quality jobs that dampen wage and income growth, not just for those who work in Wal-Mart but for surrounding communities as well."[21]

The potential dangers for Wal-Mart are many. What if consumers begin to worry about the impact the company is having on the economy and society more than they welcome the lower prices the company brings? Communities that worry about a megastore's impact on rural downtowns have already restricted Wal-Mart's growth.[22] Will employees continue to apply for positions at Wal-Mart if better paid alternatives exist? As the company continues to expand, will the government begin to fear the monopolistic characteristics of such a huge market influence? Suppliers are stakeholders who both relish Wal-Mart's market size and reach and fear their pricing pressures. How will these various stakeholder reactions affect Wal-Mart's business strategy over the longer term? What is the outlook for the company from a CSR perspective?

**Figure 2.2**   Is Wal-Mart Good for the U.S. Economy?

| Yes | No |
| --- | --- |
| ☑ Lower prices for consumers (lower inflation) | ☒ Loss of U.S. jobs to overseas suppliers |
| ☑ Jobs in economically deprived regions | ☒ Strong opposition against union representation of workforce |
| ☑ Wide range of products | ☒ Low employee wages, benefits |
| ☑ Redefinition of supply chain management (SCM) and general pursuit of technologically driven efficiencies | ☒ Competitors (and sometimes suppliers) go out of business, reducing competition and, ultimately, consumer choice |
| ☑ Increased productivity | ☒ Increase in litigation against the company on issues of alleged discrimination, employment of illegal immigrants, refusal to pay employee overtime, and so forth. |

## Prices

Wal-Mart has grown to such an influential point that it now dominates any industry it enters by driving down prices and imposing punishing margins on competitors. Wal-Mart accounts for about 30% of household goods sold in the United States (predicted to rise to 50% by 2010), including 32% of disposable diapers, 30% of hair care products, 26% of toothpaste sales, 20% of pet food, and 13% of home textiles. In addition, the company accounts for 15–20% of CD, video, and DVD sales; for 15% of all single-copy magazine sales;[23] and for 21% of toy sales.[24]

Wal-Mart arrives at its low prices by reducing costs through two separate strategies. First, it has revolutionized the management of supply chains and inventory within the retail industry. Now, thanks to Wal-Mart's innovations, many firms are better able to manage the flow of goods and materials that form an interconnected chain from providers (such as subcontractors and suppliers), through the firm, to the customer. The company uses information technology to track products—from the supplier to the warehouse to the shelf to the cash register—and ensure, as soon as they are sold, that replacements are back on the shelf waiting for the next customer. And with this greater refinement in managing the flow from suppliers around the world, it has become easier for firms like Wal-Mart and others to outsource supplies globally. In turn, due to Wal-Mart buying on a global basis, this trend of outsourcing has led higher-cost domestic producers to lose their supplying relationship to Wal-Mart, sometimes with disastrous results for the suppliers. The company's insistence that its top 100 suppliers integrate radio frequency identification (RFID) technology (its "RFID Mandate,"[25]) within their distribution systems by 2005 further pushes the technological boundaries of supply chain management. Wal-Mart's innovations have created savings across the board. And it strives to pass these savings on to customers in the form of lower prices.

Second, however, Wal-Mart also seeks to cut costs in other areas by pursuing activities that impose specific outcomes. Examples include paying some of the lowest wages in the retail sector or delaying payments to suppliers. It achieves this advantage, as in other areas, by virtue of its size and importance within the economies in which it operates:

> Wal-Mart's prices are about 14 percent lower than other groceries' because the company is aggressive about squeezing costs, including labor costs. Its workers earn a third less than unionized grocery workers, and pay for much of their health insurance. Wal-Mart uses hardball tactics to ward off unions. Since 1995, the government has issued at least 60 complaints alleging illegal anti-union activities.[26]

And Wal-Mart's impact is always industrywide. It was accused of causing great dislocation within the toy industry during the 2003 holiday season (leading to the bankruptcies of both F.A.O. Schwarz and KB Toys) and reducing the margins of all the other major industry retailers, in particular Toys R Us:

> The toy war is merely the most recent manifestation of what is known as the Wal-Mart effect. To the company's critics, Wal-Mart points the way to a grim Darwinian world of bankrupt competitors, low wages, meager health benefits, jobs lost to imports, and devastated downtowns and rural areas across America.[27]

This relentless driving down of costs above all else is good in the short term for consumers. In the long term, however, competition and quality are diminished, as all elements of the production process become potential cost savings that need to be made to compete, from research and development (R & D) to the components used to make the product.

## Suppliers

Wal-Mart's size increases its importance for any supplier "lucky" enough to have the company as a client, and the company's growing influence among certain brands is astounding. In 2003, it was reported that 28% of total sales for Dial were made from Wal-Mart stores.[28] Similar figures are true for Del Monte, Clorox, and Revlon, among others.

This growing dependence, however, can be a double-edged sword for stakeholders who find themselves out of favor for whatever reason. From the point of view either of governmental or supplier stakeholders, overdependence on one company can cause societal harm or supplier collapse. More important, it also presents the company with disproportionate negotiating power and an advantage over suppliers when times are good. Wal-Mart is able to dictate the cost at which goods should be supplied and enforces its demands by sourcing elsewhere, leaving the supplier unable to plug the gap such an important client leaves behind.

## Jobs

Often in rural areas, Wal-Mart is the only large employer in town, which gives the company additional clout:

> Wal-Mart's reputation for bringing a wide variety of goods to small towns and rural communities gives the company leverage over town councils and planning boards, which are often asked to grant zoning concessions or relax environmental standards. And, Wal-Mart's frequent position as the only big employer in town allows it leeway to hire workers at low wages.[29]

Lee Scott, Wal-Mart's CEO, defends the company's employment policies:

> We pay more than our competitors. We opened a store in Phoenix recently and 5,000 people applied for 500 openings.[30]

> If Wal-Mart were as greedy as its detractors say, it would never have attracted 8,000 job applicants for 525 places at a new store in Glendale, Ariz., or 3,000 applicants for 300 jobs in outlying Los Angeles.[31]

Nevertheless, alleged poor employment policies, an accusation that has dogged Wal-Mart for some time, may well indicate some of the CSR-related dangers facing the company down the road. When employees do have a choice, they may start choosing not to work for Wal-Mart. A reputation as a poor employer leads to low morale, which reduces productivity, and high turnover rates, which raise costs and disrupt service as new employees retrain. The operating practices that create such a reputation do not make good business sense in the long term:

By Wal-Mart's own estimate, about 44% of its 1.4 million employees will leave in 2003, meaning the company will need to hire 616,000 workers just to stay even.[32]

Where an employer's bad practices become inherent in the way the company conducts business, the fallout can have even more expensive repercussions. Wal-Mart faces a growing number of lawsuits (including class-action suits[33]) from disgruntled past and present employees alleging illegal overtime pay rates, sexual discrimination in promotion policies, and the hiring of illegal immigrants at even lower wage levels:[34]

Questions over whether the retailer's relentless drive to cut costs is causing it to stray too close to the boundary of legality. . . . Many powerful businesses eventually run into issues that threaten to hold back their progress. . . . Could labor issues become the kind of thorn in the side for Wal-Mart that antitrust probes became for Microsoft?[35]

## Quality and Variety

Another component of Wal-Mart's pricing strategy enabling it to lower prices is stocking the most profitable top tier of products in an industry, for example, the top 10% of best-selling toys from the biggest brands. Wal-Mart can afford to market these best sellers at lower margins (or even as loss leaders) because of the volume and extra business they generate for the store. The concern for product quality and variety in the long term is related to future R & D. By cherry-picking today's most profitable products and selling them at low margins, Wal-Mart is taking away the profits that other industry-focused companies use to fund current and future R & D. Without these profits to finance the innovation that drives product development, creates choice, and produces the hits of the next generation, consumers may be ensuring future quality and variety will be diminished. Is Wal-Mart also hurting its own future business strategy by narrowing the number of best-seller products it is able to market at low margins over time?

## WAL-MART IS KING . . . TODAY

None of the issues above mention the paradox that Wal-Mart's promise to produce "everyday low prices" appeals to the very workers who cannot afford to pay more. Many of these workers have had their wages driven down and their job security threatened because of Wal-Mart's pursuit of ever lower costs, whether they work for the company itself, a supplier, a competitor, or another company in the affected labor pool.

A CSR perspective, however, argues that Wal-Mart's business model will only remain viable while its attractions offset the consequences of its actions. In the end, a strategy of lower prices that alienates increasing numbers of stakeholders will gradually erode the innovation, choice, and support of needed constituents. Already coalitions of unions, environmentalists, community organizations, state lawmakers, and academics are planning coordinated attacks on Wal-Mart to force it to change its methods.[36] Wal-Mart's actions in some communities have already been restricted, leading Wal-Mart to mount large-scale media campaigns to influence public perceptions of its actions;[37] even holding its "first-ever media event," to defend its policies and actions.[38] In April 2005, Wal-Mart announced a $35 million campaign in partnership with the National Fish and Wildlife Foundation "to offset the amount of land [Wal-Mart] develops to use for its stores and other facilities" over the next 10 years by purchasing 138,000 acres "of land in sensitive habitats" for conservation.[39] What if these public relations and advertisements are not sufficient?

CSR is an argument about business today and an ability to understand what business will be about tomorrow. Today Wal-Mart is king. But, in order to sustain its dominant market position, stakeholder theory argues that a CSR perspective should be integrated into the organization's strategic planning processes and throughout day-to-day operations. Absent this perspective, CSR theory suggests Wal-Mart will eventually lose societal legitimacy, particularly among the key constituents (such as local community zoning boards) that are so crucial to its growth mandate.

Of course, the answer to the questions raised by Wal-Mart cannot be resolved definitively at present. Much will depend on the individual decisions made by the company's 20 million daily customers. Nevertheless, it does seem that CSR concerns raised by Wal-Mart's actions already affect its future strategies, limiting management freedom and discretion to pursue shareholder value.[40]

## MARTHA STEWART LIVING OMNIMEDIA

The case study of Martha Stewart gives insight into a firm's (sometimes fragile) relations with its stakeholders, particularly customers and shareholders. Here the issues and consequences were not only different, but societal reactions varied as this protracted case played out in the media. The case shows the importance of a positive perception of the product and brand but also indicates the danger that a lingering hint of "unacceptable' behavior can bring over the long term.

Martha Stewart and her company gained widespread media visibility after the sale of her 3,928 shares in ImClone Systems Inc. on December 27, 2001 (the day before the Food and Drug Administration announced a negative report about the biotech company's new cancer drug). Her trial, on federal charges of obstruction of justice and securities fraud, began in January 2004;[41] however, in discussing this case, it is not our intention to consider the issue of Martha Stewart's guilt or innocence.[42] Instead, addressed here are the reactions by consumers, investors, and other relevant stakeholders to the chain of events surrounding the stock sale. We also address how the perceptions of these stakeholders affected economic transactions involving Martha Stewart Living Omnimedia (MSLO), the company's products, and the brand. Here, concern focuses primarily on consumer and investor reactions to the tainted image of the firm.

## CONSUMER REACTION

Martha Stewart's company reflects the media-dominated entertainment age in which we live—a powerful and successful brand, inseparable from the superstar leading the company.[43] What makes this case interesting from a CSR standpoint is that the sale of her ImClone shares had no direct connection with the company's business as opposed to, say, a product recall, accounting irregularities, or the polluting of the local stream as part of the manufacturing process. Therefore, it is more likely that the public would be willing to separate the two (individual and company) and continue buying Martha Stewart products. This sense was supported by initial reaction from consumers to the investigation and allegations, reported by Joan Quigly in a November 2002 article in the *Miami Herald*:

> People don't care. . . . It goes in one ear and out the other. . . . [At Kmart] Martha Stewart remains a strong seller. . . . The customer appreciates the Martha Stewart name. . . . Her brand name still has clout.[44]

What appeared more important to customers was the value they derived from the products themselves and the difference Martha Stewart was able to make to their lives on a personal level rather than activities that they perceived as having no direct impact on their daily lives and no relation to the products they were buying.

In the longer term, however, as the allegations lingered and Martha Stewart's profile dropped, sales suffered. As her trial approached, sales continued to decline overall;[45] however, a significant number of consumers continued buying the company's products, at least reserving judgment until a pronouncement of innocence or guilt was made. Likewise, even after her conviction and jail sentence, her branded products continued to be sold throughout leading retail outlets.

## INVESTOR REACTION

MSLO is an example of the roller-coaster effects a fair-weather institutional reaction can induce. Martha Stewart became damaged goods, and, in investors' eyes, her negative halo extended to the firm. Perceptions that the firm was socially conscious, even virtuous, had previously made it a *safe* investment—one with a strong brand, unlikely to be soiled by controversy. Attractively positioned in the minds of consumers, institutional support for Martha Stewart's television and magazine products was evidenced by the long list of advertisers seeking to affiliate their offerings with her brand. This positioning of the brand earned considerable advertising revenue for her magazine and television show. The allegations of wrongdoing, however, produced a swifter reaction from investors than from consumers, stopping this virtuous momentum in its tracks. The investigation into Martha Stewart erased the socially conscious image the company once enjoyed, harming its potential moneymaking ability. In the minds of stockholders,

> Her legal woes have harmed the corporate bottom line, causing a plunge in advertising revenues for the flagship magazine and television show. Ratings for Stewart's syndicated television show, *Martha Stewart Living*, have dropped and she shelved plans for her annual holiday special. . . . MSLO's stock price, which traded around $18 before the allegations surfaced, has also tanked, closing . . . at $8.48.[46]

Institutional flight from a company's stock, or withdrawal of financial support in general (e.g., advertising), can be termed "distressed investing."[47] Although consumer support for

Martha Stewart products seemingly changed little during the first year of the controversy, institutional support from advertisers and networks and brokerage recommendations during the same period quickly shifted.[48] The potential consequences of such ostracism can be great for companies in today's investing environment:

> What's at stake is a company's very survival. In a changing investment climate, capital will flow only to those the market judges to be the savviest risk managers. The rest face a dim future in which they pay much more for credit and their stocks trade at big discounts.[49]

It is important to note, however, that in cases such as this, institutional investors are primarily interested in perceptions rather than the more complicated issue of actual guilt or innocence. For example, in late 2002 and early 2003, as rumors swirled that the prospect of an indictment seemed unlikely, MSLO's stock price began to recover. Nevertheless, Martha Stewart herself estimated the damage to her company caused by the allegations made against her amounted to $400 million.[50] Ultimately, "the brand has taken an enormous hit."[51]

Time has powerful healing abilities, however. Following Martha Stewart's conviction and during her incarceration, the company's stock price shot up from levels that had been depressed by the uncertainty surrounding her trial; and subsequent to her release from jail, she was offered the chance to participate in a number of television programs and other lucrative "image revival" projects—all of which suggest, perhaps, that the ImClone incident has had no lasting impact on future expectations for the company, although advertising dollars, profits, and stock price certainly suffered along the way:

> Prison has been a good thing for Martha Stewart—at least for her company's stock. . . . Ever since Ms. Stewart was sentenced on July 16 [2004], the shares have been on a tear. . . . For Ms. Stewart, who owns more than 29 million shares of the company's Class A stock, the gains have meant about $600 million in paper profit, all while Ms. Stewart sat in prison.[52]

## SO, DO STAKEHOLDERS CARE?

The central question of this chapter is this: Do stakeholders care?

In these two extended examples, Wal-Mart and Martha Stewart Living Omnimedia, cross-currents exist, reinforcing the idea that different stakeholders have different perspectives. In other examples, corporate actions may be seen as less ambiguous with more direct consequences. Think of Bhopal, India, where a Union Carbide plant accident killed thousands or Enron's self-destruction due to the lack of social responsibility among some of its leaders or the crises surrounding Adelphia Communications, Tyco, and other firms that resulted in lost jobs and shareholder value, as well as criminal indictments. In these examples, among many others, a lack of strategic CSR has led to uniform and universal condemnation, along with significant legal and market penalties.

In general, firms that ignore societal tradeoffs do face limits, as suggested by the "iron law of social responsibility" (introduced in Chapter 1) and evidenced by the growing coalition of organizations intent on changing Wal-Mart's operations. The stakeholder backlash, however, to a firm's indifference to CSR is not necessarily felt immediately. The tobacco and fast-food industries stand as prime examples. Nevertheless, a company that does not reflect the evolving interests of its stakeholders is ultimately putting itself, its reputation, and its brand or image at risk. Companies understand this today, which is why they go to such strenuous efforts to avoid the negative publicity CSR lapses bring.

Many consumers cannot afford the luxury of the choice between economic and social issues. On that basis, the low-wage jobs offered by Wal-Mart may well be a cause for praise: Most people would agree that a low paying job is better than no job at all. This does not, however, negate the central idea of this book: The long-term interests of a company depend on a broad stakeholder perspective. Short-term perspectives that allow economic necessity to take precedence over social concerns will eventually catch up with the perpetrators. But, as the examples of the tobacco and fast-food companies illustrate, it is fair to say that firms in certain industries can delay the CSR day of reckoning for a significant period of time. This is because the threshold of concern varies for each stakeholder and within each industry.

Stakeholders' CSR concerns depend on a unique mix of individual priorities and available options, both of which change over time. They also reflect the interwoven battle among conflicting constituent interests. In the short run, even a flagrant disregard for CSR may be ignored by some, or even all, stakeholders. On the other hand, reaction may be swift and unequivocal. Mostly, however, reactions will be mixed. Initially, for example, consumers continued to buy Martha Stewart's products at the same time institutionalized supporters (advertisers and investors) began to flee (a flight driven largely by economic factors rather than CSR concerns). Other stakeholders—employees and leaders—undoubtedly cared as they faced insecurities brought about by the consequences of poor CSR. And yet it was another stakeholder group, the regulating governmental agencies, that initiated the legal action against Stewart.

Putting aside motives and attributions, however, it is clear that firms suffer the consequences of stakeholder disillusionment for a perceived lack of commitment to CSR. Wal-Mart has had its requests for zoning variations denied because its operations were deemed contrary to community interest, for example. Growing unionization efforts within the company's stores in the United States, Canada, and elsewhere seem at least partially attributable to revolt against its human resource policies. Likewise, Martha Stewart's firm was severely affected as advertisers, institutional investors, and other stakeholders reduced their support as the ImClone case unfolded.

So, finally, do stakeholders care about CSR? Though a decisive answer must be hedged by the tradeoffs between stakeholder groups—as when company profits compete with paying a living wage to foreign factory workers—and differences between industries, it is apparent that stakeholders do care about the consequences of CSR and the moral, rational, and economic impact those consequences hold. CSR is not a short-term issue, however. The job for boards of directors is to choose leaders who are able to anticipate shifting stakeholder concerns, respond, and aim their firm toward a more successful future. In an increasingly globalizing business environment, this future-oriented vision offers benefits for all stakeholders, particularly stockholders.

## QUESTIONS FOR DISCUSSION AND REVIEW

1. What is meant by *stakeholder advocacy*?

2. Would you report a classmate you suspected of cheating at school? Why? Why not?

3. If you were a member of Wal-Mart's top management, what arguments would you make to a community group that is trying to stop the building of a Wal-Mart in their community? If you were the leader of the community group resisting Wal-Mart's expansion into your community, what arguments would you make?

4. Is a low paying job better than no job at all?

5. Would you ever consider boycotting a certain brand or store because of the parent company's actions or stance on a particular issue? Illustrate with an example.

6. Martha Stewart's sale of her ImClone stock (which led to government investigations, indictment, trial, and prison) had nothing directly to do with her firm, Martha Stewart Living Omnimedia. Why was her firm so significantly affected by her actions?

7. Why are large, multinational firms more likely to be concerned about CSR?

## NOTES

1. *BSR News Monitor,* December 17, 2003, No. 358, p6. Co-Op Bank Sustainability Reports and other CSR-related work can be found at http://www.co-operativebank.co.uk/servlet/Satellite?cid=1078822537303&pagename=CoopBank%2FPage%2FtplPageStandard&c=Page

2. Warren Bass, 'A Brave New World in 9/11 Aftermath,' *Miami Herald,* April 10, 2005, p7M. Review of 'The World is Flat: A Brief History of the Twenty-First Century,' by Thomas L. Friedman, Farrar Straus Giroux, 2005.

3. 'The Leaders Who Run Toward Crises,' *New York Times,* December 22, 2002, Section 3, p12.

4. 'You Mean Cheating Is Wrong?' *BusinessWeek,* December 9, 2002, p8.

5. http://www.net-impact.org/

6. For an analysis of the awareness and importance of CSR to the public and other corporate stakeholders, see Jenny Dawkins & Stewart Lewis, 'CSR in Stakeholder Expectations: And Their Implication for Company Strategy,' *Journal of Business Ethics,* May 2003, Vol. 44, pp 185–193: "Over ten years of research at MORI has shown the increasing prominence of corporate responsibility for a wide range of stakeholders, from consumers and employees to legislators and investors. . . . Traditionally, the factors that mattered most to consumers when forming an opinion of a company were product quality, value for money and financial performance. Now, across a worldwide sample of the public, the most commonly mentioned factors relate to corporate responsibility (e.g., treatment of employees, community involvement, ethical and environmental issues)."

7. Anthony Bianco & Wendy Zellner, 'Is Wal-Mart Too Powerful?' *BusinessWeek,* October 6, 2003, pp 100–110.

8. Tim Weiner, 'Wal-Mart Invades, and Mexico Gladly Surrenders,' *New York Times,* December 6, 2003, Section A, p1.

9. *New York Times,* December 6, 2003, op. cit., Ibid.

10. *BusinessWeek,* October 6, 2003, op. cit., pp 100–110.

11. Editorial, 'The Wal-Martization of America,' *New York Times,* November 15, 2003, Section A, p12.

12. Daren Fonda, 'Will Wal-Mart Steal Christmas?' *Time,* December 1, 2003. http://www.time.com/time/archive/preview/0,10987,1006375,00.html

13. Amy Tsao, 'Wal-Mart: Cruising for a Bruising?' *BusinessWeek,* November 14, 2003, http://www.businessweek.com/bwdaily/dnflash/nov2003/nf20031114_9758_db014.htm.

14. Steve Lohr, 'Is Wal-Mart Good for America?' *New York Times,* December 7, 2003, Section 4, p1.

15. *BusinessWeek,* October 6, 2003, op. cit., pp 100–110.

16. Steven Greenhouse, 'Wal-Mart, a Nation Unto Itself,' *New York Times,* April 17, 2004, pB7.

17.  John Helyar, 'COSTCO: The Only Company Wal-Mart Fears,' *Fortune,* November 10, 2003, http://www.fortune.com/fortune/investing/articles/0,15114,538834,00.html

18.  *BusinessWeek,* October 6, 2003, op. cit., pp 100–110.

19.  Ibid.

20.  Ibid.

21.  Constance L. Hays, 'When Wages Are Low, Discounters Have Pull,' *New York Times,* December 23, 2003, pp C1&C4.

22.  For example, see, John M. Broder, 'Stymied by Politicians, Wal-Mart Turns to Voters,' *New York Times,* April 5, 2004, pA12; Steven Malanga, 'The War on Wal-Mart,' *Wall Street Journal,* April 7, 2004, pA18; Ann Zimmerman, 'Wal-Mart Loses Supercenter Vote,' *Wall Street Journal,* April 8, 2004, pB7; and, providing some degree of balance in the coverage, George F. Will, 'Waging War on Wal-Mart,' *Newsweek,* July 5, 2004, p64.

23.  *BusinessWeek,* October 6, 2003, op. cit.

24.  Daren Fonda, 'Will Wal-Mart Steal Christmas?' *Time,* December 1, 2003.

25.  Demir Barlas, 'Wal-Mart RFID Mandate Lag,' *E-Business News,* November 19, 2004, http://www.line56.com/articles/default.asp?ArticleID=6147

26.  *New York Times,* November 15, 2003, op. cit., Section A, p12.

27.  *New York Times,* December 7, 2003, op. cit., Section 4, p1.

28.  *BusinessWeek,* October 6, 2003, op. cit.

29.  Sharon Zukin, 'We Are Where We Shop,' *New York Times,* November 28, 2003, pA31.

30.  Ann Zimmerman, 'Defending Wal-Mart,' *Wall Street Journal,* October 6, 2004, pB1.

31.  Steven Greenhouse, 'Can't Wal-Mart, A Retail Behemoth, Pay More?' *New York Times,* May 4, 2005, http://aolsvc.news.aol.com/business/article.adp?id=20050504071909990033&ncid=NWS0001000 0000001

32.  *BusinessWeek,* October 6, 2003, op. cit., pp 100–110.

33.  The largest lawsuit facing Wal-Mart was allowed to proceed as a class-action suit in June 2004 (a decision that is under appeal as this book goes to print: 'Wal-Mart CEO Defends Wages, Health Benefits,' *Wall Street Journal,* April 6, 2005, pA6). This court decision, involving a lawsuit initially filed by six former employees who felt they were not treated equally to male employees, presents "the world's largest retailer with the prospect of fighting a lengthy legal battle or potentially paying a multibillion-dollar settlement. . . . [involving] as many as 1.6 million current and former female U.S. employees." Ann Zimmerman, 'Judge Certifies Wal-Mart Suit as Class Action,' *Wall Street Journal,* June 23, 2004, pp A1&A6.

34.  In March 2005, Wal-Mart agreed "to pay $11 million to settle a federal investigation into allegations it knowingly hired floor-cleaning contractors who employed undocumented workers." The settlement was "about four times as large as any other single payment received by the government in an illegal-alien employment case." Ann Zimmerman, 'Wal-Mart Settles Immigration Case,' *Wall Street Journal,* March 21, 2005, pB3.

35.  'Labor Issues a Thorn at Wal-Mart,' *Financial Times,* in *Miami Herald,* November 22, 2003, p2C.

36.  Steven Greenhouse, 'Opponents of Wal-Mart to Coordinate Efforts,' *New York Times,* April 13, 2005, p16.

37.  For example, Emily Kaiser, 'Wal-Mart Goes on PR Offensive to Repair Image,' Reuters, February 2, 2004.

38.  'Wal-Mart CEO Defends Wages, Health Benefits,' *Wall Street Journal,* April 6, 2005, pA6.

39.  Ryan Chittum, 'Wal-Mart to Give $35 Million for Wildlife Areas,' *Wall Street Journal,* April 13, 2005, pB4; and Stephanie Strom, 'Wal-Mart Donates $35 Million for Conservation and Will Be Partner With Wildlife Group,' *New York Times,* April 13, 2005, pA16.

40.  In spite of growing revenues and profits, Wal-Mart's share price continues to underperform those of its competitors: "while Wal-Mart has won on Main Street, it's been the loser on Wall Street. . . . [From 2004 to 2005] its shares have fallen 19%. An owner of Kmart stock . . . is more than 200% ahead." Justin Lahart, 'Ahead of the Tape: Wall and Main,' *Wall Street Journal,* April 29, 2005, pC1.

41. For a comprehensive timeline of events leading up to the trial, see http://www.savemartha.com/martha_stewart_trial_when.html

42. Martha Stewart pleaded not guilty to the charges in advance of her trial, but was found Guilty on March 5, 2004, "on all four counts of obstructing justice and lying to investigators" about the stock sale. 'Stewart convicted on all charges,' *CNNMoney,* March 5, 2004, http://money.cnn.com/2004/03/05/news/companies/martha_verdict/ Stewart served 5 months in jail and was released on March 4, 2005. She then served a further 5 months under house arrest, followed by 2 years of probation. Krysten Crawford, 'Martha Out and About,' *CNNMoney,* March 4, 2005, http://money.cnn.com/2005/03/03/news/news makers/martha_walkup/

43. For a selection of Martha Stewart cartoons and humor commenting on her trial and prison sentence, go to http://cagle.slate.msn.com/news/MarthaStewartinJAIL/main.asp and also http://politi calhumor.about.com/od/marthastewart/

44. Joan Quigley, 'Stewart Customers True Blue,' *Miami Herald,* November 16, 2002, pp C1&C2.

45. Note: a significant part of this drop in sales was due to Kmart's economic difficulties at the time, leading to continued store closures (Kmart carried a wide range of Martha Stewart goods), as well as anticipation in terms of possible outcomes of the trial.

46. *Miami Herald,* November 16, 2002, op. cit., pp C1&C2.

47. David Rocker, general partner at Rocker Partners LP, a New York hedge fund, quoted in Robin Sidel & Matthew Rose, 'Contrarian Says, Don't Sell Martha Short,' *Wall Street Journal,* December 6, 2002, pp C1&C3.

48. For example, "[In 2004] advertising pages were down a staggering 47% from the previous year at Martha Stewart Living, which is responsible for one-third of the company's revenue." Gregory Zuckerman & James Bandler, 'Martha Stewart Living: No Bars,' *Wall Street Journal,* March 3, 2005, pp C1&C4.

49. Emily Thornton, 'A Yardstick for Corporate Risk,' *BusinessWeek,* August 26, 2002, pp 106–108.

50. Jeffrey Toobin, 'Lunch at Martha's,' *The New Yorker* (http://www.newyorker.com) February 2, 2003.

51. Eric Wahlgren, 'Crunch Time for the Martha Mess,' *BusinessWeek* online, December 4, 2003.

52. *Wall Street Journal,* March 3, 2005, op. cit. pp C1&C4.

# Chapter 3

## THE STRATEGIC CONTEXT OF CSR

There are three kinds of organizations: nonprofit, governmental, and for-profit. Each exists to meet needs in society. Those needs may be altruistic, such as feeding the poor, in the case of a nonprofit; they may be civic, such as providing for the safety and security of the public, in the case of government agencies; or they may be primarily economic, such as organizing resources to meet societal needs in ways that yield a surplus for the owners, called profit. In a free society, organizations that do not meet needs go away. Restated, no publicly traded company, government, or nonprofit initially sets out to do harm. Yet, as the first two chapters have illustrated, organizations can create undesired consequences. These often unintended consequences spring not from the goals of the organization but from the methods or strategies deployed in the pursuit of organizational goals—thus the need to understand the strategic context of CSR.

In pursuing societal needs, all organizations face constraints on their methods and results. For example, the economics of survival requires each entity to produce the *results* that generate the donations, taxes, or profits needed to operate. At the same time, these results must be attained by *methods* that are deemed acceptable to the larger society. Leaders of all organizations constantly grapple with the balance between methods and results. When these issues involve for-profits, CSR helps businesses balance the means they use and the ends they seek. It does this by ensuring that profit-seeking businesses plan and operate from the perspective of multiple stakeholders.

The problem that a firm's decision makers face is simple to state: Which stakeholders and what issues matter under the broad heading of corporate social responsibility as it pertains to their organization? The simple (if not simplistic) answer depends on the for-profit's strategy. And, because these strategies vary widely, the right mix will differ from firm to firm and will evolve over time as firms adapt both their strategy and execution to increasingly turbulent operational environments. The result? It is impossible to prescribe the exact issues that any firm is likely to face at any given time. Instead, we argue that a strategic lens offers the best viewpoint through which to study CSR.

# THE STRATEGIC LENS: VISION, MISSION, STRATEGY, AND TACTICS

Companies need to view CSR through a strategic lens. Although businesses exist for many reasons, survival depends on profits. These profits depend on revenues that only come about through customers who are satisfied with the value the firm offers through its competent and motivated employees.[1] The pursuit of profits, however, is so broad a mandate that it offers little guidance about where to begin or what to do. Instead, insight comes from understanding the need in society that the business seeks to meet. That need, toward which the organization strives, forms the basis of its aspirations or vision. Ideally, an organization's *vision* is an ennobling, articulated statement of what it seeks to be and become. A vision that ignores the larger role that a firm plays in society is likely to be neither ennobling nor sustainable. Vision statements must appeal to multiple stakeholders, including customers, members of the organization (employees), its direct beneficiaries (owners), and the larger community in which the organization operates (society, broadly defined).

From these aspirations, the firm's *mission* identifies what the organization is going to do to attain its vision or aspirations. For example, a food bank may have the vision of "ending hunger in the community," and its mission is to "feed the poor." A business may have the vision of "providing the best personal transportation vehicles" and a mission of "making cars." But here again, the mission must balance both the methods and the results to be considered socially responsible. Vision identifies what the organization is striving toward, and the mission tells us what the organization is going to do to get there. Both these statements are constrained by what society deems as acceptable.

*Strategy* explains how the organization is going to go about achieving its vision and mission. It defines the organization's response to its competitive environment. Thus, the food bank may have a strategy of using a mobile soup kitchen that can transport the food to where the poor live, whereas the auto firm may have a strategy of producing high-end sports cars.

*Tactics* are the day-to-day management decisions that implement the strategy. Tactics are the actions people in the organization take every day. Restated:

---

- The *vision* answers *why* the organization exists. It identifies the needs the firm aspires to solve for others.
- The *mission* states *what* the organization is going to do to achieve its vision. It addresses the types of activities performed for others.
- The *strategy* determines *how* the organization is going to undertake its mission. It sets forth the ways it will negotiate its competitive environment.
- The *tactics* determine *when* and *where* the strategy will be implemented and by whom. They are the actions necessary for success.

---

Effective strategy results in providing businesses with a source of sustainable, competitive advantage. For any competitive advantage to be sustainable, however, the tactics must be executed in ways that are at least minimally acceptable to the societies in which they are deployed. Otherwise, social, legal, and other forces may conspire against the firm, as when lawsuits punish a manufacturer for polluting the air and water.

**Figure 3.1**   The Tactics, Strategy, CSR, Mission, Vision Constraints

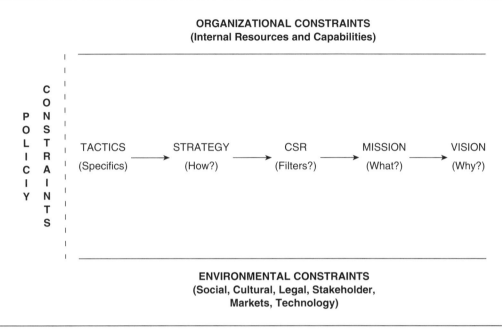

NOTE: A sustainable effort to attain a firm's mission and vision depends on a strategy and tactics that are evaluated through the CSR filter within the organizational policy and external environmental constraints under which the firm must operate.

Both CSR and strategy are primarily concerned with the firm's relationship to the environments within which it operates. Whereas strategy addresses how the firm competes in the marketplace, CSR considers the strategy's impact on relevant stakeholders. In turn, both CSR and strategy are constrained by these environments.

As illustrated in Figure 3.1, vision, mission, strategy, and tactics are limited. Limitations come from the organization's resources and capabilities. Other constraints on pursuing strategy include company policies that require and forbid specific actions, though these are internally imposed and can be changed by management—thus the dashed line suggesting that policy constraints are more porous or flexible. Similarly, the sociocultural-legal-stakeholder environments, along with markets and technology, limit the firm's actions. The tactics society and stakeholders expect and permit (a key component of CSR) determine the environment in which the firm pursues its strategic goals and which, in turn, enable it to perform its mission and strive toward its vision. Compounding the complexity of integrating CSR into the vision-mission-strategy-tactics linkages are the ever changing expectations of society.

## THE STRATEGIC LENS: THE E.S.C.S. FRAMEWORK

For a business strategy to provide a source of sustainable competitive advantage assumes a marriage of the firm's internal strengths (its competencies) with its external (environmental)

**Figure 3.2**   The Environmental-Strategic-Competency-Structure Framework

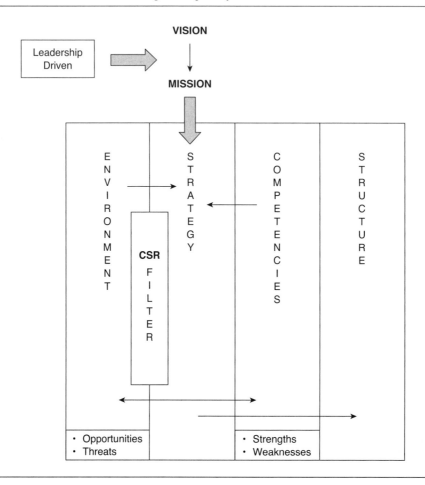

opportunities. As illustrated in Figure 3.2, the multiple arrows show that vision and mission shape strategy. Additionally, strategy is influenced by both the firm's internal competencies and the demands of the external environment in which it must operate. In turn, strategy helps influence the organizational structure. The connection among the internal strengths and the external opportunities (needs in society) is driven by the strategic axiom that success depends on a position of competing from strengths; however, for the strategist to connect strengths with opportunities in a globalizing business environment requires an intimate understanding of both, while implementing the competitive strategy through a CSR filter. Figure 3.2 shows how the CSR filter fits between strategy and the environment in which the strategy operates.

A better understanding of the role CSR plays in a firm's strategic success (the CSR filter) requires an understanding of the interplay among a firm's competencies, strategy, and structure as it faces its environment.

## Competencies

For a firm to compete from strengths, it must have and be able to identify them. These strengths represent the critical factors that determine how the firm will compete in the external environment. To facilitate an understanding of strengths, a clear differentiation among *capabilities, competencies,* and *core competencies* is required:

- *Capabilities* are actions that a firm can do, such as pay its bills and produce some value-added good or service.
- *Competencies* are actions a firm can do and can do very well.
- *Core competencies* are actions a firm does very well, and it is so superior at performing these activities that it is difficult (or at least time consuming) for other firms to match its performance in this area.

Consider how Wal-Mart is able to manage the flow of goods from suppliers to customers, often referred to as *supply chain management.*

An example: Wal-Mart has a *capability* to produce advertisements; it has a *competency* to locate stores where they will be successful; and it has a *core competency* of maintaining and distributing its inventory throughout the supply chain. In fact, Wal-Mart is so very good at managing its supply chain that it minimizes both the amount of inventory it carries and the number of times items are out of stock in its stores. Other firms have the capability to maintain their inventory; some even have a competency at doing that. But none of Wal-Mart's competitors appear to match its core competency of supply chain management.

## Strategy

Wal-Mart's *vision* of offering the best customer value in retailing gives rise to a *mission* of delivering groceries and other consumer products efficiently. That vision and mission are attained by a *strategy* of passing on cost savings to customers by continually seeking to roll back their "everyday low prices." In turn, that strategy is built upon *competencies* and *core competencies,* which are the competitive weapons with which Wal-Mart competes. How Wal-Mart folds its competencies into a strategy and then how it deploys that strategy vis-à-vis stakeholders determines how society views the degree to which Wal-Mart is socially responsible.

Certainly, a firm like Wal-Mart must advertise and do hundreds, even thousands of other activities. But its competitive advantage comes from its network of store locations, backed by an unmatched ability to manage and deliver its inventory in optimal ways. These competencies interact, reinforcing each other. Without its exceptionally efficient and effective supply chain management competencies, it would not be a low-cost provider of groceries and other goods. But with these competencies supporting its strategy, it creates a *virtuous cycle* in which Wal-Mart's lower prices attract more customers. More customers, in turn, mean greater volumes, which lead to increased economies of scale in operations and greater power in demanding price reductions from its suppliers. The result is still lower costs that allow the firm to lower prices further, which in turn continues the virtuous cycle by attracting still more customers. The increased economies of scale in distribution and purchasing perpetuate the cycle of still lower costs. Thus, the strategy rests upon the competencies of the firm and supports its mission and vision. Although not all firms are able to create a virtuous cycle like Wal-Mart, all successful strategies ultimately rest upon a firm's competencies . . . until the competitive environment changes.

When the competitive environment demands a different strategy, the existing capabilities or competencies of the firm may no longer be sufficient. For example, if Wal-Mart is seen as exploiting its low-paid workers, the accompanying negative publicity will eventually harm its image. This may cause customers to shop elsewhere or cause communities to deny Wal-Mart's applications for zoning variances needed to build or remodel stores. Evolving societal expectations force changes in Wal-Mart's competitive environment (as with all firms), requiring new competencies in public relations, advertising, and human resource management.

When environmental changes like these or others occur, leaders face a *make-or-buy* decision. Should the needed competencies be developed internally (*make*) or acquired from others outside the firm (*buy*)? Historically, many large firms like Wal-Mart have had the resources to develop the needed competencies internally through hiring and training. Today, the external environment is changing so rapidly that firms often buy the needed skills from others because of the need for speed of execution. If the decision makers decide to *buy* the needed capabilities or competencies, leaders then face a second decision: whether to bring the needed capabilities under the control of the organization structure or to outsource those activities via contractual relationships with suppliers. When the activity is seen as a core competency—managing inventory at Wal-Mart, for example—most firms seek to capture that activity within the structure of the firm to strengthen this vital component of their strategic advantage. If the activity is seen as peripheral, such as calculating and printing payroll checks, the firm will often outsource the activity if it is cheaper or faster to do so.

Wal-Mart's approach is primarily a cost-based form of competition, or business strategy. Mercedes-Benz, on the other hand, does not seek to produce the lowest-priced cars by operating as efficiently as possible. Instead, it competes based on *differentiation*. By differentiating its products along the lines of safety, prestige, and durability, Mercedes-Benz (and other luxury goods producers) can charge a premium for the differentiation (real or perceived) that consumers receive. McDonald's strives for a focused strategy that embraces both low costs and product differentiation. Relatively low costs result from its high volume and standardization, leading to economies of scale; however, McDonald's also differentiates the product it offers by providing fast service, putting it in the fast-food segment (or niche) of the restaurant industry.

Whether firms compete on costs, differentiation, or a focused strategy that embraces either cost or differentiation (or both), strategy seeks ways for the firm to provide customer-focused value added as a means of gaining a competitive advantage.

## Structure

The structure—the organizational design—exists to support the strategy of the firm. What architects say of a building, organization designers say of the firm's structure: The form follows the function. Thus, expertise is often concentrated into a *functional* organization design, in which site location, store construction oversight, information systems, warehousing, distribution, store operations, and other like activities are grouped together by their common functions into specialized departments. This organizational *form* supports the *functions* necessary for the firm to implement its strategy successfully and thus is called a functional organization design.

In the case of Wal-Mart, different parts of the company might pursue different structural designs. For example, support activities like accounting or finance may be grouped by function at corporate headquarters. At the same time, because Wal-Mart is spread across many geographical areas, the store management oversight and distribution systems may be organized along geographical lines, such as a northeastern warehouse division or overseas store operations. At Nike, CSR is such an important function that it is built into the firm's structure in the form of a separate CSR department, headed by a vice president.

The optimal organizational design is the one that best supports the firm's strategy, giving attention to key functions. Therefore, organization structure varies from industry to industry and from company to company within an industry.

## The CSR Filter

Competencies molded into a strategy and supported by structure are no longer sufficient for success. It is vital that firms also consider the societal and stakeholder implications of these aspects of operations. The *CSR filter* is a conceptual screen through which strategic and tactical decisions are evaluated for their impact on the firm's various stakeholders. Here the intent is to take a viable strategy and make it *optimal* for the stakeholder environment in which the strategy must be executed. Although CSR is only one part of the strategic big picture, even clever strategies can fail if the strategy or its implementation is perceived as socially *irresponsible.* The CSR filter injects multiple considerations into the decision mix beyond the profit maximization goals that are central to the firm's survival. The application of these societal-based considerations screens strategies for their impact on the firm's multiple constituents. Together, these stakeholders form the larger environment, called society, within which the firm operates and seeks to implement its tactics, strategy, mission, and vision.

Part II of this book discusses the various considerations that compose the ever changing mosaic labeled collectively as the "CSR Filter" in Figure 3.2. Beyond identifying some of the scores of issues embedded in the CSR filter, Part II also provides company-specific case studies outlining the practical impact of these considerations, as well as Web-based resources for further exploration. But before turning to specific issues that make CSR such an intellectually challenging and operationally vital subject, changing societal expectations underscore the growing impact of CSR on strategy.

## THE STRATEGIC LENS: ENVIRONMENTAL CONTEXT

Customers, competitors, economics, technology, government, sociocultural factors, and other forces all drive changes in the firm's external environment. Often, these changes are gradual and imperceptible to all but the keenest observers. But over time, their cumulative impact redefines the competitive environment and what organizational strategies and actions are deemed socially acceptable. As Professor Archie Carroll observed,[2] this evolution of what is socially expected of organizations typically migrates from discretionary to ethical to mandatory (legal and economic).

Over time, actions previously considered discretionary or ethical can be codified as laws or government rulings and, finally, as economic components of operations. For example, many firms in the United States once blatantly paid women less than men for the same work. For whatever justifications that were applied, this behavior was within the discretionary decision-making authority of businesses. Gradually, such discrimination was seen to be unfair, even unethical. Then, in 1963, the federal government enacted the Equal Pay Act, which outlawed discrimination in pay solely based on one's gender. This legislation immediately served to limit this once discretionary area of management decision making. Today, diversity in the workplace is viewed as an economic imperative, helping firms respond effectively to their consumers' needs.

More generally, once society recognizes a particular form of discrimination, or other socially unacceptable action, the perceived abuse can lead to a legally mandated correction, such as the Equal Pay Act. Consequently, the range of socially acceptable employment policies used to facilitate competitive strategies has changed greatly in the last half century.[3] Similar changes can be identified with regard to environmental pollution, product safety standards, financial record keeping, and scores of other, previously discretionary behaviors. Once discretionary issues evolve into legal constraints, meeting societal expectations becomes an absolute requirement, enforced by criminal or civil sanctions.

More difficult to identify are issues not yet subject to legal mandates. If leaders exercise discretionary authority to attain economic ends but that use of their authority is deemed socially irresponsible, the consequences may damage sales, employee recruitment and retention, financial support from investors and markets, and a host of other important relationships. What should a company do?

At one extreme are the views of Milton Friedman,[4] that to consider CSR-related issues is a distraction from the firm's profit-seeking and wealth-creating functions. Friedman has stated that as long as a company can remain in business (i.e., consumers continue buying its products or services), it should be entitled to do so because it provides jobs for society and a return on investment for shareholders. At the other extreme lies the argument that society has the right, even the obligation, to restrain the negative excesses of businesses. This position states that just as societies rely on the commerce and industry businesses create, companies unarguably rely on the resources of the societies within which they are based. No organization exists in isolation, and businesses, without exception, have an obligation to contribute to the communities on which they rely so heavily for employees and financial or other resources.

*Strategic CSR* bridges both these arguments. True, a business cannot ignore its profit-seeking and wealth-creating functions if it is to remain in existence; however, if the firm is to survive beyond the short run, it must pursue these ends of profits and wealth creation by means that are deemed acceptable to the larger society. Ultimately, as was argued in Chapter 1, stakeholders have the right and the power to determine what is acceptable corporate behavior. At its most basic level, customers can exercise this right by redirecting their purchases elsewhere. The standards society applies to define socially responsible behavior embrace moral, cultural, ethical, historical, economic, and other issues. Regardless of what those standards are or how they are promulgated, long-term business success demands at least minimum compliance with societal expectations. Otherwise, stakeholders can limit the firm's ability to earn profits and create wealth. Simply put, businesses are increasingly expected to pursue their strategies in ways that do not harm others; and as societies become more affluent and interconnected, the definition of *harm* changes constantly.

Our starting point is that, in terms of CSR, very little is discretionary any more. Past expectations that viewed businesses narrowly as profit engines and little more have been altered beyond recognition both by globalization (and particularly the free flow of information that drives globalization) and growing affluence. Wealthier societies, given information about firm behaviors that are deemed irresponsible, have the resources to demand responsibility, even if those actions cost society more. For example, wealthy societies around the world uniformly demand that car producers make safer and less polluting cars because developed societies have the knowledge about the implications of unsafe or polluting autos and can afford to pay extra for seat belts and pollution control equipment. In today's globalizing world, shareholder value can be maximized over the long term only if the firm addresses the needs of as many stakeholder groups as possible. Satisfying stakeholders is often most efficiently achieved by adopting a CSR perspective as part of strategic planning, especially within informed and affluent societies.

# ENVIRONMENTAL FORCES PROPELLING GREATER CSR

Four environmental forces are driving CSR to the forefront of corporate strategic thinking: growing affluence, globalization, communications technologies, and brands. Any one of these drivers might be ignored by managers not convinced of the strategic benefits to the firm of CSR. Collectively, they are reshaping the business environment by empowering stakeholder groups. And, because each of these trends interacts with the others, the reinforcing effects mean that the environmental context will not only change but will change at an increasingly rapid rate, often in ways not foreseen by today's best strategists. Though each is discussed separately, their interactive effects ensure the importance of the CSR filter for corporate strategists.

## CSR and Growing Affluence

As we mentioned in Chapter 1, CSR issues tend to gain a foothold in societies that are more affluent—societies where people have jobs, savings, and security and can afford the luxury of choosing between, for example, low-cost cars that pollute and those that do not. As public opinion evolves and government regulation races to catch up, actions previously thought of as discretionary often become legal obligations.

As a result, the greatest attention to CSR is found in developed economies; however, it would be shortsighted to assume that CSR is only applicable where there is affluence.

An example: In the past, manufacturers have often been able to externalize some of their production costs to the larger society by polluting the environment. When the majority of people are desperately focused on the need for jobs to feed their families, pollution seems of limited concern. When most members of a society are desperately seeking food, shelter, and other necessities of life, CSR seems a luxury of little relevance. As societies become increasingly affluent, however, the collective understanding of social issues, like pollution, grows, as does the ability of society to afford solutions.

Increasingly, multinational corporations are being held to high standards for their overseas activities in developing countries. Nike, for example, typically requires its subcontractors in developing nations to provide wages and working conditions above the local norms. Even so, activists have still taken Nike to task, criticizing the pay and working conditions of its subcontractors because local standards often are well below those that prevail in its home country, the United States. Similarly, protests against pollution, deforestation, and civil disruption by international petroleum companies have occurred (both internationally and at home) when the companies' operating standards overseas have been construed as harmful to host countries' societal interests. The obvious conclusion is that competitive strategies must consider the ever shifting pattern of societal expectations that become emboldened by the greater choices affluence affords societies.

## CSR and Globalization

Increasingly, corporations operate in a global business environment. The Internet, which drives this global environment, is a powerful enabling tool for communication and education; however, it also depersonalizes relations between individuals and reduces our sense of an immediate community. This, in turn, affects a business's sense of self-interest and can loosen the self-regulating incentive to maintain strong local ties. As Dr. Peter Whybrow[5] observes:

> Historically, . . . built-in social brakes reined in our acquisitive instincts. In the capitalist utopia envisioned by Adam Smith in the 18th century, self-interest was tempered by the competing demands of the marketplace and community. But with globalization, the idea of doing business with neighbors one must face the next day is a quaint memory, and all bets are off.[6]

Globalization, therefore, transforms the CSR debate and magnifies its importance exponentially. A domestic context is not the only lens through which the issue of CSR should be viewed. Today, no multinational company can afford to ignore CSR, even if employees or consumers appear not to care. For example, European consumers are just as likely to look to a company's operations in the United States, or elsewhere in the world, when judging to what extent a U.S. company's actions are acceptable and whether they are going to buy the company's products. Differences in cultures across the globe lead to widely varying expectations of workers, customers, governments, and citizens. Actions that may be acceptable, even required, in one culture may be prohibited in another.

---

An example: Discrimination based on gender is generally prohibited in developed societies, albeit with varying degrees of enforcement; however, in some cultures, like Saudi Arabia, women are segregated from male workers and face gender-based limitations on the type of work available. A firm operating in Europe and Arabia may well be considered socially irresponsible and culturally insensitive if it applied the same human resource policies across all operating locations. Yet, if women are treated differently in Saudi Arabia, criticisms may arise in Europe or elsewhere. Ignoring inconsistencies in company practices can place multinational firms in very awkward positions: On one hand, they must adapt their strategies to local expectations; but on the other hand, strategies based on varying standards can leave the firm open to negative publicity, lawsuits, or other harmful outcomes at home.

CSR is more relevant today than ever before because of globalization. In terms of the relationship between corporations and their various stakeholders, this process of globalization appears to be progressing through two phases, as suggested by Figure 3.3.

Phase I of globalization greatly empowered corporations, enabling them to expand operations on a worldwide basis, shift manufacturing offshore, reform supply chain management, and develop powerful global brands. Merger and acquisition activities blossomed (because it was a quick way for companies to grow) and, as they grew, their power increased significantly. Many commentators today claim one consequence of this growth is that corporations now have greater economic power than most nation states:

Of the world's 100 largest economies, 49 of them are countries and 51 are companies. General Motors has greater annual sales than the gross national products of Denmark, Thailand, Turkey, South Africa, or Saudi Arabia. Wal-Mart's economy is larger than that of Poland, Ukraine, Portugal, Israel, or Greece. Because of the size and influence of modern corporations, business ethics take on special significance.[7]

**Figure 3.3**   The Two Phases of Globalization

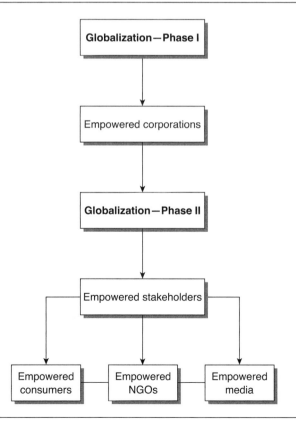

As globalization transcends the control of nation states, the power of global firms expands further. Companies today are free to incorporate offshore to avoid paying higher tax rates in their home country. They are also increasingly able to move their manufacturing operations or production processes to lower-cost environments, often in countries with less rigorous labor and environmental regulations. In addition, corporations benefit from establishing global brands because of greater sales and worldwide customer loyalty. The brand's value proposition may entice consumers with price, quality, or other features not otherwise available. Even regulating authorities may fear losing jobs, tax revenues, or even public support by fighting back against corporate power. Imagine, for example, if the European Union banned Microsoft products because of unfair or monopolistic operating practices. Microsoft's leverage over both consumers and regulating authorities may be too strong for such an outcome to be politically or economically feasible.

Globalization, however, creates countervailing forces that are capable of curtailing corporations' expanding power (as depicted in Phase II of Figure 3.3). Corporations are losing control over the flow of information, which empowers NGOs and consumer activists to communicate and mobilize. A growing list of examples suggests that companies are no longer able to dictate the quality and quantity of information about their company and how that information affects the social debate. Nike, ExxonMobil, and Gap are just a few examples of companies that have been damaged at some point by global information flows. Companies may be well advised to try to anticipate stakeholder needs and begin promoting operations from a CSR perspective rather than fight against the free flow of information:

> Thanks to instant communications, whistle-blowers and inquisitive media, citizens and communities routinely put firms under the microscope. And the Internet is a central focus and organizing force for all these activities. . . . Transparency is on the rise, not just for legal or purely ethical reasons but increasingly because it makes economic sense. Firms that exhibit openness and candor have discovered that they can better compete and profit.[8]

This self-feeding cycle of globalization, triggering reactions that are met with reformulated strategies and CSR policies, may well be leading to what Malcolm Gladwell refers to as "the tipping point"[9]—the point of critical mass after which an idea or social trend spreads wildly (like an epidemic) and becomes generally accepted and widely implemented. CSR is nearing its tipping point largely because of globalization and will increasingly become a mainstay of strategic thinking for businesses, especially global corporations.

The approaching CSR tipping point is reinforced by the gradual institutionalization of CSR in society. This institutionalization is evidenced by the numerous publications, references, and articles related to CSR found in the endnotes of this book. A Google search of the term *corporate social responsibility* (in quotation marks) reveals 1,430,000 hits, and the number is growing daily.[10] Perhaps more relevant to CSR professionals, the institutionalization of the field is documented by the growing number of organized CSR-related consultancies, think tanks, and advocacy groups, many of which are listed in Part III of this book. CSR organizations of like-minded individuals meeting regularly around the world, organized through the Web site meetup.com, already number 45 groups, with members from 47 cities and 12 different countries (http://csr.meetup.com/about/).

# CSR and Communications Technologies

Phase II of globalization (see Figure 3.3) suggests a shift in the balance of power concerning control over the flow of information back toward stakeholders in general and three important constituent groups in particular. First, the Internet has greatly empowered consumers because of the access it provides to greater amounts of information, particularly when an issue achieves a critical mass in the media. Second, globalization has increased the influence of NGOs because they, too, are benefiting from easily accessible and affordable communications technologies. These tools empower NGOs by enabling them to inform, attract, and mobilize geographically dispersed individuals and consumer segments, helping to ensure that socially nefarious activities achieve visibility. And third, new tools of communication and the demand for instantaneous information have enhanced the power of media conglomerates. Media companies have responded by increasing both their size and scope of operations, which ensures corporations today are unable to hide behind the fig leaves of superficial PR campaigns:

> We are approaching a theoretical state of absolute informational transparency. . . . As individuals steadily lose degrees of privacy, so, too, do corporations and states. . . . It is becoming unprecedentedly difficult for anyone, anyone at all, to keep a secret. In the age of the leak and the blog, of evidence extraction and link discovery, truths will either out or be outed. This is something I would bring to the attention of every diplomat, politician and corporate leader: the future, eventually, will find you out. . . . In the end, you will be seen to have done that which you did.[11]

The new kind of activism this technology is stimulating among consumers and NGOs, combined with the insatiable demand of the always-on global media conglomerates, is increasingly extending CSR concerns and awareness. And globalization is continuing to enhance the power of the Internet. For example, developing economies will enjoy increasing access via wireless technology (mobile phones and text messaging) rather than via the desktop computers and land telephone lines that were the foundation of the Internet in the developed economies. The result is an ever widening, free flow of information in a globalizing world, as suggested by Figure 3.4 and by the following examples:

- Seattle protests against the World Trade Organization in 1999 being organized entirely over the Internet by groups with little financial resources.
- Citizens overthrowing President Estrada of the Philippines in 2001 using text messages spread via cell phones to mobilize and coordinate actions.
- A youth political movement in South Korea (the country with the most advanced broadband infrastructure and highest proportion of per capita connections),[12] revitalized and mobilized by a campaign conducted largely on the Internet by the online newspaper *OhmyNews*.[13] The Web site's coverage of the 2002 presidential elections heavily influenced the outcome, helping deliver victory to President Roh Moo Hyun.
- Citizens in China using their increasingly ubiquitous cell phones[14] and e-mail or text messaging to spread concerns about SARS in 2003, forcing a brief political opening-up and government recognition of the crisis.

**Figure 3.4**   The Free Flow of Information in a Globalizing World

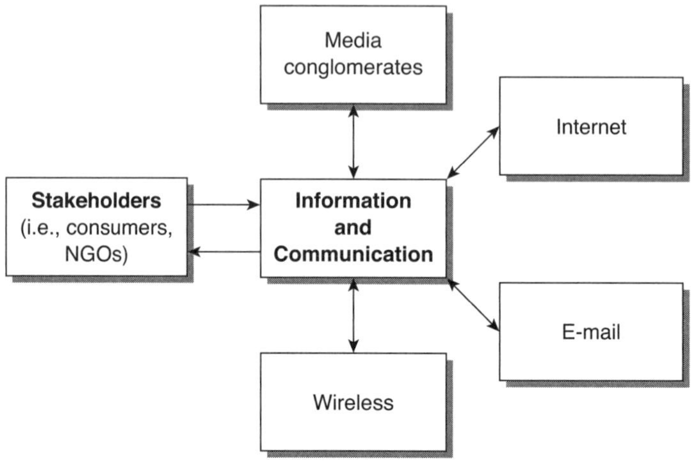

- Cell phones aiding the democracy movement Orange Revolution[15] in the Ukraine, which overturned the presidential election of Prime Minister Viktor Yanukovych in 2004 (widely suspected to have been engineered fraudulently) and forced a revote, eventually won by the opposition leader Viktor Yushchenko:

Using the phones' SMS messaging technology, demonstrators sent messages to meet. . . . Meanwhile, community Websites in Ukraine would post the numbers of tents on the [Independence] square where medical help was needed, or . . . recruit people with specific TV skills needed at . . . the lone independent TV station. The Ukrainian Supreme Court's historic Dec. 3 [2004] decision, declaring the election a fraud, was streamed on the Internet live from a Kiev courtroom . . . [and] sent out on e-mail distribution lists so the next steps could be discussed by the reform network and put in motion within an hour.[16]

Admittedly, these examples are all political movements, for now. This technology will affect corporate targets, too. It is only a matter of time. Whether it is via flash mobs[17] (http://www.flashmob.com/), moblogs[18] (using mobile camera phones to construct blog-type diary Web sites), or simply playing Pac-Manhattan[19] (adapting the computer game Pac-Man to the streets of Manhattan using mobile phones and global positioning system [GPS] technology), the power of information technology to mobilize strangers and unite them under a common agenda is mind-boggling. Harnessing this power and directing it at a corporate target has the potential to inflict significant damage to any firm's product, brand, or reputation.

Success today assumes companies reflect accurately the values and aspirations of a broad range of stakeholder groups. For companies that promote lifestyle brands, such as Nike, this rule is even more significant. Corporations moving to take the initiative and meet stakeholder expectations (while avoiding confrontation) need to put in place clear and open channels of communication that allow stakeholder concerns to find their way through to the strategy and decision-making table.

A key component of this dialog can be joining with NGOs (and other nonprofits) to pursue talks or projects in areas of common concern. NGOs and consumers (both independently and together) use the free flow of information, with the help of the media, to spread knowledge and build coalitions. These coalitions can occur spontaneously or as part of coordinated campaigns. One consistent factor, however, is their fluidity, encouraged by the nature of the technology, with groups bonding together for a particular issue then disbanding and joining other partners for a different issue. Besides avoiding conflict, developing a dialog with stakeholders offers potential benefit for firms. NGOs and nonprofits can help companies understand the rapidly evolving markets in which they are operating, help them stay in touch with the consumers they are targeting, and contribute in areas such as product development and trend identification.

Simply put, "The Internet makes it possible to organize a global community around a certain issue in a split second."[20] Consider two brief examples:

1. *Media conglomerates—the CNN test. A few giant media companies control large percentages of the information we receive across a wide range of media.* The CNN test has been a criterion that causes CSR sensitive decision makers to ask, "How will this be viewed by watchers of CNN when broadcast around the world?" Even U.S. military commanders used this test to select bombing targets during the second Iraq war in 2003. This test shows the influence of the media in shaping government policy as well as public opinion today and why the CNN test is part of the CSR filter for some organizations.

2. *Internet Web sites—knowledge. The Internet conveys information rapidly to large numbers of people.* Howard Dean's fund-raising dominance early in the race for the 2004 Democratic presidential nomination[21] is another example of how Web sites and e-mails can drive social change (the tactics Dean used were later adopted by the Democratic nominee, John Kerry, and are expected to be widely used by both political parties from now on).

In short, for companies to enjoy sustained success in a globalizing business environment, CSR will increasingly form a central component of strategy and operations, particularly in relation to a firm's brand management.

## CSR and Brands

Brands today are often a focal point of corporate success. Companies try to establish popular brands in consumers' minds because it increases any competitive advantage they hold that is then directly reflected in sales and revenue. We have identified three benefits of CSR to brands:

### *Positive Brand Building*

### *The Body Shop*

Anita Roddick had long championed the power of an influential global brand to enact meaningful social change. In doing so, she helped distinguish her firm in the minds of consumers, gaining a strategic advantage. Whether you agree with the stance that The Body Shop adopted on a number of fair trade and other social issues, many consumers were drawn to purchase the company's products because of the positions it took.[22] Its fair trade stance helps differentiate the firm's offerings and stands out in the minds of consumers. Likewise, Benetton has also set itself apart through advertising, using its voice to comment on the social issues that it thinks are relevant to its consumers.[23] Ben & Jerry's is another activist-alternative brand in a similar vein,[24] although its cult-like status has faded somewhat since being bought by Unilever in 2000.

## BP

With a $200 million rebranding exercise, BP has repositioned itself as the most environmentally and socially responsible of the extraction companies. The company stands in stark contrast to ExxonMobil, which faces ongoing NGO attacks, consumer boycotts, and activist-led litigation because of its decision to oppose the environmental movement. Shell has also done a good, if less high-profile, job of rebranding itself in a similar way to BP, although it was tainted by a scandal concerning the reporting of proven oil reserves in 2004.

### Brand Insurance

### Nike

Today, this company is one of the most progressive global corporations in terms of CSR, largely because of past mistakes and attacks by NGOs. Nike has become more proactive in arguing the positive impact of its operations and products worldwide. Nike has created a vice president for corporate responsibility and publishes CSR reports to institutionalize a commitment to CSR in its corporate structure and operations as well as help protect the company's brand against future CSR lapses.

### Merck & Co.

Reflecting a socially responsible stance, George W. Merck, son of the pharmaceutical company's founder, announced, "Medicine is for the patients, not for the profits." This "radical" corporate vision translates into an often cited example of the company donating the medicine Mectizan to combat the devastating disease river blindness. Since the decision was announced in 1987, the company says that it has given the medicine away free to more than 30 million people every year and will continue to do so "for as long as necessary."[25] It could be argued that Merck's actions bought a degree of insurance against attacks by social activists because of the company's up-front commitment to such a worthwhile, unselfish, and unprofitable cause. Perhaps this socially responsible viewpoint has enabled Merck to enjoy a relatively free run from the activist criticism visited on other pharmaceutical companies. The reputation it gained from this act has also been cited as a significant reason for the company's success in entering new markets, most notably Japan, where its socially responsible reputation preceded it. Yet even Merck's proactive CSR efforts may not save it from the economic and legal implications of Vioxx, a Merck product voluntarily withdrawn from the market in 2004 after a growing number of heart-related health problems among users.

### Crisis Management

#### Johnson & Johnson

Johnson & Johnson's transparent handling of the Tylenol crisis in 1982 is widely heralded as the model case in the area of crisis management. J&J went beyond what had previously been expected of corporations in such situations, instigating a $100 million recall of 31 million bottles of the drug following a suspected poisoning incident. In acting the way it did, J&J saved the Tylenol brand, enabling it to remain a strong revenue earner for the company to this day.[26]

Brand value is critical to firms, whether on the local or global stage. Today, the value of the intangible brand may even exceed the value of the firm's tangible assets. The Coca-Cola brand, for example, is worth significantly more than half of the company's total market capitalization.[27] And CSR is important to brands within a globalizing world because of the way brands are built: on perceptions, ideals, and concepts that usually appeal to higher values. CSR is a means of matching corporate operations with stakeholder values at a time when these values are constantly evolving. Thus, given the large amount of time, money, and effort companies invest in creating them, a good CSR policy has become a vital component of a successful corporate brand—an effective means of maximizing its market appeal while protecting the firm's investment over the long term.

Companies today need to build a watertight brand with respect to all stakeholders. The attractiveness of a company—whether as an employer, producer, buyer, supplier, or investment—is directly linked to the strength of its brand. CSR affects all aspects of operations within a corporation because of the need to consider the needs of all constituent groups. Each area builds on all the others to create a composite image of the corporation and its brand in the eyes of all its stakeholder groups.

## STRATEGIC CSR

The Strategic CSR Model, Figure 3.5, visually summarizes the relationship between CSR and strategy. Corporate success assumes that strategy matches internal competencies with external opportunities in such a way that the firm achieves its mission as it strives toward its vision. An effective CSR policy requires proactive action (regarding strategic initiatives) that helps the company achieve its strategic and CSR objectives. We, therefore, see CSR as a competitive differentiator for a firm, as well as a form of brand insurance, in which the brand represents the perception of the company by each of its key stakeholder groups.

As societies in general become more affluent, societal expectations evolve, and communication technologies become even more widespread, greater and greater demands for CSR will result. Certainly, moral and rational arguments exist for companies to act in a socially responsible manner; however, a strong economic incentive also exists to be perceived as a net contributor within a society and provides the strongest reason for the implementation of CSR with the long-term viability of the organization.

This economic argument surfaces daily in advertising and public relations campaigns. The sophisticated level to which the crisis management industry has evolved in the United States further demonstrates the value of reputation. Investors, as one stakeholder, "are willing to give higher valuations to companies that are deemed good citizens. Put another way, investors give some companies with good track records the benefit of the doubt."[28]

**Figure 3.5**  The Strategic CSR Model

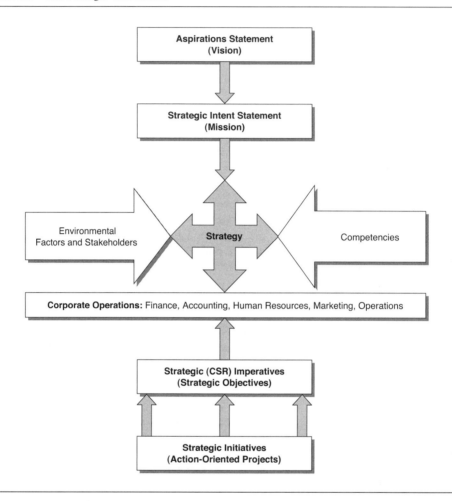

Companies understand the value of being perceived as friendly neighbors and good corporate citizens. Until now, however, managers have largely confined this to public relations because they were able to control the information that determined the public face of the corporation. Figure 3.3 (outlining the current shift from the first to the second phase of globalization) and Figure 3.4 (documenting elements of the increasingly free flow of information) show why this situation is changing as the momentum swings away from multinationals and toward their various constituent groups. As globalization progresses, the Internet and global media will further democratize and feed the exchange of information in developed and developing societies. Thus, strategic CSR goes beyond just good public relations. It is about substantive actions—good or bad—that flash around the world through electronic technologies and the global media.

Companies need to reflect the concerns of society through substantive actions, especially regarding the consumer base of their target market. Ideally, progressive companies seek to stay ahead of these evolving values and are able to meet new stakeholder demands as they arise. Significantly, core constituent groups are increasingly acquiring the information necessary to see past superficial advertising campaigns, as well as the means to communicate their message and mobilize where necessary. The balance of power and influence is shifting between corporations and their stakeholders because of this change in control of the flow of information. An effective CSR policy allows firms to take advantage of these changes and maximize their economic performance in an increasingly globalizing world.

Key to the practical impact of CSR, therefore, is the ability to persuade business leaders that CSR offers strategic and economic benefits. Firms can only maximize *shareholder* value in a globalizing world by utilizing strategies that address the needs of key *stakeholders*. CSR, driven by stakeholder theory, delivers these results. It is a means of allowing firms to analyze the total business environment and formulate appropriate organizational strategies. It can protect the firm and its assets, while also offering a point of competitive differentiation. When the business community perceives CSR in this way (and this is increasing as globalization affects more and more of our lives), CSR will receive greater attention from 21st century leaders.

## QUESTIONS FOR DISCUSSION AND REVIEW

1. Why is it important to view CSR from a strategic context?

2. Define and explain the relationship among vision, mission, and strategy.

3. How do competencies, strategy, structure, and the external environment combine to create a successful organization?

4. What advantages does a CSR filter give to a company? If you were CEO of a firm, how would you go about implementing the CSR filter—what form might it take? Can you think of a company that is successfully utilizing a CSR filter today?

5. What are the four environmental forces propelling greater interest in CSR? Explain using real-life examples to illustrate your points. Do you see emerging forces that may reshape CSR in the future?

6. Why are lifestyle brands more susceptible to CSR than more traditional companies and products?

7. What are the three aspects of brand management that benefit from CSR?

## NOTES

1. Bruce D. Henderson, 'The Origin of Strategy,' *Harvard Business Review,* November–December, 1989, pp 134–143.

2. Carroll, Archie B., 'A Three-Dimensional Conceptual Model of Corporate Performance,' *Academy of Management Review,* 1979, Vol. 4, No. 4, pp 497–505.

3. Same sex partner employee benefits will likely be the next form of discrimination to be corrected by legal mandate. Many progressive firms today are proactively implementing such policies so as to avoid being forcefully sanctioned by litigation as the tide of social acceptability turns.

4. Milton Friedman, 'Capitalism and Freedom,' University of Chicago Press, 1962; and, 'The Social Responsibility of Business Is to Increase Its Profits,' *New York Times Magazine,* September 13, 1970.

5. Peter Whybrow is the Director of the Semel Institute of Neuroscience and Human Behavior at the University of California at Los Angeles.

6. Summarized by Irene Lacher, 'In New Book, Professor Sees a "Mania" in U.S. for Possessions and Status,' *New York Times,* March 12, 2005, pA21.

7. O. Lee Reed, et al., 'The Legal and Regulatory Environment of Business,' 12th edition, McGraw-Hill, 2002, p133.

8. Don Tapscott & David Ticoll, 'The Naked Corporation,' *Wall Street Journal,* October 14, 2003, pB2. Tapscott and Ticoll are coauthors of 'The Naked Corporation: How the Age of Transparency Will Revolutionize Business,' Free Press, 2003.

9. Malcolm Gladwell, 'The Tipping Point: How Little Things Can Make a Big Difference,' Little Brown, 2000.

10. Search performed in May 2005 at http://www.google.com/

11. William Gibson, 'The Road to Oceania,' *New York Times,* June 25, 2003, pA27.

12. 'Progress at a Snail's Pace,' *The Economist,* October 11, 2003, p43.

13. http://english.ohmynews.com/ (original site in Korean: http://www.ohmynews.com/)

14. "Chinese society is saturated with mobile phones. . . . There are more than 260 million cell-phone users, according to government figures, a tenfold increase from five years ago." Gladys A. Epstein, '"Cell Phone" Rings True,' *Miami Herald,* February 1, 2004, p25A.

15. For an "objective and unbiased" view of the events in the Ukraine, see: http://www.crocodile .org/UA-Election-2004/

16. Daniel Henninger, 'Wonder Land: Here's One Use of U.S. Power Jacques Can't Stop,' *Wall Street Journal,* December 17, 2004, pA14.

17. Daniel Chang, 'Flash Mobs Come (Late) to South Florida' *Miami Herald,* August 30, 2003, p1E; and Wanda J. DeMarzo, 'Dollars, and Jaws, Drop as "Flash Mob" Fad Hits S. Florida,' *Miami Herald,* August 31, 2003, p4A.

18. Ann Grimes, 'Moblog for the Masses,' *Wall Street Journal,* April 29, 2004, pB4.

19. Warren St. John, 'Quick, After Him: Pac-Man Went Thataway,' *New York Times,* May 9, 2004, Section 9, p1.

20. Michael Elliott, 'Embracing the Enemy Is Good Business,' *Time,* August 13, 2001, p29.

21. "[From March 2003 to March 2004, Howard Dean's] campaign raised more than $50 million [online]—most of it through donations of less than $100." John H. Fund, 'Bookshelf: Caught in the Web,' *Wall Street Journal,* July 28, 2004, pD10. "[John Kerry] emerged as the largest online fund-raiser in [the 2004 political campaign], bringing in about $82 million over the Internet. . . . The one-day record of $5.7 million was set when Mr. Kerry accepted the Democratic nomination." Glen Justice, 'Kerry Kept Money Coming With Internet as His A.T.M.' *New York Times,* November 6, 2004, pA10.

22. 'Our History and Values: A Message From Dame Anita Roddick, The Body Shop Founder,' http://www.thebodyshop.com/bodyshop/company/index.jsp;jsessionid=0F1NXOKOQTJX1ULSIIX FAFOROJBC0UP4

23. http://www.benettongroup.com/en/whatwesay/campaigns.htm

24. http://www.benandjerrys.com/our_company/our_mission/index.cfm

25. http://www.merck.com/about/cr/mectizan/home.html

26. Mallen Baker, 'Companies in Crisis: What to Do When It All Goes Wrong,' CSR Case Studies in Crisis Management: Johnson & Johnson, http://www.mallenbaker.net/csr/CSRfiles/crisis02.html

27. Coca-Cola's brand was consistently ranked number 1 in value in *BusinessWeek's* annual brand surveys from 2002 to 2004. The brand was estimated to be worth $67.39 billion in the 2004 survey: Gerry Khermouch, 'The Best Global Brands,' *BusinessWeek,* August 5, 2002, pp 92–99; Gerry Khermouch et al., 'Brands in an Age of Anti-Americanism,' *BusinessWeek,* August 4, 2003, pp 69–78; and Diane Brady et al., 'Cult Brands,' *BusinessWeek,* August 2, 2004, pp 64–71.

28. Paul J. Lim, 'Gauging That Other Company Asset: Its Reputation,' *New York Times,* April 10, 2004, pA18.

# Chapter 4

## IMPLEMENTATION: THE INTEGRATION OF CSR INTO STRATEGY AND CULTURE

The first three chapters of this book set out the case for CSR, addressed the anti-CSR argument, and analyzed CSR's strategic importance within the global economy. This chapter provides insights as to what a firm must do to integrate strategic CSR into the organization's culture and actions. That is, *when* and *how* does a company become more socially responsible?

For example, when should a company begin adopting CSR as a strategic determining factor? Is there a standard point of organizational evolution at which this should occur, or does it differ from company to company and among industries? How should management construct CSR policies that can then filter down throughout the organization? How will stakeholders determine a genuine CSR strategy from a cynical attempt to create positive public relations?

We address the *when* by focusing on the *CSR threshold*, a tipping point that triggers firms to move toward strategic CSR. Then we turn to the *how* by outlining the design, timing, and implementation of strategic CSR, introducing the necessary corporate infrastructure and key policy ideas.

## THE CSR THRESHOLD

The decision of *when* to implement a CSR policy is compounded by *why, where*, and *how* it should be implemented, not to mention *who* should oversee the process. The industry context complicates things further because of the varied stages of acceptance of CSR by different competitors. Although the value of an effective CSR policy within specific industries and companies is becoming increasingly accepted, the point at which such a policy becomes ripe for implementation (or unavoidable to those unconvinced of the benefits) varies. It varies with many factors, including the industry, the current business environment, the CEO's attitude toward CSR, and other factors.

Companies can pursue an effective CSR policy for either offensive or defensive reasons. The innovative, proactive CEO who is convinced of the intrinsic value of CSR sees it as an opportunity[1] that can maximize company capabilities and identify new competitive advantages. Examples abound. Creative, environmentally sound ideas (Grand Hyatt Singapore),[2] innovative building design (*Jie Fang Daily News,* Shanghai),[3] and efficient recycling policies (Anheuser-Busch)[4] can significantly reduce energy costs. Employee volunteer programs (Timberland)[5] can raise morale and increase retention, therefore lowering training costs while inducing new skills and stoking corporate pride. Companies with a progressive and innovative mind-set capable of designing and implementing effective CSR policies see benefits, ranging from being an attractive employer (helping retention and recruitment) to greater acceptance among government agencies (such as needed zoning) and social activists (such as Greenpeace).

On the defensive side, CSR still has value for a company, primarily by avoiding criticism and other attacks on the firm or its offerings. In this instance, CSR acts like a brand insurance policy, minimizing or offsetting stakeholder disillusionment in response to perceived lapses in CSR.[6]

Either approach assumes an up-front investment in creating CSR policies; however, *when* to introduce CSR into the strategic process depends on the driving force behind its implementation. For those managers convinced of the potential benefits of strategic CSR, there is no time like the present. Innovative ideas and policies that maximize market opportunities, minimize costs, and increase productivity can produce immediate benefits. For managers yet to be persuaded of the argument for CSR and reluctant to invest up front for potential future gains, however, the temptation exists to look around at industry competitors and delay as long as possible. Worse, cynical managers might see CSR as merely a public relations exercise or, worse still, postpone hard CSR choices by assuming they can avoid the expense altogether. Perhaps this is analogous to staying healthy so one can avoid outlays for health insurance— a risky, if not foolhardy, approach.

Nevertheless, a crisis point can arise. Once reached, and stakeholder backlash becomes sufficient to warrant the introduction of a reactionary CSR policy, it may be too late. For example, as mentioned in Chapter 2, in April 2005 Wal-Mart announced that it would donate $35 million during the next decade to the National Fish and Wildlife Foundation. Though commendable, this action took place "barely a week after environmentalists forged a broad alliance with organized labor and community groups to attack Wal-Mart and its business practices."[7] Complicating matters further, this threshold ebbs and flows with public perceptions and media spin, which can change with the next news cycle. Even more confounding is the variability that exists among industries, as well as among companies within the same industry.

In summary, firms introduce CSR for different reasons. Implementing CSR proactively throughout the firm generates the business benefits listed above and may yield additional benefits associated with first-mover status. The genuine implementation of CSR, whether for offensive or defensive reasons, generates the insurance-like benefits, which render CSR lapses less damaging if committed due to factors outside the firm's control.

Whatever the motivation, however, there is a CSR threshold in every industry that acts as a last-resort, CSR point of no return. The sooner CSR is introduced, the less likely a firm is to cross this "tipping point,"[8] which varies for each company (depending on whether it is the market leader or a smaller player) and within each industry (some industries are more susceptible to stakeholder backlash than others). The variable nature of this CSR threshold suggests why some companies perceive CSR to be of greater or lesser importance to their particular organization.

Why is it that different companies and industries have different CSR thresholds for different reasons? Our research indicates that the business-level strategy a company pursues is key to answering this question.

## The CSR Threshold—Variations Between Companies

Analyzing a company's business-level strategy reveals how it distinguishes itself in the marketplace. Its value proposition is captured in its strategy and attracts stakeholder groups, particularly customers. In turn, strategy has a direct impact on the CSR threshold for that company within its industry.

Consider these comparisons in light of Figure 4.1. Wal-Mart's cost strategy, for example, probably raises the company's CSR threshold; that is, it has more CSR leeway and can "get away with" more because its value proposition is based on low cost. Thus, a Wal-Mart shopper is unlikely to be surprised to discover that the company pays its employees some of the lowest wages in the retail industry.

For a company like The Body Shop, however, which has built its reputation and customer base largely on the social justice issues it chooses to advocate (such as no animal testing), the CSR threshold at which customers, media, and society in general react may have a much lower tipping point. Thus, The Body Shop's stakeholders are more likely to have a lower threshold of tolerance for perceived CSR violations. Restated, a Body Shop consumer would expect the company to live up to the values that attracted them in the first place, which translates into a correspondingly lower CSR threshold for the firm. For example, one CSR error by The Body Shop may well be equal, in terms of stakeholder perception, to multiple CSR oversights by Wal-Mart.

**Figure 4.1**   The Business-Level CSR Threshold

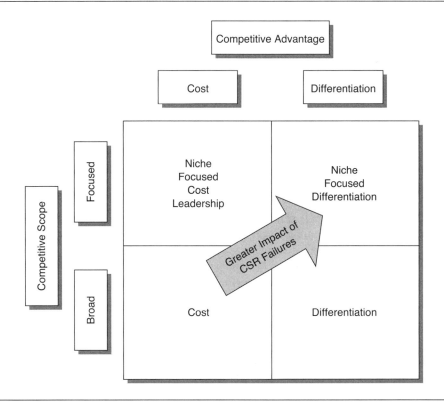

As suggested by Figure 4.1, business-level strategies can be divided into those pursuing low costs and those pursuing differentiation. The low-cost approach suggests an ability to deliver products or services at a price below that of competitors. Because what Wal-Mart sells is not fundamentally different from what other competitors offer, Wal-Mart gains its competitive advantage from its "everyday low prices." Differentiation strategies, however, seek to offer the customer something unique, such as a luxury car from Rolls Royce.

These low-cost and differentiation strategies can be further categorized as either broad (e.g., a wide product range) or narrowly focused (e.g., pursuing only high-end cars, but not SUVs, station wagons, or pickup trucks). As a result, Wal-Mart has a scope of business that can be labeled *broad,* while Rolls Royce's offerings are *focused.*

Overall, therefore, Rolls Royce's business strategy offers a *differentiated* product, focused on the *niche* market of high-end cars, whereas Wal-Mart's strategy pursues *cost leadership* (low costs) across a *broad* base of customers. A firm like McDonald's, however, seeks a focused strategy of low cost (cheap food) *and* differentiation (fast service).[9]

Whether a company pursues a cost- or differentiation-based strategy shapes the firm's CSR threshold, the point at which CSR becomes obviously critical to strategic success. The most vulnerable strategy will be focused differentiation, particularly for those products dependent on lifestyle segmentation, such as products targeted at specific customers based on their approach to life. For example, Nike tries to associate its products (athletic wear and shoes) with people who have a positive and physically active lifestyle. If, however, Nike is seen as socially irresponsible by its target customers, they are less likely to want to associate their lifestyle with these products. Market segments, or niches, such as lifestyle brands, are especially valuable to a company because they often rest more heavily on subjective impressions—such as the fickle sense of fashion—as opposed to objective price and quality comparisons. Moreover, customers who associate the brand's appeal with their lifestyle are often willing to pay a greater premium for the product. Yet, paradoxically, those able to pay this premium are precisely those with the widest range of alternatives, backed by the resources to make different choices. Thus, a CSR-related failure that might inflict limited harm on a firm relying on a broad, cost-based strategy could prove significantly damaging to one reliant on a strategy of focused differentiation.

The petroleum industry, where consumers draw less distinction between similar gasolines from different companies, offers another example. The nature of this industry allows ExxonMobil to adopt a lower CSR profile than either BP or Shell (which have made greater strides in this area) without penalty.[10] This implies a higher CSR threshold for ExxonMobil because it has both lower visibility among environmentalists and its products are hardly differentiated from either BP's or Shell's.

As different companies range across the chart in Figure 4.1 (in the direction of the shaded arrow) from cost- to differentiation-based strategies, the CSR threshold that they face is likely to fall, making those firms more susceptible to stakeholder backlash. This, therefore, increases the importance of an effective and well-implemented CSR policy within the firm. A similar tendency is visible when analyzing the industries within which these firms operate.

## The CSR Threshold—Variations Between Industries

Different industries also evoke different stakeholder emotions. For example, a company operating within the apparel industry (with its reputation for sweatshop labor in developing countries) may face a higher CSR threshold if it sells unbranded clothing based on low costs.

But the CSR threshold may drop dramatically for a company using a focused differentiation strategy that offers a "lifestyle brand" aimed at well-to-do customers who have choices and include more than just cost in their value calculations. If a well-known fashion brand, for example, is seen as violating CSR expectations, customers can quickly abandon the brand and products by shopping elsewhere. But, a large nonbranded producer, particularly one offering just low-cost styles, may have a much higher threshold, simply because the connection between product, brand, and customer aspirations is weaker.

By comparison, in the financial or banking industry (with its strategy of broad differentiation), the CSR threshold may be relatively higher than for apparel. Here it may be harder for consumers to identify a victim or accurately quantify the degree of harm caused by any CSR violation. For example, the U.S. mutual fund scandals in 2003—"One of the biggest financial scandals in U.S. history, which has so far implicated 15 mutual funds, 12 brokerage firms, 4 banks, and dozens of individuals,"[11] suggests that when it comes to personal finance, the average American is more willing to separate ethics from personal benefit:[12]

> There's little evidence that scandal is hurting mutual fund sales. In October [2003], net inflows to equity funds hit an estimated $31 billion. . . . A strong stock market trumps some funds' bad behavior.[13]

> Net inflows to U.S. mutual funds rose to almost $300bn in 2003, the highest for seven years [32.77% average increase for the year[14]]. . . . Despite the widening scandal over mutual fund trading abuses, the surge in new money continued in January [2004] with an estimated $40bn flowing into equity and balanced funds. . . . The figures suggest the scandal has had only a short-term impact on a few fund managers.[15]

The issues that determine the CSR threshold for an industry seem more complicated than those for individual companies, with specific industries being more vulnerable than others. Indeed, a number of industries have already passed their CSR threshold, which has forced companies operating within those industries to take significant corrective action. One example is the fast-food industry and its recent conversion to the benefits of health foods.[16] Another example, the tobacco industry, passed its CSR threshold long ago. To hear Philip Morris warning against the dangers of smoking in its advertising campaigns—recommending tips on how to give up smoking, while providing URL links on the company's Web site (http://www.philipmorrisusa.com/) to help smokers quit—is to know that the industry long ago passed the point of no return with its CSR threshold.

## The CSR Threshold—Variations Between Cultures

Complicating the picture still further are CSR thresholds driven by different cultural expectations among different societies. Even among developed economies, there are stark differences. For example, it was legal action in the United States that determined the CSR thresholds for the tobacco and fast-food industries, likewise for the asbestos industry, given the ongoing litigation surrounding asbestos-related illnesses. In Europe, by contrast, instead of litigation-driven activism, it is NGO and nonprofit activism that has largely driven the CSR agenda. Again, examples abound and include the extraction industry (Shell and Greenpeace[17]), genetically modified foods (Monsanto and Friends of the Earth[18]), and Fair Trade Coffee (Starbucks and Oxfam[19]). In much of the developing world, however, the perception of CSR revolves around issues of corporate philanthropy, a subsection that consumes only a fraction of the CSR debate in developed economies.

Given these differences, however, globalization and the free flow of information help drive down CSR thresholds across the board and across cultures (reducing stakeholder tolerance and increasing the chance of backlash) as the news media expose corporate CSR lapses. Consider the results of a survey among 138 companies in eight East Asian countries that reviewed their corporate governance, social, and environmental performance:

> "On the whole the East-West difference is rather overblown and for a long time used by governments and ultra-nationals to defend the status quo" on corporate social and environmental performance, Mr. Choo (a researcher in the area of socially responsible investing) said. "I personally believe almost all SRI issues are universal and are not culturally based—it doesn't matter if Asians consider tobacco industries unethical or not, they are just plain bad and it doesn't take a Ph.D. to understand this."[20]

This greater availability of information helps forge, for better or worse, a more recognizable link between stakeholders and the company or product. Furthermore, as levels of affluence and living standards rise generally, the CSR threshold is likely to become lower still as issues of societal necessity evolve into greater social choice.

Just reporting on corruption among different countries, for example, highlights environments where CSR lapses are more likely and suggests areas where even greater controls are needed. Consider, for example,

> While some countries (such as index-toppers Finland, New Zealand, Denmark, and Iceland) are relatively "clean," the vast majority (106) of the 146 countries studied score less than 5 on a scale from 0 (most corrupt) to 10 (least corrupt). More than a third (60) of the countries scored less than a 3, and six countries (Bangladesh, Haiti, Nigeria, Chad, Myanmar, Azerbaijan, Paraguay) scored less than 2.[21]

The combination of globalization, rising living standards, and media applications of first-world standards to developing-world operations suggests that an effective CSR policy, which prevents CSR lapses and insulates against stakeholder backlash, is increasingly advisable for all firms and will grow in importance as these trends continue into the future. The theoretical CSR threshold model presented here argues that the different points at which CSR jumps onto the radar screens of leaders in different industries and between different companies varies based on a host of strategic and stakeholder factors. Best practice, in response to the uncertainty, is to implement a proactive CSR policy, which provides business benefit to the firm as well as a means of avoiding, or at least minimizing, negative publicity and societal backlash.

## WHERE DO FIRMS STAND TODAY?

Research provided by the Center for Corporate Citizenship at Boston College, a membership-based research organization (http://www.bcccc.net/), found from a sample of 515 firms that,

Like financial controls and human resource management, corporate citizenship is integral to keeping a business healthy. Most accept the notion that businesses have responsibilities that go beyond the traditional making money, providing jobs, and paying taxes. Most respondents report that their commitment is rooted in tradition and values; eight of ten say corporate citizenship helps the bottom line; and more than half indicate it is important to their customers. The attitude about and commitment to corporate citizenship by small- and medium-sized business leaders are just as strong as they are in the largest corporations.[22]

The study also found that good corporate citizenship was driven by a variety of internal and external forces. Traditions and values, reputation or image, and business strategy were internal forces, with consumers forming the most significant external pressures cited by more than 50% of the respondents. Lack of resources and a lack of top-management commitment, however, were perceived to be the greatest barriers to good corporate citizenship. Encouragingly, only 9% of the respondents reported seeing no benefit to the firm for good corporate citizenship.[23]

These research findings are supported by anecdotal evidence from a variety of top firms. Companies such as Nike,[24] Starbucks,[25] Ford,[26] Microsoft,[27] Timberland,[28] and a growing number of others have grouped CSR-related activities into CSR departments, led by executives. Though not all firms have interwoven CSR into their operations to such an extent, the leadership of these and other proactive firms suggests that such internal organizational structures are likely to be increasingly common as CSR gains attention and grows in importance.

But, how do firms become socially responsible?

# CSR BUSINESS PLAN OF ACTION—SHORT TERM

The urgency with which CSR policies are implemented depends on the perceived CSR threshold and the priority the issue holds with the firm's leaders. Implementation is about common-sense policies that represent a means of integrating a stakeholder perspective into all aspects of operations, thus protecting the often huge investments corporations make in their public image, investor confidence, and brands. The eventual goal should be for CSR to form an inherent component of a business's culture, as reflected in its day-to-day operations. The challenge is to move to a position at which all employees approach their work using a CSR filter (see Figure 3.2).

The following steps offer an overview of how any corporation can further the integration of CSR into its operational culture.

## From the Top Down With Sincere Commitment

The CEO must establish the necessary components of an effective CSR policy and ensure that CSR is institutionalized within the firm as a core component of day-to-day operating practice. Ideally, the CEO will consider himself or herself the chief CSR officer.[29] At a minimum, the CEO must remain in touch with the effectiveness of the company's CSR policy by receiving regular updates, while granting a clear line of access to the top for the CSR officer. This commitment from senior management is crucial for effective implementation.

Executives must exhibit leadership to infuse a stakeholder perspective. Otherwise, any CSR policy or statement will quickly become a hollow public relations gesture. A perfect example is Enron and its "award-winning" *Code of Ethics:*

> Look at this list of corporate values: Communication. Respect. Integrity. Excellence. They sound good don't they? Strong, concise, meaningful. Maybe they even resemble your own company's values, the ones you spent so much time writing, debating, and revising. If so, you should be nervous. These are the corporate values of Enron, as stated in the company's 2000 annual report. And as events have shown, they're not meaningful; they're meaningless.[30]

---

**Figure 4.2**   Top-Down Support for CSR—How It Should Not Be Done!

---

As officers and employees of Enron Corp., its subsidiaries, and its affiliated companies . . . we are responsible for conducting the business affairs of the Company in accordance with all applicable laws and in a moral and honest manner.[31]

Enron stands on the foundation of its Vision and Values. Every employee is educated about the Company's Vision and Values and is expected to conduct business with other employees, partners, contractors, suppliers, vendors and customers keeping in mind respect, integrity, communication and excellence. Everything we do evolves from Enron's Vision and Values statements.[32]

Employees of Enron Corp., its subsidiaries, and its affiliated companies (collectively the "Company") are charged with conducting their business affairs in accordance with the highest ethical standards. An employee shall not conduct himself or herself in a manner that directly or indirectly would be detrimental to the best interests of the Company or in a manner that would bring to the employee financial gain separately derived as a direct consequence of his or her employment with the Company. Moral as well as legal obligations will be fulfilled openly, promptly, and in a manner which will reflect pride on the Company's name.[33]

---

Some choice extracts from Enron's award-winning *Code of Ethics* appear in Figure 4.2. Clearly, a well-crafted position statement is not enough, nor is senior management's less than complete support. For example, ostensibly, CSR at Enron had top-management support: CEO Kenneth Lay signed off on all the documents. The point is that not only must injecting a CSR perspective be supported by top management, but that commitment must be enforced in practice on a day-to-day basis.

## CSR Officer

Top-management support must be translated into tangible action. CSR needs both visibility and sponsorship within the organization. Backing by the CEO equals sponsorship, and the creation of a CSR officer position staffed by a company executive (and with a direct reporting relationship to the board of directors) creates visibility. Influencing the corporate culture toward greater CSR requires time, effort, and details. Given other demands, CEOs are forced to delegate their efforts to a CSR officer. This CSR executive needs to formulate the direction that the company will pursue in terms of CSR. Thus, the champion must have access to the highest levels of decision making to ensure a CSR perspective is part of the strategic direction of the company. Starbucks[34] and Nike[35] provide good examples of this approach.

The CSR officer defines, implements, and audits the company's CSR policies. This includes assisting with legal and regulatory compliance, as well as compliance with discretionary—but advantageous—configurations, such as the ISO (International Organization for Standardization) standards (primary among which include ISO 9000 standards for quality management and ISO 14000 standards for environmental management).[36] It also includes input to strategy formulation. In addition, a CSR officer may lead innovations—such as the introduction of a Stakeholder Relations Department in place of the existing Investor Relations Department—to actively demonstrate the CSR commitment of the firm.

All these policies need an organizationwide perspective to ensure effective implementation and dissemination of benefits and goals. Ideally, but rarely found, the CSR officer must create awareness with a blend of rewards and, where necessary, penalties to organizational members who act in contrary ways. At a minimum, the CSR officer must be able to influence rewards and penalties. Thus, the CSR position is all encompassing. In particular, the CSR officer should be part risk manager, part ethics officer, part crisis manager, part brand builder and insurer, and part beacon bearer. Additionally, the CSR officer will need to develop contingency plans for the unexpected emergence of CSR crises.

Ideally, all departments will eventually grow a CSR perspective. In the short term, however, this effort must begin with a focal point in the form of a corporate officer whose first thoughts and contribution to the strategic decision-making process come from a CSR perspective. Over time, CSR will become more ingrained throughout the organization. But initially at least, focused leadership, supported by the CEO, is vital to strengthening the CSR perspective within the organizational culture.

## CSR Position Statement

All stakeholders (internal and external) need to understand the firm's CSR position and how that stance affects them. The value of a statement outlining the vision and mission for the organization is part of the awareness process, as mentioned in Chapter 3. Equally important for the company's CSR direction is a CSR position statement. The development of an effective CSR position statement

- *Engages* the organization's key stakeholders to determine their perspectives
- *Helps* map out a conflict resolution process that seeks mutually beneficial solutions
- *Involves* the CEO's necessary endorsement and active support
- *Reinforces* the importance of CSR through rewards and sanctions
- *Provides* policies on how CSR is to be implemented on a day-to-day basis

## Awareness Creation: Measurement and Rewards

Collectively, top-management support, the creation of a senior executive CSR position, and the elaboration of a CSR position statement address a critical element in implementing CSR—awareness. Although the intent of CSR may be noble, people tend (as the saying goes) to do "what is inspected not expected." Many CSR violations arise from decision makers at different levels of the organization sincerely trying to make good decisions for the organization. Faced with a choice between a minor violation of company rules about pollution, for example, or meeting a key performance deadline, a decision maker at any level of the firm might make a tradeoff that results in a CSR backlash. Why? Because in most firms, rewards (pay, promotions, bonuses, and the like) are based on performance results, not CSR compliance. If an incentive is tied to meeting a goal and CSR is neither measured nor rewarded, reasonable people inside the firm conclude that CSR is of secondary importance, whether it is or not.

---

An example: Third World subcontractors to Nike must comply with company employment standards that dictate pay, rest breaks, and other terms and conditions of employment. These standards are enforced by inspections. Those subcontractors who perpetuate sweatshop conditions that are contrary to Nike's requirements risk the penalty of losing their production contracts, even if these firms are in full compliance with local human resource laws and practices.

---

Whether internal to the firm or subcontractors, as in Nike's case, rewards and measures serve a fundamental role in changing the organizational culture to one of greater sensitivity to CSR. The creation of rewards and measures, particularly if those involved in applying CSR standards are involved in their development, increases awareness of CSR and its profile within the firm. Then, the reporting of CSR measures and assignment of rewards further reinforce CSR as part of the firm's strategy. These measures become part of the basis for auditing the firm's CSR performance.

## CSR Audit and Report

A genuine organizationwide CSR audit, with published results, furthers awareness among internal and external stakeholders. For example, environmental audits are now widely conducted, with the results included in companies' annual reports, because consumers and the public began demanding greater accountability for the environmental consequences of businesses' actions. In general, poor countries often put economic needs ahead of environmental controls. That is, poorer countries are more likely to permit firms to externalize, or push, environmental or other costs onto society—a tradeoff made to gain or retain jobs. The poorer a country is, the more desperate it is likely to be for jobs and the more willing it may be to allow firms to avoid costs like pollution cleanup or worker safety. As consumer and employee choice increase, usually related to increased affluence, the willingness to accommodate undesirable behavior decreases. Although many companies recognize the importance of being held publicly accountable for the consequences of operations, this realization does not always permeate the countless tactical decisions made by employees throughout the firm. The result can be lapses in a firm's CSR: The avoidable *Exxon Valdez* accident in 1989 provides a well-known example.[37]

Figure 4.3 suggests the entirety of the CSR auditing process. A company wanting to be transparent and accountable with respect to all of its stakeholders should seek to expand the scope of its annual report to incorporate the "triple bottom line"[38]—in equal parts, a consideration of a

**Figure 4.3**   A Broader Perspective: The CSR-Focused Triple Bottom Line

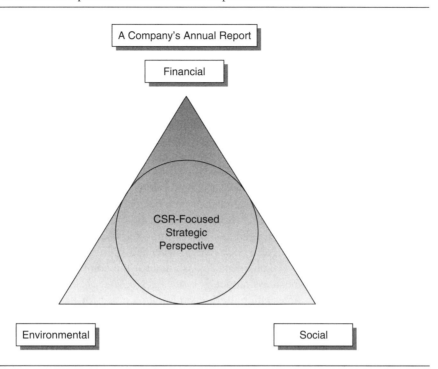

company's financial, environmental, and social performance—all centered on a CSR-focused strategic perspective. More and more firms are incorporating a CSR audit and the triple bottom line into their reporting process:

> From a point in 1992 when only 26 stand-alone corporate social responsibility reports were published, we now have a world where 81% of FTSE 100 companies produce one—and in 2003 a total of 1,791 PDFs and hard-copy versions were published.[39]

Beginning in April 2005 in the UK, an evaluation of social and environmental risks, as related to operations, is legally mandated as part of a company's financial reports:

> The Operating and Financial Review regulation (OFR) is part of the UK government's response to corporate scandals. . . . The OFR requires all UK-listed companies to report on non-financial impacts to the extent necessary to enable shareholders to make informed decisions about the company's future.[40]

Similar requirements have been in place in France since 2002 and, regarding environmental reporting, also in the Netherlands since 1999.[41]

An example of a CSR audit and its implications comes from the Gap. The 2003 launch of Gap's *Social Responsibility Report*,[42] which was well received by NGOs monitoring the industry,[43] shows the extent to which CSR has advanced for apparel companies. Imagine the likelihood of strongly enforced, CSR-related human resource policies among Gap's employees and subcontractors if they knew there would be no audit or social responsibility report. Key findings of the first report:

- 3,000—Number of factories worldwide that contract with Gap
- 8,500—Number of visits by Gap compliance officers to factories
- 90—Percentage of factories that fail initial inspection
- 136—Number of factories with severe enough violations that Gap pulled out[44]

Another good example of a company leading the way in CSR auditing and reports is Shell, which was prompted to reanalyze its business practices in 1995. This followed two separate NGO-orchestrated campaigns that attacked the company's decision to sink the *Brent Spar,* an old oil rig, in the ocean and its failure to prevent the execution by the Nigerian government of an environmental activist, Ken Saro-Wiwa, who had been campaigning against Shell's operations in Nigeria. The stakeholder backlash against the company over these two issues threatened its underlying business model.[45]

Following the intense international criticism Shell received for its reactions to these two high-profile events, "The company decided it needed to become a better global citizen."[46] One component of the drive to change the corporate culture and increase awareness of CSR at Shell was the *Shell Report:*

The report has become famous for disclosing Shell's successes and failures in human rights and environmentalism, including oil spills and community protests, as well as the profits and losses of its multibillion-dollar business. . . . "I don't know any American oil company that produces anything as comprehensive and candid about its global social responsibility programs as the Shell Report," said Frank Vogl, co-founder of Transparency International, a European watchdog group that tracks corruption around the world. ". . . there is a tremendous level of sincerity behind what [the company] is trying to do."[47]

In general, this phenomenon is growing faster outside of the United States than within. A report released by the organization Stratos that analyses the extent of corporate sustainability reporting in Canada states that "60 percent of large Canadian firms publish CSR reports, up from 35 percent in 2000."[48] Similarly, a listing of the 100 most sustainable firms is produced each year by the Canadian corporate social responsibility magazine *Corporate Knights.*[49]

Another positive step (vital for validity) is to have the audit conducted, or at least verified, by an independent third party in the same way that an independent auditor verifies a company's financial reports. Some form of objective verification lends credence to the information included. The sooner industry standards can be agreed upon and applied, the more meaningful CSR audits and reports will become.[50] As one research study concluded,

The majority of nongovernmental organizations, who play an increasingly important role in evaluating corporate social responsibility (CSR) reports, are skeptical. . . . Of the 56 NGOs surveyed . . . 79 percent find CSR reports "very" or "fairly" useful, but only

44 percent consider the reports "believable." . . . According to the survey, companies can gain credibility for their reports by disclosing poor sustainability performance, or significant challenges, or noncompliance with social or environmental laws or regulations. Other factors that boost confidence in CSR reporting include comprehensive performance metrics, third-party certification, and standardization of reporting.[51]

## CSR Ombudsman

A key component of the continuous internal reinforcement necessary for a CSR policy to remain effective is an anonymous feedback–complaint–whistle-blowing procedure. This process should be available via a third party or CSR ombudsman. This requirement was a key component of the Sarbanes-Oxley Act. As a result, a number of independent companies have emerged offering to provide this service (often online) to firms wishing to contract it out:

> Shareholder.com[52] is typical of online services. Employees of a company that hires Shareholder.com can file their complaints with the . . . firm. The complaints then are forwarded electronically to the appropriate people back at the company—but only after all identifying information is stripped away.[53]

An independent third party performing this job is ideal because it guarantees the protection of employees' identities, which prevents retaliation from within the organization. The online provision conveys the sense of an additional degree of anonymity. This infrastructure encourages the reporting of any breaches of policy, particularly in terms of ethics compliance, that would affect the company's stated CSR position. It should also encourage positive feedback in the form of contributions and ideas from employees, who are often best placed to evaluate the organization's CSR policies in action.

## CSR Framework—Organizational Structure

In order for all these CSR elements to coalesce into an effective CSR policy that represents stakeholder interests within the strategic decision-making process of the firm, an organizational CSR framework is essential. The CSR effort must have visibility. Ideally, the day-to-day operationalization of CSR demands the direct involvement of top management with board commitment and oversight. Evidence among firms of the growing importance of CSR will be found when the board of directors puts CSR on the same level as other key corporate governance issues, such as the integrity of the firm's financial information. Further, the access of the CSR officer to the CEO, with a direct reporting relationship to the board of directors, suggests further operational and symbolic support for CSR. Many firms, however, are lagging in terms of instituting the necessary structural support for CSR. A report from Sustainable Asset Management (SAM), based on questionnaire responses by the CEOs of public, private, and state-owned companies from 16 countries in 18 industries, found that,

> Only 16 percent of the 1,336 companies SAM assessed . . . have established specific board committees on CSR and sustainability. . . . A mere 29 percent of the companies assessed by SAM had boards that have taken formal responsibility for CSR or sustainability.[54]

Although board-level visibility and support are rare and may seem like overkill, especially in otherwise well-run, ethical, and socially responsible firms, strong support and visibility demonstrate the firm's genuine commitment in ways that mere memos, posters, hollow speeches, or press releases fail to do.

# CSR BUSINESS PLAN OF ACTION—MEDIUM TERM

Beyond minimum start-up conditions for CSR, the organization must seek to institutionalize and externalize the substance of its CSR policies. Over the medium to long term, the organization should communicate its perspective, while seeking feedback from stakeholder groups to make them feel both informed and involved.

## Stakeholder Involvement

All large, publicly held corporations have well-developed investor relations departments. They have become the norm because of the primacy shareholders have typically enjoyed as a company's main stakeholder, particularly in English-speaking economies. As a company's share price has become the key indicator of corporate and management success, keeping investors happy has become central to a CEO's ability to retain his or her job (see Figure 1.4).

As part of moving CSR to the center of a company's strategic outlook, this two-way avenue of communication needs to be expanded to other stakeholders. One approach would be to change the focus of the investor relations department to become the "stakeholder relations department." Though the scope and skills of these two departments vary, suggesting the expansion of the investor relations department would be far more substantive than merely changing the title and charter. The goal should be to develop relationships with all stakeholder interests, including NGOs. Of course, this assumes that the skills in the investor relations department exist or can be expanded, perhaps a change more demanding than might first be imagined, given the very different roles this transformation suggests. An online article by SRI Compass discusses how investor relations has become more complex vis-à-vis CSR. The piece notes how investor relations officers from 20 companies connect investors' interest in their companies with social and environmental performance.[55]

Of course, external activists also demand attention from these stakeholder relation departments:

NGOs—nongovernmental organizations—have won significant influence over global companies. The demonstrations against global capitalism at the G-8 summit in Genoa were the latest manifestation of a trend that—mostly quietly and behind the scenes—is defining our age. From companies like the coffee shop giant Starbucks (attacked for the treatment of workers on plantations and the price it pays for coffee), to Big Oil (a perennial target for environmentalists), to tuna canners (think dolphins), companies are increasingly changing their business practices when pressured by activists.[56]

As Paul Tebo, DuPont's corporate vice president for safety, health, and environment and "an advocate for social responsibility," more succinctly put it: "The closer [Dupont] can align with social values . . . the faster we will grow."[57]

## Manage the Message

Strategic CSR is more than mere public relations. Communicating a company's CSR efforts to the outside world is a sensitive area. Excessive self-promotion soon comes to be interpreted as a cynical effort of going through the CSR motions only to receive the public relations benefits. Avoiding the impression of spin is crucial; however, it is also important to let stakeholders know that the company values their input and interests. The aim is to meet stakeholder expectations by matching promises with reality.

Examples of companies that have failed to take the lead in determining the public perception of their organization are many. Often the perception of a company in the public mind, once created, is difficult to shift. For example, in spite of the company's more recent progressive CSR work, Nike's initial failure to anticipate the reaction by its stakeholders to manufacturing offshore in low-cost environments and the failure to work closely with NGOs in this area has tagged it with an image that still prevails in many eyes. In Dave Barry's humorous review of 2003, he noted that,

> In May . . . Nike signs a $90 million endorsement deal with 18-year-old basketball player and Humvee owner LeBron James Incorporated. To pay for this, Nike raises the average price of a pair of its sneakers to $385, which includes $1.52 for materials, and 17 cents for labor.[58]

Go to Nike's corporate Web site[59] today, and it soon becomes apparent that the company has redefined the way it presents its operations and corporate message to the outside world along CSR lines; however, because of its early lapses, the company continually finds itself having to play catch-up, with some stakeholders refusing to grant the company any concessions at all.

## Corporate Governance

Corporate governance matters.[60] In a study of 1,500 firms, researchers concluded that "there is a premium associated with good governance as far as we measured it."[61] In another study of 3,220 global firms by GovernanceMetrics International evaluating the effectiveness of corporate governance, the 1% of firms that scored best had superior financial returns.[62] The importance of corporate governance has grown in recent years, even leading to the formation of the International Corporate Governance Network (http://icgn.org/index.php) to exchange information about corporate governance and raise governance standards generally.

*Transparency* and *accountability* have become the watchwords of effective corporate governance, which has also become a vital aspect of an effective CSR policy. Increased legal requirements reinforce this change in sentiment for all but the most narrow-sighted of corporate boards; however, equally important is the ability to move ahead of today's legal requirements and anticipate the legal expectations of tomorrow. Shareholder activism is increasing and is driving reform in this area of corporate law. Ensuring a company's policies and procedures are transparent, that its managers are accountable to the company's owners, and that the process by which these policies are created and board members appointed is democratic are all crucial to ensuring the traditional conflict between principal and agent is minimized.

### Corporate Activism

Both The Body Shop and Ben & Jerry's found that activism alone is insufficient to remain viable in the long run. In both cases, the founders have been forced to take a backseat to professional managers, in terms of running day-to-day operations, as their organizations have grown. Activism of any sort, particularly CSR-related efforts, must support an economically viable business strategy. CSR-focused organizations benefit few if they are stuck in bankruptcy court. Economic viability and operating within society's legal parameters are minimum conditions for business survival. That said, a sincere CSR focus throughout the organization helps further that viability over the long term. It does not, however, preserve any operation if basic economical, legal, or other business fundamentals are missing.

## OVERVIEW OF IMPLEMENTATION

The primary CSR responsibility of the CEO is to actively support CSR and the CSR officer. The CSR officer's role is to hold the company accountable to its own CSR position statement. The main method of achieving this is to conduct a substantive, annual CSR audit of the company. And though few have that audit independently verified, such verification is advised and may become necessary for firms that have lost creditability because of past actions. The final report, released to all stakeholders (including investors), forms an integral and prominent aspect of the company's triple bottom line annual report, along with information detailing the company's environmental and financial performance. The overall job perspective of the CSR officer is to ensure congruity among the firm's CSR goals and its actions.

Other stakeholders can be expected to hold the organization accountable to the standards it has set for itself. Emboldened by technology and growing expectations for CSR, stakeholders will grow increasingly assertive in ensuring their best interests are represented. And stakeholder activism may be the final piece of the CSR jigsaw puzzle that pushes CEOs and legislatures past the CSR threshold, ushering in a greater commitment to CSR. The real question is will that commitment by firms be proactive or reactive?

## IMPLEMENTATION FROM A STRATEGIC PERSPECTIVE: PLANNING

Though CSR involves the firm's overall direction and day-to-day activities, its implementation begins with the annual planning process. Most firms large and sophisticated enough to implement a CSR perspective undertake strategic planning, usually on an annual basis. The planning process seeks to identify targeted goals, strategies to attain those goals, and an allocation of financial, human, and other resources in pursuit of those goals.

Typically, long-range planning and goal setting begin early in the calendar (or fiscal) year of the firm. *Long range,* however, has vastly different meanings from one industry to another. In electricity utilities, for example, the planning horizon might stretch 10, 15, or more years into the future, given the complexity of estimating future electricity demand: designing, permitting, and building a base-load power plant and connecting long distribution lines from facilities to users, with often contentious regulatory and hearing requirements coupled with a not-in-my-backyard mentality. In a consumer products firm, however, the long term might be measured in months, from idea to product introduction and obsolescence.

Nevertheless, the goal of long-range planning is to agree on the future objectives the firm will seek. In turn, business goals (growth rates, market share, and the like) must be translated into realizable objectives for each business unit and within these units for operating and support groups—from production to finance to human resource departments. Broad, overarching goals form the basis for specific strategies. An example might include the goal of being the most widely admired firm in the industry because of the firm's attention to societal issues. Though such a goal might not lead to immediate financial gains, it may be indispensable to hiring hard-to-find employees with unique skills. In fact, the ability to hire and retain key players may be a necessity for survival, further justifying the allocation of time and resources toward socially responsible goals.

Long-term goals and their strategies for attainment must then be translated into more specific, short-term objectives. Ideally, short-term objectives are SMART, that is, Specific, Measurable, Action-oriented, Responsible, and Time-targeted. Then, the resources necessary to implement these objectives are allocated. The unifying approach to the allocation of resources to future objectives is the budgeting process. Usually done near the end of the previous fiscal or calendar year, the budgeting process allocates money and resources (and, through salaries and capital budgets, people and investments) for the upcoming year.

Because this approach traditionally focuses on business investments selected on some objective basis (such as the payback period or return on investment), hard-to-measure objectives (such as social responsibility) may fail to register. And because most firms seek multiple objectives, the relative importance of goals must be weighed by a correspondingly appropriate allocation of resources and rewards. CSR can fall through the cracks without an appropriate mandate from senior management or the board of directors and a dedicated CSR officer.

The ease with which CSR can be overlooked in this planning process, therefore, only further emphasizes the importance of adopting a methodical approach to ensuring uniform implementation throughout the organization. The integration of CSR within the strategic decision-making process and organizational culture along the lines outlined in this chapter goes a long way to ensuring CSR achieves the position of prominence within the organization that is increasingly necessary in today's business environment.

## IMPLEMENTATION FROM A FIRM PERSPECTIVE: ACTION

At the firm level, CSR is meaningless unless it is translated into action. Public relations releases to the media, speeches to employees or trade groups, or assertions of CSR in annual reports are not the end goal of CSR, necessary as they may be to raise awareness within the firm and the larger environment of stakeholders. Nevertheless, CSR must be operationally integrated into the firm's day-to-day activities. For CSR to become integrated in this way requires a CSR filter to be applied to the vision, mission, strategy, and tactics of the firm. Granted, in a capitalist system, for-profit firms face an absolute economic imperative. Businesses do not exist merely to be nice to constituents; they exist to meet needs in society and make a profit. Increasingly, however, these needs include societal expectations. Ultimately, the viability of the firm—its ability to grow, make stockholders wealthy, and meet the needs of customers and other stakeholders—presupposes both an external and internal environment that is conducive to success.

With the primacy of economics, however, other components of the firm's activities can easily be relegated to a distant concern. The result may be a hostile environment that impairs the firm's economic performance, even its long-term viability. A CSR perspective, integrated throughout the organization, offers an alternative business approach, one that is more likely to provide the long-term stability companies require; however, top-management support, a dedicated CSR officer (at least until CSR is fully integrated into the processes and culture of the firm), a well-defined CSR position statement, awareness built through measurements and rewards, a CSR audit and public report to relevant stakeholders, an internal or external ombudsman, and a structure that institutionalizes these elements are merely a beginning.

Ideally, stakeholder involvement will include all affected constituencies to as great a degree as possible. Inclusion is more than just an attempt to co-opt relevant constituents. Whether internal or external, inclusion means giving stakeholders a voice and requires leaders that are both receptive and proactive to stakeholder concerns. Admittedly, the message must be managed, if for no other reason than to assure the firm's efforts are communicated and recognized. How else can stakeholders react and become involved in the process? With transparency and corporate activism added to the mix, a firm has the basic ingredients for a successful CSR orientation.

The ultimate test of a firm's CSR, however, is its actions. And for those actions to mean more than mere public relations window dressing, CSR must form part of the firm's larger strategic plan. Here concern must focus not only on the results but also on the methods used. This focus must also be recalibrated to accommodate, as much as possible, the differing perspectives of the relevant constituents that the firm touches. Initially, long- and short-term objectives are translated into action through the planning process. Then plans are converted into budgets, which directly allocate financial and other resources. The way these actions are received by those most affected by them indicates the success of the process by which the socially responsible organization matches plans and intentions to actions and results.

The varied stakeholder roles and issues that define CSR are the focus of Part II of *Strategic Corporate Social Responsibility*. Taking advantage of the Internet, which is reshaping the role of CSR within the competitive business landscape, current CSR issues are identified, offering Internet links to relevant Web sites that provide both the specifics and implications of these issues.

## QUESTIONS FOR DISCUSSION AND REVIEW

1. What is meant by the phrase "CSR as brand insurance?" Can you think of a firm that has benefited from CSR in this way?

2. Why do some firms and industries have different "CSR thresholds" than others?

3. What role do stakeholders play in establishing the level of the CSR threshold for a particular firm or within a particular industry?

4. Think of an example firm and/or industry; what event do you think would push that firm or industry over its CSR threshold?

5. Why is top-management support for CSR so critical? Can CSR be delegated? If so, why and to whom?

6. What elements should be present for a firm to change the organizational culture toward a more CSR outlook? Which one do you think is the most important? Why?

7. How does a firm avoid the perception that its CSR report is merely a public relations–generating exercise? Does it matter whether the reasons behind an action are genuine or cynical if the outcome is the same?

## NOTES

1. David Grayson & Adrian Hodges, 'Corporate Social Opportunity! Seven Steps to Make Corporate Social Responsibility Work for Your Business,' Greenleaf, 2004.

2. Barry Wain, 'Chill Pill: One Singapore Hotel Becomes Very Cool, Uniquely Green,' *Wall Street Journal,* October 20, 2004, pB2C.

3. David Hobstetter, 'In the Fray: Seeing the Light About Daylight,' *Wall Street Journal,* October 19, 2004, pD6.

4. Lisa Roner, 'Anheuser-Busch Reports Recycling 97% of Solid Waste,' *Ethical Corporation Magazine,* June 21, 2004, http://www.ethicalcorp.com/content.asp?ContentID=2228

5. http://www.timberland.com/timberlandserve/timberlandserve_index.jsp

6. William Werther & David Chandler, 'Strategic Corporate Social Responsibility as Global Brand Insurance,' *Business Horizons,* Vol. 48, No. 4, 2005. pp 317–324.

7. Stephanie Strom, 'Wal-Mart Donates $35 Million for Conservation and Will Be Partner With Wildlife Group,' *New York Times,* April 13, 2005, pA16.

8. Malcolm Gladwell, 'The Tipping Point: How Little Things Can Make a Big Difference,' Back Bay Books, 2002.

9. Although there are disagreements as to which categorization best fits different business models, what all these firms have in common is that their strategies seek to provide their customers with superior value.

10. In April 2005, ExxonMobil announced the largest ever fourth quarter profit for a publicly traded U.S. company: "$8.4 billion. That translated into $3.8 million an hour. . . . Politically, [Exxon's CEO] has become a lightening rod for his skepticism about global warming, continuing to question the science behind such worries. . . . Earlier [in 2005] Exxon became the biggest publicly traded company in the U.S. in terms of market value." Jeffrey Ball, 'Mighty Profit Maker,' *Wall Street Journal,* April 8, 2005, pp B1&B6.

11. Paula Dwyer, 'Breach of Trust,' *BusinessWeek,* December 15, 2003, pp 98–108.

12. Jesse Eisinger, 'Year of the (Shrugged Off) Scandal,' *Wall Street Journal,* January 2, 2004, pR3.

13. Strategic Insight, a New York fund–research firm in 'Mutual Funds,' *BusinessWeek,* December 8, 2003, p116.

14. Karen Damato, 'Stock Funds Were No Scandal,' *Wall Street Journal,* January 2, 2004, pC1.

15. Deborah Brewster, 'Scandal Stems Mutual Fund Surge,' *Financial Times* (U.S. Edition), February 6, 2004, p1.

16. Richard Gibson, 'McDonald's Seeks Ways to Pitch Healthy Living,' *Wall Street Journal,* May 27, 2004, pD7.

17. http://archive.greenpeace.org/comms/brent/brent.html and http://archive.greenpeace.org/comms/ken/

18. http://www.foei.org/corporates/gmoaid.html

19. Lisa Roner, 'Starbucks and Oxfam Team Up on Ethiopian Development Programme,' *Ethical Corporation Magazine,* October 18, 2004, http://www.ethicalcorp.com/content.asp?ContentID=2961 and Alison Maitland, 'Starbucks Tastes Oxfam's Brew,' *Financial Times* (U.S. Edition), October 14, 2004, p9.

20. William Baue, 'Corporate Social and Environmental Performance Varies Widely Across Far-East Asia,' *CSRWire,* March 19, 2004, http://www.csrwire.com/sfarticle.cgi?id=1372

21.  William Baue, 'Graphing Graft: Transparency International Finds Rampant Corruption in 60 Countries,' *CSRWire,* November 3, 2004, http://www.csrwire.com/sfarticle.cgi?id=1563

22.  May 2005, http://www.bcccc.net/index.cfm?fuseaction=Page.viewPage&pageId=694&node ID =1&parentID=473

23.  Ibid.

24.  http://www.nike.com/nikebiz/nikebiz.jhtml?page=24

25.  http://www.starbucks.com/aboutus/csr.asp

26.  http://www.ford.com/en/company/about/corporateCitizenship/report/default.htm?referrer= home

27.  http://www.microsoft.com/mscorp/citizenship/

28.  http://www.timberlandserve.com/

29.  The Ethics Officer Association in the United States (http://www.eoa.org/) believes the CEO acronym should also stand for "chief ethics officer."

30.  Patrick M. Lencioni, 'Make Your Values Mean Something,' *Harvard Business Review,* Vol. 80, No. 7, July 2002, pp 113–117.

31.  Memorandum from Kenneth Lay to All Employees, Subject: Code of Ethics, July 1, 2000.

32.  Enron Corp's "Code of Ethics," p5.

33.  Ibid, p12.

34.  'What Does It Mean to Be VP of CSR? A Conversation With Sandra Taylor of Starbucks,' *Business Ethics Magazine,* Summer 2004, p4.

35.  Lisa Roner, 'Ethics Cited in Choice of New Nike Chief Executive,' *Ethical Corporation Magazine,* November 24, 2004, http://www.ethicalcorp.com/content.asp?ContentID=3248

36.  http://www.iso.org/iso/en/is09000–14000/index.html

37.  The National Oceanic and Atmospheric Administration's Web site provides details of the *Exxon Valdez* oil spill at http://response.restoration.noaa.gov/spotlight/spotlight.html and images from the event at http://response.restoration.noaa.gov/photos/exxon/exxon.html. Another authoritative Web site is administered by the Exxon Valdez Oil Spill Trustee Council at http://www.evostc.state.ak.us/

38.  The phrase *triple bottom line* was first introduced in 1994 by John Elkington of SustainAbility (http://www.sustainability.com/) "to describe social, environmental, and financial accounting." The term was used in conjunction with the launch of SustainAbility's "first survey benchmarking non-financial reporting." William Baue, 'Sustainability Reporting Improves, but Falls Short on Linking to Financial Performance,' November 5, 2004, http://www.socialfunds.com/news/article.cgi/article1565.html

39.  'Comment: Buttering Parsnips,' *Ethical Corporation Magazine,* October 5, 2004, http://www .ethicalcorp.com/content.asp?ContentID=2881

40.  Deborah Doane, 'Mandated Risk Reporting Begins in UK,' *Business Ethics Magazine,* Spring 2005, p13. Note: Guidance from the UK Accounting Standards Board concerning reporting standards for these risks can be found at http://www.asb.org.uk/asb/press/pub0645.html

41.  Ibid.

42.  http://ccbn.mobular.net/ccbn/7/645/696/index.html

43.  Matthew Gitsham, 'Book and Publication Reviews: Gap's 2003 Social Responsibility Report,' *Ethical Corporation Magazine,* June 21, 2004, http://www.ethicalcorp.com/content.asp?ContentID =2231

44.  Amy Merrick, 'In Candid Report, Gap Details Violations in Its Factories,' *Wall Street Journal,* May 12, 2004, pA9.

45.  Elizabeth Becker, 'At Shell, Grades for Citizenship,' *New York Times,* November 30, 2003, Section 3, p2.

46.  Ibid.

47.  Ibid.

48.  http://www.stratos-sts.com/pages/publica012.htm

49.  William Baue, 'List of Global 100 Most Sustainable Companies Highlights Alcoa, BP, and Toyota,' *CSRWire,* February 2, 2005, http://www.csrwire.com/sfarticle.cgi?id=1628

50. The Global Reporting Initiative (http://www.globalreporting.org/) is leading the push for international standards in the area of CSR and social reporting.

51. William Baue, 'Survey Says: NGOs Believe Corporate Social Responsibility Reports That Reveal Faults,' *CSRWire,* November 14, 2003, http://www.csrwire.com/sfarticle.cgi?id=1268

52. http://www.shareholder.com/. Another company providing a similar service is EthicsPoint Inc. (http://www.ethicspoint.com/), where "about 78% of the complaints channeled through [the company] had arrived via the Web," (Phyllis Plitch, 'Making It Easier to Complain,' in the supplement, 'Corporate Governance: The Journal Report,' *Wall Street Journal,* June 21, 2004, pR6).

53. Ibid.

54. William Baue, 'World Economic Forum Surveys CEO Attitudes Toward Corporate Citizenship,' *CSRWire,* February 6, 2003, http://www.csrwire.com/sfarticle.cgi?id=1028

55. 'CSR and the Role of Investor Relations 2003,' *SRI Compass,* http://www.sricompass.org trends/investorrelations2003_page108.aspx

56. Michael Elliott, 'Embracing the Enemy Is Good Business,' *Time,* August 13, 2001, p29.

57. Marc Gunther, 'Tree Huggers, Soy Lovers, and Profits,' *Fortune,* June 23, 2003, pp 98–104.

58. Dave Barry, '2003: A Dave Odyssey', *Miami Herald,* December 28, 2003, pp 1M&5M–7M.

59. http://www.nikebiz.com/

60. Michael Hopkins, 'The Planetary Bargain: Corporate Social Responsibility Matters,' Earthscan, 2003.

61. Paul J. Lim, 'Gauging That Other Company Asset: Its Reputation,' *New York Times,* April 10, 2004, pA18.

62. Ibid.

# Part II

# CSR: THE ISSUES AND CASE STUDIES

**P**art II reveals the unique nature of *Strategic Corporate Social Responsibility*. Chapters 5, 6, and 7 explore the breadth of corporate social responsibility (CSR) through 45 issues and case studies, each of which serves as a practical introduction to a much larger element of the CSR debate. Chapter 8 adds 40 additional corporate examples of CSR in action. Collectively, these case studies form a basis for discussion and explanation that is enriched by Internet links for further investigation.

Topics range from issues of governance and accountability to self-interest and economic viability. They illustrate the direct impact of CSR on corporate behavior, decisions, and strategies, within the organization and within the marketplace and society. These CSR issues, along with the actions and reactions they prompt, can harm or benefit the bottom line. They directly influence stakeholders' relationships with the organization and their perceptions of the corporate brand, product, or behavior.

In Chapters 5, 6, and 7, each issue is divided into four sections:

- *Issue:* A definition of the issue and its relation to the wider field of CSR.
- *Case Study:* An illustration of the issue via a real-life situation and corporate action or reaction.
- *Web-Based Examples and Resources:* Internet-linked resources and Web sites directly relating to the issue and case study.
- *Questions for Discussion and Review:* Three questions that provide initial guidance for further investigation and a starting point for class discussion.

**Figure II.1**   CSR Issues—Stakeholder Classification

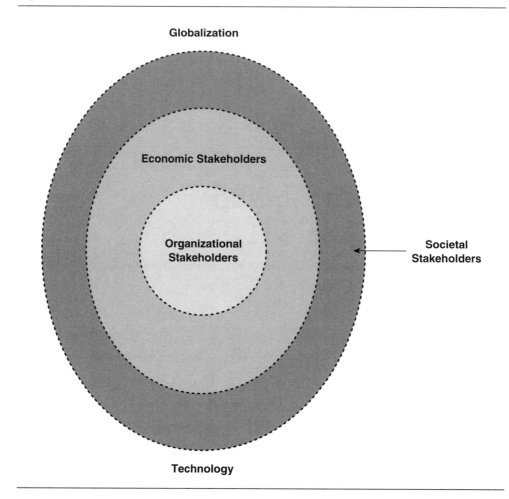

To grasp the spectrum of CSR issues that affect corporate behavior, consider Figure II.1. We use this model to classify broadly the 45 issues within the three kinds of stakeholders that we initially described in Chapter 1, Figure 1.1: Chapter 5 contains issues and case studies primarily involving organizational stakeholders; Chapter 6 economic stakeholders; and Chapter 7 societal stakeholders.

The 15 examples for each stakeholder group chosen in Part II (45 in total) are intended to be illustrative and do not cover every issue within each demarcation. Similarly, each issue is designed as a brief introduction to its CSR-related topic and is not intended to be a comprehensive analysis of the subjects covered, many of which are complex. The Internet-based sources provided are there to lead to whatever depth of discovery is relevant and appropriate. Within this framework, many of the issues are broad, stretching across organizational, economic, and societal boundaries. As such, our goal here is to classify each issue in terms of its primary impact.

## Chapter 5: Organizational Stakeholders

First, stakeholders exist within the organization. The business functions and practices that affect organizational stakeholders are presented from a CSR perspective. Examples of organizational stakeholders include stockholders, employees, and managers.

## Chapter 6: Economic Stakeholders

Second are economic stakeholders, examples of which include consumers and creditors. They serve as the interface between the organization and its larger social environment. Not only do the issues in this section affect the financial aspects of the organization, they create bonds of accountability between the firm and its wider operating context.

## Chapter 7: Societal Stakeholders

Third, topics that affect societal stakeholders determine the business environment in which the firm operates. Examples of societal stakeholders include government agencies and regulators, communities, and the environment itself.

Finally, the twin forces of globalization and technology frame this bull's-eye model of concentric circles and provide the overall business context within which CSR and stakeholder theory have become more relevant for corporations today (see Chapter 3).

This model is not limited to for-profit organizations and can be applied equally to governments and nonprofits. Economic stakeholders serve as the accountability interface between any organization and the society within which it operates. Among businesses, the accountability mechanism is profit and loss: If a company fails to make a profit over the long term, it will be unable to remain in business. For democratic governments, the accountability mechanism is twofold: The campaign contributions that finance the democratic process and the votes of stakeholders (taxpayers), which determine the outcome. And for nonprofits, the accountability mechanism is the organization's ability to generate sufficient operational funds by justifying its continued existence to economic stakeholders, its funder(s).

Without these economic interfaces, organizations lose their mechanism of accountability and, therefore, their legitimacy over the long term. This is true regardless of whether the organization is a business, government, or nonprofit.

The issues selected below illustrate CSR's practical effects. Being as topical as today's newspaper headlines, they form the basis for active discussion and further inquiry using the Web-based resources provided. All of these issues and case studies are key elements of corporate social responsibility:

## ISSUES AND CASE STUDIES

| Organizational Issues | Case Studies |
| --- | --- |
| Action versus intention | Enron |
| Auditing CSR | Sweatshops |
| Compliance—Ethics | Ethics officers |
| Compliance—Approaches | Voluntary versus mandatory |
| Corporate charters | Federalization |
| Corporate governance—Reporting | Sarbanes-Oxley Act (2002) |
| Corporate governance—Boards | Corporate boards |
| Corporation | The U.S. corporation |
| Employee relations | Ohio Employee Ownership Center |
| Hypocrisy | The Body Shop |
| Principal-agent conflict | Expensing stock options |
| Research and development | Asbestos |
| Shareholder activism | GlaxoSmithKline |
| Stakeholder relations | Ben & Jerry's |
| Volunteering | Timberland |

| Economic Issues | Case Studies |
| --- | --- |
| Advertising | Benetton |
| Brands | BP |
| Consumer apathy | SUVs |
| Cultural conflict | Nike |
| Diversity—Discrimination | U.S. Masters |
| Diversity—Helpful intent | Goodwill Industries |
| Environmental sustainability | Ford |
| Fair trade | Starbucks |
| Finance | Citigroup |
| Investing | SRI Funds |
| Loans | Microloans |
| NGO and corporate cooperation | Greenfreeze |
| Philanthropy | Merck |
| Profit | Hewlett-Packard |
| Wages | McDonald's |

| Societal Issues | Case Studies |
|---|---|
| Community | Fannie Mae |
| Corruption and bribery | Legislation |
| Country of origin | Conflict diamonds |
| Ethics | Teaching ethics |
| Globalization | U.S. judicial activism |
| Human rights | Union Carbide |
| Internet | NGO activism |
| Legislation | Company Responsibilities Bill |
| Litigation | Chiquita Brands |
| Media | CNN |
| Patents | Generic drugs |
| Patriotism | Tyco |
| Science and technology | Cloning |
| Sex | Abercrombie & Fitch |
| Universities and CSR | West Coconut Grove |

## Chapter 8: Special Cases of CSR

Chapter 8 supplements these issues and mini–case studies with 40 additional examples of CSR in action. These include examples of companies implementing CSR in ways that are beneficial to firms and in ways that lead to criticism. Other examples include businesses that are attempting to implement CSR, as well as firms that persevere with CSR against all the odds:

## SPECIAL CASES OF CSR

## Companies Doing CSR Well

Bank of America

Coca-Cola

Fast-food industry

Heineken

IKEA

Johnson & Johnson

Mattress Giant

Microsoft (Bill Gates)

Newman's Own

Nike

Pepsi

Procter & Gamble

Prudential Insurance

September 11, 2002

Sony PlayStation

Southwest Airlines

Starbucks

## Companies Criticized for Their CSR Efforts

American Airlines

Bridgestone/Firestone

Defense contractors

ExxonMobil

Ford

Genetically modified (GM) labeling

Hewlett-Packard

McDonald's

Video game industry

## Companies Trying to Do CSR Well

Berkshire Hathaway

Cadbury

Kraft

Malden Mills

Monsanto

Nestlé

PETA

Shell

University of Nottingham

Wal-Mart

## Companies Persevering Against All the Odds

British American Tobacco

McDonald's

NBC

Philip Morris Companies

# Chapter 5

## ORGANIZATIONAL ISSUES AND CASE STUDIES

### ACTION VERSUS INTENTION

☑ *CSR Connection:* This issue reflects the importance of distinguishing between the cynical corporation, superficially addressing CSR, and the corporation genuinely seeking to introduce sustainable business practices.

### Issue

What drives a company to pursue CSR? Is it the expected public relations returns, or is it a genuine intent to value key stakeholder groups? To what extent will results match stated intentions?

The underlying reasons for Enron's collapse can be traced to characteristics common to all corporations: obsession with profits and share prices, greed, lack of concern for others and a penchant for breaking legal rules. [It shows] what can happen when the characteristics we take for granted in a corporation are pushed to the extreme.[1]

Without attempting to explain, much less justify, the well-documented details and events surrounding the collapse of the Enron Corporation, we offer the following case study as an example of action and intention being out of sync.

# Case Study: Enron

Enron is a good example of an organization that on the surface had excellent CSR credentials. It is also a good example of the danger presented by a firm's CSR policy that is ill defined and superficially championed. Without leadership from the top, a company's CSR policy merely presents the organization with sufficient rope to hang itself:

> Take a look at this list of corporate values: Communication. Respect. Integrity. Excellence. They sound pretty good don't they? Strong, concise, meaningful. Maybe they even resemble your own company's values, the ones you spent so much time writing, debating, and revising. If so, you should be nervous. These are the corporate values of Enron, as stated in the company's 2000 annual report. And as events have shown, they're not meaningful; they're meaningless.[2]

To what extent are a company's efforts at social responsibility window dressing? To what extent is there a genuine intention to recognize and reflect the shifting consumer market globalization is producing, as well as a company's larger responsibility to all its stakeholders and the wider social context within which it operates?

CSR advocates understand that it is very easy for a company to say one thing while intending to do another. To what extent is the CSR movement a façade, providing short-term relief to companies that are not willing to adopt a broader perspective? *Business Ethics Magazine* questions Enron's mission and whole purpose:

> Enron rang all the bells of CSR. It won a spot for three years on the list of the 100 Best Companies to Work for in America. In 2000 it received six environmental awards. It issued a triple bottom line report. It had great policies on climate change, human rights and (yes indeed) anti-corruption. Its CEO gave speeches at ethics conferences and put together a statement of values emphasizing 'communication, respect, and integrity.' The company's stock was in many social investing mutual funds when it went down. Enron fooled us.[3]

How can the stakeholders of an organization trust a firm's actions if all CSR pronouncements are intended to mislead people into believing the firm is something that it is not?

> As officers and employees of Enron Corp., its subsidiaries, and its affiliated companies . . . we are responsible for conducting the business affairs of the Company in accordance with all applicable laws and in a moral and honest manner.[4]

These are some key extracts from Enron's *Code of Ethics:*

> Enron stands on the foundation of its Vision and Values. Every employee is educated about the Company's Vision and Values and is expected to conduct business with other employees, partners, contractors, suppliers, vendors and customers keeping in mind respect, integrity, communication and excellence. Everything we do evolves from Enron's Vision and Values statements.[5]
>
> We are dedicated to conducting business according to all applicable local and international laws and regulations . . . and with the highest professional and ethical standards.[6]
>
> Employees of Enron Corp., its subsidiaries, and its affiliated companies (collectively the "Company") are charged with conducting their business affairs in accordance with the highest ethical standards. An employee shall not conduct himself or herself in a manner which directly or indirectly would be detrimental to the best interests of the Company or in a manner which would bring to the employee financial gain separately derived as a direct consequence of his or her employment with the Company. Moral as well as legal obligations will be fulfilled openly, promptly, and in a manner which will reflect pride on the Company's name.[7]

Increasingly, firms are being held accountable for all aspects of their operations by the societies within which they are located. Those companies that do not appreciate this, or attempt to circumvent responsibility with superficial commitments to CSR, risk exposure in our always-on, media-driven world. Each industry and each company has a different CSR threshold level, as we discussed in Chapter 4. Companies that avoid crossing that threshold by adopting an effective CSR perspective stand a much better chance of long-term survival. Those companies that ignore the threshold, like Enron, eventually are held accountable for their actions.

## Web-Based Examples and Resources

*Business Ethics Magazine:* http://www.business-ethics.com/

> The mission of *Business Ethics* is to promote ethical business practices, to serve the growing community of professionals striving to work and invest in responsible ways.

*Ethics & Enron* (ethics Web bookstore) has a collection of books on ethics and Enron and papers, SEC filings, and other documents about the company and its downfall at http://www.ethicsweb.ca/books/enron.htm

From the Web site of Art Berkowitz, CPA, author of *Enron: A Professional's Guide to the Events, Ethical Issues and Proposed Reforms* at http://www.enronguide.com/

> Enron is more than a passing scandal that will be overtaken by new headlines tomorrow. It is a business failure, an accounting failure, a political failure, and, most important of all, an ethics failure. Accountants, attorneys, corporate executives, investment bankers, and security analysts need to understand what the scandal will mean to the regulatory structure, their professions, and their everyday business dealings.

*The Smoking Gun* (TSG, Web site) presents a copy of Enron's in-house *Code of Ethics* at http://www.thesmokinggun.com/enron/enronethics1.shtml

> TSG is understandably proud to present a copy of a truly valuable artifact, Enron's in-house "Code of Ethics." The 64-page booklet was distributed to employees along with an introductory letter from Chairman Kenneth Lay noting the "moral and honest manner" in which the energy firm's business affairs should be conducted.

## Questions for Discussion and Review

1. What is your impression of Enron? What legacy does it leave for the business world? Do you think the scandal presents lasting lessons, or will the company be forgotten during the next business cycle?

2. Review Chapter 4 in Part I of this book. Outline the key components of a policy to successfully implement a CSR perspective throughout the organization. What is the key feature and starting point?

3. Does it matter if a company's commitment to CSR is genuine or superficial, as long as the outcome is the same?

## AUDITING CSR

☑ **CSR Connection:** This issue reflects the large amount of work regarding auditing and social reporting that is taking place within the field of CSR.

### Issue

What is the real driving force behind a company adhering to CSR behavior and policy—expected public relations returns or genuine intent? How can a company be held accountable for its CSR actions in a way that is objectively measurable yet not financially crippling?

A CSR audit provides some answers. The benefit of transparency and honesty in all aspects of an organization's operations is that it allows external observers to better evaluate the organization, its managers, and policies. The less than transparent reporting of a corporation's activities can have a negative impact on the perception of that organization in the outside world. Transparent and independent auditing, however, can enhance public perception of an organization and its operations.

GovernanceMetrics International (GMI) releases reports rating companies in the S&P 500, comparing the rating received with the company's stock performance over the past 1, 3, and 5 years and producing an overall corporate governance score:

> In the S&P 500, the average decline of a stock for the three years ended March 20, 2003, was 2.3 percent. . . . But the five companies earning the highest score rose 23.1 percent on average. The top 15 averaged total returns of 3.4 percent. . . . Top-ranked companies also outperformed their peers in measures like return on assets, return on investment and return on capital, [CEO, Gavin] Anderson said. Stock prices of the 50 companies with the lowest scores fell 28.2 percent in the last year, on average, and 11.1 percent in the last three years.[8]

CSR auditing is evolving rapidly. The field is moving beyond the foundation of the triple bottom line[9] into the search for objective standards that can be consistently applied among companies and across industries. In addition to presenting a more complete CSR perspective of a company's operations, establishing these standards represents an essential component for those seeking to establish a holistic approach to business risk:

> "We are not social activists; we're independent risk assessors," says George Dallas of S&P. The information in non-financial reports "contributes to building up a company's risk profile." And although it has still not been convincingly demonstrated that good environmental and social practices create value for shareholders, it is clear, says Mr. Dallas, that bad ones can destroy it.[10]

# Case Study: Sweatshops

Establishing objective CSR standards is an important goal within the audit industry. The issue has gained much publicity following attempts to audit companies' operations in foreign, often developing, countries. High-profile apparel brands have drawn much interest and criticism when they operate sweatshops overseas, out of sight of their customers.

The evolution of environmental reporting from its beginnings in the 1970s and 1980s offers a model for CSR reports. In time, this will hopefully lead to established CSR audits. Today, an environmental report is increasingly considered a vital component of an organization that aims to produce a comprehensive annual report:

> Sony was . . . one of the first Japanese firms to take environmental issues seriously, setting up its Environmental Conservation Committee in 1990. It produces an in-house newsletter on environmental issues in both Japanese and English, as well as environmental reports for wider distributions, also in both languages. . . . Sony pays a great deal of attention to its environmental profile, producing separate environmental reports for each of its plants and setting up the Sony Eco Plaza at the entrance to its head office.[11]

There are many organizations that are operating within the audit field and working toward establishing generally accepted standards:

The Global Reporting Initiative (GRI) is the leading light in the field. Initiated in 1997, GRI works with the United Nations and today is

> the only tool standardizing non-financial reports . . . [with] a broadly supported checklist of dozens of questions to which almost all of the best reporting firms pay lip service.[12]

AccountAbility, a British organization, has also been at the forefront of the push to establish a credible objective means by which the CSR performance of companies can be evaluated. In March 2003, the organization launched its assurance standard:

The AA1000 Assurance Standard is the world's first assurance standard developed to ensure the credibility and quality of reporting on social, environmental and economic performance.[13]

Social Accountability International (SAI), founded in 1997, is another organization that has done pioneering work in this area. SAI was one of the eight founding members of the auditing and accreditation alliance ISEAL (International Social and Environmental Accreditation and Labeling). ISEAL is important because of the international scope the organization's different members lend to the project and shows the willingness among accreditation organizations to move toward a set of internationally recognized standards.

Verité, founded in 1995, is also a major influence in the social auditing field and is "the only major nonprofit doing global factory inspections."[14]

The Fair Labor Association (FLA), founded in 1999, is taking the industry one step further by encouraging multinational organizations to allow their overseas factories to be audited by FLA auditors. Significantly, the FLA pushes to allow the final reports to be made public, something often resisted by corporations in the past. This occurred for the first time in June 2003. A list of companies that belong to the Fair Labor Association and have allowed their audits to be available to the public is at http://www .fairlabor.org/all/companies/index.html. The Web site claims,

> In joining the FLA, the following companies have committed to a rigorous program of Code of Conduct implementation, internal and external monitoring, and remediation in order to promote compliance with international labor standards in their supply chains.

While allowing these companies to take the moral high ground in the sweatshop debate, this move by the FLA also places a great deal of pressure on other brands (which have been the subject of unwanted NGO attention in the past) to submit their factory operations to the same level of public scrutiny. Nevertheless, FLA, under pressure from its member companies, is not implementing the highest level of standards to which other organizations would like to see multinational companies held:

> For example, the FLA doesn't even try to make sure that factories pay a living wage by the standards of the countries in which they operate—a frequent activist demand. Nor do FLA inspectors report on whether factories respect the right to form independent unions in countries like China that represses them. The FLA. . . . also declined to require that the actual factories inspected be named, making it more difficult for watchdog groups to check up on the reports.[15]

In addition, other complaints have focused on the relatively low percentage of a company's total factories (only 5%) that need to be inspected before FLA will release a report. This low number makes it difficult to release a report that could be considered representative of the company's operations as a whole. And criticism has also been leveled at the for-profit inspectors that FLA uses who tend not to interview workers off-site, considered to be the best means of obtaining the most accurate information about disreputable procedures and operations. Off-site interviews are more expensive to conduct and are often avoided by companies that want to spend as little as possible on these projects. Nevertheless, the frankness of the reports released by the FLA offers hope that this is a positive step forward. The reports are deemed to be genuine simply because the depressing operating practices they reveal are still being continued in these factories. One bright spot is the steps they note companies are taking to attempt to redress the negative practices that still exist. This, as well as the reports themselves, offers a benchmark by which all companies can be measured moving forward.

As the field develops, new tools are being introduced to help observers evaluate different firms' operations from a CSR perspective. In November 2004, SustainAbility, an independent think tank, strategy consultancy, and expert in corporate responsibility and sustainable development, released its sixth triple bottom line survey together with the UN Environment Program (UNEP) and, for the first time, Standard & Poor's, "the first time a credit-rating agency has been involved."[16] SustainAbility predicts the "full integration of sustainability and financial reporting by 2010,"[17] no doubt buoyed by the British government's proposal to make such reporting requirements mandatory for large firms.[18]

## Web-Based Examples and Resources

AccountAbility—The Institute of Social and Ethical AccountAbility, http://www.account ability.org.uk/

> AccountAbility is an international membership organization committed to enhancing the performance of organizations and to developing the competencies of individuals in social and ethical accountability and sustainable development.

CoreRatings, http://www.coreratings.com/

> CoreRatings is the leading European rating agency providing independent investment analysis of corporate responsibility risks.

EU Eco-Management and Audit Scheme, http://www.emas.org.uk/

> EMAS—the Eco-Management and Audit Scheme, is a voluntary initiative designed to improve companies' environmental performance. It was initially established by European Regulation 1836/93, although this has been replaced by Council Regulation 761/01.

Fair Labor Association, http://www.fairlabor.org/

The Fair Labor Association (FLA) is a nonprofit organization combining the efforts of industry, non-governmental organizations (NGOs), colleges and universities to promote adherence to international labor standards and improve working conditions worldwide. The FLA was established as an independent monitoring system that holds its participating companies accountable for the conditions under which their products are produced. To advance fair, decent and humane working conditions, the FLA enforces an industry-wide Workplace Code of Conduct, which is based on the core labor standards of the International Labour Organization (ILO).

Global Reporting Initiative, http://www.globalreporting.org/

The Global Reporting Initiative (GRI) is a multi-stakeholder process and independent institution whose mission is to develop and disseminate globally applicable Sustainability Reporting Guidelines. These Guidelines are for voluntary use by organisations for reporting on the economic, environmental, and social dimensions of their activities, products, and services. The GRI incorporates the active participation of representatives from business, accountancy, investment, environmental, human rights, research and labour organisations from around the world. Started in 1997, GRI became independent in 2002, and is an official collaborating centre of the United Nations Environment Programme (UNEP) and works in cooperation with UN Secretary-General Kofi Annan's Global Compact.

GovernanceMetrics International (GMI), http://www.gmiratings.com/

GovernanceMetrics International [was] the world's first global corporate governance ratings agency. GMI's premise is straightforward: companies that emphasize corporate governance and transparency will, over time, generate superior returns and economic performance and lower their cost of capital. The opposite is also true: companies weak in corporate governance and transparency represent increased investment risks and result in a higher cost of capital. . . . While companies with weak governance structures and practices are the subjects of newspaper headlines, there are as many companies with outstanding governance policies and disclosure levels that go unrecognized. GMI's ratings hope to correct that.

International Social and Environmental Accreditation and Labeling (ISEAL) Alliance, http://www.isealalliance.org/

The ISEAL Alliance is a formal association of the leading international voluntary standards, certification and accreditation programs focused on social and environmental issues. The member organizations of ISEAL have a common vision of a world where ecological sustainability and social justice are the normal conditions of business.

International Organization for Standardization (ISO), ISO-14000, http://www.iso.ch/iso/en/ prods-services/otherpubs/iso14000/index.html

Environmental Management—The ISO 14000 Family of International Standards.

Rating Research LLC, http://www.ratingresearch.com/

> Rating Research LLC (RRC) is a public rating agency that measures the critical intangible assets that constitute corporate reputation. RRC's broadly disseminated Reputation Ratings and Ethics Reputation Ratings on leading companies—and the Industry Reputation Studies that support and explain those ratings—provide interested third parties, relevant stakeholders, and the general public with greater insight into corporations' performance—both present and future.

Social Accountability International, http://www.cepaa.org/

> Social Accountability International (SAI) works to improve workplaces and combat sweatshops through the expansion and further development of the international workplace standard, SA8000, and the associated S8000 verification system.

Verité, http://www.verite.org/

> Verité is an independent, nonprofit social auditing and research organization established in 1995. Our mission is to ensure that people worldwide work under safe, fair and legal working conditions. Where Verité auditors identify exploitation of workers or health and safety violations in the workplace, we develop concrete steps to correct them through a combination of trainings for management and workers, education programs and remediation programs.

For an article outlining the history of social auditing ("A Brief History of Social Reporting"), see http://www.mallenbaker.net/csr/CSRfiles/page.php?Story_ID=857. The article is written by Alice Tepper Marlin and John Tepper Marlin, Adjunct Professors of Markets, Ethics and Law at the Stern School of Business, NYU.[19]

## Questions for Discussion and Review

1. Why is it important that an audit of any aspect of a company's operations be conducted by an independent organization?

2. What benefits are there for a firm in working together with NGOs to conduct a social audit of operations? What are the dangers? Which approach would you use if a major client wanted you to demonstrate your CSR commitment?

3. Respond to the following quote concerning Nike's relationship with its global network of over 700 independent supplier factories:

The relationship is delicate. . . . NGOs have berated firms such as Nike for failing to ensure that workers are paid a "living wage." But that can be hard, even in America. . . . In developing countries, the dilemma may be even greater: "In Vietnam, [Nike's] workers are paid more than doctors. What's the social cost if a doctor leaves his practice and goes to work for [Nike]? That's starting to happen."[20]

# COMPLIANCE—ETHICS

> ☑ *CSR Connection:* This issue reflects the growth in the compliance industry, due to the increase in legislation and SEC oversight that resulted from the corporate scandals at the turn of the century.

## Issue

In response to allegations of corporate financial abuses, government has limited the discretion of companies in reporting their financial information. The Sarbanes-Oxley Act of 2002 has added specific responsibilities to management and board of directors. The goal of the Act is to guarantee the accuracy of information produced concerning operations, as well as ensure operations are conducted within the law. Compliance, in terms of ethics and corporate governance, is now legally mandated and has become an important—and expensive—measure of a company's effectiveness of operations:

> A survey of board members conducted by RHR International for *Directorship* magazine found that big companies with $4 billion or more in revenues are spending an average of $35 million to comply with the act. Another survey by Financial Executives International found $3.1 million in added costs for companies with average revenues of $2.5 billion.[21]

---

## Case Study: Ethics Officers

In the United States, the evolution of corporate compliance programs—and the growth in the ethics and compliance officers that enforce these programs—has been driven largely by the desire to avoid the legal consequences of a failure to comply:

> The first corporate-ethics office was created in 1985 by General Dynamics, which was being investigated by the government for pricing scams.[22]

In 1991, this desire to avoid litigation was enhanced by an additional incentive provided by federal sentencing guidelines, which empowered judges to act leniently when penalizing those companies that had an established ethics program and accompanying implementation policies in place.[23]

This compliance incentive was further heightened with the passing of the Sarbanes-Oxley legislation in 2002 and again in November 2004 with the announcement of updated federal sentencing guidelines:

> New amendments to the guidelines raise the bar on what it means to have an effective ethics program. The amendment requires boards and executives to assume responsibility for the oversight of ethics programs. At a minimum, the guidelines require organizations to identify areas of risk where criminal violations may occur, train employees in their obligations, and give ethics officers sufficient authority and resources.[24]

As a result of the shifting compliance landscape, a compliance industry within the United

States has blossomed and a new career path has opened up for potential ethics officers:

The [Ethics Officer Association's] membership has increased from 632 in 2000 to more than 1,200 members today. That's a far cry from 1992, the year the EOA began, when it had just 12 members.[25]

[The EOA's] more than 1,200 members include ethics officers representing about 40% of the Fortune 500. Recent surveys show that 50% of North America's biggest companies have ethics officers reporting to chief executives. And many experts believe that number will rise with the revision of the sentencing guidelines.[26]

The appointment of chief governance officers (CGOs) in large companies is seen as helping prevent negative publicity or legal action as well as promoting a more positive image of a company. Both factors encourage investor confidence in the company's management and strategic perspective:

Pharmaceutical company Pfizer Inc. is widely credited with hiring the first chief governance officer in 1992. . . . [As late as 2002], the number of chief governance officers could be counted on one hand. . . . CGOs currently number only about 60, [but] their ranks are expected to grow exponentially over the next year or so.
    Disney . . . recently appointed . . . [a] CGO in the wake of heavy criticism for a board largely perceived as a rubber stamp for CEO Michael Eisner's decisions. Disney has twice topped *BusinessWeek's* list of companies with the worst boards of directors.[27]

These appointments are also being made in reaction to the increasing profile corporate governance has enjoyed in the wake of the Sarbanes-Oxley legislation. Institutional investors, as well as the credit-rating agencies—Moody's Investors Service and Standard & Poor's—are now demanding action in this area:

Deloitte Touche Tohmatsu, for example, recently appointed a chief ethics partner at about one-third of its 85 member firms, including one in each of the major countries where the firm operates. . . . The firm has also created a Web-based ethics course for employees in all 150 countries where it operates. It has the kind of 1-800 hotline mandated by Sarbanes-Oxley for the anonymous reporting of malfeasance.[28]

Some companies, however, are more reluctant to comply. Sometimes it takes unwelcome media attention before they are encouraged to implement significant reform in this area and create such compliance positions:

[Chief Executive of Wal-Mart, Lee] Scott complained about the criticism that has been heaped on [Wal-Mart] in the last couple of years but said the glare of the spotlight has helped the company function better. Wal-Mart created a compliance office [in 2004] that has 140 people working to ensure the company follows the rules and procedures.[29]

A key part of compliance, and the Sarbanes-Oxley legislation, includes the responsibility to identify and publicize the wrongdoing of senior officers when it is found:

The Sarbanes-Oxley law . . . protects whistle-blowers from retaliation and requires lawyers and senior executives to report wrongdoing to their superiors. Outside lawyers and auditors who alert corporate executives or directors of suspected wrongdoing are required by law to quit if no action is taken. Many corporations now have internal rules requiring employees to bring concerns to a top corporate lawyer or the board—a trend encouraged by the U.S. Sentencing Commission, which oversees sentencing guidelines and looks kindly on companies with strong legal-compliance programs.[30]

An effective ethics officer, combined with the infrastructure of an independent compliance program, encourages a healthier work environment and the ability for employees to come forward in confidence.[31]

It appears, however, that even the ethics and compliance officers themselves have little faith that the programs their companies are putting in place are any more than fig leafs designed to appease those calling for reform:

About 45 percent [of ethics and compliance officers attending the Conference Board's ethics conference in May 2003] said that their ethics and compliance programs would reduce the likelihood of an ethics scandal at their companies only "a little" or "not at all." . . . [In 2003] 20 percent said they expected more than 10 major ethics scandals among the Fortune 500 companies in the next 12 months. . . . An additional 41 percent said they expected 6 to 10 major scandals the next year. . . . Asked to describe the compensation of senior executives in general, only 7.5 percent said it was fair and appropriate, while 67 percent said it was "out of control."[32]

## Web-Based Examples and Resources

Conference Board—Council on Corporate Compliance, http://www.conference-board.org/knowledge/knowledgeCouncil.cfm?Council_ID=170&nav=cg

Recent developments have encouraged U.S. corporations to establish the position of Chief Compliance Officer. Chief Compliance Officers are facing new challenges and developing trail blazing agendas. U.S. Corporations are codifying policies and procedures, establishing criteria and reallocating their resources. The Conference Board's Council on Corporate Compliance provides a unique opportunity to learn and discuss compliance issues with peers in a confidential environment.

Ethical Leadership Group, http://www.ethicalleadershipgroup.com/

In 1993, we set out to create the premier ethics, values and compliance consulting firm in the world.

Ethics Officer Association, http://www.eoa.org/

The Ethics Officer Association (EOA) is the professional association exclusively for managers of ethics, compliance and business conduct programs.

George R. Wratney and Patrick J. Gnazzo, "Are You Serious About Ethics? For Companies That Can't Guarantee Confidentiality, the Answer Is No," *Across the Board,* July/August, 2003, http://www.conference-board.org/articles/atb_article.cfm?id=206

## Questions for Discussion and Review

1. What do you imagine the day-to-day work of an ethics or compliance officer entails? Do you think it is viewed as a position of importance within companies today? Why or why not?

2. From looking at the list of member companies available at the Ethics Officer Association Web site (http://www.eoa.org/MemberDirectory/EOA_Company_List.pdf), you can see

that many companies now have ethics officers in place—or at least support the work of the EOA. What is your reaction to the list when you see it?

3. What do you think when you read about the survey of ethics and compliance officers attending the Conference Board's ethics conference in May 2003, which reported as follows:

About 45 percent said that their ethics and compliance programs would reduce the likelihood of an ethics scandal at their companies only "a little" or "not at all."?[33]

## COMPLIANCE—APPROACHES

☑ *CSR Connection:* This issue reflects an ongoing debate within CSR: the extent to which companies should be compelled or encouraged to adhere voluntarily to more socially responsible practices.

### Issue

Some argue that companies only act in their best interests and that those interests are narrowly defined. Therefore, the only way to get companies to act in a way deemed more socially acceptable is to force them to act through legislation. The alternative argument assumes that only if an organization commits to CSR voluntarily will it pursue those goals with sufficient enthusiasm to produce genuine and meaningful change.

At one end of the spectrum is an argument in favor of mandatory controls:

Existing laws do not compel a high enough standard of social behavior. Companies will never do more than is required of them if the action is considered a cost to business. Therefore, new and stricter legislation is required to compel more responsible corporate behavior.

At the other end of the spectrum is an argument in favor of encouraging voluntary action:

Companies will eventually come to realize that it is in their best interests to make sure the communities in which they do business accept them. It is those communities' expectations and shifting standards that will define what is and is not acceptable behavior. Adequate behavior cannot easily be defined or mandated. If CSR behavior is tied to corporate success, then the profit motive will provide the ideal incentive for compliance.

Needless to say, there are several shades of gray between these two points of view.

# Case Study: Voluntary Versus Mandatory

Compliance goes to the heart of CSR because it largely dictates the degree to which a company is going to be accepted by society. Those companies that add value will be welcomed and those that are perceived to be detracting from the general well-being will be criticized, even rejected. How the notions of *contributing* or *adding value* and *detracting* are defined is constantly shifting; therefore, there is self-interest driving companies to determine in advance what will be expected of them:

> Companies are more mindful that their reputation is a precious asset which today's media can destroy in hours. Hence their interest in responding to the demand for CSR.[34]

There is a strong case for the strict regulation of a company's actions when they come into (potentially negative) contact with society. For example, left to its own devices, a company transporting nuclear waste might be tempted to avoid undertaking all the costly precautions necessary to ensure a completely safe journey. There is also, however, a strong case that a company has to be genuinely committed to implementing CSR in order for it to be effective and that no amount of regulation can dictate such commitment:

> Mandatory disclosure requirements would not help—especially if they were highly prescriptive. If requirements were too rigid, the result would be a bureaucratic compliance culture, where disclosure would relate not to any real commitment to good behavior but to a desire to tick the right boxes. . . . If corporate social responsibility means anything, it must involve some voluntary recognition by companies that they cannot thrive in isolation or opposition to the society in which they are trying to do business.[35]

Alan Greenspan, chairman of the Federal Reserve Board in the United States, has long been an advocate of self-regulation, or voluntary compliance, within the finance industry:

> "It is in the self-interest of every businessman to have a reputation for honest dealings and a quality product," he wrote . . . in 1963. Regulation, he said, undermines this "superlatively moral system" by replacing competition for reputation with force. . . . [Greenspan] still admires the laissez-faire capitalism of the mid-19th century. At that time, competition, not regulation, kept financial markets honest. Banks, for example, issued their own currency whose value fluctuated with the issuer's reputation.[36]

Government regulatory interventions—such as producing a national currency and guaranteeing individual savings deposits—Greenspan argues, reduced

> the incentive for bankers and businessmen to act prudently . . . [and made] depositors less concerned about the reputation of the bank to which they entrusted their money.[37]

The European Multi Stakeholder Forum on Corporate Social Responsibility (CSR EMS Forum) indicates a growing awareness of the need to encourage voluntary change:

> Participants agreed [on] a definition of corporate social responsibility. They reaffirmed that it is the voluntary integration of environmental and social considerations into core business operations over and above legal obligations, and is based on dialogue with stakeholders.[38]

It is also true, however, that given half a chance, many companies would determine where to cut costs based on self-interest (i.e., the lowest cost) rather than on what they feel would be best for society in general, if money were no object. Hence the case for stricter legislation as a safeguard:

Enron, for example, proudly presented its CSR credentials as a giant PR exercise while internally betraying them. Unless companies really own CSR it is only window-dressing, argue the voluntarists. . . . The best instrument is to show business that behaving well is good business, so that it adopts CSR willingly and internalizes it.[39]

There is definitely a place for regulation in areas of greatest interest to the largest number of people:

> In France, since 2002 all public companies have been required to report social and environmental information as part of the annual report.[40]

> Belgium has a national kitemarking scheme so that consumers can identify companies that follow CSR principles.[41]

Too much regulation stifles entrepreneurship and encourages inefficiency. Yet business's best interests require an understanding that consumer definitions of what is and is not acceptable are shifting. If firms ignore consumer expectations, a potentially more damaging backlash of widespread regulation may stifle the business environment and make the whole situation worse.

A pattern that is emerging in global business is that those corporations that have felt the brunt of the attention of CSR campaigners up until now are often those that are most proactive regarding CSR. These companies see the self-interest in reacting positively to their experiences and instigating CSR protection to try and avoid similar problems in the future:

> Shell's experience with *Brent Spar* and in Nigeria convinced it to take relations with its stakeholders more seriously, becoming an exemplar of best practice in its environmental and social reporting.[42]

It is always difficult to tell, of course, whether these incidents prompt a company genuinely to reevaluate its operations and strategic perspective to incorporate the importance of CSR or whether the company merely recognizes a need to *appear* concerned about issues that can harm it. The debate continues.

## Web-Based Examples and Resources

EurActiv.com, http://www.euractiv.com/

> EurActiv.com is now the leading online media on European Union policies.

> Corporate Responsibility: Voluntary vs. mandatory to remain point of contention in CSR. (02/07/2004)

http://www.euractiv.com/Article?tcmuri=tcm:29–110211–16&type=Overview

> European Multi Stakeholder Forum on Corporate Social Responsibility (CSR EMS Forum)

http://forum.europa.eu.int/irc/empl/csr_eu_multi_stakeholder_forum/info/data/en/csr%20em s%20forum.htm

> The (CSR EMS Forum) . . . brings together European representative organisations of employers, business networks, trade unions, and NGOs, to promote innovation, convergence, and transparency in existing CSR practices and tools. The Forum's mandate was approved at the launch on 16th October 2002.

FiCom, http://www.ficom.fi/en/lyhyesti.html

Finnish Federation for Communications and Teleinformatics, FiCom, is a co-operation and lobbying organisation in the field of industrial policy concerning the Finnish communications, teleinformatics and message transfer sectors.

"Karoliina Rasi-Hedberg, European Commission Discusses the Corporate Social Responsibility—Should It Be Mandatory or Voluntary?" (May 30, 2002), http://www.ficom.fi/en/issue_a.html?Id=1022684046.html

IIED—International Institute for Environment and Development, http://www.iied.org/index.html

IIED is an independent, nonprofit organization promoting sustainable patterns of world development through collaborative research, policy studies, networking and knowledge dissemination.

Halina Ward, 'Legal Issues in Corporate Citizenship,' February 2003. http://www.iied.org/cred/execsumm/legalissues.html

Royal Dutch/Shell Group, http://www.shell.com/

Do you still think of Shell as an oil company? In fact we are a global group of energy and petrochemicals companies, operating in over 145 countries and employing more than 119,000 people.

Shell's *Brent Spar* Dossier, http://www.shell.com/brentspar/

Shell Nigeria, http://www.shell.com/nigeria/

## Questions for Discussion and Review

1. Which argument do you favor—persuading a company to change to incorporate a CSR perspective voluntarily or forcing them to change using legislation? Why?

2. Have a look at Shell's Web site and the way it presents the two issues that prompted the company to reinvent itself as a CSR-oriented organization: *Brent Spar* (http://www.shell.com/brentspar/) and Nigeria (http://www.shell.com/nigeria/). Do you think Shell's reaction to these problems shows a genuine commitment to change or simply recognition of the need to appear to be listening to key external stakeholders?

3. Enter the search terms *csr, mandatory, voluntary* into Google. Have a brief look at some of the relevant documents this search produces. What is your sense of the argument that is playing out within the business world? Where would most corporations like the balance to fall? Is that the same as the nonprofit organizations or NGOs that are also participating in the debate?

# CORPORATE CHARTERS

☑ *CSR Connection:* This issue analyzes a company's responsibilities and obligations as determined by corporate law and founding charters.

## Issue

What responsibilities and obligations do corporations have, as determined by their founding charters?

The corporation, as created by law, compels executives to prioritize the interests of their companies and shareholders above all others. The law forbids any other motivations for company actions, whether to assist workers, improve the environment, or help consumers save money. Corporate social responsibility is thus illegal—at least when it is genuine.[43]

Is this ideal from a CSR perspective? And what is the most appropriate authority (federal vs. state government) to regulate this area of corporate law?

## Case Study: Federalization

Issues of corporate governance are currently regulated under state rather than federal law. Those who support this system argue that this encourages competition between states (to entice corporations to incorporate within their state) and therefore produces effective and efficient legislation; however, critics of this system rebut the benefits of this interstate competition because the result is a race to the bottom, as states bend over backwards to craft legislation that appeases corporations. States want corporations to incorporate within their jurisdiction because of the lucrative fees they receive for each company that registers there, wherever the company is actually headquartered:

Corporations don't have to incorporate where a firm is headquartered, or even where it employs the most people. Managers can go jurisdiction-shopping, looking for the most advantageous set of laws, since getting a corporate charter is easier than getting a driver's license. As a result, some 60 percent of the Fortune 500 is

incorporated in Delaware, which is most protective of managerial interests.[44]

Delaware is perceived as having the *most advantageous* system of regulation for companies, which translates as having the *least* regulation. In terms of oversight, liability, responsibility, and regulation, Delaware has "long been reluctant to disturb the decisions of corporate boards."[45] Other states attempt to reproduce Delaware's lax environment simply to keep companies currently headquartered within the state from reincorporating to Delaware:

If another state wants to be more aggressive in fighting corporate crime or protecting shareholders, employees, or communities, it runs the risk that its companies will simply re-incorporate in Delaware. So most states end up mimicking Delaware law.[46]

There is a growing belief that meaningful reform in the area of governing corporations can only take place if the federal government takes control of the process. This would allow either Congress or the SEC to raise the bar for all corporations without having to worry that companies would simply flee in protest to the state with the weakest rules, although here the risk would be that firms would incorporate overseas in such places as Bermuda, for example, with its favorable tax treatment.

A good starting point for the federal government would be a law stating that corporations have to incorporate where their true headquarters are or where they employ the most people or have the greatest percentage of their operations. This would make corporations accountable for their actions to the community within which they actually operate. By introducing these changes, the government would also go a long way toward closing the loophole in the tax code that allows corporations to incorporate offshore (again, irrespective of where their headquarters are) to avoid paying the higher rates of corporation tax levied in the United States.

As a first step in this campaign toward federalization, various attempts have been made to introduce a "Code for Corporate Responsibility" at the state level, which would reform the law with regard to director's duties:

> For public corporations, the corporate purpose of maximizing returns for shareholders is now held in place by the state law of director's duties, which in all states say that directors must act in the best interests of the corporation and its shareholders. Attorney Robert Hinkley has drafted a model Code for Corporate Responsibility which would change this to say, in effect, directors may not pursue shareholder gain at the expense of employees, the community, and the environment. If these parties can demonstrate harm, they would have a right to sue under the proposed law.[47]

The potential impact of this simple but far-reaching change to the law would be huge. The whole purpose of the corporation would necessarily shift, and the new law would give stakeholders a tool by which to hold the corporations operating within the community accountable for their actions and policies. Forcing this multiconstituency approach would result in U.S. firms increasingly acting like European ones, which tend to define

their stakeholders more broadly and actively. Groups in both Minnesota and California have begun campaigning for this change, with states such as Maine and Massachusetts also showing interest. Legislation has been introduced in California to put the new code into effect:

> In California—where the state legislature is controlled by Democrats—corporate purpose legislation was introduced . . . by Senate Majority Whip Richard Alarcon (D—San Fernando Valley). While current law says directors must maximize profits for shareholders, Alarcon's Good Corporate Citizen bill (SB 917) says companies may not do so at the expense of the environment, human rights, the public health, the community, or the dignity of employees. The attorney general could bring civil action against violators. Under certain conditions, directors would be personally liable.[48]

There are legitimate issues relating to implementation. For example, "What happens if a company moves a plant to a more environmentally friendly facility, thereby helping the environment but harming the employees and community of the previous locality?"[49] Also, what would be the proposed penalties for directors that fail the new test? Would they be individually liable? Nevertheless, there is also growing support for the idea. A *BusinessWeek*/Harris Poll in 2000 asked which of the following options was preferable:

> Corporations should have only one purpose—to make the most profit for their shareholders—and pursuit of that goal will be best for America in the long run.
> —or—
> Corporations should have more than one purpose. They also owe something to their workers and the communities in which they operate, and they should sometimes sacrifice some profit for the sake of making things better for their workers and communities.
>
> An overwhelming 95 percent of Americans chose the second proposition. . . . When 95 percent of the public supports a proposition, enacting that proposition into law should not be impossible.[50]

## Web-Based Examples and Resources

Background information and a copy of the "Code for Corporate Responsibility," press cuttings, examples of existing state laws, reports of attempts to reform state laws, and other resources, can be found at Citizen Works (founded by Ralph Nader), http://www.citizen works.org/enron/corp_code.php

According to Corporate Law, Corporations make decisions based only on maximizing profits and increasing stock prices. The Code for Corporate Responsibility seeks to add protections for the environment, human rights, public health and safety, the welfare of our communities and the corporate employees.

Code for Corporate Responsibility activity in Minnesota: http://www.c4cr.org/

C4CR envisions a world in which corporations work for a just, peaceful and sustainable global society.

Code for Corporate Responsibility activity in California: http://groups.yahoo.com/group/ c4cr_california/?

For information concerning Bill SB 917 and an update on its progress, see: http://info. sen.ca.gov/cgi-bin/postquery?bill_number=sb_917&sess=PREV&house =B&site=sen

Common Dreams NewsCenter, http://www.commondreams.org/views02/0119–04.htm

Robert Hinkley, "How Corporate Law Inhibits Social Responsibility: A Corporate Attorney Proposes a 'Code for Corporate Citizenship' in State Law," published in the January/February 2002 issue of *Business Ethics: Corporate Social Responsibility Report.*

## Questions for Discussion and Review

1. What is the argument for having corporate governance issues regulated at the federal rather than state level? Do you agree?

2. Do you agree with the goals contained within the "Code for Corporate Responsibility"?

3. What would be the argument against the "Code for Corporate Responsibility"?

# CORPORATE GOVERNANCE—REPORTING

☑ *CSR Connection:* This issue highlights the growing importance of corporate governance within CSR.

## Issue

Issues of corporate governance were central to the corporate scandals that came to light so prominently in the early years of the 21st century. The system of corporate governance, developed over time to provide oversight of a company's managers and operations, was failing the very people it was set up to protect: the company's owners, its shareholders. This failure resulted from a relatively recent shift in emphasis of corporate outlook: from managing the relationships between the organization and its many stakeholder groups over the medium to long term to focusing on short-term measures of success above all else (for example, emphasizing quarterly earnings reports in order to bolster a company's share price):

> Before the 1980s one tenet of corporate governance was that company management served several constituencies: shareholders, yes, but also employees, customers, and perhaps others too. . . . But the shareholder-value crowd insisted that the only clientele that mattered was stockholders. If they were rewarded, then all other players would reap benefits as a byproduct of an even higher stock price. This mantra of shareholder value, however, could be taken to an extreme and perverted—you can see how this bit of dogma could become a handy all-purpose justification for mass firings, shoddy products, and the dumping of chemicals into rivers.[51]

As a result of the public outcry at the extent of the corrupt excesses brought to light by the corporate scandals, the U.S. legislature stepped in to regulate further the area of corporate governance. One result was the Sarbanes-Oxley Act of 2002.

---

## Case Study: Sarbanes-Oxley Act (2002)

The reforms introduced by the Sarbanes-Oxley legislation can be loosely divided into three sections:

Significantly, the legislation also created the Public Company Accounting Oversight Board

| | |
|---|---|
| Certification | High-ranking company executives are required to certify the accuracy and validity of the company's financial statements, including detailed explanations of any divergence from generally accepted accounting principles (GAAP). |
| Auditability | Adequate internal controls are required to ensure that the governance of the company is both transparent and free of corrupting influences and that this can be determined objectively. These internal controls will need to be compatible with standards established by organizations such as COSO (see http://www.coso.org/). |
| Disclosure | Financial results and other relevant information must be publicly disclosed much more rapidly (real-time where possible) than had been previously required. |

(http://www.pcaobus.org/) to provide further objective oversight in the area of corporate governance.

The timeline listed at http://www.pwc.com/sarbanes-oxley details the various reforms that the Sarbanes-Oxley legislation introduces, as well the date on which they become effective.

A key part of the legislation is the provision for greater responsibility placed on executive officers, holding them personally accountable for the actions of the organization:

> Under new federal sentencing guidelines after the Sarbanes-Oxley Act, corporate crooks can get life in prison if crimes involve some combination of the following: over 250 victims, a loss of at least

$400 million, involvement of a public company, or threat to a financial institution's solvency.[52]

As the full impact of the legislation becomes clearer with time, however, the business community has begun to complain about the burdens the new act places on them (both in terms of time and money), as well as its relative inability to prevent similar corporate excesses from reoccurring:

> Corporate America is now being turned upside-down by a law that was ill-considered and certainly unread by most of those who voted for it. . . . No wonder that the annual bill for Sarbox [compliance] is going through the roof, with the

latest estimates being about $6 billion for the Fortune 1000 alone. . . . No wonder, too, that the number of companies alerting the SEC that their latest financial reports will be late doubled [in the third quarter of 2004], adding to a backlog of late filers that recently topped 600.[53]

Further information about Sarbanes-Oxley can be found at the following Web sites:

U.S. Securities and Exchange Commission, http://www.sec.gov/spotlight/sarbanes-oxley.htm

PricewaterhouseCoopers, http://www.pwc.com/sarbanes-oxley

Most observers would agree that the Sarbanes-Oxley Act (SOA) is the single most important piece of legislation affecting corporate governance, financial disclosure and the practice of public accounting since the U.S. securities laws of the early 1930s. . . . With this site, PricewaterhouseCoopers aims to help the user make some sense of it all.

Sarbanes-Oxley, http://www.sarbanes-oxley.com/

Sarbanes-Oxley allows firms to stay abreast of the proposed and final rules and regulations issued by the SEC to implement the Sarbanes-Oxley Act (SOX).

## Web-Based Examples and Resources

Committee of Sponsoring Organizations of the Treadway Commission (COSO), http://www.coso.org/

COSO is a voluntary private sector organization dedicated to improving the quality of financial reporting through business ethics, effective internal controls, and corporate governance.

CorpGov.net, http://www.corpgov.net/

Since 1995 the Corporate Governance site has . . . [served] as a discussion forum and NETwork for shareholders and stakeholders who believe active participation by concerned shareholders in governing corporations will enhance their ability to create wealth.

http://www.corpgov.net/links/links.html (An extremely comprehensive list of corporate governance Web site links.)

Global Corporate Governance Forum (OECD & World Bank), http://www.gcgf.org/

Helping countries improve the standards of governance for their corporations, by fostering the spirit of enterprise and accountability, promoting fairness, transparency and responsibility.

The Global Corporate Governance Forum is sponsored by the governments of India, Luxembourg, the Netherlands, Norway, Sweden, Switzerland, the United Kingdom, the United States, the Organisation for Economic Co-operation and Development (OECD), and the World Bank Group.

GovernanceMetrics International, http://governancemetrics.com/

Academic studies and investors' own experiences have taught us there is a link between governance practices and investment risk. . . . GMI was formed in April 2000 by a small group of people who recognized the need for a new, easy-to-use tool to monitor corporate governance. GMI Rating Reports for 500 U.S. companies are now available on a subscription basis.

Institutional Shareholder Services, http://www.issproxy.com/

> Institutional Shareholder Services, Inc. (ISS) is the world's leading provider of proxy voting and corporate governance services. ISS serves more than 950 institutional and corporate clients throughout North America and Europe with its core business—analyzing proxies and issuing informed research and objective vote recommendations for more than 10,000 U.S. and 12,000 non-U.S. shareholder meetings each year.

International Corporate Governance Network, http://www.icgn.org/

> One of the objectives of the ICGN is to facilitate international dialogue on issues of concern to investors.

Investor Responsibility Research Center, http://www.irrc.org/

> IRRC is an independent research firm that has been the leading source of high quality, impartial information on corporate governance and social responsibility issues affecting investors and corporations, for 30 years. Founded in 1972. . . . IRRC is unique in the industry as it does not advocate on any side of the issues it covers.

PIRC (Pensions & Investment Research Consultants Ltd.), http://www.pirc.co.uk/

> PIRC is the guardian of good corporate governance—and shareholder responsibility—in the UK. [*Investor Relations Magazine*]

Public Company Accounting Oversight Board, http://www.pcaobus.org/

> The PCAOB is a private-sector, nonprofit corporation, created by the Sarbanes-Oxley Act of 2002, to oversee the auditors of public companies in order to protect the interests of investors and further the public interest in the preparation of informative, fair, and independent audit reports.

SigmaFLOW, http://www.sigmaflow.com/solutionareas/sarbanes-oxley.html

> The Sarbanes-Oxley legislation directly references COSO (Committee of Sponsoring Organizations of the Treadway Commission) as a framework to assist management with better controlling their business activities by providing a consistent approach to review business entities. . . . Forward thinking companies that recognize Sarbanes-Oxley and COSO as an opportunity to extend Six Sigma to the Audit function are accomplishing these benefits:

> 1. Arming Audit staff with Improvement Tools such as RPN (Risk Priority Number), Pareto Charting of Risks, and Value Analysis so they can transition from inspection and documentation—to facilitating improvement workshops.

> 2. Use Six Sigma to Eliminate Waste and transition from multiple manual reactive controls to defining a key predictive control.

> 3. Use Sarbanes-Oxley to identify high priority Six Sigma projects.

Sir Adrian Cadbury, *Corporate Governance and Chairmanship: A Personal View*, 2002. [book]

The Corporate Library ("a corporate governance research service"),[54] http://www.the corporatelibrary.com/

The Corporate Library is intended to serve as a central repository for research, study and critical thinking about the nature of the modern global corporation, with a special focus on corporate governance and the relationship between company management, their boards and shareholders.

The OECD's initiative to strengthen Corporate Governance, http://www.oecd.org/topic/ 0,2686,en_2649_37439_1_1_1_1_37439,00.html

The OECD Principles of Corporate Governance, link at http://www.oecd.org/depart ment/0,2688,en_2649_34813_1_1_1_1_1,00.html

Transparency International, http://www.transparency.org/

Purpose: To curb corruption by mobilising a global coalition to promote and strengthen international and national Integrity Systems.

Weinberg Center for Corporate Governance (University of Delaware), http://www .be.udel.edu/ccg/

The Center for Corporate Governance operating out of the Lerner College of Business and Economics at the University of Delaware has been established to propose sensible and progressive changes in corporate structure and management through education and interaction. It provides a forum for business leaders, members of corporate boards, corporate legal scholars and practitioners, jurists, economists, graduate and undergraduate students and all other persons interested in corporate governance issues to meet, to interact, to learn and to teach.

## Questions for Discussion and Review

1. What is the job of a corporation's board of directors? Whose interests do they serve?

2. Many CEOs complain that the result of the Sarbanes-Oxley legislation has been only to further complicate the auditing process and push up fees that the auditing companies charge corporations:

   Companies . . . have spent at least $1 billion adopting new Sarbanes-Oxley rules meant to address the crisis of confidence that wiped out $35 billion in investor wealth.[55]

   Do you think that this is an area of law that can be left to market forces (after all, Enron and Arthur Anderson no longer exist), or do you think that if corporations cannot regulate their own behavior, then it is the duty of government to step into the void?

3. Look at the eight categories used by The Corporate Library in measuring the effectiveness of a corporation's board (http://www.thecorporatelibrary.com/Products-and-Services/board-effectiveness-ratings.html). Which do you think are the most important categories? Why?

# CORPORATE GOVERNANCE—BOARDS

☑ *CSR Connection:* This issue reflects the growing importance of the effectiveness of boards of directors within the field of corporate governance.

## Issue

The performance (and independence) of corporate boards has come under increased scrutiny in the early years of the 20th century. The Enron scandal, among others, showed the damage a weak board can allow to happen. The corporate scandals at the turn of the century raised the profile of corporate governance in general. Rather than being a theoretical ideal to which lip service is paid but not acted on, board effectiveness is now a key investment criterion in terms of evaluating a large corporation and establishing investor confidence. Corporations ignore the opacity of their boards at their peril, especially in an investment environment in which easily obtained dollars are the exception.

## Case Study: Corporate Boards

The rise in importance of *BusinessWeek's* ranking of the best and worst boards reflects this change in attitude toward the issue of corporate governance in the United States:

Bad boards, in particular, have made extraordinary strides in confronting [difficult corporate governance issues]. Spurred in many cases by scandal, crisis, or a plummeting stock price, former laggards have become ardent believers in good governance.[56]

The *BusinessWeek* survey ranks corporate boards according to four principles of good governance:

*Independence.* The number of directors who were previously company executives or have existing business relationships with the company (e.g., consulting contracts).

*Stock ownership.* The amount of stock each member of the board owns in the company, therefore aligning personal interests directly with shareholder interests. *BusinessWeek* has stipulated an ideal minimum of $150,000 per director.

*Director quality.* Directors should have experience in the same industry of the company's core business, as well as experience of managing similar-sized organizations. "Fully employed directors should sit on no more than four boards, retirees no more than seven. Each director should attend at least 75% of all meetings."[57]

*Board activism.* Boards should meet regularly, should also meet without management present, and should show restraint in areas such as executive compensation.

The survey, begun in 1996, launched its fourth list of rankings in October 2002:

For three years after the list appeared, the stocks of companies with the best boards outperformed those with the worst by 2 to 1. But as the economy slowed starting in 2000, the Best Boards companies retained much more of their value, returning 51.7%, vs. –12.9% for the Worst Boards companies.[58]

Some, however, are still skeptical regarding the potential scope for meaningful reform. Observers refer back to the wide-ranging corporate governance reform movement of 1993—when many boards sought to reassert their independence and control over management and CEOs in particular—and ask whether anything has really changed since then:

"It now seems that what we had in 1993 was sporadic and random action by high-profile directors at high-profile companies, but no countrywide improvement in corporate performance," said Peter C. Clapman, the chief counsel of TIAA-CREF, the huge pension and mutual fund manager that has long fought for better boardroom vigilance. "I'm just mildly optimistic that the latest reforms will stick if we go into another bull market now."[59]

A recent PriceWaterhouseCoopers survey found that the number of executives with a favorable opinion of Sarbanes-Oxley had fallen from 42% last October [2002] to 30% this June [2003]. . . . "There is a sense that if the capital markets simply recover and the stock market goes up, this whole focus on governance will lose steam."[60]

One of the biggest factors regarding the operational effectiveness of corporate boards in the United States—and a barrier to significant progress—is the issue of whether the jobs of CEO and chair of the board should be legally separated. Traditionally in the United States, power is concentrated in one person who both chairs the board and is the top employee of the company, the CEO. In Canada, Britain, and continental Europe, however, the separation of these two jobs is standard practice. For corporate governance to be effective within an organization, the performance of the board of directors is crucial. And for this performance to be effective, the board's independence from management is important. Many in the United States are now arguing that the board cannot possibly oversee the effectiveness of the CEO in terms of day-to-day operations if that same person is also the chair of the board:

Andrew S. Grove, who is chairman of Intel Corp., while Craig R. Barrett is its CEO, made the point . . . this way: "The separation of the two jobs goes to the heart of the conception of a corporation. . . . If [the CEO is] an employee, he needs a boss, and that boss is the board. The chairman runs the board. How can the CEO be his own boss?" In a recent survey of board members from 500 large U.S. companies, McKinsey & Co. found similar views. Nearly 70% of respondents said a CEO should not run the board.[61]

The oversight role played by the board is growing in importance as individual investors (who rely on boards to protect their investments, especially retirement investments) are taking charge of their personal finances. The position of chair of the board, as chief representative of investors, is also growing in importance. Add in the different skills required by both positions and the difficulty in having one person in both roles becomes increasingly apparent:

[Before 2003], the share of companies separating the two jobs was rising about 2% annually. [In 2003], the share of companies whose CEOs didn't also hold the chairman's reins increased to 25% of the S&P 500 from 21% in 2002.[62]

As shareholders become aware of the conflict of interest inherent in one person holding both positions, the backlash against companies that ignore calls for reform is also increasing. Within the pharmaceutical industry,[63] shareholder resolutions tabled in 2005 garnered support for dividing the two roles and appointing an independent director chair of the board at Wyeth (39%); Eli Lilly & Co. (25%); Abbott Laboratories (17%); Merck & Co. (46.5%); and Pfizer Inc. (42.1%).[64]

In March 2004 at the company's annual general meeting (AGM), 43% of Disney shareholders voted in favor of a no-confidence motion against Michael Eisner. In response, the board removed him as chairman of the company, allowing him to retain his position as CEO; however, in spite of the growing support for the idea of splitting the CEO and chair positions, many corporations in the United States maintain unified responsibilities:

> Of the 30 large companies that make up the Dow Jones Industrial Average [in 2002], only eight have split functions.[65]

One compromise that has grown in popularity is the appointment of independent lead directors of boards, allowing companies to avoid splitting the CEO and chair roles:

> The percentage of S&P 500 companies appointing a lead or presiding director more than doubled [in 2003] to 53% from 26% [in 2002]. . . . The proportion of companies that divide the CEO and chairman's position also accelerated [in 2003], but at a slower pace, with the overall numbers still trailing the companies opting for a lead director structure.[66]

A 2005 survey, "including most of the nation's largest companies," released by the Business Roundtable reported that this trend is continuing:

> Seventy-one percent [of responding companies] said they now hold executive sessions ["without company managers present"] at every board meeting, up from 68% [in 2004] and 55% [in 2003]. Moreover, 83% of the companies said they now have an independent chairman, a lead director or a presiding director—up 12 percentage points from [2004].[67]

It is important to remember, however, that *independence* from the organization does not automatically mean effectiveness:

> The Sarbanes-Oxley Act requires public companies to have a majority of independent directors. . . . But the SEC still allows director nominations to be closely controlled by management. So as James McRitchie of Corp.Gov.net put it, independent directors "can still be the CEO's golfing buddies." Enron, we might recall, had 12 out of 14 independent directors.[68]

## Web-Based Examples and Resources

See *Web-Based Examples and Resources* under the previous topic, Corporate Governance—Reporting.

## Questions for Discussion and Review

1. Are "independent" board members truly independent? What would you do to ensure greater independence of board members?

2. Look at the four principles of good governance used by *BusinessWeek's* ranking in "The Best & Worst Boards." Which of these do you think is the most important? Why?

3. What is your opinion regarding the issue of splitting the roles of chair and CEO? Justify your position.

# CORPORATION

☑ *CSR Connection:* This issue reflects the focus on the corporation throughout this book. To what extent is the firm a part of the problem versus part of the solution?

## Issue

The corporation is the focus for much of the criticism put forward by CSR advocates. It is also blamed for many of the ills created by globalization and free trade:

> One hundred and fifty years ago, the corporation was a relatively insignificant entity. Today, it is a vivid, dramatic and pervasive presence in all our lives. Like the Church, the Monarchy and the Communist Party in other times and places, the corporation is today's dominant institution. But history humbles dominant institutions. All have been crushed, belittled or absorbed into some new order. The corporation is unlikely to be the first to defy history.[69]

To what extent is the corporation a positive factor in the CSR debate? And how can a corporation's contribution to the wider good be measured and evaluated?

## Case Study: The U.S. Corporation

*Fortune* magazine heralds the corporation as one of "the most significant innovations of the past 50 years":

> Without [corporations] and their proven ability to marshal and allocate resources, organize and harness the ingenuity of people, respond to commercial and social environments, and meet the ever more elaborate challenge of producing and distributing goods and providing services on a global scale, we would have far less innovation—and less wealth.[70]

This belief is shared by Micklethwait and Wooldridge in their book, *The Company: A Short History of a Revolutionary Idea*, published in 2003:

> Hegel predicted that the basic unit of modern society would be the state, Marx that it would be the commune, Lenin and Hitler that it would be the political party. Before that, a succession of saints and sages claimed the same for the parish

church, the feudal manor, and the monarchy. The big contention of this small book is that they have all been proved wrong. The most important organization in the world is the company: the basis of the prosperity of the West and the best hope for the future of the rest of the world. Indeed, for most of us, the company's only real rival for our time and energy is the one that is taken for granted—the family.[71]

Bill Gates is even more effusive:

> [The] modern corporation is one of the most effective means to allocate resources we've ever seen. It transforms great ideas into customer benefits on an unimaginably large scale.
>     Drucker and Collins, likewise, think [all organizations] would benefit if they learned to behave more like corporations. . . . Whether or not the ever-evolving modern corporation can be a panacea for the ills and dysfunctions of other kinds of institutions, there's no question

that it is peerless at creating wealth and providing meaningful employment for tens of millions of people.[72]

When a corporation attempts to infuse the corporation with a CSR perspective, it is important to remember that, merely by existing—by providing a return on investment to shareholders, by providing jobs for employees, and by paying taxes to government—the corporation is benefiting society. If you add to that mix the constant product innovation necessary to maintain sales and profits (only products that are in demand are purchased), then the corporation, as a concept, can be considered a positive and productive component of a healthy society.

The corporation, however, can also do harm to the societies within which it is based. Doing all of the above does not ensure an organization's long-term viability and does not replace the need for an effective CSR policy implemented throughout the organization. Our discussion of Wal-Mart in Chapter 2 shows that a company that is successful and producing products customers want can still be accused of behavior that is harmful to society as a whole. But the positive aspects of Wal-Mart's operations are often hidden by the negative publicity the company receives:

> Wal-Mart [in 2003] added 99,000 jobs in the U.S., making it the country's biggest job creator.[73]

Nevertheless, it is important to recognize that corporations exist because their products are in demand and that, generally, it is in society's best interests to encourage healthy and wealthy corporations because they bring many benefits. On top of this healthy foundation, it is then important to build an integrated CSR policy. The Center for Corporate Citizenship at Boston College and the U.S. Chamber of Commerce's Center for Corporate Citizenship, released a 2004 report (*The State of Corporate Citizenship in the U.S.: A View From Inside*), which analyzes the level of CSR (corporate citizenship) awareness within the modern U.S. corporation. The report, a survey of 515 business leaders from firms across the U.S. business landscape,

> concludes that regardless of company size, business executives see corporate citizenship as a fundamental part of business and central to good business practice. Eighty-two per cent of respondents say good corporate citizenship helped the bottom line and 59% feel these practices improve company image and reputation. Fifty-three per cent report corporate citizenship is important to their customers. More than half of the executives surveyed say corporate citizenship is part of their business strategy.[74]

We, as a society, benefit if we are progressing. Corporations help us progress and generate much of the wealth on which we measure that progress. The business world is society's most important stakeholder and is the key to future progress. CSR helps corporations understand the environment within which they operate and helps them chart a more sustainable path forward. CSR helps corporations maximize their potential and benefit for the widest number of constituent groups.

## Web-Based Examples and Resources

Bakan, Joel, *The Corporation: The Pathological Pursuit of Profit and Power,* Free Press, 2004.

Micklethwait, John, and Wooldridge, Adrian, *The Company: A Short History of a Revolutionary Idea,* Modern Library, 2003.

The Center for Corporate Citizenship at Boston College, http://www.bcccc.net/

The Center for Corporate Citizenship at Boston College is a membership based research organization. We work with global corporations to help them define, plan and operationalize their corporate citizenship. Our goal is to help business leverage its social, economic and human assets to ensure both its success and a more just and sustainable world.

*The Corporation,* http://www.thecorporation.com/

In this complex and highly entertaining documentary, Mark Achbar . . . [seeks] to examine the far-reaching repercussions of the corporation's increasing preeminence. Based on Bakan's book *The Corporation: The Pathological Pursuit of Profit and Power,* the film is a timely, critical inquiry that invites CEOs, whistle-blowers, brokers, gurus, spies, players, pawns and pundits on a graphic and engaging quest to reveal the corporation's inner workings, curious history, controversial impacts and possible futures. Featuring illuminating interviews with Noam Chomsky, Michael Moore, Howard Zinn and many others, *The Corporation* charts the spectacular rise of an institution aimed at achieving specific economic goals as it also recounts victories against this apparently invincible force.

U.S. Chamber of Commerce's Center for Corporate Citizenship, http://www.uschamber .com/ccc/

The U.S. Chamber of Commerce Center for Corporate Citizenship (CCC) is a 501(c)(3) nonprofit organization that serves as a resource and a voice for businesses and their social concerns.

## Questions for Discussion and Review

1. Make the case for the corporation as a force for good in society today.

2. Then point out why that argument is insufficient in terms of measuring a firm's level of CSR commitment.

3. Go to the Web site for the movie documentary, *The Corporation* (http://www.thecor poration.com/). Have a look at the trailer posted on the site. Is this kind of commentary helpful to those promoting CSR? Do you agree with the message it is conveying? Why, or why not?

## EMPLOYEE RELATIONS

☑ *CSR Connection:* This issue supports the business case for CSR: that firms benefit by meeting their stakeholders' needs and concerns rather than by focusing on minimizing costs and maximizing profits in the short term.

## Issue

Employees are a central stakeholder of the firm. To the extent that the organization fosters a feeling of commitment and loyalty within its workforce, the firm benefits. Employees are proud to work for organizations with an ethical reputation,[75] a sense that carries over into the quality of work that is produced:

> Evidence from the *Sunday Times'* "100 best companies to work for" list shows that the share prices of the quoted companies on the list outperform the FTSE All Share Index by between 10% and 15%, a result that is seen in every country that produces a list.[76]

There are many causal-related benefits for companies ensuring their employees are happy and healthy at work:

• Employee retention reduces costs associated with advertising for and training new staff, as well as lost productivity as they gain experience in their new positions:

> Workers are six times more likely to stay in their jobs when they believe their company acts with integrity, according to Walker Information, a research company that measures employee satisfaction and loyalty at the workplace. But when workers mistrust their bosses' decisions and feel ashamed of their firm's behavior, four out of five workers feel trapped at work and say they are likely to leave their jobs soon.[77]

• Increased employee safety leads to reduced amounts of lost time and productivity due to injuries. Intel's approach to this issue makes both moral and business sense:

> At Intel (No. 3), based in Santa Clara, Calif., good citizenship . . . includes careful attention to employee safety—so much that CEO Craig Barrett insists he be sent an e-mail report within 24 hours any time one of his firm's 80,000 employees loses a single day of work to injury. . . . In 2000, Intel's worldwide injury rate was just .27 injuries per 100 employees, compared to an industry average of 6.7.[78]

• An effective employee share-ownership scheme ensures that the workers', managers', and owners' interests are more closely aligned and that employees will feel more committed to generating positive outcomes for the company as a whole. In spite of the criticism leveled at stock options—and their debatable impact on performance for top management—companies that distribute ownership of the company throughout the organization do see notable improvements in job motivation and satisfaction:

> Evidence suggests that smart use of options and other compensation do boost performance. Companies that spread ownership throughout a large portion of their workforce, through any form—options, Employee Stock Ownership Plans, or other means—deliver total shareholder returns that are two percentage points higher than at similar companies. . . . Better stock performance isn't the only benefit. Companies with significant employee ownership do better on a wide range of performance metrics, including productivity, profit margins, and return on equity, according to the studies.[79]

William Greider argues in his book, *The Soul of Capitalism,* that employee ownership is central to the goal of altering "the basic operating values of American capitalism so that the priorities of society [over the narrow financial priorities of stockholders] become dominant":

Most Americans, in current life, go to work daily and submit to what is essentially a master-servant relationship inherited from feudalism. . . . The solution is for workers to own their work. The forms for doing so—employee-owned firms, partnerships, cooperatives and other hybrids—are alive and growing. To be effective, they must incorporate not only employee ownership but collaborative decision making as well.[80]

## Case Study: Ohio Employee Ownership Center

One further illustration of a company's commitment to a transparent and honest relationship with its workforce is exemplified by the presence of employee-worker directors on company boards. The possibility of this position developing in the United States has been complicated by the Sarbanes-Oxley Act, 2002, which requires independent board members (i.e., nonemployees) for public companies. The principle, however, is one that has not figured significantly in ownership debates in the United States and should be part of the discussion:

> The U.S. needs what practically all our European counterparts have long had: a "loyal opposition" of non-managerial employee representatives on company boards . . . [to provide] a counterweight to the failure of conventional corporate boards to protect stakeholder—or even shareholder—interests.[81]

Employee board representatives are commonly found within German corporations, a feature of corporate governance in Europe that was initiated in the rapid economic expansion of Germany following the Second World War:

> The law [in Germany], commonly known as Mitbestimmung, or co-determination, entitles workers and union representatives to half the seats on supervisory boards of big corporations; the remainder are held by shareholder representatives. That gives workers a powerful voice in their company's decision making: Under Germany's two-tier board structure, the supervisory board has ultimate authority over all major management decisions. . . . Shareholders still have an edge, because most decisions require a simple majority and the board chairman has a second vote in case of a tie. But major moves, such as mergers or appointment of a chief executive, require a two-thirds majority.[82]

Although such a board structure also can lead to obstruction of progress and inefficiencies with employee representatives not wanting to do anything that would endanger jobs, there is much to be said for managers having employee buy-in to any major policy decision adopted by the firm. Could a system that has been successful in Europe for decades in terms of reducing workplace tension work in the United States? A study, titled The Real World of Employee Ownership,[83] indicates that, in Ohio at least, worker representation can be effective:

> Among Ohio employee-owned companies, about one out of six have worker directors on their boards. . . . [The study] shows that employee-owned companies with worker directors tend to outperform those without.[84]

The existence of employee representatives as members of audit committees of many European and Asian companies is now causing difficulties for those companies that want to list on the New York Stock Exchange because of the new requirements contained within the Sarbanes-Oxley Act, signed into law by President George Bush on July 30, 2002.

Sarbanes-Oxley requires audit committee members to be drawn from independent directors; however, in Germany "supervisory board audit committees must include employee representatives; by definition, they aren't independent. . . . Independent audit committees are almost unheard of at many European and Asian companies."[85]

There is some doubt as to whether independence in itself will guarantee the kind of objective oversight that is sought:

> The nostrum widely recommended today is more "independent directors"—yet firms like Enron and WorldCom had many prominent outside directors, and still routinely rubber-stamped management schemes that impoverished employees, communities and shareholders alike.[86]

There are also more general fears expressed regarding the claustrophobic nature of Sarbanes-Oxley and the hasty, knee-jerk manner in which it was passed into law:

> This law requires audit committees to be entirely composed of outside directors and chief executives to certify personally that a company's financial reports accurately reflect its financial condition. It also establishes a Public Oversight Accounting board with vast but vague powers. Since Enron satisfied many of the requirements of this law, Sarbanes-Oxley probably would not have prevented the debacle at the company. Moreover, an overly aggressive oversight board and the threat of criminal prosecution to CEOs are likely to make U.S. business leaders less flexible and more cautious.[87]

Will the crisis in corporate credibility end in 2003? Only 26% of investors surveyed by the Securities Industry Association believe that the Sarbanes-Oxley corporate reform act of 2002 will reduce fraud.[88]

## Web-Based Examples and Resources

Fair Labor Association, http://www.fairlabor.org/

> The Fair Labor Association (FLA) is a nonprofit organization combining the efforts of industry, non-governmental organizations (NGOs), colleges and universities to promote adherence to international labor standards and improve working conditions worldwide.

Investors in People (UK), http://www.investorsinpeople.co.uk/

> Investors in People is the national Standard which sets a level of good practice for training and development of people to achieve business goals.

National Center for Employee Ownership, http://www.nceo.org/

> The National Center for Employee Ownership (NCEO) is a private, nonprofit membership and research organization that serves as the leading source of accurate, unbiased information on employee stock ownership plans (ESOPs), broadly granted employee stock options and related programs, and ownership culture.

Ohio Employee Ownership Center, http://dept.kent.edu/oeoc/

> The Ohio Employee Ownership Center (OEOC) is a nonprofit, university-based program established in 1987 to provide outreach, information, and preliminary technical assistance to Ohio employees and business owners interested in exploring employee ownership.

Work Foundation, http://www.theworkfoundation.com/

The Work Foundation, a not-for-dividend public interest company, exists to inspire and deliver improvements to performance through improving the quality of working life. It believes that productive, high performance organisations are those committed to making work more fulfilling, fun, inspirational and effective, and through engaging their work-forces succeed in integrating the many aims crucial to organisational success.

## Questions for Discussion and Review

1. What are the benefits of employee loyalty and retention?

2. Do you think it is important to have employees involved with the management and oversight of a company? What are the potential benefits? Drawbacks?

3. Which do you think is the more important principle—independent board members or board members with a direct interest in the company?

# HYPOCRISY

☑ *CSR Connection:* This issue highlights the difficulties that can arise for firms that establish themselves as being guided by motives other than profits.

## Issue

To what extent can companies that claim to be ethically conscious and socially responsible live up to the high standards they claim or hold to others?

## Case Study: The Body Shop

The Body Shop has made a name for itself as a progressive, conscience-driven, campaigning corporation. Many of its consumers are drawn to the company because of its activism as much as the quality and range of its products:

A growing number of companies such as the Body Shop, a global skin- and hair-care retailer, make corporate virtue part of their value proposition: Buy one of our products, the Body Shop tells its customers, and you improve the lives of women in developing countries, promote animal rights, protect the environment, and otherwise increase the supply of social responsibility.[89]

One of the first issues the company focused on, and became famous for campaigning against, was the issue of using animals for the testing of human cosmetic products:

The use of animals to test cosmetics and toiletries products and ingredients continues around the world today. It is estimated that over 35,000 animals are used in cosmetics tests every year throughout the European Union alone.

In some cases the tests can cause suffering and even death.

The Body Shop believes cosmetics testing on animals is unethical, unnecessary and should be banned.[90]

A significant section of its customers are loyal to the organization because of the ethical stand it adopts:

In 1999 The Body Shop brand was voted the second most trusted brand in the UK by the Consumers Association. According to the 1997 Interbrand survey criteria, the company was named 28th top brand in the world, second in the retail sector. In a 1998 report, a survey of international chief executives in *The Financial Times* ranked The Body Shop the 27th most respected company in the world.[91]

There is evidence, however, to suggest that there may be a degree of public relations gloss covering much of the company's ethical position in its history and perhaps not quite as much substance as many customers believe. Animal testing is only one of several issues that have been raised by various campaigning and interested parties:

Beyond balance-sheet woes, the company that likes to insist it puts principles before profits has been buffeted for two years by allegations, which Roddick angrily denies, that it has misled the public about everything from its stand against animal testing to the ingredients of elderflower eye gel.

All the bad news has tarnished the Body Shop's image as one of Britain's most glamorous growth stocks. Its share price has dropped 65%, from a high of $6.55 in 1992 to around $2.29 today.[92]

Although the Body Shop may not itself test on animals, it is benefiting from the knowledge gained by others who have previously tested on animals:

During 1989, The Body Shop switched from "not tested on animals" to "against animal testing" labeling after a lawsuit by the German government. The lawsuit claimed that Body Shop labeling was misleading, since their products' ingredients may have been tested on animals.[93]

The company's claims of innocence in this regard are disingenuous at a minimum and probably misleading to a significant percentage of its customers:

Helping animals?—Although the Body Shop maintains that they are against animal testing, they do not always make clear that many of the ingredients in their products have been tested on animals by other companies, causing much pain and suffering to those animals. They accept ingredients tested on animals before 1991, or those tested since then (if they were animal-tested for some purpose other than for cosmetics). There continue to be concerns about the enforcement of their policy. Also, some Body Shop items contain animal products such as gelatine (crushed bone).[94]

## Web-Based Examples and Resources

*Animal People*: "Body Shop Animal Testing Policy Alleged 'a Sham,'" http://www.animal peoplenews.org/94/8/body_shop.html

*Animal People* is the leading independent newspaper providing original investigative coverage of animal protection worldwide. Founded in 1992, *Animal People* has no alignment or affiliation with any other entity.

Beyond McDonald's, http://www.mcspotlight.org/beyond/index.html

The Beyond McDonald's pages provide information about the unethical practices of many other companies and industries.

PETA—People for the Ethical Treatment of Animals, http://www.peta.org/

> People for the Ethical Treatment of Animals (PETA), with more than 800,000 members, is the largest animal rights organization in the world. Founded in 1980, PETA is dedicated to establishing and protecting the rights of all animals. PETA operates under the simple principle that animals are not ours to eat, wear, experiment on, or use for entertainment.

The Body Shop, http://www.thebodyshop.com/

> The Body Shop has always believed that business is primarily about human relationships. We believe that the more we listen to our stakeholders and involve them in decision making, the better our business will run.

The Humane Society of the United States, http://www.hsus.org/

> The Humane Society of the United States makes a difference in the lives of animals here at home and worldwide. The HSUS is dedicated to creating a world where our relationship with animals is guided by compassion. We seek a truly humane society in which animals are respected for their intrinsic value, and where the human-animal bond is strong.

## Questions for Discussion and Review

1. In your own experience, think of an example of a corporation that you felt has been hypocritical in terms of its ethical or CSR stance. What is your reaction to the company's actions?

2. Read the essay titled, "Body Shop Animal Testing Policy Alleged 'a Sham'" (http://www.animalpeoplenews.org/94/8/body_shop.html). Then compare it with the Body Shop's Web site dealing with the same issue (http://www.uk.thebodyshop.com/web/tbsuk/values_aat.jsp). Which of the two accounts do you believe? Does The Body Shop's stance on this issue matter?

3. Would you consider boycotting the products of a company that you felt had acted in a socially irresponsible way? How about one you felt had acted in a hypocritical way?

## PRINCIPAL-AGENT CONFLICT

☑ *CSR Connection:* This issue reflects the central role of the conflict between a company's *principals* (shareholders) and *agents* (managers) in understanding the stakeholder approach to CSR.

## Issue

Principal-agent theory describes the inherent tension that exists between the owners of an organization (collectively, the principals, which include the shareholders and their representatives, the board of directors) and the managers (the agents), whom the owners appoint to operate the business and protect their investment.

The conflict of interest that arises between these two groups is a problem that has plagued limited liability joint stock companies ever since they were established in the Companies Act of 1862.[95] In its modern reincarnation, this conflict eventually resulted in the corporate scandals that peppered the business world around the turn of this century:

> The Enron scandal—and those at WorldCom, Tyco, Adelphia and others—exposed a glaring flaw in the oversight of America's top executives. . . . In the textbooks, capitalism works because corporate managers are kept in check by shareholders, who operate through directors they elect. The truth, however, is that many American directors are handpicked and handsomely compensated by the very executives they oversee.[96]

What is the best way to align the interests of the owners of the organization with those of the agents entrusted to operate the organization on the owners' behalf? In the 1990s, stock options rose as the new Holy Grail: By awarding executives options, the theory held that they would have a direct interest in the performance of the company. If the company performed well, stock prices would rise and the executives would benefit personally; however, this theory was quickly shown to be flawed, as some executives saw the short-term stock price as their most important focus (maximizing personal benefit) rather than the long-term health of the organization.

---

## Case Study: Expensing Stock Options

One of the reasons why stock options, which grant employees the right to purchase company stock at a fixed price at a future point in time, were adopted so enthusiastically by companies during the 1990s is that they were viewed as having minimal impact on a firm's accounts:

> In recent years, especially during the halcyon days of the technology boom, stock options were handed out liberally with no direct impact on companies' bottom lines, because most of these options, which critics contend impose a real economic cost on companies, weren't booked as expenses. They simply were referenced in footnotes in annual reports.[97]

Requiring the expensing of stock options would force companies to attribute a value to the options and treat that value as an expense, which would count against earnings. The move is being fought by some corporate interests, such as technology firms, which are generally younger organizations and which might not have the established cash flows necessary to pay higher salaries or other traditional forms of compensation.

How a company approaches the issue of expensing stock options is an important indicator of that company's approach to transparency, corporate governance, and reporting financial statements and company information that are as accurate as possible. Many of the scandals that have plagued corporate America resulted from a lack of these three characteristics. Many of the problems revolved around violating the spirit, if not the letter, of the law and deceiving investors for personal, self-motivated corporate gain.

There are many technical difficulties with expensing stock options, principally involving what value to assign to them, as it is unknown when and at what price they will be vested. There are many ways to assign such a value and until the Financial Accounting Standards Board (FASB) chooses a standard, different companies have begun using different formats.[98] The accounting industry, however, has found ways around other similarly difficult issues (e.g., amortization, depreciation, as well as valuing intangibles, such as goodwill) and companies are beginning to see the benefit in being perceived as proactive on this issue. The wider goal should be to promote to companies the value of presenting financial reports that are as accurate as possible:

> You might think that investors would punish companies that have decided to expense stock options. . . . And yet, as a small but growing band of big-name companies makes the switch, investors have for the most part showered them with love. With a few exceptions, the stock prices of the expensers . . . have outpaced the market since they announced the change. What's going on? One possibility is that investors are rewarding companies for something that is sorely missing these days: honesty.[99]

The calls for companies to expense stock options reflect a growing public sentiment in support of greater transparency in corporate management. In April 2003, Apple computer's shareholders voted to enforce such a move at the company, "rejecting the company's wishes to keep the costs off the books." Although nonbinding, the majority vote was a rare example of shareholders being able to gather together enough support to carry a motion against management's wishes:

> The outcome marks the first time a Silicon Valley company has been told to include stock option expenses on its income statement. Similar shareholder proposals recently failed by narrow margins at Knight Ridder . . . and Palo Alto computer giant Hewlett-Packard.[100]

Initially, the idea behind options-based compensation was that by aligning CEO and top management interest more closely with that of the

shareholders (e.g., via the company's share price), management would have an incentive to maximize company performance. This, in turn, would lead to maximum sustainable growth for the company and share price over time. In practice, however, many CEOs did whatever they could to raise the company's share price in the short term, sometimes irrespective of the legality or honesty of their actions or the long-term impact on the interests of the company.

> These huge [compensation packages] bolster a system in which executives have incentives to manage the numbers for short-term gain and personal payout, and not manage their businesses for long-term growth and shareholder value. Exorbitant compensation feeds the worst instincts and egos of powerful CEOs, fueled by their desire to win at all costs and resulting, too often, in the cutting of ethical corners.[101]

Consequently, the value of stock options essentially fell out of correlation with company performance:

> Compensation researcher Equilar studied 450 companies in the Standard & Poor's 500 and found something curious: The worst-performing companies in 2002 were those that gave their chief executives the biggest option grants in 2001. The median grant for those CEOs was $9.4 million. Median shareholder return the next year: -50%. CEOs with the best performances received much smaller grants—the median size was $3.7 million—and delivered returns of 17%.[102]

In the past decade, companies that granted 90% of all options to CEOs and a few top managers performed worse than those that distributed options more evenly and fairly among employees. There is no justification for increasing the compensation of CEOs from 40 times that of the average employee in the 1960s to nearly 600 times today.[103]

Consider: If you had invested $10,000 in the stock market (as represented by the Standard & Poor's average of 500 stocks), you would have more than doubled your money over 10 years, accumulating $22,170 by the end of 2002, despite the bear market. . . . But if you were investing in the companies with the highest-paid executives over the same period of time, the value of your investment would have fallen 71 percent to $2,899.[104]

The goal should be to refocus compensation incentives on the long-term health of the company and find ways to best encourage workers throughout the organization to work toward that goal. Some companies have stopped giving out earnings estimates to investors as one way of reducing pressure on the short-term share price:

Critics worry that a lack of guidance could lead to more earnings surprises, greater stock volatility, or even less vigorous oversight of management. In fact, it's a great leap forward. Successful strategies are not executed in three-month time slots. By refusing to play the quarterly guessing game, companies reduce the focus on short-term performance. That lessens incentives for accounting shenanigans aimed only at juicing the numbers.[105]

The drive to expense stock options was first tried as early as 1993. Then, however, the FASB faced so much lobbying pressure from companies and political pressure from Congress that it was forced to back down. Companies at the time (as they still do today) feared the effect expensing would have on profits and, therefore, income statements. The lobbying movement is lining up for the second time round:

Already, 40 lawmakers, led by California Representatives David Dreier (R) and Anna Eshoo (D), warned FASB in a Jan. 30 letter that treating options as an expense "results in the disclosure of inaccurate corporate financial information and a flawed picture of company performance."[106]

This time, however, the political and corporate environment has shifted, and many politicians are advocating change in support of the FASB, while some of the largest corporations are setting an example:

Coca-Cola's decision [in July 2002] to treat options as an expense set off a stampede that has resulted in more than 170 companies [updated to 270 companies[107]] pledging to adopt expensing voluntarily. . . . And unlike a decade ago . . . Senators Carl Levin (D—Mich.) and John McCain (R—Ariz.), longtime advocates of expensing, on Feb. 3 sent a letter signed by 28 other lawmakers, urging FASB to follow through on its quest.[108]

The FASB proposed a rule change in March 2004 that would have required

publicly traded companies to record as an expense all forms of share-based payments to employees, including stock options.[109]

The impact of the move would have been to affect significantly the annual earnings of large companies, particularly in those sectors (notably the high-tech industry) in which stock options continue to be widely used as employee incentives. The FASB's opponents won again, however, and the proposal was defeated in a 312–111 vote on July 20, 2004. Instead a measure was passed that would

limit required expensing of options to those owned by a corporation's top five executives. It would also allow newly public companies to delay expensing for top executives in the first three years.[110]

Never mind that this [bill] has no basis in accounting theory. . . . Members of the House know a lucrative compromise—Read: humungous Silicon Valley campaign contributions—when they see it. They passed the bill overwhelmingly. . . . During 2002's summer of fraud, politicians passed lots of reforms. Now that they think investors have shaken off losses, many politicians are doing what their big tech donors want instead. . . . Another wink here, another nod there, and soon the book-cookers may figure that once again they are officially condoned.[111]

This conflict between Congress and the FASB is the focus of the debate. Many expect the FASB to carry the argument eventually, as the momentum throughout the developed economies is toward expensing options. Another important factor is that the intransigence in the House of Representatives seems not to be shared by the Senate:

> The rules are likely to change, perhaps as early as [2005]. . . . The FASB said it planned to impose the rule, and while a bill to block it had passed the House of Representatives, it appeared unlikely to be approved by the Senate. A similar rule is scheduled to go into effect next year in countries that follow rules laid down by the International Accounting Standards Board, including those in the European Union.[112]

Why is the opposition so set against expensing stock options?

> It costs companies. . . . For example, a Credit Suisse First Boston report issued in June [2004] estimates that at Yahoo, options eat up 27 cents a share, 62 percent of the 44 cents a share that the company is expected to earn in 2005. . . . One estimate from Bear Stearns figures the earnings of companies in the NAS-DAQ 100 would have fallen 44 percent [in 2003] if options had been expensed. For the S&P 500, Credit Suisse put the cost of options at $35 billion [in 2005].[113]

In December 2004, the FASB announced it would proceed with the introduction of its plan to require companies to expense stock options, starting in 2005. Following a 6-month delay, the proposal was due to take effect with third-quarter financial statements beginning after June 15 for all large U.S. publicly traded companies.[114] Then in April 2005,

> The SEC's staff recommended that SEC commissioners vote to change the deadline, so that the rules instead would take effect for fiscal years starting after June 15 [Essentially a further six month extension for companies whose fiscal years end in December].[115]

Ironically, given the long period of notice and public debate concerning this rule change, companies have had plenty of time to limit the possible impact. Due to improved corporate earnings, significantly reduced options grants, and accelerated options vesting, companies seem well placed to weather the storm:

> Even some of the biggest opponents of stock-option expensing are seeing much lower expected cost: Options expensing would have dented Intel's earnings [in 2004] by 16%, down from 37% in 2002, its filings show.[116]

## Web-Based Examples and Resources

Cato Institute, http://www.cato.org/

> The Cato Institute was founded in 1977 by Edward H. Crane. It is a nonprofit public policy research foundation headquartered in Washington, D.C.

Reynolds, Alan, "Expensing Stock Options is a Faddish Fraud," July 18, 2002, http://www.cato.org/research/articles/reynolds-020718.html

Citizen Works—Expense Stock Options, http://www.citizenworks.org/corp/options/options-main.php

> CEO greed and stock options. Stop the stock options con game.

Employment Policy Foundation, http://www.epf.org/

The Employment Policy Foundation (EPF) is a nonprofit, nonpartisan public policy research and educational foundation based in Washington, D.C. that focuses on workplace trends and policies.

"The Economic Impact of Expensing Stock Options," September 17, 2002, http://www.save stockoptions.org/pdf/studies_03.pdf

Financial Accounting Standards Board, http://www.fasb.org/

The mission of the Financial Accounting Standards Board is to establish and improve standards of financial accounting and reporting for the guidance and education of the public, including issuers, auditors, and users of financial information.

International Accounting Standards Board, http://www.iasb.org/

The International Accounting Standards Board is an independent, privately-funded accounting standard-setter based in London, UK. . . . The IASB is committed to developing, in the public interest, a single set of high quality, understandable and enforceable global accounting standards that require transparent and comparable information in general purpose financial statements.

myStockOptions.com, http://www.mystockoptions.com/

The goal of myStockOptions.com is to help you profit from employee stock options, stock purchase plans, and restricted stock. Our calculators, content, and community will make you smarter about the financial planning, tax, and legal issues that surround equity compensation.

SaveStockOptions.org, http://www.savestockoptions.org/

SaveStockOptions.org provides a wealth of accurate and up-to-date information about the debate over expensing employee stock options and the negative effects that mandatory expensing will have on employees, investors, businesses, the economy and the future of broad-based employee stock option plans.

## Questions for Discussion and Review

1. Are stock options a good form of employee or manager compensation? Do they begin to heal the inherent conflict that exists between principals and agents?

2. Look at some of the Web sites listed in the subsection, *Web-Based Examples and Resources*. Is expensing stock options a good idea?

3. Some companies award stock options to all employees. Starbucks is a good example of the loyal employees and good press coverage such a policy can generate. Have a look at some information about the company's Bean Stock program written in a case study at http://www.mhhe.com/business/management/thompson/11e/case/starbucks-1.html (under the heading "Schultz's Strategy to Make Starbucks a Great Place to Work").

Would such a policy encourage you to join one company over another, or is salary level still the most important determining factor in deciding between compensation packages?

# RESEARCH AND DEVELOPMENT

☑ **CSR Connection:** This issue looks at the balance between adequate research into the safety aspects of a product and the pressure to minimize development costs and bring the product to market as soon as possible.

## Issue

Some companies today are accused of rushing products to market before they have been adequately tested or enough is known about the products' uses and any side effects that may result from their use. Consumer activists argue that a company should bear the burden of proving that a product is safe before releasing it rather than assume it is safe as long as there is no evidence that it is not.

---

**Figure 5.1**   "The Price of Safety"[117]

Safety, like CSR, often comes at a price. Whether the price is worth paying—whether it provides a sufficient return on investment—is crucial to the argument for or against:

How efficient are safety regulations? To decide, economists estimate how many lives a regulation saves, then compare that with the cost of implementing the rule. By this measure, the labeling of trans-fat content in foods is a clear winner.[118]

The AEI-Brookings Joint Center for Regulatory Studies reports that the cost of including the trans fat content on food labels is only $3,000 for each life this action saves. This can be compared with the cost of $300,000 for each life saved by insulating airplane cabins to protect against fire.

Automobile safety regulations tend to be more expensive: It is estimated that state seat belt laws cost $500,000 for each life saved, whereas one life is saved for every $1.1 million spent on reinforcing car side doors.

The most expensive regulation highlighted, however, was reducing the exposure of factory workers to asbestos. This move was estimated to cost $5.5 million for each life the regulation saves.

---

This reasoning gave rise to the Food and Drug Administration (FDA), which came into existence in 1906. The agency evolved slowly as ideological opposition to the idea of government regulation faded in the wake of several deaths and other disasters caused by products that had not been adequately tested. It was not until 1938, however, that substantial progress was enacted:

> It took 107 deaths from a liquid antibiotic preparation using highly toxic diethylene gly-
> col (a common ingredient in today's antifreeze) to get Congress to pass a landmark 1938
> law. At last, before a product could be sold, a company would have to submit data proving
> that it was safe. Similarly, the thalidomide tragedy of the early 1960s . . . [allowed the
> Kennedy Administration] to push through the then startling idea—bitterly opposed by the
> American Medical Association as well as conservatives—that drugs should be tested to see
> if they actually work before they can be sold.[119]

Nevertheless, in spite of the best initial intentions of the FDA, many products (non–food and drugs) still reach market today without passing through any significant testing proce-dures. Currently, the product must be proven unsafe before it is banned rather than the com-pany having to prove the product is safe before it is released:

> Existing laws [in the EU] allow most chemical-based products to be introduced without
> prior assurances by the company of their safety. The result is that 99% of the total chemi-
> cals sold in Europe have not passed through any environmental and health testing process.[120]

In an attempt to alter this balance, the EU Commission has proposed regulation that is built around the concept of "the precautionary principle":

> [The proposed directive] would force companies to prove chemical products introduced
> into the marketplace are safe before being granted permission to market them . . . [and rep-
> resents] a radical new approach to science and technology based on the principle of sus-
> tainable development and global stewardship of the Earth's environment.[121]

The proposal is termed the REACH directive, which stands for the *R*egistration, *E*valuation, *A*uthorization, and restriction of *CH*emicals.[122] It has angered the U.S. chemical industry, which sees the move as a threat to the more than $20 billion of chemicals it sells in Europe every year. Companies would be required to register and test the safety of up to 30,000 chemicals at an estimated cost of approximately €6 billion.[123]

In spite of the EU amending the proposed regulation in the face of strong lobbying from U.S. firms backed by Washington,

> still, the U.S. government fears $150 billion of its exports could be affected, and the
> American Chemistry Council estimates the proposal could cost U.S. companies $8 billion
> during the next decade.[124]

This move within the EU marks a shift in the modern-day regulation of product safety. Placing a higher priority on risk prevention than risk taking is gaining support, at least in Europe, especially as the penalties for mistakes seem to become higher by the day.

## Case Study: Asbestos

Companies that launch a product just because there is no reason not to do so see only their good intentions and the product's benefits, not the position of the consumers they are attempting to service. Consumer fear—often expressed through product boycotts or large-scale protests but more commonly expressed through a refusal to purchase the product—can be the result. Today a good example of this concern is genetically modified (GM) foods, particularly in Europe:

> Worried about falling behind its global competition, much of Asia is rushing forward with the development and cultivation of genetically modified crops. . . . Critics of genetically modified crops say these moves in Asia could leave consumers around the world with little choice but to accept them. . . . But in the absence of any solid evidence that genetically modified crops are harmful to humans, scientists in Asia are experimenting on everything from genetically modified corn, potatoes and papaya to biotech mustard and chili peppers.[125]

A past example of the potentially massive penalties for getting this wrong can be seen in the problems surrounding asbestos. Asbestos litigation in the United States has involved

> some 600,000 plaintiffs, more than 6,000 defendants, 61 companies in bankruptcy, and up to $275 billion in liability costs.[126]

The Rand Institute for Civil Justice, a Santa Monica, Calif., research organization, estimates there are now more than 600,000 asbestos claimants and 8,400 defendants. Litigation has cost more than $54 billion to date and eventually could total over $200 billion, says the institute. The financial pressure has pushed nearly 70 companies to seek bankruptcy protection, including several contractors and material suppliers.[127]

With 100,000 new claims filed [in 2003] and 70 companies already pushed into bankruptcy . . . the latest asbestos scandal is threatening the integrity of the judicial system itself.[128]

Both sides of the debate, however, disagree on actual numbers, and the process of assisting those who have become sick from exposure to asbestos has been complicated by the large number of claims filed by those who are yet to show any symptoms from their work with the material:

> More than 100,000 American workers (300,000, say trial lawyers) have died after being exposed to [asbestos]. . . . [The President has been advised that] "out of approximately 850,000 claimants since asbestos litigation began, perhaps 600,000 of these are largely baseless claims." Worse, more than half of the cost of litigation is paid to lawyers or spent on administration.[129]

Halliburton is the headline company whose name became synonymous with the controversy surrounding asbestos:

> Halliburton became exposed to a mountain of asbestos claims through its acquisition of Dresser Industries Inc. in 1998. . . . The claims, totaling more than 400,000 due to asbestos and silica, were filed against former Dresser subsidiary Harbison-Walker Refractories.[130]

In spite of individual companies having already announced settlements addressing claims made against them (e.g., Halliburton, in December 2002, agreed to pay $4 billion in cash to settle all current and future claims against the company,[131] a trust fund that eventually ballooned into a $5.1 billion settlement),[132] the prospect of a broad legislative solution carried political support. In early July 2003, the Senate Judiciary Committee approved legislation to be considered by the Senate. The legislation creates a general trust fund, backed by the companies concerned, which would end all asbestos claims. The fund greatly reduces the amount of money each company was potentially going to have to pay:

> Over its 27-year life, the fund is supposed to have $108 billion to pay people who develop cancer or other health impairments from their

exposure to asbestos in the workplace. The money in the trust fund would come from about 8,500 companies that made or sold asbestos products either directly or through their subsidiaries, as well as the companies' insurers. But most of the firms would pay no more than $25 million per year.[133]

It has been estimated, for example, that "Halliburton would pay about $675 million under the proposed legislation,"[134] compared with the $4 billion it had agreed to before the prospect of legislation appeared. The chance of the legislation passing both houses, however, is still unclear. There is no general consensus and companies may be forced to settle the claims against them separately:

In September [2004], Senate leaders Bill Frist and Tom Daschle agreed to $140 billion for the proposed fund to be paid by defendant companies and insurers. But they failed to reach agreement on whether pending asbestos claims would remain in the courts or shift to the fund.[135]

With the amount in the proposed trust fund getting ever larger, the prospects of legislation proceeding were thrown even further into doubt when more than a dozen insurance companies retracted their support in April 2005:

This makes it less likely that Congress will approve legislation on the subject [in 2005], leaving hundreds of U.S. companies unsure how much money they owe in asbestos claims. . . . The insurers joined conservative Republicans and a growing number of corporations that believe the trust fund would be too large and wouldn't adequately limit their liability.[136]

Halliburton's woes in relation to asbestos continue in the meantime. In June 2004, the company was forced to record another one-time charge of $615 million, or $1.40 a share, to bolster the agreement it had made in 2002.[137] The asbestos saga has significantly affected the organization:

The asbestos lawsuits have taken a huge financial toll on Houston-based Halliburton, resulting in more than $3 billion in charges since 2002. . . . Halliburton created a $5.1 billion trust fund to pay current and future asbestos liabilities from a combination of 59.5 million company shares and $2.8 billion in cash.[138]

## Web-Based Examples and Resources

Asbestos Alliance, http://www.asbestossolution.org/

The Asbestos Alliance is a nonprofit organization comprised of asbestos defendant companies, trade associations, insurers and others seeking congressional legislation to solve America's asbestos litigation crisis.

Association for Science in the Public Interest, http://www.public-science.org/

The Association for Science in the Public Interest (ASIPI) is a professional society dedicated to fostering the participation of scientists in public processes, the conduct of community research and the promotion of scientific work that supports the public good.

Food and Drug Administration, http://www.fda.gov/

The FDA is responsible for protecting the public health by assuring the safety, efficacy, and security of human and veterinary drugs, biological products, medical devices, our nation's food supply, cosmetics, and products that emit radiation. The FDA is also responsible for advancing the public health by helping to speed innovations that make medicines and foods more effective, safer, and more affordable; and helping the public get the accurate, science-based information they need to use medicines and foods to improve their health.

Halliburton, http://www.halliburton.com/

Details of the agreement made by Halliburton can be found on the company's Web site: http://www.halliburton.com/ir/agreesum.jsp

Also posted are other company statements related to the asbestos issue: http://www.halliburton.com/ir/asbestos_primer.jsp

Monsanto, http://www.monsanto.com/

A pledge outlining Monsanto's approach to its business can be found on the company's Web site: http://www.monsanto.com/monsanto/layout/our_pledge/default.asp

## Questions for Discussion and Review

1. Do you support the motives behind the EU's "precautionary principle"?

2. Halliburton's liability in relation to asbestos claims was assumed when it acquired the company Dresser Industries in 1998. Do you think this absolves Halliburton (because the initial offenses were not committed by them), or do you think a CSR perspective obligates them as the parent company? What is the government's role or responsibility?

3. Based on your general knowledge of the company and what you see in the news, what is your impression of Halliburton? The company receives much negative publicity. What do you think is the cause of this? Is it simply the nature of the businesses in which it is involved, or do you think it indicates a lack of CSR within the organization?

# SHAREHOLDER ACTIVISM

☑ *CSR Connection:* This issue reflects the significant rise in shareholder activism in recent years. As this trend continues, companies will face increasing pressures to respond to the concerns of these vital stakeholders.

## Issue

To what extent do demands for greater management transparency and honest information, both from large institutional investors and individual shareholders, lead to more accurate evaluations of corporate performance and investment opportunities?

In the 2003 proxy season,

1,040 shareholder resolutions were filed, up 20 percent from [2002], according to the Investor Responsibility Research Center.[139]

# Case Study: GlaxoSmithKline

The surge in shareholder activism found a focal point in the UK in May 2003 when almost 51% of GlaxoSmithKline (GSK) shareholders (a total that rises to 61% if abstentions are included[140]) voted against the company's *Remuneration Report* in a direct rebuke to the leadership of CEO Jean-Pierre Garnier. The report, which included the CEO's remuneration package and an estimated £22–23 million (approximately US$40 million) compensation clause for the CEO if the company is taken over, caused widespread anger in its excess at a time when GSK's share price had been falling. The rebellion was widely reported in the UK press as "historic," and a sign that greater shareholder involvement in corporate annual general meetings (AGMs) was here to stay.

Although more dramatic than most, the GSK shareholder rebellion is only part of a growing trend:

Reuters, Barclays, Hilton, Amvescap Reckitt Benckiser and Granada are just a few of the companies to have endured significant votes against approval of remuneration policies at their annual general meetings.[141]

Michael Eisner, CEO of Disney, saw 43% of shareholders support a vote of no confidence in his leadership at the company's AGM in March 2004:

Eisner isn't the only king whose subjects want him deposed. His 43% no-confidence vote was the highest in recent memory, but according to an analysis by Institutional Shareholder Services, six other companies have seen between 28% and 42% of shares voted against a sitting CEO in the past year: Starwood Hotels & Resorts (42%); Boise Cascade (38%); Ryder System (37%); CSX (32%); Wisconsin Energy (29%); and Delphi (29%).[142]

The rapid rise in the number of shareholder resolutions being filed is one of the strongest indicators of this trend. Early on in the 2003 season, the increase was already apparent:

The annual meeting season is about to start, and already the number of shareholder resolutions dealing with corporate governance, such as executive pay and board elections, has reached a record 680, up from 529 for all of last year, according to the Investor Responsibility Research Center's survey of about 2,000 companies.[143]

Some 265 shareholder resolutions to limit executive pay have been submitted so far [in 2005]. [In 2004], 182 actually came to a vote, up from 163 in 2003 and 25 in 2002, according to the Investor Responsibility Research Center in Washington.[144]

What the *Financial Times* refers to as

the trend towards investor activism amid a crisis of confidence in corporate America . . . investors are no longer content merely to make money, but want to ensure they are doing so responsibly.[145]

To indicate how big and unusual a rejection the shareholder majority vote at GSK's AGM was, the SEC stipulates a threshold of only 3% of shareholder votes for a proposition to be deemed to have sufficient shareholder support for it to be resubmitted for a vote the following year.[146] This is due to the disproportionate weight of individual shareholder votes:

Institutional investors hold more than 50% of all listed corporate stock in the United States (about 60% in the largest 1,000 corporations). The largest 25 pension funds accounted for 42% of the foreign equity held by all U.S. investors.[147]

Institutional votes make up the vast majority of votes (and therefore influence) at AGMs, and these investors have traditionally tended to vote with the company's management; however, this is changing as individual shareholders become increasingly strident in expressing their opposition to the excesses in corporate management that appeared early this century. In response to the shareholder rebellion at GSK, the board eventually fired two nonexecutive members, both of whom were on the Remuneration Committee (one of whom was the chair) that had produced the CEO's unpopular pay package. They also agreed to withdraw the *Remuneration Report* and instigate a full review of remuneration across the company. As a result, at the company's 2004 AGM,

82 percent of shareholders voted in favor of a revised pay package for GlaxoSmithKline's chief executive, Jean-Pierre Garnier. . . . [The Association of British Insurers] said "Dialogue with shareholders really helps. GSK was prepared to listen and the result, though not perfect, is a vast improvement."[148]

Alternative shareholder resolutions that seek directly to counter board recommendations, as well as votes of 20% and up in support of those resolutions, are becoming increasingly common. As pressure increases on institutional investors to ensure corporate governance reflects general shareholder and public values, the number of votes approaching and exceeding the 50% barrier looks set to increase. One example of shareholder pressure resulting in policy change: In July 2003, Dell Computer launched a recycling campaign ("Asset Recovery" program) to help customers dispose of their computers. Correct dismantling ensures the toxic chemicals they contain do not end up in landfill waste sites. Dell will charge customers $49 per computer for this service. The company was pressured into this move by a proxy-session campaign to improve recycling efforts by all the major computer manufactures instigated by

a group of activist shareholders led by Calvert Group and the As You Sow Foundation. . . . Dell, which has been blasted for not taking a lead role in keeping toxic-laden PCs from ending up in landfills, will set specific recycling targets, disclose its progress to the public, and make sure its recycled goods are handled properly. Dell also pledged to study how to use its direct distribution model to lower the cost of recycling tech waste.[149]

Initially, issues of management remuneration have attracted the greatest ire from investors. In response to terms of basic pay, bonuses, severance agreements, and pension provision, more and more shareholders are rebelling against management, who still manage to receive increasing compensation packages at a time of decreasing company performance and increasing job losses.

The company, however, is usually not bound by the result of a shareholder vote, even if the vote is

a majority of total shareholder voters. For example, legislation now in place in the UK requires companies to produce a remuneration report every year, which then must be voted on at the AGM. This produces a great deal more information for shareholders and investors on issues surrounding various elements of a corporation's remuneration package such as contract terms, takeover clauses, and pension arrangements, as well as clauses inserted into CEO contracts that result in large payments in the event that the company is taken over (the main point of contention in GSK's case). Such information has previously been very difficult for interested parties to discover; however,

while voting on it is mandatory, the company is not obliged to make any changes even if the report is rejected, and no heads will roll.[150]

In the United States shareholder activism has also been increasing, which has drawn institutional support in the prevailing atmosphere of tighter control over corporate governance:

Under current rules, companies can ignore votes on resolutions proposed by shareholders. But the Securities and Exchange Commission has instituted a review of the proxy system. . . . If it makes shareholder votes mandatory the effect could be dramatic.[151]

The SEC is particularly focusing on easing the rules to allow shareholders to more easily nominate alternative candidates for board positions.[152] The AFL-CIO supports the change and other calls of support are growing:

Direct shareholder nominations will not fix all that ails Corporate America. But SEC Chairman William H. Donaldson has an historic opportunity. In one bold stroke, his agency can give greater voice to America's frustrated investors and improve accountability in the boardroom.[153]

There is great conflict between businesses, investors, and the SEC on how this, and other, ideas should proceed. The SEC is facing strong lobbying from business, in particular, which is causing it to back away from some of its more ambitious reform ideas.[154] In the resulting vacuum, however, concerned groups are finding ways to advance the agenda:

> One SEC commissioner is publicly railing against the delay [in the proposal granting shareholders greater power to nominate directors to the board]. Four public pension funds have filed a shareowner resolution at Disney to implement the rule there despite the fact it has not been broadly implemented.[155]

The SEC has also declared that from 2004, mutual funds' proxy votes are to be made public, thus revealing how each fund votes on any particular issue or resolution at a company's AGM. Until companies take an approach to management that emphasizes making decisions that incorporate all the company's stakeholders' concerns, the amount of conflict expressed at corporate AGMs seems set to grow.

## Web-Based Examples and Resources

Association of British Insurers, http://www.abi.org.uk/

> The Association of British Insurers is the trade association for the UK's insurance industry. We represent around 400 companies.

Corporate Library, http://www.thecorporatelibrary.com/

> The Corporate Library is an independent investment research firm providing corporate governance data, analysis & risk assessment tools.

GlaxoSmithKline, http://www.gsk.com/

GlaxoSmithKline—UK Web site, http://www.gsk.com/countryhubs/uk/docs/index.html

> GlaxoSmithKline—one of the world's leading research-based pharmaceutical and healthcare companies—is committed to improving the quality of human life by enabling people to do more, feel better and live longer.

Institutional Shareholder Services, http://www.issproxy.com/

> Institutional Shareholder Services, Inc. (ISS) is the world's leading provider of proxy voting and corporate governance services. ISS serves more than 950 institutional and corporate clients throughout North America and Europe with its core business—analyzing proxies and issuing informed research and objective vote recommendations for more than 10,000 U.S. and 12,000 non-U.S. shareholder meetings each year.

Investor Responsibility Research Center, http://www.irrc.org/

> IRRC is an independent research firm that has been the leading source of high quality, impartial information on corporate governance and social responsibility issues affecting investors and corporations, for 30 years.

National Association of Pension Funds, http://www.napf.co.uk/

> NAPF promotes workplace pensions. Its priority is to ensure a regulatory and fiscal environment which encourages the provision and take up of employer-sponsored pensions, as well as sound stewardship of pension fund assets.

NAPF concentrates the power of its membership into an influential voice to government, parliament, regulators and the media. It also provides its members with valuable information and other services to assist them in the effective running of their schemes.

Securities and Exchange Commission (U.S.), http://www.sec.gov/

Proposed Rule: Security Holder Director Nominations, http://www.sec.gov/rules/proposed/34–48626.htm

We are proposing new rules that would, under certain circumstances, require companies to include in their proxy materials security holder nominees for election as director.

Social Investment Forum's Advocacy and Public Policy Program, http://www.sriadvocacy.org/

The Advocacy and Public Policy Program . . . provides communication, research, and advocacy on public affairs related to socially responsible investing.

## Questions for Discussion and Review

1. Do you own any shares of a company? If so, do you vote at the company's annual general meeting (either in person or by proxy)? Is it important for shareholders to be actively involved with the company they own? Why, or why not?

2. What are your feelings regarding executive and CEO pay in general? Companies say that they will not attract qualified candidates to be their CEO unless they include clauses in their remuneration package such as the one included by GlaxoSmithKline granting an estimated £22–23 million (approximately US$40 million) for the CEO if the company is taken over. Is that a fair argument? What if the alternative is the potential sudden resignation of the CEO when a hostile takeover emerges?

3. What are your thoughts about the legislation, now in place in the UK (outlined in the case study above), that requires companies to produce a remuneration report every year, which then must be voted on at the AGM? Is it a good idea or unnecessary interference in day-to-day management?

# STAKEHOLDER RELATIONS

☑ *CSR Connection:* This issue builds on the shareholder activism issue and discusses the extent to which corporate managers are willing to listen and respond to all stakeholders' needs and concerns.

## Issue

To what extent are stakeholders considered within the company's strategic perspective? Stakeholder relations involves a number of issues, which reflect the wide variety of groups that can be defined as an organization's stakeholders in today's globalizing world (see Figure 1.1). The size and complexity of this issue, therefore, indicates the importance of a stakeholder perspective as part of a comprehensive approach to CSR. By implementing an effective stakeholder relations policy, companies can counter the prevailing perception, created in the wake of the corporate scandals in the United States, that executives only look out for themselves. A *BusinessWeek*/Harris Poll found that

> 79 percent of those surveyed felt the CEOs of large companies put their own interests ahead of workers and shareholders.[156]

The extent to which a company's stakeholders are being considered and consulted before making significant company decisions is increasing. The benefits of such a policy are also getting much wider recognition:

> "The collaboration with other stakeholders provides stability and predictability for the peaceful resolution of conflicts. Establishing a level of mutual trust, respect and understanding of each one's needs is a requirement for any public-private partnership. We, at Novartis, believe that this is an important factor for a successful and sustainable development," said Dieter Wissler, Head of Novartis Communications, during a speech at the World Bank Forum on 27 November 2000 in Berlin.[157]

One of the earliest corporate pioneers in this field of stakeholder relations was Ben & Jerry's. The company's cofounders, Ben Cohen and Jerry Greenfield, set new standards in defining the concept of a concerned and responsive employer.

---

## Case Study: Ben & Jerry's

Ben & Jerry's was one of the first corporations to adopt significantly the concept of stakeholders. The company specifically began to recognize the importance of addressing stakeholder needs and concerns as part of its groundbreaking *Social Audit*, which was first commissioned in 1989. Ben & Jerry's was the first major corporation to allow an independent social audit of their business operations:

> This social auditor recommended that the report be called a "Stakeholders Report" (the concept of stakeholders existed but this was possibly the first-ever report to stakeholders) and that it be divided into the major stakeholder categories: Communities (Community Outreach, Philanthropic Giving, Environmental Awareness, Global Awareness), Employees, Customers, Suppliers, Investors. After this first social audit in 1989, B&J continued to issue annual social reports, rotating to different social auditors as they sought to develop the concept.[158]

Ben & Jerry's has continued developing the concept of a business that takes its stakeholder concerns into consideration ever since. The company's mission statement reads as follows:

> Ben & Jerry's is dedicated to the creation & demonstration of a new corporate concept of linked prosperity. Our mission consists of three interrelated parts.
>
> Underlying the mission is the determination to seek new and creative ways of addressing all three parts, while holding a deep respect for individuals inside and outside the company, and for the communities of which they are a part.
>
> **Product:** To make, distribute and sell the finest quality all natural ice cream and related products in a wide variety of innovative flavors made from Vermont dairy products.
>
> **Economic:** To operate the Company on a sound financial basis of profitable growth, increasing value for our shareholders, and

creating career opportunities and financial rewards for our employees.

**Social:** To operate the Company in a way that actively recognizes the central role that business plays in the structure of society by initiating innovative ways to improve the quality of life of a broad community—local, national, and international.

One practical example is the issue of executive pay, on which Ben & Jerry's took a dramatic stance: No employee could earn more than seven times the salary of the lowest paid worker in the company:

The gap between CEO salaries and those on the factory floor is widening. In 1973, for example, the typical CEO made 45 times the wage of the average worker. Today, it's as much as 500 times [in the US]. . . . Japanese executives earn 20 to 30 times the lowest-paid worker while, in Europe, the ratio is about 40 times. Ben Cohen and Jerry Greenfield, the quirky entrepreneurs behind Ben & Jerry's ice cream, kept the [salary] ratio of top to bottom earners at 7:1— though that did not last after the two stepped down in 1995.[159]

Getting the balance right, in the eyes of all stakeholders, is not easy, however:

Costco Wholesale Corp. often is held up as a retailer that does it right, paying well and offering generous benefits. But Costco's kind-hearted philosophy toward its 100,000 cashiers, shelf-stockers and other workers is drawing criticism from Wall Street. Some analysts and investors contend that the Issaquah, Wash., warehouse-club operator actually is too good to employees, with Costco shareholders suffering as a result.[160]

Ben & Jerry's cult status was tarnished somewhat, however, when they sold out to the corporate giant Unilever in August 2000.[161] One example: *Business Ethics* dropped Ben & Jerry's out of its list of 100 Best Corporate Citizens in 2001 because of its unfavorable evaluation of Unilever, the new parent company. A second example: The top-to-bottom compensation ratio, referred to above, (including benefits and bonuses) had jumped to an average of 16:1 in 1999, 2000, and 2001.

The company's managers, however, still stress their support for the cofounders' original values and social goals. At several points on the company's Web site, they reaffirm the message. For example, the following comment was posted on the company's Web site (http://www.benjerry.com/) in March 2003:

Ben & Jerry's continues to support the progressive principles on which the company was founded. Ben & Jerry's has a progressive, nonpartisan Social Mission that seeks to meet human needs and eliminate injustices in our local, national and international communities. We have long supported nonviolent initiatives that seek to achieve peace. In all of our dealings, we are guided by a mission statement which makes the community's quality of life integral to and inseparable from our product and financial goals.

## Web-Based Examples and Resources

Ben & Jerry's, http://www.benjerry.com/

Ben & Jerry's Homemade, Inc., the Vermont-based manufacturer of ice cream, frozen yogurt and sorbet, was founded in 1978 in a renovated gas station in Burlington, Vermont, by childhood friends Ben Cohen and Jerry Greenfield, with a $12,000 investment ($4,000 of which was borrowed). . . . The company currently distributes ice cream, low fat ice cream, frozen yogurt, sorbet and novelty products nationwide as well as in selected foreign countries in supermarkets, grocery stores, convenience stores, franchised Ben & Jerry's scoop shops, restaurants and other venues.

Boxes and Arrows, http://www.boxesandarrows.com/

> Boxes and Arrows is the definitive source for the complex task of bringing architecture and design to the digital landscape.

Jonathan Boutelle, "Understanding Organizational Stakeholders for Design Success," May 6, 2004, http://www.boxesandarrows.com/archives/understanding_organizational_stake holders_for_design_success.php

Multi-stakeholder Processes (UNED Forum), http://www.earthsummit2002.org/msp/

> The term multi-stakeholder processes (MSPs) describes *processes which aim to bring together all major stakeholders* in a new form of communication, decision-finding (and possibly decision-making) on a particular issue.

SustainAbility, http://www.sustainability.com/

> Founded in 1987, SustainAbility is the longest established international consultancy specializing in business strategy and sustainable development—environmental improvement, social equity and economic development.

## Questions for Discussion and Review

1. What is a stakeholder? Define the term in your own words.

2. Do you think Ben & Jerry's does a good job of interacting with its stakeholders and presenting its stakeholder approach on its Web site? Did Unilever's assurances that this approach would not change after they bought the company in August 2000 do enough to safeguard this important element of Ben & Jerry's? Why, or why not?

3. Have a look at the wide variety of stakeholders that form a key component of Mallen Baker's definition of CSR, including the diagram, at http://www.mallenbaker.net/csr/CSRfiles/definition.html. How can an organization begin to balance such an array of competing stakeholder interests?

# VOLUNTEERING

> ☑ **CSR Connection:** This issue builds on the employee relations issue. Volunteer programs, effectively implemented, are an established means of increasing employee productivity and retention, while decreasing costs.

## Issue

When companies ask for a "bottom-line" benefit for implementing a comprehensive CSR perspective, employee volunteer programs deliver. In terms of employee loyalty and retention, employee volunteer programs revitalize employees. Such programs expose employees to a new environment away from their everyday position, allowing them to feel pride in their company and its standing within the community while also leading to the development of new skill sets:

> Marc Benioff, CEO of Salesforce.com, promotes what he calls "the 1 percent solution": 1 percent of the company's equity, 1 percent of its profits, and 1 percent of its employees' paid work hours are devoted to philanthropy.
>
> U.S. software maker SAS, which for six years has been among the Top 20 in *Fortune's* annual list of the 100 best companies to work for, offers a volunteer initiative that lets employees use flexible schedules to take paid time off for projects in the community, or even work in teams with their managers on a volunteer effort during business hours.[162]

In response to the growing popularity of volunteer programs in the UK,[163] the British government (Home Office) designated 2005 as the Year of the Volunteer.[164]

## Case Study: Timberland[165]

Timberland is committed to its employee volunteer program (timerberlandserve.com[166]) and even reports the program's results along with the quarterly financial reports it releases in its annual *Corporate Social Responsibility Report.*

The company's CEO, Jeffrey Swartz, inspired the volunteer program. Swartz saw the power the company possessed to evoke social change and also had the foresight to see the potential benefits this activism would bring:

> Timberland launched an in-house volunteer program in 1992, the Path of Service.[167] . . . Due to strong employee participation, the program expanded to . . . forty hours in 1997, where it remains today.
>
> Workers . . . choose their own volunteer activities. Service can range from serving meals in a homeless shelter to coaching a Little League baseball team. Above all, the company wants to make it as easy as possible for workers to find a service program that matches their interests. It's

effective: more than 90 percent of Timberland workers take part in the Path of Service.

> The company added . . . a service sabbatical program. Up to four employees each year are awarded three to six months of leave to work full time with a nonprofit organization of their choosing. The sabbatical comes with full pay and benefits, and participating employees return to their same job after completing their assignment.
>
> Although community well-being ranks high on Timberland's agenda, the Path of Service is first and foremost an avenue for employee enrichment. "We believe that investing in our community begins by investing in our employees," declares Swartz.[168]

Research indicates that volunteerism at the workplace is a key driver for positive worker attitudes. One study finds that individuals who participate in employer-sponsored community activities are 30 percent more likely to want to continue working for that company and to help make it a success.[169]

# Web-Based Examples and Resources

SERVEnet, http://www.servenet.org/

SERVEnet.org is the premier website on service and volunteering. Through SERVEnet, users can enter their zip code, city, state, skills, interests, and availability and be matched with organizations needing help. SERVEnet is also a place to search for calendar events, job openings, service news, recommended books, and best practices. YSA's commitment to America's Promise is to have volunteer opportunities on SERVEnet for every zip code in America. SERVEnet is a program of Youth Service America (YSA), a resource center and the premier alliance of 200+ organizations committed to increasing the quantity and quality of opportunities for young Americans to serve locally, nationally, or globally.

timberlandserve.com, http://www.timberlandserve.com

Timberland believes in making a difference and through timberlandserve.com, we invite people everywhere to join us. Timberlandserve.com brings consumers a searchable database of about 30,000 volunteer opportunities and information about our commitment to corporate social responsibility.

Other examples of corporate volunteer programs can be found at Salesforce.com, SAS, Shell, and Verizon.

http://www.salesforce.com/foundation

We are the global leader in fully integrating business and the community by providing an inspiring and innovative service model for integrated philanthropy

- 1% Time
- 1% Equity
- 1% Profits

SAS, http://www.sas.com/corporate/community/index.html

SAS is committed to being a contributing corporate citizen. Through a generous philanthropic program, including corporate support for a robust employee volunteer initiative, we seek to better the communities where we live and work by supporting education, community creativity and efforts where SAS is uniquely qualified to make a difference.

Shell Project Better World (since 1998), http://www.shell.com/home/Framework?siteId= careers-en&FC2=&FC3=/careers-en/html/iwgen/inside_shell/project_better_world_ 0912.html

Verizon Volunteers (launched January 1, 2001), http://foundation.verizon.com/07001.shtml

## Questions for Discussion and Review

1.  What are some of the benefits to companies operating a volunteer employee program stated in the case study? Do you agree?

2.  How can companies encourage employees to participate in volunteer programs and avoid having employees feel that "by volunteering, they are potentially derailing their chances for a promotion because of the time they'll spend out of the office"?[170]

3.  Go to Timberland's main Web site at http://www.timberland.com/ and also the company's volunteer Web site at http://www.timberlandserve.com. Do you get the sense that Timberland is genuine in its commitment to CSR? Does that create a good impression of the company or not make much difference in your perception of it?

# NOTES

1.  Joel Bakan, 'The Corporation: The Pathological Pursuit of Profit and Power,' Free Press, 2004. Quoted in *Business Ethics Magazine,* Spring 2004, p6.

2.  Patrick M. Lencioni, 'Make Your Values Mean Something,' *Harvard Business Review,* Vol. 80, No. 7, July 2002, pp 113–117.

3.  'The Next Step for CSR: Economic Democracy,' *Business Ethics Magazine,* Cover Story, Summer 2002, http://www.business-ethics.com/NextStepforCSR.htm

4.  Memorandum from Kenneth Lay to all employees, Subject: Code of Ethics, July 1, 2000.

5.  Enron Corp.'s "Code of Ethics," p5.

6.  Enron Corp.'s "Code of Ethics," p5.

7.  Enron Corp.'s "Code of Ethics," p12.

8.  Gretchen Morgenson, 'The Shares of Corporate Nice Guys Can Finish First,' *Miami Herald,* April 27, 2003, p6E.

9.  The triple bottom line represents the inclusion of financial, environmental, and social data within a company's annual report—see Chapter 4, Figure 4.3.

10.  'Wood for the Trees,' *The Economist,* November 6, 2004, http://www.economist.com/business/displayStory.cfm?story_id=3364578

11.  'Taking care of shareholder needs,' *Focus Japan,* JETRO, March 2001, pp 3–6.

12.  *The Economist,* November 6, 2004, op. cit., http://www.economist.com/business/displayStory.cfm?story_id=3364578

13.  The Institute of Social and Ethical AccountAbility, http://www.accountability.org.uk/

14.  Aaron Bernstein, 'Sweatshops: Finally, Airing the Dirty Linen,' *BusinessWeek,* June 23, 2003, p100.

15.  Ibid.

16.  *The Economist,* November 6, 2004, op. cit., http://www.economist.com/business/displayStory.cfm?story_id=3364578

17.  William Baue, 'Sustainability Reporting Improves, But Falls Short on Linking to Financial Performance,' November, 5, 2004, http://www.socialfunds.com/news/article.cgi/article1565.html

18.  Poulomi Mrinal Saha, 'OFR Regulations to Be Relaxed, Reports Financial Times,' *Ethical Corporation Magazine,* November 18, 2004, http://www.ethicalcorp.com/content.asp?ContentID=3189

19.  Mallen Baker, 'News Summary,' *Ethical Corporation Magazine online,* March 10, 2003, http://www.ethicalcorp.com/content.asp?ContentID=430

20. 'Business Ethics: Doing Well by Doing Good,' *The Economist,* April 22, 2000, pp 65–68.

21. David Henry & Amy Borrus, 'Death, Taxes and Sarbanes-Oxley?' *BusinessWeek,* January 17, 2005, pp 28–31.

22. *The Economist,* April 22, 2000, op. cit.

23. 'New Benchmarks for Ethics Programs Set by Sentencing Guidelines,' *BizEthics Buzz* (the online news report from *Business Ethics Magazine*), November 2004, http://www.business-ethics.com/email_newsletter/sample.html.

24. Ibid.

25. 'Ethics Officers Double in Four Years,' *Business Ethics Magazine,* Spring 2005, p9.

26. Editorial, 'Ethics officers—a growing breed?' *Ethical Corporation Magazine,* February 7, 2005, http://www.ethicalcorp.com/content.asp?ContentID=3466

27. Tamara Loomis, 'Scandals Spur New Kind of Corporate Exec,' *New York Law Journal,* May 2, 2003, http://www.law.com

28. Kris Maher, 'Global Companies Face Reality of Instituting Ethics Programs,' *Wall Street Journal,* November 9, 2004, pB8.

29. Chuck Bartels, 'Wal-Mart to Alter Pay System,' *Miami Herald,* June 5, 2004, p1C.

30. Kara Scannell & Almar Latour, 'Raising a Red Flag Isn't Enough,' *Wall Street Journal,* April 21, 2004, pC1.

31. George R. Wratney & Patrick J. Gnazzo, 'Are You Serious About Ethics? For Companies That Can't Guarantee Confidentiality, the Answer Is No,' *Across the Board,* July/August, 2003, http://www.conference-board.org/articles/atb_article.cfm?id=206

32. Patrick McGeehan, 'Most Corporate Ethics Officials Are Critical of Top Officers' Pay,' *New York Times,* June 17, 2003, pC8.

33. Ibid.

34. Will Hutton, 'Capitalism Must Put Its House in Order,' *The Observer,* November 24, 2002, http://observer.guardian.co.uk/business/ethics/story/0,12651,846563,00.html

35. Peter Montagnon, 'Companies Need to Get a Social Life,' *Financial Times* (insert), April 22, 2002, http://specials.ft.com/ftfm/FT3VAPKG80D.html

36. Greg Ip, 'A Less-Visible Role for the Fed Chief: Freeing Up Markets,' *Wall Street Journal,* November 19, 2004, pp A1&A8.

37. Ibid.

38. Alex Blyth, 'EU Multi-Stakeholder Forum Presents Final Report,' *Ethical Corporation Magazine,* July 5, 2004, http://www.ethicalcorp.com/content.asp?ContentID=2327

39. *The Observer,* November 24, 2002, op. cit.

40. Deborah Doane, 'Mandated Risk Reporting Begins in UK,' *Business Ethics Magazine,* Spring 2005, p13.

41. *The Observer,* November 24, 2002, op. cit.

42. Ibid.

43. *Business Ethics Magazine,* Spring 2004, op. cit.

44. Kent Greenfield, 'It's Time to Federalize Corporate Charters,' *Business Ethics Magazine,* Fall 2002, p6, http://www.business-ethics.com/constitEconDemoc.htm

45. Ibid.

46. Ibid.

47. Kent Greenfield, 'State Chartering Initiatives,' *Business Ethics Magazine,* Fall 2002, p6.

48. Marjorie Kelly, 'Despairing Globally, Hoping Locally,' *Business Ethics Magazine,* Spring 2003, p4.

49. Susan Wennemyr, 'Code for Corporate Responsibility Considered by Two State Legislatures,' *BizEthics Buzz,* e-mail newsletter, March 2004, http://www.business-ethics.com/email_newsletter/sample.html

50. Robert Hinkley, 'How Corporate Law Inhibits Social Responsibility,' *Business Ethics Magazine,* Spring 2002, http://www.business-ethics.com/constitEconDemoc.htm

51. Andy Serwer, 'Wall Street Comes to Main Street,' *Fortune,* May 3, 2004, pp 132–146.

52. 'Quick Takes,' *Business Ethics Magazine,* Summer 2003, p8.

53. Holman W. Jenkins Jr., 'Thinking Outside the Sarbox,' *Wall Street Journal,* November 24, 2004, pA13.

54. *BusinessWeek,* December 23, 2002, p33.

55. Christopher Davies, portfolio manager at David Advisors. Quoted in Nanette Byrnes et al., 'Reform: Who's Making the Grade,' *BusinessWeek*, September 22, 2003, pp 80–84.

56. Louis Lavelle, 'Special Report: The Best and Worst Boards,' *BusinessWeek,* October 7, 2002, pp 104–114.

57. Ibid.

58. Ibid.

59. '10 Years Later, Corporate Oversight Is Still Dismal,' *New York Times,* January 26, 2003, pp A1&A12.

60. *BusinessWeek,* September 22, 2003, op. cit.

61. 'Don't Let the CEO Run the Board, Too,' *BusinessWeek*, November 11, 2002, p28.

62. Phyllis Plitch, 'Post of Lead Director Catches On, Letting CEOs Remain Chairmen,' *Wall Street Journal,* July 7, 2003, pB2B.

63. Paul Davies, 'Drug Firms Urged to Split Top Jobs,' *Wall Street Journal,* April 22, 2005, pC3.

64. Interfaith Center on Corporate Responsibility, http://www.iccr.org/shareholder/proxy_book05/05statuschart.php

65. 'Survey: U.S. Directors Favor Splitting CEO, Chairman Roles,' *Daily Yomiuri,* May 30, 2002, p17.

66. *Wall Street Journal,* July 7, 2003, op. cit.

67. Alan Murray, 'Emboldened Boards Tackle Imperial CEOs,' *Wall Street Journal,* March 16, 2005, pA2.

68. Marjorie Kelly, 'Eureka: An Opening for Economic Democracy,' *Business Ethics Magazine,* Summer 2003, p4.

69. 'The Corporation,' Movie-documentary, http://www.thecorporation.tv/about/. The documentary is summarized in the *Wall Street Journal* as "a documentary that functions as a 2½-hour provocation in the ongoing debate about corporate conduct and governance." 'The Corporation,' July 9, 2004, pW2.

70. Brent Schlender, 'The New Soul of a Wealth Machine,' *Fortune,* April 5, 2004, pp 102–110.

71. John Micklethwait & Adrian Wooldridge, 'The Company: A Short History of a Revolutionary Idea,' Modern Library, 2003, pp xiv–xv.

72. *Fortune,* April 5, 2004, op. cit.

73. Ann Zimmerman, 'Costco's Dilemma: Be Kind to Its Workers, or Wall Street?' *Wall Street Journal,* March 26, 2004, pB1.

74. Lisa Roner, 'More Than Half of U.S. Executives Surveyed Say Corporate Citizenship Is Part of Their Business Strategy,' *Ethical Corporation Magazine,* July 12, 2004, http://www.ethicalcorp.com/content.asp?ContentID=2363

75. *The Economist,* April 22, 2000, op. cit.

76. Newsdesk, 'The great company contribution,' *Ethical Corporation Magazine,* October 5, 2004, http://www.ethicalcorp.com/content.asp?ContentID=2884

77. David Batstone, 'Saving the Corporate Soul—and (Who Knows?) Maybe Your Own,' Jossey-Bass, 2003, p3.

78. Peter Asmus, '100 Best Corporate Citizens of 2003,' *Business Ethics Magazine*, Spring 2003, pp 6–10.

79. Nanette Byrnes et al., 'Beyond Options,' *BusinessWeek*, July 28, 2003, pp 36–37.

80. William Greider, 'Beyond Scarcity: A New Story of American Capitalism,' *Business Ethics Magazine*, Fall, 2003, pp 9–11.

81. John Logue, Executive Director of the Ohio Employee Ownership Center, quoted in *BizEthics Buzz*, December 2002. *BizEthics Buzz* (http://www.business-ethics.com/email_newsletter/sample .html) is an online news report from *Business Ethics* magazine.

82. Matthew Karnitschnig, 'German Board Law Targeted,' *Wall Street Journal*, October 28, 2004, pA13.

83. Cornell University Press, 2001.

84. *BizEthics Buzz*, December 2002, op. cit., http://www.business-ethics.com/email_newsletter/sample.html

85. 'Will Overseas Boards Play by American Rules?' *BusinessWeek*, December 16, 2002, p36.

86. BizEthics Buzz, December 2002, op. cit., http://www.business-ethics.com/email_newsletter/sample.html

87. Gary S. Becker, 'What the Scandals Reveal: A Strong Economy,' *BusinessWeek*, December 30, 2002, p30.

88. Mike McNamee with Howard Gleckman, 'Capital Ideas,' *BusinessWeek*, December 30, 2002, p69.

89. Roger Martin, 'The Virtue Matrix,' Harvard Business Review, March 2002, Vol. 80, No. 3, pp 68–75.

90. The Body Shop's Web site, http://www.thebodyshop.com/bodyshop/index.jsp, December, 2002.

91. The Body Shop's Web site, http://www.thebodyshop.com/bodyshop/index.jsp, December, 2002.

92. Charles Wallace, 'Can the Body Shop Shape Up?,' *Fortune*, April 1996, http://www.business2.com/articles/mag/0,1640,1696,00.html?ref=cnet

93. Aisha Ikramuddin, 'The Cosmetic Mask: Decoding Cruelty-Free,' November 1, 1996, http://www.checnet.org/healthehouse/education/articles-detail.asp?Main_ID=322

94. 'What's Wrong With The Body Shop?-A Criticism of "Green Consumerism,"' London Greenpeace, March, 1998, http://www.mcspotlight.org/beyond/companies/bodyshop.html

95. Micklethwait & Wooldridge, op. cit., pp xvi&xviii.

96. Alan Murray, 'Political Capital: CEO Responsibility Might Be Right Cure for Corporate World,' *Wall Street Journal*, July 13, 2004, pA4.

97. Gene Colter, 'Stock Options Lose Appeal as an Option,' *Wall Street Journal*, October 12, 2004, pC3.

98. Anne Tergesen, 'Options: Cutting Through the Thicket,' *BusinessWeek*, June 23, 2003, pp 122–124.

99. David Stires, 'A Little Honesty Goes a Long Way,' *Fortune*, September 2, 2002, p186.

100. 'Apple Advised on Options,' *Miami Herald*, April 26, 2003, p3C.

101. Arthur Levitt Jr., 'Money, Money, Money,' *Wall Street Journal*, November 22, 2004, Op-ed page.

102. Louis Lavelle, 'Wretched Excess: Mega Options, Mega Losses,' *BusinessWeek*, June 23, 2003, p14.

103. Editorial, 'What We Learned in 2002,' *BusinessWeek*, December 30, 2002, p170.

104. Kathy Kristof, 'Shareholders Should Look for Signs of Excessive Exec Pay,' *Miami Herald*, June 22, 2003, p6E.

105. Nanette Byrnes, 'Earnings Guidance: Silence Is Golden,' *BusinessWeek*, May 5, 2003, p87.

106. Amy Borrus, 'Expensing Options: This Time, Silicon Valley Can't Shout Down FASB,' *BusinessWeek*, February 24, 2003, p49.

107. Anne Tergesen, 'Options: Cutting Through the Thicket,' *BusinessWeek*, June 23, 2003, pp 122–124.

108. *BusinessWeek*, February 24, 2003, op. cit.

109. Marcy Gordon, 'Divided House Votes to Block Stock-Option Bill,' *Miami Herald*, July 21, 2004, p3C.

110. Ibid.

111. Jonathan Weil, 'Ahead of the Tape: Not an Option,' *Wall Street Journal*, July 22, 2004, pC1.

112. Floyd Norris, 'Proposals on How to Handle Options,' *New York Times*, September 6, 2004, pC2.

113. Harriet Johnson Brackey, 'Expensing Options Bill Stirs Debate,' *Miami Herald*, August 1, 2004, pp 1E&5E.

114. AP, 'FASB to Require Expensing of Options Starting Next Year,' *Wall Street Journal*, December 17, 2004, pC3.

115. Jonathan Weil & Joann S. Lublin, 'Companies Get Reprieve on Expensing Options,' *Wall Street Journal*, April 13, 2005, pC3.

116. Diya Gullapalli, 'Ahead of the Tape: Underwhelming Stock Options,' *Wall Street Journal*, March 21, 2005, pC1.

117. 'The List: The Price of Safety,' *BusinessWeek*, September 15, 2003, p12.

118. Ibid.

119. John Carey, 'The Hundred Years' War at the FDA,' *BusinessWeek*, July 28, 2003, p20. Review of the book 'Protecting America's Health: The FDA, Business, and One Hundred Years of Regulation,' by Philip J. Hilts, Knopf, 2003.

120. Jeremy Rifkin, 'A Precautionary Tale,' *The Guardian*, May 12, 2004, p23.

121. Ibid.

122. Editorial, 'Incredibly Shrinking Europe,' *Wall Street Journal*, April 28, 2005, pA18.

123. Rifkin, op. cit.

124. 'EU Chemicals Regulation Workable, Study Says,' Wall Street Journal, April 27, 2005, pA12.

125. David Barboza, 'Development of Biotech Crops Is Booming in Asia,' *The New York Times*, February 21, 2003, pA3.

126. Lorraine Woellert, 'Will a Chance for Asbestos Reform Be Missed?' *BusinessWeek*, January 13, 2003, p43.

127. Debra Rubin et al., 'Potential Asbestos Deal Nears,' *Engineering News-Record*, enr.com, May 5, 2003, http://enr.construction.com/news/bizlabor/archives/030505.asp

128. Editorial, 'The Latest Asbestos Scam,' *Wall Street Journal*, June 1, 2004, pA16.

129. 'A Bid to Bypass the Lawyers,' *Economist*, January 29, 2005, pp 69–70.

130. Russell Gold, 'Halliburton Finalizes Settlement For $5.1 Billion Over Asbestos,' *Wall Street Journal*, January 4, 2005, pA3.

131. Susan Warren & Alexei Barrionuevo, 'Halliburton to Settle Asbestos Claims,' *Wall Street Journal*, December 19, 2002, pp A3&A5.

132. *Wall Street Journal*, January 4, 2005, op. cit.

133. David Savage, 'Asbestos Fund Advances to the Senate Floor,' *Miami Herald*, July 15, 2003, p16A.

134. Susan Warren, 'Halliburton to Request Extension on Stay for Asbestos Obligations,' *Wall Street Journal*, July 21, 2003, pA3.

135. Lisa Roner, 'U.S. Insurers Weigh Options on Asbestos,' *Ethical Corporation Magazine*, November 19, 2004, http://www.ethicalcorp.com/content.asp?ContentID=3218

136. Brody Mullins, 'Insurance Firms Withdraw Support for Asbestos Fund,' *Wall Street Journal,* April 5, 2005, pp A3&A12.

137. Russell Gold & Neil King Jr., 'Halliburton to Take Big Charges for Brazil Project, Asbestos Fund,' *Wall Street Journal,* June 30, 2004, pA3.

138. *Wall Street Journal,* January 4, 2005, op. cit.

139. 'Quick Takes,' *Business Ethics Magazine,* Summer 2003, p8.

140. Jill Treanor, 'Investors Fear Garnier Revenge,' *The Guardian,* May 21, 2003, http://www.guardian.co.uk/business/story/0,3604,960220,00.html

141. 'Investors in Revolt Against Bosses' Feeding Frenzy,' *The Observer,* May 25, 2003, http://www.observer.co.uk/business/story/0,6903,962775,00.html

142. Christopher Tkaczyk, 'by the Numbers,' *Fortune,* March 22, 2004, p38.

143. Eileen Ambrose, 'The New Activist Shareholder,' *Miami Herald,* March 9, 2003, p3E.

144. Shabina S. Khatri, 'Who's Winning?' *Wall Street Journal* CEO Compensation Survey, April 11, 2005, pR3.

145. Sheila McNulty, 'Shareholder Activists Hijack Exxon's AGM,' *Financial Times,* May 9, 2003, p17.

146. Quoted by an officer from the Investor Responsibility Research Center on *The NewsHour With Jim Lehrer,* PBS, June 10, 2003.

147. http://www.corpgov.net/, June 2003.

148. Alex Blyth, 'GSK Wins Battle Over Chief Executive's Pay,' *Ethical Corporation,* May 20, 2004, http://www.ethicalcorp.com/content.asp?ContentID=2077

149. Andrew Park, 'Dell Gets Greener,' *BusinessWeek,* May 5, 2003, p89.

150. *The Observer,* May 25, 2003, op. cit.

151. Ibid.

152. To view the proposed rule: 'Security Holder Director Nominations,' visit the SEC's Web site at: http://www.sec.gov/rules/proposed/34–48626.htm

153. Louis Lavelle, 'A Fighting Chance for Boardroom Democracy,' *BusinessWeek,* June 9, 2003, p50.

154. Deborah Solomon, 'Tough Tack of SEC Chief Could Relent,' *Wall Street Journal,* January 12, 2005, pC1.

155. Newsdesk, 'SEC Dallies on Fundamental Shareholder Nomination Right,' *Ethical Corporation Magazine,* November 2, 2004, http://www.ethicalcorp.com/content.asp?ContentID=3083

156. Kris Axtman & Ron Scherer, 'Enron Lapses and Corporate Ethics,' *The Christian Science Monitor,* February 4, 2002, http://www.csmonitor.com/2002/0204/p01s01-ussc.html

157. Novartis Web site, January, 2003, http://www.novartis.com/corporate_citizenship/en/stakeholder_dialog.shtml

158. Alice & John Tepper Marlin, 'A Brief History of Social Reporting,' *Ethical Corporation Magazine,* March 10, 2003, http://www.ethicalcorp.com/content.asp?ContentID=430

159. Axtman & Scherer, op. cit., http://www.csmonitor.com/2002/0204/p01s01-ussc.html

160. Ann Zimmerman, 'Costco's Dilemma: Be Kind to Its Workers, or Wall Street?' *Wall Street Journal,* March 26, 2004, pB1.

161. 'Unilever Scoops Up Ben & Jerry's,' BBC News, April 12, 2000, http://news.bbc.co.uk/1/hi/business/710694.stm

162. Richard Pound & Karl Moore, 'Volunteering to Be a Better Manager,' *Strategy + Business e-news,* April 29, 2004, http://www.strategy-business.com/press/enewsarticle/enews042904?pg=0

163.   "[The UK's Home Office] estimates that the number of Britons engaged in 'active community participation' rose from 18.8 million to 20.3 million between 2001 and 2003." Simon Kuper, 'Office Angels,' *FT Weekend,* December 31, 2004 to January 2, 2005, pW2.

164.   http://www.yearofthevolunteer.org/

165.   In *Fortune* magazine's list of 'The 100 Best Companies to Work For' in 2003, Timberland placed number 50. "[Timberland] gives employees up to 40 hours a year of paid time off for community service. 'Businesses should do more than just make money,' says planning analyst Anthony Gow, and his does: Last year Timberland granted him a six-month sabbatical to help a local food pantry." Christopher Tkaczyk, 'The 100 Best Companies to Work For,' *Fortune,* January 12, 2004, p68.

166.   http://www.timberland.com/timberlandserve/timberlandserve_index.jsp

167.   Note: The Path of Service program has been renamed timberlandserve.com.

168.   David Batstone, 'Saving the Corporate Soul—and (Who Knows?) Maybe Your Own,' Jossey-Bass, 2003, p83.

169.   Batstone, op. cit., p87.

170.   Pound & Moore, op. cit.

# Chapter 6

# ECONOMIC ISSUES AND CASE STUDIES

## ADVERTISING

☑ *CSR Connection:* This issue reflects the importance of advertising as a key tool that a company uses to communicate with its external stakeholders—in particular its customers.

## Issue

Consumer perception plays a large role in the success of a company, especially among global brands. Therefore, advertising is an influential element of CSR because it plays a significant role in conveying the company's values to its stakeholders.

How a company is perceived by the societies within which it is based and operates goes a long way to determining whether that company is welcomed or rejected by that society—the loyalty of local consumers, the company's employees, suppliers, relationships with local interest groups, the relevant regulating authorities, and so on.

The goal of an effective CSR policy is to ensure the company is both welcomed and successful. Increasingly, it is becoming impossible to separate the two.

## Case Study: Benetton

Communication should never be commissioned from outside the company, but conceived from within its heart.

—Luciano Benetton[1]

Benetton's advertising has always been colorful and unique, highlighting trends ahead of their time and challenging conventions and stereotypes.

A history of the company can be found at http://www.museedelapub.org/pubgb/virt/mp/benetton/index.html

A history of the company's advertising campaigns can be found at: http://www.museedelapub.org/pubgb/virt/mp/benetton/pub_benetton.html

In the late 1980s and early 1990s, the theme of racial harmony, which had run throughout Benetton's early ad campaigns, turned to a more challenging look at race within contemporary Western society. In 1990 and 1991, the company started to tackle confrontational issues and present their positions using controversial images in its advertising. In 1992, Benetton stepped up the tone even further with the result that many French advertising billboard companies refused to carry the most radical of the images, including death, race, AIDS, religion, sexuality, war, and environmental pollution.

The institutional and general public's reaction to Benetton's increasing cries for attention reflected the company founder's perception of the role of advertising within corporate operations:

The purpose of advertising is not to sell more. It's to do with institutional publicity, whose aim is to communicate the company's values. . . . We need to convey a single strong image, which can be shared anywhere in the world.

—Luciano Benetton[2]

Oliviero Toscani, the photographer who took many of the Benetton radical campaign photographs, attempts to implement this philosophy in his work:

"I am not here to sell pullovers, but to promote an image." . . . Benetton's advertising draws public attention to universal themes like racial integration, the protection of the environment, Aids . . . [3]

Examples of some of the most controversial of the company's advertising campaigns can be found on the company's Web site: http://www.benetton-group.com/en/whatwesay/sottosezioni/campaigns_photo_gallery.htm

In order to create the ideas behind the company's positions on a number of wide-ranging issues combining art and research, Benetton created Fabrica, what it calls its "communication research center." The group is active in many areas—including photography, cinema, design, music, and art in general—and acts as a resource similar to a think tank with the assignment of reaching out and promoting the company name and image to various constituents. The group's magazine *Colors* (http://www.colorsmagazine.com) is a particularly high-profile project that spreads Benetton's message around the world:

Sold in more than 30 countries, with three editions published in four languages and a critically acclaimed web presence, *Colors* is a successful, trend-setting magazine. Founded in 1991 under the direction of Tibor Kalman, it is based on the conviction that differences are a richness to be protected, and that all cultures have the same value.[4]

The company has the following to say about its controversial advertising campaign:

Benetton Group's advertising campaigns are not only a means of communication but an expression of our time. Through their universal impact, they have succeeded in attracting the attention of the public and in standing out amid the current clutter of images. The campaigns have gathered awards and acclaim worldwide; by the same token, they have aroused strong reactions—at times ferocious, at times simply curious, confirming once again that they are always a focal point of discussion and of confrontation of ideas.[5]

Whatever the stance an individual adopts about a particular image or campaign the company adopts, it is impossible to ignore their impact. Benetton significantly altered the general perception of the company in the eyes of their consumers (for good or bad):

Those provocative images, with their pointed social messages, helped turn Benetton's colorful sweaters into a casual-wear empire in the 1980s, creating one of the world's best-known brands.[6]

Although not necessarily guaranteeing corporate success, Benetton's public image ensures that the company means something in the public mind. One foundation of successful branding today rests on the assumption that it is better to stand for something than nothing. Benetton's radical stance ensures it enjoys a loyal following among some (who feel the company is passionately committed to the causes it highlights) but alienates others (who feel it is resorting to shock value in order to sell clothes).

The key to a successful CSR policy is to ensure the stance that a company adopts reflects the sentiments of enough of the company's target market and key stakeholder groups to enable corporate success that is sustainable over the medium to long term.

## Web-Based Examples and Resources

Adbusters, http://www.adbusters.org/

We are a global network of artists, activists, writers, pranksters, students, educators and entrepreneurs who want to advance the new social activist movement of the information age. Our aim is to topple existing power structures and forge a major shift in the way we will live in the 21st century.

Benetton, http://www.benetton.com/

Today, the Benetton Group is present in 120 countries around the world. Its core business is clothing: a group with a strong Italian character whose style, design expertise and passion are clearly seen in the United Colors of Benetton. . . . The Group produces over 110 million garments every year, over 90% in Europe.

## Questions for Discussion and Review

1. Do you like Benetton's clothes? Depending on your answer, does that mean the company does a good or bad job about advertising its products?

2. Respond to the statement by Benetton's most famous photographer, Oliviero Toscani, that his role is not "to sell pullovers, but to promote an image." Do you agree? Why or why not?

3. Go to the following page on the company's Web site: http://www.benettongroup .com/en/whatwesay/sottosezioni/campaigns_photo_gallery.htm

   What is your opinion about the example ads shown there? Is the company just trying to shock people, or is it important for a high-profile company like Benetton to be raising difficult issues such as those?

# BRANDS

☑ *CSR Connection:* This issue is related to the issue of advertising. A company's brand, along with its mission statement, should set out the organization's values, its goals, and how it intends to achieve them.

## Issue

To what extent does a corporation's integration of a CSR perspective benefit its brand value?

The biggest challenge that any organization has in communicating its brand promise is finding a common ground between what it wants to be known as and how the target audience it wants to influence perceives it to be.[7]

Brands have become a central part of corporate value in recent years. Brands are something that companies pay a lot of money to build and maintain:

In 2000, Nike paid £300 million [US$450 million] to ensure that Manchester United would wear its shirts and shorts for the next 13 years.[8]

The flip side of the brand loyalty that companies try to build is the growing importance of consumer perception of a company and the products it produces. A negative perception raises the risk of possible consumer boycotts, organized by activist NGOs. Their influence among consumers has been heightened by the Internet, which allows them to identify and target the widest possible audience with much greater efficiency.

Studies suggest that as consumers become more sophisticated, different approaches from companies are needed to maintain brand loyalty. Straightforward marketing and advertising is now no longer enough. As societies develop and become more affluent, CSR advocates believe that consumers want to become responsible members of their communities and purchase products from companies that reflect their beliefs and values.

---

## Case Study: BP

BP is the world's largest oil company, in terms of both production and refining operations. BP has 27,800 service stations worldwide (14,700 in the United States) and had 102,900 employees in 2004.[9]

In 2000, BP began an enormous attempt to reinvent itself as a company with the aim of altering the public perception of what it does and the role it plays in wider society. The cost of the rebranding exercise, created by Ogilvy & Mather Worldwide, was $200 million and included a new name, "BP," rather than "British Petroleum," a new slogan, "Beyond Petroleum," and a new logo:

Out went the old British Petroleum shield . . . and in came a green, yellow and white sunburst that seemed to suggest a warm and fuzzy feeling about the earth. BP press officers were careful not to explain exactly what "Beyond Petroleum" meant, but the slogan . . . sent the message that the company was looking past oil and gas toward a benign, eco-friendly future of solar and renewable energy.[10]

BP has essentially made itself a very wealthy company by contributing to the climate change that it is now publicly warning about. Lord John Browne, group chief executive since 1995, is leading the charge, suggesting it is time that companies like BP recognize the impact of their operations:

Companies composed of highly skilled and trained people can't live in denial of mounting evidence gathered by hundreds of the most reputable scientists in the world.[11]

BP was the first oil company in the world to begin addressing the issue of global climate change—and its role in creating the problem in the first place—with environmental penalties that have been levied against the company posted on its Web site.[12]

Without doubt, the company is still first and foremost an oil-producing company. BP seeks to persuade the public that it produces oil in a way that minimizes the impact on the earth's environment. It is also looking for alternatives in hydrogen, wind, and solar energy but is much more vague about the chances of shifting its emphasis from being an oil producer to being a producer of alternative energy sources at some future point.

Browne, however, is leading the oil industry to the need for change. Everything indicates he is acting with conviction, as well as attempting to use BP's initiative to create a competitive point of differentiation in the marketplace for the company. And, although it is difficult for an oil company to brand itself as distinctive (many people consider one company's oil to be much like another), BP is making a start.

## Web-Based Examples and Resources

"bp: Beyond Petroleum?"—An alternative viewpoint of BP's rebranding, http://www.uow.edu.au/arts/sts/sbeder/bp.html [excerpted from Sharon Beder, *Battling Big Business: Countering Greenwash, Infiltration and Other Forms of Corporate Bullying*, edited by Eveline Lubbers, Green Books, Devon, UK, 2002, pp 26–32.]

BP's "Environment and Society" Web page, http://www.bp.com/genericsection.do?categoryId =4445&contentId=7005392

I am convinced that BP must be a force for good wherever we operate and that corporate responsibility must remain at the heart of our business, driving everything we do.

BP Group chief executive's introduction: BP Solar, http://www.bpsolar.com/

BP Solar is a BP Group Company. The BP Group represents over 100,000 employees worldwide united around a vision of environmental leadership and recognition that the challenge to develop a cleaner energy must be met. Our core purpose is to provide the energy which make it possible for people all across the globe to have more choices, more opportunity and a better way of life, today and tomorrow.

BP Solar manufactures, designs, markets, and installs a wide range of photovoltaic solar electric products and systems.

We are a recognized leader in protecting the environment and believe solar power is a key element in reducing the threat of global climate change and improving air quality.

BP—The New BP Brand, http://www.bp.co.nz/about/brand.html

In 2000, BP introduced a new, unified global brand which is now beginning to appear across all company offices, manufacturing plants and retail service stations.

Greenpeace, http://archive.greenpeace.org/climate/arctic99/html/content/news.html

BP runs to courts to prevent Greenpeace ships from protecting the climate.

## Questions for Discussion and Review

1. Think of a company with a brand that you like and one with a brand that you dislike. What accounts for the difference between the two? Is CSR related at all?

2. Read Sharon Beder's essay listed first in the *Web-Based Examples and Resources* subsection. What do you think of her perspective?

3. *Greenwash* is a term that suggests firms talk about environmental responsibility to gain public relations benefits. After reviewing the BP Web site in the *Web-Based Examples and Resources* subsection above, are you convinced that BP is genuine in its commitment to CSR? What arguments can you advance that support the claim of some that BP's branding campaign is little more than "Greenwash"?

# CONSUMER APATHY

> ☑ *CSR Connection:* This issue (Do consumers care about CSR?) is crucial to the CSR debate. If consumers do not care, then there is little incentive for companies to implement CSR.

## Issue

To what extent do consumers care if companies are socially responsible? What if consumers really do not care? What if the most important thing for wealthy customers in developed economies is to buy products as cheaply as possible and that satisfy whatever personal needs they have? What if they do not want to think about the wages and general working conditions of the person who had to make the product or the effect that product may have on others, whether at home or abroad?

---

## Case Study: SUVs

Traffic fatalities in the United States fell steadily from 54,600 in 1972 to 34,900 in 1992. But then they started to rise again. . . . America's ranking has fallen from first to ninth over the last 30 years, with Australia, Britain and Canada all having better records. A big part of the difference . . . seems to be the prevalence of sport utility vehicles and pickups on American highways. Sales of light trucks—SUVs, pickups and minivans—were about a fifth of total automobile sales 30 years ago. Now they account for more than half.[13]

Although there was a slight decline in traffic fatalities in 2003 to 42,643,

one significant caution for drivers was that . . . the number of fatalities in SUVs from rollover accidents increased 7%, amid a 12% increase in the number of SUVs on the roads.[14]

SUVs have become a common feature of the U.S. automobile landscape. In terms of cars, U.S. citizens feel they should have the right to travel freely and express themselves in whatever way they feel appropriate. The open road is a way of life; and it seems the bigger the vehicle, the more suitable it is for tackling the giant highways that crisscross the country.

As Dave Barry points out, however, some manufacturers are producing truly massive cars for which there is very little use in urban America. He describes the Chevrolet Suburban subdivision as

> the current leader in the humongous-car category . . . the first passenger automobile designed to be, right off the assembly line, visible from the Moon.[15]

Slowly, as gas prices rise and the size of SUVs continues to grow, a debate is emerging around the role SUVs are playing on U.S. roads today:

> Recent events make the business case [for CSR] seem a little worn. In an article for the *Public Affairs Newsletter*, Alexander Evans of the Institute for Public Policy Research (IPPR) questioned why, if consumers are so green, Sports Utility Vehicles have been the top-selling product line in the U.S.[16]

SUVs are classed as trucks for the purposes of the Clean Air Act of 1990, passed to modernize laws on pollution. The advantage of this classification (rather than being labeled as cars) is that trucks are treated more leniently than cars in the legislation, and therefore the favorable classification was a significant victory for the automobile industry.

One example of the benefits this classification brings is that the luxury car tax, a 10% tax that applies to cars priced over $30,000, exempts light trucks (with a gross weight over 6,000 pounds); therefore, it is in the interests of the car makers to make their SUVs as heavy as possible, decreasing prices and increasing profits:

> In 2001 "sales of light trucks [which include SUVs] topped those of cars for the first time." This is despite a growing perception that SUVs "waste gas, crowd highways, and endanger motorists."[17]

Late in 2004, the administration of George Bush discussed removing the generous tax break that encouraged many small business owners to buy bigger and heavier trucks or at least limiting it to those who legitimately need such vehicles for their business:

> Those that qualify [for the tax break] must have a gross vehicle weight—which means when they are fully loaded—of more than 6,000 pounds. . . . The loophole allows [small business owners] to write off against their taxes up to $100,000 from purchases of these trucks—usually the entire price of the vehicle.[18]

In addition to the price, safety is another quoted reason why consumers choose SUVs. And it is true that SUVs are safe for those who are riding inside the SUV during a crash. It would appear, however, that safety comes at the price of increased risk for all other drivers on the road:

> "The theory that I'm going to protect myself and my family even if it costs other people's lives has been the operative incentive for the design of these vehicles, and that's just wrong," said Dr. Runge, the administrator of the National Highway Traffic Safety Administration (NHTSA).[19]
>
> [SUVs] are three times more likely than cars to roll over and cause deaths . . . according to a recent study by the National Academy of Sciences.[20]
>
> Light trucks—including SUVs, pickups and mini-vans—now outsell cars and account for nearly 40 percent of vehicles on American roads. But they are involved in a disproportionate number of fatal crashes.[21]

Dave Barry ironically points out:

> A big reason why [people buy] a Sport Utility Vehicle is "safety," in the sense of, "you, personally, will be safe, although every now and then you may have to clean the remains of other motorists out of your wheel wells."[22]

Sales, however, are booming, and SUVs are too profitable for the auto industry to begin to think of surrendering the bonanza they are receiving:

> One out of every four new cars sold last year was an SUV, and sales of the monsters grew

6.3% even as the U.S. vehicle market fell 2%, according to researcher Autodata Corp. For the first time, so-called light trucks, including SUVs and extended-cab pickups, outsold passenger cars.[23]

Mr. Bradsher describes how a single Ford factory in Michigan produced $11 billion in annual S.U.V. sales (equal to the size of McDonald's global sales) and $3.7 billion in pre-tax profits [for the company].[24]

SUV sales . . . account for 90% of the Big Three's profits.[25]

There are also political reasons why the government might feel reluctant to upset the auto industry by stepping in to try and regulate a better social outcome:

Regulating SUVs is particularly sensitive because Michigan is a swing state in presidential elections and SUVs, which are coming under increasing attack from a variety of groups, are the main profit center of the domestic automakers. Andrew H. Card Jr., President Bush's chief of staff, also served as G.M.'s top lobbyist in the 1990s.[26]

However, Jeffrey Runge (a former emergency room surgeon) at the National Highway Traffic Safety Administration (NHTSA) is trying to enforce design changes that would make SUVs safer and also advocating

non-binding recommendations for reducing SUV-related injuries by lowering bumpers, adding side air bags, and creating chassis with more "give" to soften impacts. . . . Safety and SUVs, as now designed, are mutually exclusive. . . . Per 100,000 registered vehicles, the death rate from rollovers in SUVs is more than twice that of passenger cars.[27]

Runge's criticisms are joining a growing anti-SUV voice that includes Christian environmentalists (the Evangelical Environmental Network)[28] who launched a popular "What would Jesus drive?"[29] advertising campaign in 2002.

Other anti-SUV groups and campaigns include The Detroit Project, a coalition launched in 2003 that tenuously criticized SUV drivers for supporting terrorists because the high gas consumption of SUVs increases U.S. reliance on Middle East oil. As the campaign's head, Arianna Huffington, succinctly puts it,

Welcome to "The Detroit Project," our grassroots campaign to prod Detroit automakers to build cars that will get Americans to work in the morning without sending us to war in the afternoon—cars that will end our dependence on foreign oil.[30]

In Europe, a number of governments (including the Swedish, French, and British) are considering applying significant category-specific taxes to inflate SUV prices to consumers. The aim is to encourage the purchase of smaller vehicles and stem the tide of new models being planned for the market:

More than one in 20 cars sold [in Europe] is now an SUV. Volkswagen, Ford, Opel, Fiat and Audi are all planning SUVs in the next two years to take advantage of rising demand.[31]

However, do consumers care? Or are they just not researching issues, preferring ignorance to enlightenment? The only blip in SUV sales this decade has been caused by high gasoline prices rather than a reconsideration of the social value of the vehicle itself. General opinion seems to attach some of the indifference to the wider consequences of widespread SUV ownership to differing generational values and expects change to come with younger, more environmentally conscious, generations:

Mostly, though, carmakers are warily eyeing Gen X and Gen Y, the car buyers who will dictate the companies' future. They're idealistic and care more about the environment than their elders. . . . By the time those youngsters have the cash to call the shots, you can be sure Detroit will offer the environmentally correct products they'll want to buy.[32]

As time goes on, however, others expect consumer opinion to evolve. It is only those companies that are able to see beyond the immediate business horizon that will avoid the damage to a brand that comes with producing a product that has suddenly become socially unacceptable:

> German automaker BMW already runs anti-SUV ads, likening the vehicles to dinosaurs while touting its Mini Cooper.[33]

> While they don't yet provoke the kind of violent reaction that GM's Hummers do, there is growing concern that high gas prices and worries about future supply will eventually make SUVs socially unacceptable, like smoking in the 1980s and wearing fur in the 1990s.[34]

Already companies like Ford are advertising the Escape Hybrid as "the first and only gas/electric SUV," as well as other environmental initiatives the company is exploring.[35] And in Europe, governments are keen to impose taxes that penalize excessive greenhouse gas emissions, "giving customers a disincentive for buying [SUVs]."[36]

## Web-Based Examples and Resources

Bradsher, Keith, *High and Mighty—SUVs: The World's Most Dangerous Vehicles and How They Got That Way*, Public Affairs, 2002. [book]

The Detroit Project[37], http://www.thedetroitproject.com/

> Americans for Fuel Efficient Cars (AFEC) is a nonprofit group dedicated to decreasing America's reliance on foreign oil. Our goal is to mount a citizens' ad campaign aimed at getting people to stop driving SUVs and other gas-guzzling vehicles—and jolting our leaders into taking action.

U.S. Department of Energy and U.S. Environmental Protection Agency: http://www.fueleconomy.gov/ (fuel economy homepage). For the U.S. government's ranking of the most and least fuel-efficient trucks and SUVs, go to http://www.fueleconomy.gov/feg/bestworst EPAtrucks.htm

What Would Jesus Drive?, http://www.whatwouldjesusdrive.org/

> WWJDrive is organized and sponsored by the Evangelical Environmental Network (EEN), a biblically orthodox Christian environmental organization. (See http://www.creation-care.org/ for more information.)

## Questions for Discussion and Review

1. Do you own an SUV? Would you buy one if you had the opportunity? What points raised in this case seem most relevant to you in the SUV debate?

2. Are consumers apathetic? If not, explain the growth of SUVs.

3. If he were alive today, what car would Jesus drive? Why?

## CULTURAL CONFLICT

☑ *CSR Connection:* This issue highlights the complexities of CSR when dealing with conflicting values in different cultures, particularly for multinational corporations that operate in many different countries but are expected to please all stakeholders.

### Issue

To what extent does operating in a foreign environment, with different cultural values and norms, render the corporation vulnerable to cultural conflict? To what extent is this conflict a CSR issue, and how might it be dealt with? Also, what is the potential damage for the company back in its home market, where observers and consumers do not judge the company by the standards of the foreign culture?

> When a corporation from an advanced economy does business in a developing country, it may . . . establish a level of corporate virtue consistent with the host country's civil foundation. Notoriously, Nike, by running its Southeast Asian athletic footwear plants and paying its workers in accordance with local customs and practices, opened itself to charges of operating sweatshops. In essence, it was accused of averaging down its level of corporate responsibility. Although the company protested that its conduct was virtuous by local standards, angry U.S. consumers made it clear that they expected Nike to conform to [the standards of] the U.S. civil foundation.[38]

### Case Study: Nike

Nike has long been plagued by allegations that it oversees sweatshop conditions in its factories abroad. The allegation is made against the company whether the factories are Nike owned and operated or merely contractors producing shoes and clothing on behalf of the firm:

> A recent report on factories in Bangladesh found that Nike workers' average up to 78 hours a week and are paid less than 20 U.S. cents an hour.[39]

Even after ten years of campaigning against Nike over alleged abuse of workers in "sweatshops" of its developing world subcontractors, NikeWatch and its cohorts are still going strong. This reinforces how much harder it is to restore a

reputation than to lose it. Nike is still demonized by many despite impressive sustainability initiatives, including workplace monitoring.[40]

Once an image is established, it is difficult to dislodge within the minds of the public. Questions about Nike's sweatshops have even dogged the famous athletes that represent the company wherever they go. The goal has always been to balance diplomacy with capitalist instinct. Dan Le Batard calls it "sole-selling" and compliments Michael Jordan's ability to have walked the fine line ever since he joined forces with Nike:

> It's why [Jordan] famously recused himself from opining on controversial Jesse Helms in his

home state of North Carolina because, in his words, "Republicans buy sneakers, too."[41]

In 2003, the issue of Nike's overseas operations rose to the level of the U.S. Supreme Court in a case brought against the company by a private citizen from California, Marc Kasky.[42] Kasky challenged Nike's claims that it does not operate sweatshops in Southeast Asia, that it pays its workers there competitive wages, and that they enjoy better-than-average working conditions. Nike v. Kasky originally emerged out of an exchange of opinions between the *New York Times* columnist Bob Herbert and Nike CEO Phil Knight in 1996 and 1997. Herbert initially wrote two op-ed articles criticizing the conditions faced by Nike laborers in the company's Southeast Asian factories. He then contrasted these conditions with the huge salaries enjoyed by Knight and other Nike executives and also the company's stable of wealthy athletes who are paid to endorse Nike products. The contrast was all the greater due to the extreme poverty of Nike's factory laborers:

> More than 90 percent of the Nike workers in Vietnam are girls or young women, aged 15 to 28. . . . A meal consisting of rice, a few mouthfuls of a vegetable and maybe some tofu costs the equivalent of 70 cents. Three similarly meager meals a day would cost $2.10. But the workers only make $1.60 a day. And . . . they have other expenses. . . . To stretch the paycheck, something has to be sacrificed. Despite the persistent hunger, it's usually food.[43]

Herbert accused Nike of running the "boot camps" with military efficiency, and only "one bathroom break per eight-hour shift is allowed, and two drinks of water."[44] Herbert labeled this hierarchy a "pyramid of exploitation,"[45] with Nike executives at the top and the company's factory workers at the bottom.

Nike quickly responded to the provocation with a letter from Philip Knight to the *New York Times* defending the company's operations in Asia:

> Nike has been concerned with developing safe and healthy work environments wherever it has worked with contractors in emerging market societies.[46]

Reading this exchange was a consumer, completely unrelated to the issue, Mark Kasky. Under California law, anyone can sue a company for "false and misleading advertising." With the help of a large law firm (Milberg, Weiss, et al.) with a reputation for suing large multinational corporations and collecting large settlement fees,[47] Kasky argued that Nike, using press releases, op-ed articles, letters to the editor, its own Web site, and through other media

> has made false and misleading statements in describing the working conditions in its overseas factories where its athletic shoes are made.[48]

Putting aside the merits of the case, which were never conclusively decided, this case shows the difficulty for a company in trying to shake a negative label. It also shows the potentially significant costs (both financial and in terms of negative publicity) that can result from operations deemed to be less than socially responsible. The initial ruling broadened these consequences to any company conducting business in California. It also had the consequence of forcing many companies to review their public pronouncements on CSR-related issues and remain quiet on some issues of public interest, whereas they might previously have been encouraged to engage in public debate.[49] More worrying for businesses, perhaps, was the extent of the penalty that could have been imposed:

> Kasky seeks a court order requiring Nike to disgorge its California profits attributable to [the contested] statements. Under the California law, truth is not a defense to a charge of business fraud if the challenged statements are misleading in context.[50]

The case symbolizes a growing desire among consumers that large corporations act, both overseas and at home, in ways that are transparent and acceptable in terms of standards applied by consumers in the companies' home market.

From the corporate perspective, however, it also highlights the difficulty for companies that are trying to implement effective CSR policies within their organizations. Many commentators argued that the litigation has already had negative consequences that are detrimental to the general good and public debate of issues of public interest. If the effect of any court decision is to leave companies feeling that it is better to say nothing than defend themselves, and also to pull back from any effort to engage the communities within which they are based and improve corporate practices, then, arguably, the decision has done more harm than good:

> The potential affect of the [California Supreme Court's] ruling is devastating. Nike has shelved any plans to produce social responsibility reports in the near future because any such statement can now be attacked on the basis of being an advert for the company.[51]

In responding to any accusations made against it, any company should be able to answer freely and honestly, to the best of its ability, without having to worry that if what it says is slightly wrong, taken out of context, or misunderstood in some way, that it is going to be prosecuted.

It is also true, however, that the case has opened Nike's eyes to the danger of not ensuring all aspects of its operations are considered responsible. The company is much more sensitive to any potential criticism today, a position that is reflected in day-to-day decisions and policy implementation:

> Because of intense criticism . . . over the past half-decade, companies like Gap, Reebok, and Nike are generally alert to labor issues. Many now monitor factories, and . . . physical working conditions have improved as a result. "After we started working with Nike, we had to change our philosophy," says Philip Lo, the [Yng Hsing tannery in Taiwan's] vice-general manager. "They have strict requests about how you treat safety, health, attitude, environment." Nike is so sensitive to potential criticism that when the company learned of *Fortune's* visit to Yng Hsing, it immediately informed the tannery that unless it passed a hastily arranged inspection, it would be removed from Nike's supplier list.[52]

A press release announcing that the Nike v. Kasky case had been settled amicably was released by Nike on September 12, 2003:

> The two parties mutually agreed that investments designed to strengthen workplace monitoring and factory worker programs are more desirable than prolonged litigation. As part of the settlement, Nike has agreed to make additional workplace-related program investments (augmenting the company's existing expenditures on monitoring, etc.) totaling $1.5 million. Nike's contribution will go to the Washington, D.C. based Fair Labor Association (FLA) for program operations and worker development programs focused on education and economic opportunity.[53]

As a result,

> shares of Nike fell 11 cents, to $55.68, in trading Friday on the New York Stock Exchange.[54]

## Web-Based Examples and Resources

Fair Labor Association, http://www.fairlabor.org/

> The FLA was established as an independent monitoring system that holds its participating companies accountable for the conditions under which their products are produced. To advance fair, decent and humane working conditions, the FLA enforces an industry-wide Workplace Code of Conduct, which is based on the core labor standards of the International Labour Organization (ILO).

International Labor Organization on Fundamental Principles and Rights at Work, http://www.ilo.org/dyn/declaris/DECLARATIONWEB.INDEXPAGE

> Adopted in 1998, the ILO Declaration on Fundamental Principles and Rights at Work is an expression of commitment by governments, employers' and workers' organizations to uphold basic human values—values that are vital to our social and economic lives.

Labour Behind the Label, http://www.labourbehindthelabel.org/

> Labour Behind the Label is a membership organisation which brings together pressure groups, trade unions and individuals in support of garment workers' efforts to improve their working conditions and wages.

Nike, http://www.nikebiz.com

> As small as we feel, the Nike family is a fairly vast enterprise. We operate on six continents. Our suppliers, shippers, retailers and service providers employ close to 1 million people. The diversity inherent in such size is helping Nike evolve its role as a global company. We see a bigger picture today than when we started, one that includes building sustainable business with sound labor practices. We retain the zeal of youth yet act on our responsibilities as a global corporate citizen.

NikeWatch Campaign, http://www.caa.org.au/campaigns/nike/

> Nike promotes sport and healthy living, but the lives of workers who make Nike's shoes and clothes in Asia and Latin America are anything but healthy. They live in extreme poverty and suffer stress and exhaustion from overwork. Oxfam Community Aid Abroad is part of an international campaign to persuade Nike and other transnational corporations to respect workers' basic rights.

Social Accountability International (SAI), http://www.sa-intl.org/

> Social Accountability International (SAI) works to improve workplaces and combat sweatshops through the expansion and further development of the international workplace standard, SA8000, and the associated S8000 verification system.

Sweatshop Watch, http://www.sweatshopwatch.org/

> Sweatshop Watch is a coalition of labor, community, civil rights, immigrant rights, women's, religious & student organizations, and individuals committed to eliminating sweatshop conditions in the global garment industry. We believe that workers should be earning a living wage in a safe and decent working environment and that those who benefit the most from the exploitation of sweatshop workers must be held accountable.

Verité, http://www.verite.org/

> Verité is an independent, nonprofit social auditing and research organization established in 1995. Our mission is to ensure that people worldwide work under safe, fair

and legal working conditions. Where Verité auditors identify exploitation of workers or health and safety violations in the workplace, we develop concrete steps to correct them through a combination of trainings for management and workers, education programs and remediation programs.

Editor's Note: Verité has audited more than 1,000 factories on behalf of large corporations.

## Questions for Discussion and Review

1. Is it fair to make the comparison between the amount Nike pays its factory workers in Vietnam and the salaries of its CEO and the athletes that endorse the company's products?

2. Should Nike's operations abroad be judged by the standards (legal, economic, cultural, and moral) of the country in which it is operating or by the standards of its home market, the United States?

3. Is Nike responsible for conditions in factories it does not own but to whom it merely contracts out work? Is it sufficient for Nike to require the owners of those factories to pledge to uphold certain standards as defined by Nike?

# DIVERSITY—DISCRIMINATION

☑ *CSR Connection:* This issue represents an example of how enlightened and progressive management can produce real economic benefit for the organization.

## Issue

To what extent is diversity an essential element of any organization, enabling it to adequately reflect the society within which it is based?

In business the real impetus of change is, and always will be, the shifting marketplace. That's a force that can't be stopped. The sooner executives come to terms with it, the stronger—and more diverse—their companies will be.[55]

The 2000 Census data revealed that the ethnic makeup of the United States is changing rapidly and that organizations need to adapt their traditional structures and mind-sets to keep up. Existing impediments prevent companies from marketing products effectively to minority segments within the market:

Latinos are now the largest minority in the U.S., making up 13 percent of the overall U.S. population—a 58 percent increase from 1990. As black, Asian, and Pacific Islander populations also experience strong growth rates, whites are steadily heading toward minority status. Already in California, New Mexico, Hawaii and the District of Columbia, the majority of residents are nonwhite. That's also true in 48 of the nation's 100 largest cities.[56]

Smart companies have seen the future—and it isn't lily-white. The Census Bureau predicts that between 2000 and 2020, the number of Hispanics, African-Americans, Asians, and Native Americans in the U.S. will grow by 42 million. In contrast, Caucasians will rise by a mere 10 million.[57]

However, the majority of large organizations in the United States that should be taking a lead on this issue are lagging behind. Even innovative organizations in this respect still have much work to do:

Some companies, like forward-thinking Hewlett-Packard, adopted diversity programs in the '60s and '70s because it was the right thing to do. . . . But for most firms, serving the public interest through aggressive minority hiring has always taken a back seat to serving share-holders. It shows: Minorities made up roughly 29 percent of the U.S. workforce in 2000, but when it came to corporate officials and managers, they represented only about 14 percent.[58]

And the number of annual complaints to the Equal Employment Opportunity Commission shows that the issue of equality of opportunity is still being waged in many companies today:

There were 24,362 complaints of sex discrimination filed with the Equal Employment Opportunity Commission in the 2003 fiscal year. There were another 28,526 complaints of discrimination based on race. There were nearly 1,200 charges against employers for vio-lating the Equal Pay Act.[59]

Although a large percentage of these complaints are rejected due to insufficient evidence, to a firm having to address the complaints, the costs alone are significant.

---

## Case Study: U.S. Masters

Another vital issue surrounding diversity is gen-der equality, an issue that companies are increas-ingly expected to address. The launch of Calvert Women's Principles represents an attempt to intro-duce measurable incentives for companies to go further in this area, with the threat of financial consequences for those deemed to be acting insufficiently:

[In June, 2004] Calvert Group, which manages $10 billion in socially responsible funds, outlined actions that companies should take to promote gender equality. Calvert Women's Principles cov-ers everything from trying to source from female-owned suppliers to health issues. Calvert will use the code in screening investments, as well as in rating the 600-plus companies in its portfolio.[60]

This issue surfaced very prominently in a cam-paign against Augusta National Golf Club (home to the U.S. Masters annual golf tournament) by the National Council of Women's Organizations (NCWO). The campaign is orchestrated by NCWO via a Web site (http://www.augustadiscriminates.org/)

that includes such features as a "Hall of Hypocrisy" and a list of "Corporations that Sanction Sex Discrimination at Augusta National Golf Club:"

The club bars women from membership, while loudly citing tradition and stating flatly that sex discrimination is their right. Augusta Chairman Hootie Johnson has said that sex discrimination does not rise to the level of race discrimination (which ANGC practiced until pressured to open its doors to African American men in 1990).

While ANGC may be within the law in discriminating against women (Augusta's claim has not been tested in court, and clubs making similar arguments have lost their cases), the NCWO believes the club has a moral obligation to open its doors to women. When a club such as Augusta holds a very public event and figuratively invites the world into its living room, and that event is broadcast on the public airwaves, it has by its own choice become a de facto public facility. We believe it has a moral obligation to abide by the standards of the public at large. And the public standards of America as a nation, and of its people, are clearly opposed to discrimination.[61]

The campaign has received much media attention and had some success, forcing many companies to dissociate themselves both with the U.S. Masters golf tournament and with the private actions of their CEOs and directors whom the campaign has highlighted as members of the club. There were also some membership resignations, including that of Thomas Wyman, former executive of CBS, the TV station that owns the rights to air the U.S. Masters on TV every year.

[The NCWO's] strategy poses a dilemma for corporate communications executives. . . . Some privately acknowledge that they are concerned, not only about their company's public image, but also about how employees will react to the idea that they have to attend diversity meetings even as a top executive is being accused of discriminating against women.

"By broadening the focus to include their companies, [Martha Burk, chairwoman of the NCWO has] forced them to defend their memberships to their most important stakeholders,

including investors, employees and customers. . . . Her campaign plays right into current negative perceptions about the guys who sit in the executive suite."[62]

In spite of the strong negative tone of the NCWO's campaign, the organization is responsive to those CEOs and companies that are sympathetic to their message:

American Express Co. Chairman Kenneth Chenault has said that he thinks women should be admitted [to Augusta]. His company was left off the site.[63]

As the start date of the Masters approached, more and more companies became wary of such a sensitive issue that wouldn't die down:

With just five weeks to go . . . normally booked hotels around Augusta, Ga., are still wide open. . . . The list of no-show companies is long: former sponsors Citigroup and Coca-Cola, plus Cadillac, IBM, J.P. Morgan Chase, and Southern Co. Notes [Jeff] Bliss [president of Javelin Group, a sports marketing and hospitality firm] "Consumer-oriented companies have to be very wary. . . . In many cases, the primary purchasers of their products are women."[64]

And, perhaps worst from the point of view of Augusta National Golf Club, the Ku Klux Klan announced its intention to protest at the Masters tournament in support of the golf club's right to exclude female members. It was truly a public relations nightmare, which can be attributed directly to the club's intransigence:

"This equal rights stuff has gotten out of hand," Joseph J. Harper, imperial wizard of the American Knights of the Ku Klux Klan, said Friday. "We're not concerned with whether [Augusta National Golf Club] wants us there or not. We're concerned with their right to choose who they want to choose" as members.[65]

And, of course, the situation plays right into Martha Burk's hands and presents her with a perfect opportunity to further her cause:

"It is not a surprise that the KKK supports Augusta National Golf Club since the club embraces and flaunts discrimination," said Burk. . . . "It must expect the support of a like-minded group."[66]

To date, Augusta has stuck to its position that, as a private club, it has the right to determine the makeup of its membership. There have been financial consequences, too. As a result of the campaign, and in order to prevent the controversy affecting the companies that normally associate themselves with the tournament, the U.S. Masters ran on TV ad-free in 2003 and 2004. In August 2004, the club announced that sponsorship would return to the U.S. Masters in 2005:

> IBM will return as a sponsor, but Citigroup and Coca-Cola have been replaced by SBC Communications and ExxonMobil. . . . The chief executives of SBA and ExxonMobil are members of Augusta National. . . . Augusta gave up what has been variously reported as $7 million to $10 million in advertising revenue in each of the last two Masters, which were broadcast commercial free.[67]

And Martha Burk's campaign continues.[68]

## Web-Based Examples and Resources

Augusta National Golf Club Members List, http://www.usatoday.com/sports/golf/masters/2002–09–27-augusta-list.htm

The Augusta National Golf Club membership list obtained by *USA TODAY* covers a time frame within the last two years. The membership list is fluid and changes as members resign, die or leave the club. *USA TODAY* did not include those identified as former or deceased members.

Calvert Women's Principles, http://www.calvertgroup.com/pdf/womensprinciples.pdf

A Global code of corporate conduct to empower, advance and invest in women worldwide.

National Council of Women's Organizations, http://www.womensorganizations.org/

The National Council of Women's Organizations is a nonpartisan network of more than one hundred women's organizations, which together represent more than 6 million members. Our member organizations. . . . work together to advocate change on many issues of importance to women, including equal employment opportunity, economic equity, media equality, education, job training, women's health and reproductive health, as well as the specific concerns of mid-life and older women, girls and young women, women of color, business and professional women, homemakers and retired women.

http://www.womensorganizations.org/pages.cfm?ID=92

"The Augusta National Golf Club Story: 2003"

U.S. Masters, http://www.masters.org/

"The Official Site of the Masters Tournament."

Women and Work Commission, http://www.womenandequalityunit.gov.uk/index.htm

> The Government has a vision for a modern Britain. A vision of equality and opportunity for all. The Ministers for Women, supported by the Women and Equality Unit, are working to make this vision a reality in Britain and internationally.

## Questions for Discussion and Review

1. What is your position on this issue? Is the controversy worth it for Augusta National? Did the NCWO overstep the line in targeting individual members and the companies they work for as part of its campaign?

2. What dangers do you see for the corporate world failing to promote its employees equally into senior company positions?

3. Why would a global company such as ExxonMobil support Augusta National and the Masters? What should companies do to target more completely all groups within society?

# DIVERSITY—HELPFUL INTENT

☑ *CSR Connection:* This issue reinforces the importance of progressive management that is raised in the Diversity—Discrimination issue.

## Issue

Affirmative action is an important and controversial element of ensuring a diverse organizational membership. In the Bakke case of 1978, which dealt with diversity in higher education, the U.S. Supreme Court said that

> strict racial quotas violate the equal protection clause of the 14th Amendment. But the court did uphold colleges' right to pursue diversity by considering race as one "plus factor" among others.[69]

In spring 2003, the Supreme Court revisited this issue agreeing to hear two similar cases brought against the University of Michigan by two white students who had their applications to the university rejected. The University of Michigan's admissions policy was controversial but had strong support from the business community, which recognizes the benefits that a well-educated, culturally aware, and diverse employee base can bring. The Court eventually decided in favor of allowing the issue of race to be included as a consideration within a university's applications process but decided against allowing quotas or any other tangible preference system to be used as a means of achieving specific targets.

The key advantage to diversity is that it incorporates different perspectives within the product development process as well as provides access to resources that other companies do not have. The extent to which companies are rewarded for recognizing potential within employees, when others see little or none, is a key element of the debate surrounding diversity.

# Case Study: Goodwill Industries

Seventy percent of disabled people in America (50 million people) are unemployed, in spite of the large number of these people who would like to work:

> But the presumption that they will be a burden and the "disincentive of losing health insurance" often prevent them from doing so. . . . Although society expects and rewards an individual's life-long productivity . . . the right to a job is not seen as one of society's obligations."[70]

A social organization company in South Florida that is dedicated to providing meaningful work for the disabled is Goodwill Industries:

> In 2001, Goodwill provided services to 3,064 people with disabilities. About 1,000 were employed most of the year.[71]

The organization gained a lot of publicity during the second Iraq war because one of its major contractors is the U.S. military. The flak jacket of General Tommy Franks, the commander of the U.S.-led war in Iraq, for example, was made by Goodwill workers:

> Goodwill Industries is also a major supplier of camouflage fatigue trousers, military fleece jackets and coveralls. And . . . it is the exclusive maker of internment flags for the armed forces. What makes Goodwill Industries different from most military contractors is that the organization's primary mission is to help people with disabilities learn and develop self-confidence and employable skills. The goal is to place them with local companies.[72]

In addition to their work for the military, Goodwill Industries has the contract to package the *Miami Herald* newspaper. Its employees also provide various cleaning and catering services to two U.S. Coast Guard bases.[73]

Since July 1995, the adverts that come as inserts with the *Miami Herald* and *El Neuvo Herald* have been stuffed for the newspapers by mentally or emotionally disabled staff. These employees work for Goodwill Industries of South Florida, a nonprofit company that "trains, rehabilitates and employs people with disabilities."

The *Herald* is the only major newspaper in the country that contracts Goodwill workers with disabilities to insert the waves of advertising packets that fatten the Sunday sections.[74]

The move has helped reduce costs for the newspaper and also provided a crucial supporting role to an organization doing valuable work in its community. The *Herald* receives a high-quality service from individual workers who appreciate the chance they have been given. The work is repetitive but offers a position on the first rung of the working ladder for many who might otherwise not have been given the opportunity to progress:

> Turnover is high, on purpose. When skills are honed and confidence high, workers are turned loose to find outside jobs. "Our overall goal isn't to keep them here. We want to get them out to the real world," said Lourdes Little, a Goodwill spokeswoman.[75]

Companies are waking up to the potential contribution disabled people offer their businesses, either as employees or consumers:

> According to the Labour Force Survey 2004, nearly one in five people of working age in private households in Britain are disabled. Also, disabled people have a combined spending power of £50 billion. To the advantage of businesses, the costs of taking note of your disabled customers is very low as fewer than 10% of service providers said that it outweighed their benefits.[76]

As a consequence, companies are beginning to tailor policies to ensure that they are maximizing their performance in these areas. The world's first Disability Standard was launched by Britain's Employer's Forum in November 2004 to help firms assess how they measure up:

> The Disability Standard will help organizations accurately measure and assess their performance on disability issues. It will also enable them to identify areas of improvement and put in place action plans to bring in the changes.[77]

## Web-Based Examples and Resources

Center for Individual Rights, http://www.cir-usa.org/

CIR's decade long campaign to end the use of racial preferences in college admissions took an important step forward in June, 2003, when the Supreme Court issued decisions in Gratz v. Bollinger and Grutter v. Bollinger, CIR's twin challenges to racial preferences at the University of Michigan.

Goodwill Industries International Inc., http://www.goodwill.org/

Goodwill Industries International is a network of 207 community-based, autonomous member organizations that serves people with workplace disadvantages and disabilities by providing job training and employment services, as well as job placement opportunities and post-employment support. With locations in the United States, Canada and 23 other countries, we help people overcome barriers to employment and become independent, tax-paying members of their communities.

Goodwill Industries of South Florida, Inc.

2121 Northwest 21st Street

Miami, FL 33142–7317

305–325–9114

University of Michigan press releases and related university links: http://www.umich.edu/news/Releases/2003/Jun03/supremecourt.html

Amicus briefs filed with the U.S. Supreme Court on the University of Michigan's behalf, http://www.umich.edu/~urel/admissions/legal/amicus.html

## Questions for Discussion and Review

1.  Discuss the issues of affirmative action and quotas for groups that have traditionally been discriminated against in society. Are they valid and effective policies? Do they create more problems than they solve? Is there anything wrong with merely applying merit as the sole criterion for university admissions?

2.  Should the government and other public agencies make a point of contracting with organizations such as Goodwill Industries? Should they do so even if it means overlooking another company that might be able to do the job quicker and more cost effectively?

3.  Do we have a right to a job, or is it a privilege that has to be earned?

# ENVIRONMENTAL SUSTAINABILITY

☑ *CSR Connection:* This issue rose to public prominence ahead of the broader issue of CSR and is an important component of the CSR debate.

## Issue

To what extent should companies internalize the environmental costs of operations (e.g., clean up their own pollution) and ensure their consumption of resources is conducted in as sustainable a manner as possible?

The myth is that financial issues are "hard" while social issues are "soft"—meaning: unimportant and irrelevant, because they don't impact investor money. . . . When society forces companies to internalize social costs, via legal or other penalties, social issues *become* financial issues—which is the way to get companies to sit up and take notice.[78]

Reports increasingly suggest that there is a growing financial risk for any corporation not conducting business in what is considered an appropriate manner by contemporary society:

Munich Re, a large German insurance company, estimates that the effects of climate change could cost companies $300 billion annually by 2050 in weather damage, pollution, industrial and agricultural losses. . . . Companies may also face unexpected expenses resulting from future taxes, regulations, fines, and caps on products that produce greenhouse gases.[79]

There is also increasing evidence that there are business and financial benefits to be had by a company operating with sustainable policies:

Anheuser-Busch, the brewing giant that makes Budweiser, said it recycled more than 97 per cent of the solid waste it generated in 2003—more than 5 billion pounds of material. . . . Anheuser-Busch Recycling Corporation is the world's largest aluminum can recycler. The unit celebrated 25 years of operation and recycled more than 750 million pounds of aluminum in 2003. A-B says new technologies allowed it to save 5.1 million pounds of aluminum and 7.5 million pounds of paperboard. . . . A-B was the recipient of the Keep America Beautiful Vision Award in 2003 for its overall environmental leadership.[80]

## Case Study: Ford

In October 2001, William Clay Ford Jr. assumed the CEO position at the car company that bears the name of his great-grandfather. It was a reassuring move for employees, who hadn't had a Ford running the show for many years. It was also reassuring for environmental groups, who had long heralded Bill Ford for his progressive views in what they have traditionally viewed as a dirty manufacturing industry.

In spite of the cost-cutting pressures that are forcing his hand at the company, Bill Ford is finding innovative ways to combine his passionate views on the environment with efficient and cost-effective new ideas. Take, for example, the company's new Model U concept vehicle:

Dubbed "the Model T for the 21st century," the funky-looking utility vehicle boasts biodegradable materials—from the corn-based tires to the seats stuffed with soy-based foam.[81]

Ford, in response to a shareholder resolution filed with the company, acted to issue a report on climate change at the end of 2005:

The report will examine the business implications of greenhouse gas emissions . . . Ford's product and manufacturing facilities actions, and advanced technology development. . . . Ford began publicly sharing its perspective on climate change in 2000 with publication of its first corporate citizenship report. The report . . . has since been cited by external organizations for its candor in addressing business opportunities and challenges.[82]

Ford has also captured headlines and environmentalist hearts with a project known as

the world's largest living roof . . . 10 acres of greenery planted on top of Ford's new $1 billion factory.[83]

Bill Ford hired Bill McDonough, an environmental architect, as chief designer of the project to revamp Ford's River Rouge (Michigan) assembly plant (where Henry Ford first started making the Model T) and convert it into a showcase of environmental ideas and efficiency:

McDonough designed the main assembly building with a natural water-drainage system that saved Ford $35 million. At the old plant rainwater would pick up dangerous toxins used in manufacturing and carry them into the River Rouge. McDonough put a grass roof on the assembly plant and surrounded it with porous parking lots and wetlands. Rainwater now is absorbed by the grass roof, trickles through gravel beds under the parking lots, and drains into the wetlands. By the time it filters through to the river, it is crystal clean. McDonough's system cost $13 million to build; a conventional waste-treatment plant would have cost $48 million.[84]

The "green roof"[85] also acts as an insulator, both in hot and cold weather. It improves local air quality by trapping pollutants, creating oxygen as a by-product. And, as a filtration system sifting out pollutants, the quality of the rainwater run-off from the plant is also improved.[86]

A green roof is a roof substantially covered with vegetation. Since the 1970s, green roofs have increasingly become part of the European landscape, where there are over 100 million square feet of planted roofs today.[87]

Sources differ in the cost savings the designs are estimated to deliver, but all agree that it is the bottom line that makes the project really worthwhile for Ford:

It's costing Ford about $8 a square foot, or $3.6 million, to install the 454,000-square-foot roof. A traditional asphalt roof would cost $4 a square foot, or $1.8 million. But while green roofs might cost twice as much to build, they . . . last twice as long as conventional roofs. This alone roughly offsets the additional investment.[88]

Ford has called McDonough, "one of the most profound environmental thinkers in the world," who believes that, rather than reduce pollution by placing limits on processes and machines already in use, in order to really make a difference environmentally sustainable systems have to be designed from scratch. If done correctly, he believes these new systems should in no way limit the amount of energy used or convenience available. Ford has been able to harness his design concepts in ways that both save the company money and improve the company's standing within the environmental community—a difficult task for a Detroit-based manufacturing company.

## Web-Based Examples and Resources

Eco-Portal–The Environmental Sustainability Info. Source, an information gateway empowering the movement for environmental sustainability, http://www.eco-portal.com/

The Original and Best Environmental Portal Providing Full Text Searches of Reviewed Environmental Internet Content, News, Links & More—Over 3,000 Sites Made Fully Searchable.

Ford—Environmental Initiatives: The Rouge Center, http://www.fordvehicles.com/environmental/greenerplant/index.asp?bhcp=1

The 2004 Ford F-150 is being built under the roof of Ford's Dearborn Truck Plant at the Rouge Center. But something equally exciting is happening on the roof. Growing on the roof are 10.4 acres of plants called sedum. Why? They help to prevent storm water runoff, improve air quality and insulate the building. We've also developed "Fumes-to-Fuel" technology, which uses paint fumes to power fuel cells, producing electricity. And these are just a few of the sustainable features at the Rouge—home of the next F-150.

Friends of the Earth, http://www.foe.org/

Friends of the Earth is the U.S. voice of an influential, international network of grassroots groups in 70 countries. Founded in San Francisco in 1969 by David Brower, Friends of the Earth has for decades been at the forefront of high-profile efforts to create a more healthy, just world.

GreenBiz.com, http://www.greenbiz.com/

The Resource Center on Business, the Environment and the Bottom Line.

Greenpeace, http://www.greenpeace.org/

Greenpeace is an independent, campaigning organisation that uses non-violent, creative confrontation to expose global environmental problems, and force solutions for a green and peaceful future. Greenpeace's goal is to ensure the ability of the Earth to nurture life in all its diversity.

International Standards Organization (ISO)

Environmental Management: The ISO 14000 Family of International Standards, http://www.iso.ch/iso/en/prods-services/otherpubs/iso14000/index.html

The International Organization for Standardization (ISO) is a worldwide federation of national standards bodies from more than 140 countries, one from each country. ISO is a non-governmental organization established in 1947. The mission of ISO is to promote the development of standardization and related activities in the world. . . . ISO's work results in international agreements which are published as International Standards.

SustainAbility, http://www.sustainability.com/

Established in 1987, SustainAbility is the longest running sustainable development consultancy. We focus on how the sustainable development (SD) agenda fits within business strategy in environmental, social and economic terms—"the triple bottom line."

Sustainability Institute, http://sustainer.org/

A think-do tank dedicated to sustainable resource use, sustainable economics, and sustainable community.

UK Sustainable Development Commission, http://www.sd-commission.gov.uk/

The Commission's main role is to advocate sustainable development across all sectors in the UK, review progress towards it, and build consensus on the actions needed if further progress is to be achieved.

World Business Council for Sustainable Development, http://www.wbcsd.ch/

The World Business Council for Sustainable Development (WBCSD) is a coalition of 165 international companies united by a shared commitment to sustainable development via the three pillars of economic growth, ecological balance and social progress.

## Questions for Discussion and Review

1. Go to Ford's Web site introducing the new Rouge plant and the benefits it brings the company (http://www.fordvehicles.com/environmental/greenerplant/index.asp?bhcp=1). Is this just a public relations effort by the company, or is this really a new approach to sustainable business?

2. What is your image of the NGO Greenpeace? Do you trust the organization to provide accurate and objective assessments of the environmental impact of business? Visit the organization's Web site (http://www.greenpeace.org/). Is environmental sustainability given a high enough priority in business, politics, and society today? Why, or why not?

3. Discuss the environmental concern Ford showed in constructing its River Rouge plant. Then contrast it with a discussion around the environmental impact of the F-150 trucks that Ford makes in the plant. Is Ford Motor Company environmentally friendly? Is it a CSR company? Can a company be one without the other?

# FAIR TRADE

☑ **CSR Connection:** This issue reflects the growing support among consumers in developed economies, particularly Europe, for companies that are perceived as having healthy supply chains.

## Issue

To what extent do companies have an interest in purchasing products from suppliers at prices that are "fair"—and therefore ensuring their suppliers' well-being—rather than at a price dictated by the market? Also, what is the extent of the market in the developed economies for products with components that have been purchased in this way?

Products like coffee, tea and chocolate that we in the north have come to depend on, are produced in the warmer climates of the south. The prices paid for these commodities have not risen in real terms over the last forty years, whilst the value of fertilisers, pesticides and machinery (imported from the rich countries) has increased substantially. Consequently many of the people who grow these crops are having to work harder and longer for less money. On top of this the market price of commodities frequently drops below the cost of producing them.[89]

The non-governmental organization [Oxfam] says coffee growers around the world are suffering through a fall in prices of 70 per cent since 1997.[90]

The Fairtrade label first appeared in Europe on coffee packets toward the end of the 1980s.[91] The term can be defined in the following way:

Fair Trade is an alternative approach to conventional international trade. It is a trading partnership which aims at sustainable development for excluded and disadvantaged producers. It seeks to do this by providing better trading conditions, by awareness raising and by campaigning.[92]

The Fairtrade Foundation reports that, currently, "more than 100 coffee, tea, banana, chocolate, cocoa, juice, sugar and honey products carry the Fairtrade Mark." The market for fair trade and other socially responsible products is growing:

Last year, global sales of fair-trade goods—everything from nuts to wine—surpassed $700 million. Strong sales in Europe have caught the attention of U.S. companies, including Starbucks Corp., Procter & Gamble Co. and Dunkin' Donuts, which have all begun offering fair trade coffee.[93]

Green & Black's, a small firm that sells expensive, organic GM-free chocolate, has seen its sales rise five-fold since 1999 to £23.4m in 2003. . . . The "fair trade" segment is another impressive performer. . . . Figures from the Fairtrade Foundation show that Britain ate just over 1,000 tonnes of their chocolate in 2003, up from 82 tonnes in 1998—a 12-fold increase in five years, albeit from a very low base. . . . Most British supermarkets now offer some sort of "fair trade" chocolate.[94]

It is important to remember, however, that the market segment to which such goods appeal is limited. In general,

"Purchasing levels of green and ethically-produced goods are linked to levels of affluence. For the majority of consumers, price overrides ethical considerations as the key factor in their decision-making," the report ['Green and Ethical Consumer'] says.[95]

---

## Case Study: Starbucks

As the statistics above suggest, the issue of fair trade affects many industries in many countries. Fair trade campaigns have focused on coffee to catch the attention of consumers and corporations in the developed world.

As one of the top five coffee buyers in the world,[96] Starbucks' actions have significant influence over the industry as a whole and have been a source of negative publicity for the company in the past. Among other things, the company has been accused of profiting at the expense of others:

While company profits have tripled since 1997, to $181 million in fiscal 2000, many of the world's coffee farmers have been devastated by historically low prices. Coffee is now priced around 50¢ per pound, while production costs are around 80¢ per pound.[97]

Although not totally at fault, Starbucks has made a big effort to improve its image in this area. The company is involved

with various programs aimed at hiking the wages of farmers and improving the local environment. Starbucks recently unveiled guidelines that will pay farmers a premium price if they meet certain environmental, labor, and quality standards. Last year, the company joined TransFair, an organization that guarantees that farmers will receive most of the $1.26 per pound that coffee roasters pay for high-quality beans.[98]

Other aspects of the company's fair trade program can be found at the "Commitment to origins" page of its Web site: http://www.starbucks.com/aboutus/origins.asp. There is still more, however, that activists would like the company to do: Starbucks buys less than 10% of the 1.8 million pounds of fair trade coffee that activists would like it to buy.[99] As such, the brand remains a target for some.

For example, a campaign organized by the Organic Consumers Association has the goal to, among other things, "improve working conditions for coffee plantation workers, and brew and seriously promote Fair Trade coffee in all of their cafes." (http://www.purefood.org/Starbucks/starbucks.html)

The coffee company Green Mountain Coffee is attracting positive attention with its attempts to address this issue. Its progressive approach is one of the main reasons the company ranked number eight in *Business Ethics Magazine's* 2003 list of 100 best corporate citizens:

Today, with suppliers at small farmer cooperatives in Peru, Mexico, and Sumatra, Green Mountain pays Fair Trade prices for coffee beans—not the market price of 24 to 50 cents per pound, but a minimum of $1.26 per pound for conventional coffee and $1.41 for organically grown. In 2002, these Fair Trade purchases represented 8 percent of sales. Green Mountain also has a "farm direct" program that cuts out middlemen to deliver higher prices to farmers. Roughly a quarter of its coffee purchases are farm direct.[100]

The argument against fair trade is the argument in favor of free trade, which proponents believe would have a wider, quicker, and longer lasting impact in favor of farmers worldwide than any artificial designation of what may or may not constitute *fair:*

> What is prudence in the conduct of every family can scarce be folly in that of a great kingdom. If a foreign country can supply us with a commodity cheaper than we ourselves can make it, better buy it of them with some part of the produce of our own industry, employed in a way in which we have some advantage.[101]

> Poor people are poor because they do not participate sufficiently in the world international trading system. They are not poor because they are unjustly treated when they do.[102]

Such commentators argue that developed economies could do much more for farmers in developing countries by dropping all barriers to trade and extensive support provided by governments to domestic producers. Such assistance prevents farmers from the developing world from competing on a level playing field. Action to reduce these market inefficiencies would have a much greater impact than any artificial fair trade market, which is dismissed as a phenomenon created to appease consumer consciences:

> [The Fair Trade movement is] part of a broader movement to make shoppers feel good about themselves and the food they are buying.[103]

Nevertheless, consumers are responding to aspects of the campaign, albeit with different results in different markets:

> The growth of the grass-roots movement, combined with the success of the Fair Trade movement in Europe—where the market for Fair Trade Certified products is three times larger in dollar sales than it is in the U.S.—is now persuading mainstream companies to get on board. . . . [In 2003] about 32% of U.S. consumers qualified as LOHAS [Lifestyle Of Health And Sustainability][104]

Fair trade coffee is the fastest growing sector of the UK coffee market. Retail sales increased 42 per cent between 2002 and 2003.[105]

According to the National Coffee Association (NCA), awareness about fair trade is also growing among U.S. consumers:

> Awareness of fair-trade coffee among U.S. coffee drinkers aged 18 and over has risen to 12% [in 2004] up from 7% in 2003 and purchases among those aware have risen to 45% from 38%.[106]

Starbucks, among other companies,[107] appears to feel that this is an area in which it can improve both its operations and its image among consumers that care about fair trade issues:

> [Starbucks CEO] Orin Smith says that currently 10% of Starbucks' coffee is "socially responsible." By 2007, the company says 60% of its coffee will come from farms following strict guidelines on environmental and labour practices.[108]

Starbucks has committed to working closely with suppliers, helping them convert to sustainable practices and offering them long-term contracts as an incentive to do so. This approach helps the company meet the needs of the fair trade industry, as well as increase the quality of the product they buy and then resell.

In February 2004, Starbucks launched the Coffee Agronomy Company. It is based in Costa Rica and positioned as "the flagship vehicle for Starbucks' sustainable supply chain commitment." In March 2004, the company's Coffee and Farmer Equity (CAFE) Practices guidelines were launched, which "spell out Starbucks' expectations for its suppliers on economic, social and environmental issues."[109] Starbucks developed CAFE in conjunction with the environmental charity Conservation International. The goal for suppliers in conforming to the guidelines (Starbucks wants the majority of suppliers compliant within 5 years) is to be certified as a Starbucks' preferred supplier:

> The preferred supplier status carries the promise of preferential, long-term contracts and a price

premium. The premium stood at an average of $1.20 per pound of "green" (export-ready) coffee in 2002—a time when the prices farmers were getting from the commodity markets fell to historic lows of $0.40–$0.50. The best performing suppliers . . . are eligible for an additional $0.10 premium.[110]

This relationship between Conservation International and Starbucks was expanded further in September 2004 as the two organizations partnered with the U.S. Agency for International Development (USAID) to form the Conservation Coffee Alliance. The goal is to

promote private sector approaches that are environmentally sensitive, socially responsible and economically viable.[111]

The business case for fair trade, at least as far as Starbucks is concerned, is convincing:

Sure, by creating a healthier supply chain, [Starbucks] might end up helping some of [their] competitors. . . . But in the end, it helps the industry. And a healthier industry is better for us, better for the consumer, for the environment, for everyone.[112]

These results have been repeated elsewhere, particularly in Europe, where growth in this area is stronger. In September 2004, Marks & Spencer, the well-known UK retailer, announced it would source all of the coffee it serves in its coffee shops from fair trade sources. The move doubled the amount of fair trade coffee on sale in UK coffee shops. Significantly, it announced it would do this without raising prices. The Co-operative Group has also been a strong example of the bottom-line benefits of fair trade goods:

Since making all their own brands of coffee and chocolate Fairtrade they have seen sales soar. Chocolate sales volumes were up 24% in the 12 months following conversion to Fairtrade and a further 46% in the first half of [2004]. In both periods, sales of other more established brands have stayed static.[113]

## Web-Based Examples and Resources

Common Code for the Coffee Community, http://www.sustainable-coffee.net/

The Common Code for the Coffee Community is a joint initiative of coffee producers, trade & industry, trade unions and social as well as environmental NGOs to develop a global code of conduct aiming at social, environmental and economic sustainability in the production, post-harvest processing and trading of mainstream green coffee.

Conservation International, http://www.conservation.org/

Conservation International's (CI) mission is to conserve the Earth's living natural heritage, our global biodiversity, and to demonstrate that human societies are able to live harmoniously with nature.

Consortium of Coffee Cooperatives of Guanacaste and Montes de Oro in Costa Rica (COOCAFE), http://www.coocafe.com/

Ethical Trading Initiative (ETI), http://www.ethicaltrade.org/

The ETI is an alliance of companies, non-governmental organisations (NGOs), and trade union organisations committed to working together to identify and promote ethical trade—good practice in the implementation of a code of conduct for good labor standards, including the monitoring and independent verification of the observance of ethics code provisions, as standards for ethical sourcing. Members, including multinational companies (multinational corporations) or transnational companies (transnational corporations), are committed to business ethics and corporate responsibility, promotion of worker rights and human rights in general. In employment, ethical business includes working towards the ending of child labor, forced labor, and sweatshops, looking at health and safety, labor conditions and labor rights.

Fairtrade Foundation, http://www.fairtrade.org.uk/

The Fairtrade Foundation exists to ensure a better deal for marginalised and disadvantaged third world producers. Set up by CAFOD, Christian Aid, New Consumer, Oxfam, Traidcraft and the World Development Movement, the Foundation awards a consumer label, the Fairtrade Mark, to products which meet internationally recognised standards of fair trade.

Fair Trade Labeling Organizations International (FLO), http://www.fairtrade.net/

FLO is the worldwide Fairtrade Standard setting and Certification organisation. It permits more than 800,000 producers, workers and their dependants in more than 45 countries to benefit from labelled Fairtrade. FLO guarantees that products sold anywhere in the world with a Fairtrade label marketed by a National Initiative conforms to Fairtrade Standards and contributes to the development of disadvantaged producers.

Global Exchange—Fair Trade, http://www.globalexchange.org/campaigns/fairtrade/

In today's world economy, where profits rule and small-scale producers are left out of the bargaining process, farmers, craft producers, and other workers are often left without resources or hope for their future. Fair Trade helps exploited producers escape from this cycle and gives them a way to maintain their traditional lifestyles with dignity. Fair Trade encompasses a range of goods, from agricultural products from the global South like coffee, chocolate, tea, and bananas, to handcrafts like clothing, household items, and decorative arts. Our Fair Trade campaigns and stores offer a variety of ways for you to support this growing movement for social justice!

National Coffee Association (NCA), http://www.ncausa.org/

The National Coffee Association of USA was founded in 1911, one of the earliest trade associations formed in the United States and the first trade association for the U.S. coffee industry.

Organic Consumers Association, http://www.purefood.org/

The Organic Consumers Association is a public interest organization dedicated to building a healthy, safe, and sustainable system of food production and consumption. We are a global clearinghouse for information and grassroots technical assistance.

Trade Justice, http://www.tjm.org.uk/

The Trade Justice Movement is a fast growing coalition of organisations campaigning for fundamental change to the unjust rules and institutions governing international trade.

TransFair USA, http://www.transfairusa.org/

TransFair USA is a nonprofit monitoring organization which certifies that participating traders are following fair trade guidelines.

U.S. Fair Labor Association, http://www.fairlabor.org/

The Fair Labor Association (FLA) is a nonprofit organization combining the efforts of industry, non-governmental organizations (NGOs), colleges and universities to promote adherence to international labor standards and improve working conditions worldwide. The FLA was established as an independent monitoring system that holds its participating companies accountable for the conditions under which their products are produced. To advance fair, decent and humane working conditions, the FLA enforces an industry-wide Workplace Code of Conduct, which is based on the core labor standards of the International Labour Organization (ILO).

## Questions for Discussion and Review

1. Do you believe in *fair trade*? Why, or why not? What does *fair* mean?

2. Did you know about Starbucks involvement in this issue and the Fairtrade products the company sells? Do you think this is something the company should publicize?

3. Why do you think it is that fair trade seems to be more popular in Europe than in the United States?

# FINANCE

☑ *CSR Connection:* This issue reflects the increasing pressure being placed on financial institutions by NGOs to ensure money used to finance projects, particularly in developing economies, is not used to support socially irresponsible organizations (including governments).

## Issue

To what extent do financial institutions, whose financing is necessary to fund projects and operations in countries around the world, share responsibility for the use to which their funds are being put?

[In 2004] the website of Friends of the Earth UK invites activists to submit pro forma emails to the Chairman of both HSBC and the Royal Bank of Scotland to dissuade the banks from financing the Baku-Tbilisi-Ceyhan pipeline because of environmental concerns about the project. . . . For all this, however, private sector banking institutions have not received the sustained and broad-based scrutiny experienced by their clients, or by the international finance institutions (IFIs) and export credit agencies (ECAs) that lend in parallel to major projects.[114]

The banks ABN AMRO and Citigroup, in consultation with NGOs, are noted as taking a prominent role in developing progressive policies in this area.

## Case Study: Citigroup

One of our foremost goals, wherever Citigroup has a presence, is to make the community better because we are there. As a global institution with a presence in 100 countries, that responsibility extends throughout the world and includes appropriate sensitivity to sustainable development and environmental impacts.

—Sandy Weill (Memo to Citigroup employees, June 4, 2003)[115]

In 2000, Citigroup became the target of the latest campaign by the effective NGO Rainforest Action Network (RAN). RAN has been accused of using extreme measures to pursue a fringe agenda, largely focusing on environmental issues. "Others have accused the group of coercion, blackmail, even terrorism."[116] However, although their tactics may be controversial, what is not in doubt is that they have been extremely successful in forcing policy changes within some of the largest corporations in the United States:

This green coalition has in recent years persuaded dozens of companies, including Home Depot, Lowe's, Staples, Office Depot, and homebuilders Centex and Kaufman & Broad, to alter their conduct to protect forests, their species, and the people who live in them.[117]

In 2000, RAN began targeting Citigroup in an effort to stop the bank from lending money to finance projects that they believed involved harm to the environment and the indigenous people living in the vicinity of those projects.

In response to the bank ignoring their request, RAN slowly ratcheted up its campaign against Citigroup. Its tactics included protests at branches, high-profile media stunts, TV advertising, and personal hounding of Weill, both on bank business and on vacation. Citigroup's tarnished image in the wake of the corporate scandals around the turn of the century only encouraged RAN to turn up the heat another notch.

The campaign eventually forced Citigroup to the negotiating table, where the company agreed to a wide review of its polices toward lending in the areas RAN had highlighted. The review resulted in the publication of industry-leading standards in terms of Citigroup's lending and investment policies, as well as related environmental issues such as the company's recognition of the problem of global warming. The bank, in conjunction with RAN, did not stop there:

Shortly after RAN and Citi declared their ceasefire, ten global banks, including Citi, adopted the Equator Principles, a voluntary set of guidelines they developed to manage the social and environmental impact of capital projects that cost $50 million or more in the developing world. Citi's more recent environmental policy goes further.[118]

Details defining the Equator Principles, the goals of the pact, and means to achieve these goals are introduced by the Web site http://www.equator-principles.com/:

> The Equator Principles are a framework for financial institutions to manage environmental and social issues in project financing. . . . [The Principles represent] an industry approach for financial institutions in determining, assessing and managing environmental and social risk in project financing.[119]

The bank describes its involvement with the Equator Principles on the company's Web site:

> On June 4, 2003, Citigroup joined nine other banks from around the world to adopt the "Equator Principles," a voluntary set of guidelines developed by the banks for managing social and environmental issues related to the financing of development projects in all industries, including mining, oil and gas, and forestry. The Equator Principles are based on the policies and guidelines of the World Bank and International Finance Corporation (the private-sector investment arm of the World Bank), which provided extensive advice and guidance in drafting the new project finance principles for the banks.[120]

Many see the Equator Principles as providing the platform for developing international standards that can be used by all lending institutions to ensure all are operating on a level playing field; however, there are others that doubt the potential for real and lasting change. According to a 2004 report that aimed to establish the effectiveness of the Equator Principles 1 year after implementation, there is a large degree of uncertainty as to the effectiveness of the initiative:

> According to a report by BankTrack, the Equator Principles are having little impact. . . . "Many controversial projects have gone ahead virtually unaltered by the existence of the Principles . . ." said Michelle Chan-Fishel of BankTrack/Friends of the Earth U.S. . . . "If the Equator banks continue to finance controversial deals, pursue an anti-environmental lobbying agenda and cloak themselves in secrecy and unaccountability, public confidence will be irretrievably lost."[121]

Others worry about the extent of the impact activist groups such as RAN will have on companies unable to fight back because of successive years of corporate scandals and declining public trust:

> Over time, politicization of bank lending hurts not only the banks, but also the future of the economy. . . . Denying loans for oil drilling and timber cutting will hurt poor nations desperately trying to pull themselves out of poverty.[122]

## Web-Based Examples and Resources

ABN AMRO, http://www.abnamro.com/com/ir/ethics.jsp

> The standards of ethical conduct ABN AMRO expects from its employees are found within our Business Principles (http://www.abnamro.com/com/about/bp.jsp) . . . that build on our Corporate Values (http://www.abnamro.com/com/about/corp_values.jsp) by further clarifying what we stand for. They are the result of intensive discussions with management, employees and external audiences and are meant to act as a compass for individual and collective behaviour within ABN AMRO. . . . The Business Principles are being embedded in key organisational processes such as appraisal and promotion procedures, as well as performance contracts. They are also a guidance tool for our contribution to developing new standards on social and environmental issues, such as the Equator Principles.

BankTrack, http://www.banktrack.org/

> What is BankTrack? A new network of civil society organisations, established in September 2003, tracking the operations of the private financial sector and its effect on people and the environment.

BankTrack Report, "Principles, Profits, or Just PR? Triple P Investments Under the Equator Principles," http://www.banktrack.org/index.php?id=112

> One year after the launch of the Equator Principles (EP), a bank-led initiative to establish common environmental and social standards for project finance, NGOs have released an assessment on the implementation and effectiveness of the Principles so far.

Citigroup Corporate Citizenship, http://www.citigroup.com/citigroup/citizen/index.htm

> Citigroup has long been committed to making the communities in which it operates better, and at the same time, setting standards for business practices and corporate values that exceed industry norms.

Collevecchio Declaration on Financial Intuitions and Sustainability, http://www.foe.org/camps/intl/declaration.html

> In January 2003 a group of eight NGOs drafted the Collevecchio Declaration on Financial Institutions and Sustainability. This declaration, subsequently endorsed by over 100 civil society groups, sets out the commitments into which, the groups argues, banks should enter on issues including sustainability, doing no harm, responsibility, accountability, transparency, and sustainable markets and governance.[123]

Equator Principles, http://www.equator-principles.com/

> The Equator Principles are a framework for financial institutions to manage environmental and social issues in project financing.
>
> An industry approach for financial institutions in determining, assessing and managing environmental and social risk in project financing.

Friends of the Earth UK, http://www.foe.co.uk/campaigns/corporates/press_for_change/email_btc_banks/index.html

> Campaign to "Stop British banks from financing the Baku-Ceyhan pipeline."

Home Depot's "Corporate Responsibility" homepage, including a very detailed explanation of the company's environmental policies—"Environmental Responsibility," http://www.homedepot.com/HDUS/EN_US/corporate/corp_respon/corp_respon.shtml

> We sell less than 1 percent of all trees cut worldwide, yet the company is the largest supplier of certified wood on the planet.

International Finance Corporation, http://equatorprinciples.ifc.org/ifcext/equatorprinciples .nsf

> The International Finance Corporation (IFC) promotes sustainable private sector investment in developing countries as a way to reduce poverty and improve people's lives. IFC is a

member of the World Bank Group and is headquartered in Washington, DC. It shares the primary objective of all World Bank Group institutions: to improve the quality of the lives of people in its developing member countries. Established in 1956, IFC is the largest multilateral source of loan and equity financing for private sector projects in the developing world.

Rainforest Action Network (RAN), http://www.ran.org/

Since it was founded in 1985, the Rainforest Action Network has been working to protect tropical rainforests and the human rights of those living in and around those forests.

## Questions for Discussion and Review

1. From a CSR perspective, what is your impression of Citigroup? Should it share responsibility for the way its funds are used?

2. From the same CSR perspective, what is your impression of RAN? What do you think of the organization's tactics to bring about changes that it thinks are correct?

3. Go to the Equator Principles Web site. Is it naive to expect huge financial organizations to aspire and adhere to the values and principles contained within the document? Why or why not?

# INVESTING

☑ *CSR Connection:* This issue is a growing, if controversial, area within CSR. To what extent are investors willing to discriminate among companies and sacrifice short-term returns in order to pursue socially responsible investing strategies?

## Issue

To what extent are stock investors limiting their investments to companies deemed to be operating in an ethical and socially responsible manner? Such investments are often referred to as socially responsible investment (SRI) funds.

Related to this issue is the question of whether SRI funds are any more or less successful than regular investment funds? Critics claim SRI funds are ineffective and that ethical or virtuous stocks do not outperform so-called sin stocks. Those who support SRI funds, however, are beginning to find hope in numbers that appear to support their case. In the aftermath of the corporate scandals that occurred following the tech boom,

While investors pulled $10.5 billion out of U.S. diversified equity funds, they added $1.5 billion to socially responsible mutual funds.[124]

According to Lipper, a Reuters-owned firm that tracks 80,000 mutual funds worldwide, [investment firms tainted by the corporate scandals] from September to December 2003 experienced net outflows of a massive $43 billion. In those same four months, SRI equity funds saw net inflows of $1.1 billion.[125]

# Case Study: SRI Funds

Although still a relatively small fraction of total investments, the assets invested in SRI funds are growing rapidly, as are mutual funds claiming to be socially or environmentally responsible:

> Assets of so-called socially responsible funds grew five times faster than those of other mutual funds in the past three decades. . . . Socially and environmentally responsible mutual fund assets had reached a record $103 billion by mid-2001, up from $150 million in 1971—a growth rate of more than 68 times. The assets of all other mutual funds have grown by an average of about 13.5 times. . . . In 1971, Pax World had the category to itself. But today, there are 192 such funds, representing an increase of 9,500 percent. . . . This compares with a 4,074 percent increase for all other funds.[126]

Other figures support this sentiment that SRI funds are growing in number, size, and influence:

> [There are] 200 socially responsible mutual funds now offered in the U.S., a 44 percent increase over the past six years.[127]

> SRI funds . . . are on the rise, according to fund tracker Lipper Inc. Assets in SRI funds have increased 74 percent over the last five years, while assets in non-SRI funds have grown only 36 percent. At the end of November, Lipper tracked 169 SRI funds (up from just 22 10 years ago) with nearly every asset class, from global stock to municipal bond to index funds, represented.[128]

> A 2004 study by the Social Investment Forum . . . found that over 2.16 trillion USD was invested using "some combination of non-financial screening, shareholder advocacy, or community investment, accounting for one out of every nine professionally invested dollars in the U.S."[129]

It is questionable, however, how good a measure of social responsibility these funds really are. It is also debatable whether they have any impact in terms of encouraging more socially responsible behavior in corporations. Jon Entine, joint author of "Case-Studies in Business Ethics," believes that

there is not one iota of data that supports the idea that investing in these companies makes the world a better place.[130]

What about the returns of these funds? Some suggest an emphasis on technology stocks, during the Internet boom at the end of the last century, was the greatest contributor the growth of socially responsible funds.[131]

Other analysts have begun leading a backlash against ethical or environmental investment funds. As one consequence of this, sin funds have been developed (focusing on companies such as tobacco, alcohol, defense, and oil extraction companies) that aim to improve returns to investors:

> [Mutuals.com's] new Vice Fund went on sale to the public in September, advertising itself as a "socially irresponsible fund" that will invest clients' assets in tobacco, gambling, liquor, in addition to defence. . . . According to the fund's prospectus, only tobacco stocks underperformed the Standard & Poor's 500 index over the last five years. The largest gainer was alcoholic-beverage stocks. They gained 62.57% over the five years, compared with an 11.8% gain for the S&P 500.[132]

At present, Vice Funds is more of a marketing gimmick than a serious attempt to rival the reach and impact of SRI funds.[133] Nevertheless, although initially disappointing, results have been improving with time:

> So far [in 2003], Vice Funds [from Mutuals .com] has returned 17.2% to investors, beating both the S&P 500 (15.2%) and the Dow Jones industrial average (13.2%) by a few points. In fact, all four vice-ridden sectors [alcohol, arms, gambling and tobacco] have outperformed the overall American market during the past five years.[134]

More objective research suggests that, at the very least, there is no disadvantage to investing in SRIs:

> Researchers at Maastricht University in the Netherlands recently found that, in the long

run, there's no statistical difference in performance between SRI and non-SRI funds in the U.S. or abroad.[135]

Some analysts, however, suggest that the over-reliance on technology and communications stocks will hurt the long-term performance of SRI funds.[136] Interestingly, as this phenomenon evolves further, the thrust of SRIs may well be getting more strict rather than less:

[Sierra Club] is the first national environmental body to put its name on funds: the 'Sierra Club Stock Fund' and 'Sierra Club Balanced Fund' (http://www.sierraclubfunds.com/). Carl Pope, the San Francisco group's executive director, figures the investment guidelines are so strict that only a third of the companies in the Standard & Poor's 500-stock index will pass muster. Oil and lumber companies that could harm, among other things, endangered species, are taboo. The Sierra Club must approve all investments.[137]

Critics would no doubt point out that the smaller the degree of portfolio diversity, the greater the risk associated with the investment.

## Web-Based Examples and Resources

Calvert Social Investment Fund, http://www.calvertgroup.com/sri.html

> Calvert has been a leader in the Socially Responsible Investing field for nearly two decades. Its growth offers a glimpse of where SRI is today and where it is headed.

The Domini 400 Social Index (KLD Research & Analytics, Inc.), http://www.kld.com/benchmarks/dsi.html

> The Domini 400 Social Index (DSI) is the established benchmark for measuring the impact of social screening on financial performance. Launched in May 1990, the DSI is the first benchmark for equity portfolios subject to multiple social screens.

Dow Jones Sustainability Indexes, http://www.sustainability-index.com/

> The Dow Jones Sustainability Indexes are focused on meeting the financial market's demands for:
>
> - Rational, consistent, flexible and, most important, investable indexes to benchmark the performance of investments in sustainability companies and funds.
> - Independent reliable indexes as a basis for derivatives and funds focused on sustainability companies.

Ethical Investment Research Service, http://www.eiris.org/

> EIRIS is a leading European provider of independent research into the social, environmental and ethical performance of companies. EIRIS, a UK based organisation, and its eight international research partners together have a wealth of experience in the field of ethical investment research. EIRIS is the market leader in the UK with over 75% of UK ethical funds managed by our clients.

FTSE 4 Good, http://www.ftse4good.com/

FTSE4Good is an index series for socially responsible investment designed by FTSE, one of the world's leading global index providers. FTSE4Good is a series of benchmark and tradable indices facilitating investment in companies with good records of corporate social responsibility.

Mutuals.com—Vice Fund, http://www.vicefund.com/ (Vice Fund Prospectus, July 31, 2003, page 1, column 2)

It is our philosophy that although often considered politically incorrect, these and similar industries and products . . . will continue to experience significant capital appreciation during good and bad markets. We consider these industries to be nearly "recession-proof."

New Alternatives Fund, http://www.newalternativesfund.com/

We are a socially responsible Mutual fund concentrating our investments in:

- Environmental Investment; Renewable Energy
- Fuel Cells
- Recycling and Energy Conservation
- Organic Foods

Pax World Funds (http://www.paxworld.com/) ("oversees the oldest, and among the largest, socially responsible funds.")[138]

We were the first Environmental fund, founded in 1982.

The Pax World Funds seeks to enable persons of conscience to invest in keeping with their ethical values and to challenge corporations to establish and meet certain ethical standards.

Pro-Conscience Funds, Inc. (owner of the Women's Equity Mutual Fund), http://www.womens-equity.com/

The Women's Equity Mutual Fund (symbol: FEMMX) invests in public companies that advance the social and economic status of women in the workplace.

Sierra Club Mutual Funds, http://www.sierraclubfunds.com/

The Sierra Club (http://www.sierraclub.org/) is the largest and oldest environmental activism organization in the United States, and has over 700,000 active members. Its mission statement:

- Explore, enjoy and protect the wild places of the earth.
- Practice and promote the responsible use of the earth's ecosystems and resources.
- Educate and enlist humanity to protect and restore the quality of the natural and human environment.
- Use all lawful means to carry out these objectives.

SocialFunds.com, http://www.socialfunds.com/

SocialFunds.com features over 10,000 pages of information on Socially Responsible Investing (SRI) mutual funds, community investments, corporate research, shareowner actions, and daily social investment news.

Social Responsibility Investment Group, http://www.sriworld.com/

SRI World Group Inc. is a leading provider of social investing and corporate social responsibility information. We pride ourselves at being independent and objective sources of information that empower individuals and institutions.

Trillium Asset Management, http://www.trilliuminvest.com/

For over twenty years, Trillium Asset Management Corporation has been the leader in socially responsible investing. We are guided by a belief that active investing can offer good returns to the investor, while also promoting social and economic justice.

*SRI books.*

Ahrens, Dan, *Investing in Vice: The Recession-Proof Portfolio of Booze, Bets, Bombs, and Butts,* St. Martin's Press, 2004.

Camejo, Peter (Ed.) et al., *The SRI Advantage: Why Socially Responsible Investing Has Outperformed Financially,* New Society, 2002.

Waxler, Caroline, *Stocking Up on Sin: How to Crush the Market With Vice-Based Investing,* John Wiley & Sons, 2004.

## Questions for Discussion and Review

1.  When considering an investment in a mutual fund, would you consider the social responsibility of the companies in which the fund invested? What about SRI funds? Why, or why not?

2.  Would you think twice about investing in a sin fund if historical returns showed greater growth potential than SRI funds?

3.  Choose any one of the social investment fund companies listed in the *Web-Based Examples and Resources* subsection. What is your opinion of their home page and their stated mission and values? Are they a force for good, or are they merely lulling gullible investors into a false sense of security by allowing them to think they are investing with a conscience?

# LOANS

☑ *CSR Connection:* This issue reinforces the idea that finance and personal loans on a smaller scale can act as a force for encouraging socially positive outcomes.

# Issue

One of the biggest barriers to development in any area of the world is access to finance. This barrier is even greater in developing economies and in poorer communities in the developed world. Why is this so? Are poorer people more of a credit risk? Does the bureaucracy involved in administering loans for smaller amounts offer lower and less attractive margins for the lenders? Is there a business case and a market for companies willing to loan in smaller amounts to more-difficult-to-reach customers and markets around the world?

## Case Study: Microloans

Microlending, or microcredit, is being used to help foster capitalist activity within the poorer regions of the world. The healthier an economy becomes, the greater the likelihood of loan repayments and need for future loans. Microloans, usually defined as beginning at $50, have had a huge impact in those parts of the developing world where they have taken off:

> The movement began [in the 1970s] with Muhammad Yunus, founder and managing director of Grameen Bank in Bangladesh, which so far has provided $5 billion in loans to four million people. . . . [In total] more than 500 microfinance institutions around the world have loaned $7 billion to about 30 million small-business people.[139]

Hundreds of thousands of enterprises started with microloans have helped generate 5%-a-year economic growth for the past decade.[140]

The aim behind micro-loans is to "foster sustainable economic activity at the grassroots":

> In Uganda . . . 245,000 families have borrowed from village banks run by international and local agencies. The money has been used to start everything from rabbit farms to grocery stores. Microlenders "are reaching more people than Uganda's entire commercial banking sector." . . . A bank started by FINCA [Foundation for International Community Assistance, which runs a global network of microcredit banks] . . . has 36,000 clients borrowing an average of $137—and boasts an 11% return on equity.[141]

In an attempt to raise the profile of microcredit and encourage greater provision of this service to the poorer regions of the world, the United Nations has declared 2005 to be the International Year of Microcredit.[142] The main barrier to a more rapid expansion of microfinance, however, is the high interest rates associated with such loans. These are caused by the lack of financers competing to make loans available to poorer clients and also by the high transaction costs associated with making many smaller loans.

Nevertheless, in spite of high interest rates, companies have found that microloans have some of the highest repayment rates. An Accion[143] ad states,

> Last year, we gave $800 million to the poor. 97% of them gave it right back. . . . In the last 25 years, ACCION has changed millions of lives . . . by lending over $4.6 million to the poor—97% of which has been repaid.
>
> Returns to [microfinance institutions] rival those of commercial banks. Studies conducted in India, Kenya and the Philippines found that the average annual return on investments by microbusinesses ranged from 117% to 847%, according to the United Nations.[144]

This empirical experience demonstrating the attractiveness of the microcredit business model is supported by other companies working in the field. An article on Socialfunds.com's Web site by William Baue, "Community Investing Pays," (http://www.socialfunds.com/news/article.cgi/article945.html) outlines in detail the benefits of another form of loans to atypical finance customers: community investing. Similar to microloans, community investing seeks to advance capital to poorer areas of the developed world:

> Unlike speculative investments in the stock market—where your money may never actually reach companies—community investing puts investing dollars directly to work in ways that help the disadvantaged.[145]

In the United States, the community investment industry is

a thriving and growing field with overall assets of . . . $7.6 billion. The Social Investment

Forum (SIF) reports that between 1999 and 2001, community investing assets grew 40 percent—in part because of the One Percent in Community campaign by SIF, which encourages all social investors to put 1 percent of their assets in community investments.[146]

Examples of community investing in action:

> Community-based financial institutions have helped low-wage workers in North Carolina purchase homes, have assisted battered women in Texas in opening a shelter, and have renovated a crime-ridden neighborhood in Kentucky.[147]

## Web-Based Examples and Resources

1% in Community Campaign, http://www.communityinvest.org/investors/campaign.cfm

> The Social Investment Forum Foundation and Co-op America have launched a campaign to encourage people across the country to put their banking and investment dollars to work strengthening communities that have been left behind. The goal of the 1% in Community campaign is to triple the $5 billion already involved in community investing as of 2000.

Accion International, http://www.accion.org/

> ACCION International is a nonprofit that fights poverty through microlending. Every day, millions of enterprising women and men around the world struggle to better their lives by opening tiny businesses. They work exhausting hours yet they barely scrape by. What they need to break free is a little credit—a loan as small as $100. With ACCION, they can get it.
>
> In the last 25 years, ACCION has changed millions of lives . . . by lending over $4.6 billion to the poor—97% of which has been repaid.

Association for Enterprise Opportunity, http://www.microenterpriseworks.org/

> AEO was founded in 1991 and remains the only national member-based association dedicated to microenterprise development.

Communityinvest.org, http://www.communityinvest.org/

> Community investing helps create resources and opportunities for economically disadvantaged people in the U.S. and overseas who are underserved by traditional financial institutions.

Digital Dividend (World Resources Institute)

http://www.digitaldividend.org/

Our goal is to identify and promote business solutions to the global digital divide—sustainable models that will allow information and communications technologies (ICTs)-for-development to "go global," creating social and economic dividends in poor communities around the world.

FINCA, http://www.villagebanking.org/

FINCA provides financial services to the world's poorest families so they can create their own jobs, raise household incomes, and improve their standard of living. We deliver these services through a global network of locally managed, self-supporting institutions.

Journal of Microfinance, http://www.microjournal.com/

The *Journal of Microfinance* is an exciting forum for the sharing of ideas and information pertaining to the practice of microfinance and microenterprise development. The *Journal's* purpose is to influence practice by focusing on experiences and lessons learned from the field.

Microfinance Network, http://www.bellanet.org/partners/mfn/

The MicroFinance Network (MFN) is a global association of leading microfinance practitioners. The members of the Network are committed to improving the lives of low-income people through the provision of credit, savings and other financial services. While the members serve their clients using many different methodologies, they believe in employing commercial principles to achieve sustainable and profitable financial institutions. Such institutions can reach a large number of clients who would otherwise not have access to affordable financial services.

Microfinace Gateway, http://www.microfinancegateway.org/

The Microfinance Gateway is a public forum for the microfinance industry at large that offers a wealth of tailored services for microfinance professionals, including resource centers on specific topics in microfinance, a searchable library of electronic documents, a consultant database, a jobs listing service, and specialized discussion groups. The Gateway's resources constitute the most comprehensive source of information on microfinance on the World Wide Web, featuring 2,500 online documents, over 500 listings of microfinance institutions (MFIs) and nearly 200 consultant curricula vitae.

Socialfunds.com, http://www.socialfunds.com/

SocialFunds.com features over 10,000 pages of information on SRI mutual funds, community investments, corporate research, shareowner actions, and daily social investment news.

William Baue, "Community Investing Pays," October 10, 2002. http://www.socialfunds.com/news/article.cgi/article945.html

Women's World Banking Network, http://www.swwb.org/

The Women's World Banking network aims to have a major impact on expanding the economic assets, participation and power of low income women as entrepreneurs and economic agents by opening their access to finance, knowledge and markets.

## Questions for Discussion and Review

1. Why do you think more companies are not involved in either microloans or community investing? Are these valid reasons?

2. Visit the Accion International Web site at http://www.accion.org/. What are your impressions and thoughts regarding the work the organization is doing?

3. Have a look at the article "Community Investing Pays" on the Socialfunds.com Web site (http://www.socialfunds.com/news/article.cgi/article945.html). Does the author make a convincing case that low-income borrowers represent a lower default risk than conventional borrowers? What do you think about the CDFI Fund, establish in 1994?

# NGO AND CORPORATE COOPERATION

> ☑ *CSR Connection:* This issue forms an important element of the CSR debate. There is a strategic advantage for companies and NGOs that maintain open lines of communication.

## Issue

Increasingly, corporations around the world are seeing an opportunity to work in partnership with nongovernmental organizations (NGOs) that previously might have been campaigning against the company or its products. Perceptions of CSR stimulate consumer and other stakeholder reactions that can either advance or hold back an organization's ability to succeed. Corporations have sought to create favorable relations with NGOs as the strategic value of such relationships has become increasingly apparent:

Corporations provided more than $9 billion in gifts to nonprofit organizations and charities in 2001. Corporate sponsors spent more than $700 million in the previous year to sponsor nonprofit organizations and social causes. By 1998, businesses had paid more than $535 million to license the name or logo of nonprofit organizations for advertising and marketing. An increasing number of executives now point to collaborations with NPOs as an important component of their corporate social responsibility strategies.[148]

Getting the seal of approval from a highly visible NGO can be an effective selling point for a company trying to differentiate its products and help it gain a sustainable competitive advantage. For example,

For companies, the desire to work with NGOs stemmed from a recognition that environmental and social issues can provide business benefits, ranging from differentiating products to cutting costs.

In several instances NGOs have been willing to endorse products. In 1992 Greenpeace helped launch a hydrocarbon called "Greenfreeze" that could replace an ozone-damaging coolant in refrigerators. Its efforts resulted in 70,000 orders.

In another example, WWF, the conservation group, joined forces with Unilever, the consumer products group, in 1997 to tackle the political stalemate over fishing restrictions; together, they created the Marine Stewardship Council, a system for regulating responsible fishing.[149]

Two important points are necessary to ensure any cooperation works for all involved:

1.  The ability of corporations to separate the serious NGOs that want to engage in dialogue and reach a practical solution, from the radical who believe that "just talking to corporations is a sellout, and that only violent revolution will change the world"[150]

2.  The ability of NGOs to see the practical advantages that can be had by engaging business on business's own terms, while maintaining the integrity of core values and retaining the objectivity necessary to criticize the same companies when necessary

The attractions are obvious, but so are the dangers. Most significant, perhaps, is the danger that the concept is used simply to get businesses to [put] up money, which is more like taxation than partnership. Even within a more meaningful relationship, companies risk wasting time and money, and possibly divulging sensitive information which could be misused. NGOs risk reputational damage if a partnership goes wrong and wasting scarce resources if the desired outcomes are not achieved. The risks can be worth it, of course. For businesses, an NGO can bring knowledge and expertise, but also credibility and reputational gains. . . . For an NGO, business brings money, but more substantially a chance to change the way that particular business, and possibly a whole industry, operates.[151]

---

## Case Study: Greenfreeze

Perhaps the best example of businesses and NGOs working together was Greenpeace's approval of an environmentally appropriate refrigerator containing Greenfreeze:

> Since 1992, Greenfreeze has become the dominant technology in North Western Europe, having taken over nearly 100% of the German market. . . . By the year 2000, over 40 million Greenfreeze refrigerators will have been built in Europe alone. . . . There are over 100 different Greenfreeze models on the market. . . . All of the major European companies, Bosch/Siemens, Electrolux, Liebherr, Miele, Quelle, Vestfrost, Whirlpool, Bauknecht, Foron, AEG are marketing Greenfreeze.[152]

The decision to work in partnership with certain corporations was a conscious move on the part of Greenpeace. Many within the organization saw the importance of using markets and consumer power, where possible, rather than merely relying on direct action alone. Paul Gilding, a former executive director of Greenpeace International, saw the Greenfreeze project as a tactical deviation from direct action to "solutions campaigning" . . . work[ing] privately with individual companies, while continuing to attack business publicly. . . . Pragmatic activists are learning that "market campaigning" is the most efficient means of achieving their ends. And—civil disobedience apart—the most potent NGO tactics of the future will unquestionably revolve around redesigning and creating markets for more sustainable outcomes.[153]

Other examples of NGOs working together with multinational corporations to achieve common goals include the following:

One of the first alliances to gain significant notice was formed in 1990 when McDonald's and the Environmental Defense Fund (EDF) created a task force to seek ways of reducing waste in McDonald's operations.

Starbucks Coffee Company and the Alliance [for Environmental Innovation] joined forces to find environmentally beneficial ways for Starbucks to serve coffee in its [stores]. . . . The Starbucks and Conservation International partnership to promote the use of shade-grown coffee is [another] good example of an interactive collaboration moving towards a more intense alliance.[154]

It is important to point out, however, that there are more examples of NGO activism working to shame corporations into changing their operating practices than there are examples of constructive relationships. If corporations were looking for an incentive to begin communicating and cooperating with relevant NGOs, then the reputational damage done to companies that ignored NGOs and their supporters can be motivating. Coca-Cola's run-in with the controversial group Adbusters saw the innovative NGO successfully turn Coke's multimillion-dollar advertising campaign back on itself, making a political point and directly affecting sales:

Coca-Cola buckled within weeks after its precious brand and Olympic sponsorship were embroiled in a campaign against the company's use of greenhouse-polluting HFCs in refrigeration units. . . . Adbusters launched "culture jamming" attacks on the company's logos and slogans, demonstrating novel and creative approaches that can be a key feature of successful market campaigning.[155]

## Web-Based Examples and Resources

Adbusters, http://www.adbusters.org/

We are a global network of artists, activists, writers, pranksters, students, educators and entrepreneurs who want to advance the new social activist movement of the information age. Our aim is to topple existing power structures and forge a major shift in the way we will live in the 21st century.

Business for Social Responsibility, http://www.bsr.org/

Business for Social Responsibility (BSR) is a global organization that helps member companies achieve success in ways that respect ethical values, people, communities and the environment.

Conservation International, http://www.conservation.org/

Conservation International's (CI) mission is to conserve the Earth's living natural heritage, our global biodiversity, and to demonstrate that human societies are able to live harmoniously with nature.

Ecos Corporation, http://www.ecoscorporation.com/

> Ecos Corporation is an organisation with a dual identity. As a campaigning organisation, we steer companies toward sustainable growth. As a consultancy, we help them profit from that change.

Environmental Defense, http://www.environmentaldefense.org/

> Environmental Defense is fighting to protect human health, restore our oceans and ecosystems, and curb global warming.

Environmental Defense—Corporate Innovation, http://www.environmentaldefense.org/corporate_innovation.cfm

> Changing the way business thinks about the environment.

Greenpeace. Greenfreeze homepage, http://archive.greenpeace.org/~ozone/index.html

Leader to Leader Institute (formerly the Peter Drucker Foundation), http://www.pfdf.org/

> Continuing the work of the Foundation since its founding in 1990, the Leader to Leader Institute serves as a broker of intellectual capital, bringing together the finest thought leaders, consultants, and authors in the world with the leaders of social sector voluntary organizations. By providing intellectual resources to leaders in the business, government, and social sectors, and by fostering partnerships across these sectors, the Leader to Leader Institute works to strengthen social sector leaders of the United States and of nations around the globe.

Pact, http://www.pactworld.org/

> Since 1971 Pact has been helping globally to strengthen the capacity of local organizations and leaders to meet community needs in dozens of countries in Asia, Africa and Latin America.

For an overview of the benefits and dangers of Business/NGO partnerships, including three case-studies, see

Roger Cowe, "Analysis: Business/NGO partnerships–What's the Payback," *Ethical Corporation Magazine,* April 16, 2004.[156]

## Questions for Discussion and Review

1. List the pros and cons for businesses and nonprofits/NGOs working together. Can you think of any examples of successful partnerships?

2. Do NGOs lose their legitimacy if they begin cooperating with the very companies whose actions they are trying to affect? Where should the line be drawn?

3. Many NGOs face a real issue of accountability and transparency. Any independently wealthy individual can set up a nonprofit or NGO and claim to be an expert on a

particular issue. Using the Internet, it is relatively easy to mobilize support. How would you advise a company to deal with an NGO causing it problems if the company does not feel the NGO represents one of its significant stakeholder groups?

# PHILANTHROPY

☑ *CSR Connection:* This issue is what many think of first when CSR is mentioned. It is a very visible way in which a firm can demonstrate its commitment to the community within which it is based and operates.

## Issue

Philanthropy is a large part of U.S. society:

Americans give some $240 billion a year to private charities and a like amount in volunteer services, if you value the time they devote [based] on the hourly earnings of production workers.[157]

America's giving . . . has been 2% or more of GDP since 1998, following more than two decades below that mark, and [in 2003] total contributions were 2.2% of GDP, only a whisker below the all-time high of 2.3% in 2000.[158]

Many still argue that the way for an individual to contribute most to their society is to first become personally successful, thus generating the means to contribute:

Rich men should be thankful for one inestimable boon. They have it in their power during their lives to busy themselves in organizing benefactions from which the masses of their fellows will derive lasting advantage, and thus dignify their own lives.

—Andrew Carnegie, 1889

Andrew Carnegie wrote *The Gospel of Wealth,*

an essay calling upon the very rich to give their fortunes away during their lifetimes. Carnegie ultimately gave away virtually all the wealth he created, some $350 million, or in today's dollars, roughly $3 billion.[159]

He believed,

"The man who dies rich, dies disgraced."[160]

**Figure 6.1**    Top 10 Most Generous Philanthropists

## Individual Philanthrophy[161]

According to *BusinessWeek* (2002), "Not since the Gilded Age . . . has philanthropy been as bold and ambitious." Individual philanthropists are giving more often and in greater amounts. At the top of the top-10 list are Bill and Melinda Gates, who contributed over $25 million during the previous year. Other well-known names in the 2002 list include George Soros, Michael and Susan Dell, Ted Turner, and Bill Gates' partner at Microsoft, Paul Allen.

In comparison with this generosity, consider *BusinessWeek's* 2004 survey:

No. 1 givers Bill and Melinda Gates . . . made history this year by giving their estimated $3 billion Microsoft Corp. dividend to their foundation. It's one of the largest donations in history by a living donor. To put it in perspective, that one gift is three times bigger than the amount that America's richest family, the descendents of Wal-Mart Stores Inc. founder Sam Walton, has given during their entire lifetimes.[162]

Philanthropy today is

- More ambitious
- More strategic
- More global
- More demanding in terms of outcomes

All of which means a more hands-on approach from the donors themselves. Philanthropy today is more active and more tied to the donor's personal interests, goals, and ambitions.

## Corporate Philanthrophy[163]

*BusinessWeek's* (2003) "first annual ranking of America's most philanthropic companies," analyzed corporate giving from two perspectives: donations of cash, as well as donations of in-kind goods and services.

The list revealed that Freeport-McMoRan Copper & Gold made the most generous cash donations, giving $16.8 million (0.879% of revenues). The next-placed company, Corning, ($24.9 million) donated 0.787% of 2003 revenues. Rounding out the top 15 were the number 14 company Nike ($29.6 million, 0.277%) and number 15 Intel ($73.4 million, 0.274%).

In absolute dollars, Wal-Mart topped the list, donating $156 million in cash in 2002. Ford was number 2 ($131 million) and Altria was number 3 ($113.4 million). In spite of the large cash amounts, however, when considered as percentages of revenues, these firms placed further down the list.

In terms of in-kind donations, pharmaceutical companies dominated the top 5. The number 1 company was Eli Lilly, which donated $204.8 million in goods or services (1.848% of 2002 revenues). Pfizer placed number 2 ($528 million, 1.631%) and Merck placed number 4 ($575 million, 1.11%).

Many expect this trend to increase as the postwar generation of Americans dies and produces

the largest intergenerational wealth transfer in history . . . with at least $41 trillion estimated to change hands by 2052—$6 trillion of which is projected to go to charity.[164]

This "conservative" figure of $41 trillion

is four times the present size of the entire American economy and almost as large as the entire world's wealth today.[165]

Philanthropy, on the part of large corporations, has also been standard fare for many years now (see Figure 6.1). But does this in itself constitute an effective CSR policy? And how are progressive companies moving the issue beyond a regular payment to optimizing their position within the market (their economic strength) to make a difference:

With the economy sputtering, companies are finding it harder to justify charitable expenditures that don't contribute to the bottom line. But as recent scandals continue to taint the public's impressions of corporate behavior, philanthropy in some form is more important than ever.[166]

## Case Study: Merck

George W. Merck, the son of the pharmaceutical company's founder, always insisted that medicine was for the patients, not for the profits. In 1987, in keeping with this core value, his successors decided to give away a drug called Mectizan, which cures river blindness, an affliction in a number of developing countries.[167]

River blindness is an agonizing disease that afflicts some 18 million impoverished people living in remote villages along the banks of rivers in tropical regions of Africa and Latin America. The disease is caused by a tiny parasitic worm that is passed from person to person by the bite of the black fly, which breeds in river waters. The tiny worms burrow under a person's skin, where they grow as long as 2 feet curled up inside ugly round nodules half an inch to an inch in diameter. Inside the nodules, the worms reproduce by releasing millions of microscopic offspring called *microfilaria* that wriggle their way throughout the body moving beneath the skin, discoloring it as they migrate, and causing lesions and such intense itching that victims sometimes commit suicide.

Eventually, the microfilaria invade the eyes and blind the victim.[168]

When Merck scientists realized they might be able to convert one of the company's best-selling drugs (Ivermectin) that cured river blindness in animals into a human version, they were immediately confronted by the problem that the people who were going to need that medicine were those least able to afford it. The research and testing necessary to develop the drug alone could easily rise above $100 million, and the company had little chance of recovering its investment. Nevertheless, Merck says it decided to proceed with development of the drug because of the scale of the human suffering involved: an estimated 85 million people at risk from the disease.

The drug took 7 years to develop and, as feared, Merck was unable to persuade any organization to buy and distribute it in the regions of the world where it was needed. Further investment was therefore required by Merck to create the infrastructure necessary to distribute the drug free, with the help of the World Health Organization (WHO).

In spite of the huge investment made by Merck in developing Mectizan and the absence of any return that can be directly related to that investment, the company has come to realize the strategic benefits that creating such a high profile in a region can bring in other, less immediately obvious ways. As Merck's chairman at the time, Dr. Roy Vagelos, states,

> When I first went to Japan 15 years ago, I was told by Japanese business people that it was Merck that brought streptomycin to Japan after World War II to eliminate tuberculosis which was eating up their society. We did that. We didn't make any money. But it's no accident that Merck is the largest American pharmaceutical company in Japan today.[169]

The company's commitment to distributing the drug free continues to this day, and the company claims that more than 30 million people line up to receive it every year. The company has pledged to continue distributing the drug free of charge for as long as it is required.

## Web-Based Examples and Resources

Association of Fundraising Professionals, http://www.afpnet.org/

The Association of Fundraising Professionals (AFP) represents 26,000 members in 174 chapters throughout the United States, Canada, Mexico, and China working to advance philanthropy through advocacy, research, education, and certification programs.

Center on Philanthropy at Indiana University, http://www.philanthropy.iupui.edu/

The Center on Philanthropy at Indiana University increases the understanding of philanthropy and improves its practice through programs in research, teaching, public service, and public affairs.

Echoing Green, http://www.echoinggreen.org/

As one of the earliest practitioners of venture philanthropy, a relatively new approach to philanthropy, Echoing Green has emerged as the premiere venture philanthropy organization providing early stage funding to emerging social entrepreneurs around the world.

Foundation Center, http://fdncenter.org/

The Foundation Center's mission is to support and improve philanthropy by promoting public understanding of the field and helping grant seekers succeed. Founded in 1956, the Center is the nation's leading authority on philanthropy and is dedicated to serving grant seekers, grant makers, researchers, policymakers, the media, and the general public.

Geneva Global, http://www.genevaglobal.com/

Our passion is to see lives and communities changed in the neediest places of the world through performance philanthropy.

Independent Sector, http://www.independentsector.org/

Independent Sector is committed to strengthening, empowering, and partnering with nonprofit and philanthropic organizations in their work on behalf of the public good. Its membership of nonprofit organizations, foundations, and corporate philanthropy programs collectively represents tens of thousands of charitable groups serving every cause in every region of the country, as well as millions of donors and volunteers.

*Knowledge@Wharton*, http://knowledge.wharton.upenn.edu/

One innovative approach to Corporate Philanthropy is an idea put forward by Ms. Robbie Shell, managing editor of the online business journal of the Wharton School of Business at the University of Pennsylvania. The idea appeared as an article in the *Wall Street Journal* in November 2002: http://www.careerjournal.com/columnists/managersjournal/20021126-managersjournal.html.

Merck Pharmaceutical–Mectizan homepage, http://www.merck.com/about/cr/mectizan/home .html

Imagine the discovery of a medicine that could—with just one annual dose—treat one of the worst diseases imaginable and prevent blindness. Imagine more than 30 million people lining up each year to receive the medicine for free. Imagine defeating a disease that has blinded so many for centuries.

In October 1995, a seven-foot sculpture named "The Gift of Sight" was unveiled at Merck's corporate headquarters in Whitehouse Station, New Jersey. It shows a young boy leading a blind man along a path in an African village—a once common scene that is disappearing as a result of Merck's decision to donate Mectizan wherever needed for as long as needed to control river blindness.

New Philanthropy Capital, http://www.philanthropycapital.org/

New Philanthropy Capital (NPC) is a registered charity that works with donors and charities to channel money and resources into projects and organisations that are setting new standards in tackling deprivation, disadvantage and degradation in the UK and around the world.

## Questions for Discussion and Review

1. Does giving a lot of money excuse corporations operating in a less-than-CSR-like manner in other areas of operations?

2. What do you think about the idea that a company should be made to contribute a certain percentage of pretax profits?

3. What is your perception of Merck and its distribution of the drug Mectizan? Was it a cynical attempt to generate positive PR for the company or a genuine attempt to do some good? Does it matter what the motivating forces were?

# PROFIT

☑ **CSR Connection:** This issue forms an essential component of the CSR debate. The best of intentions aside, a bankrupt company does not benefit any stakeholder.

> Any CSR argument that does not allow the company to pursue profits is ill conceived and fighting against the tide of economic theory and human history.

## Issue

By definition, profit is what drives all for-profit organizations. This pursuit of profit underwrites market-based economies and forces companies constantly to stimulate innovation and progress to meet society's developmental needs. Profit is also cited by business leaders as a reason for not being able to pursue CSR behavior; that is, a corporation has a duty to be as profitable as possible in order to ensure it remains in business and maximizes returns for investors.

The merging of the pursuit of profit and integration of CSR within corporate strategy renders a profit-only approach increasingly untenable. Combined with the increasing pressure placed on companies today to perform consistently, managers need to be as innovative and broad-minded as possible in seeking to implement the organization's vision, mission, strategy, and tactics:

> [For business] doing good does not necessarily rule out making a reasonable profit. You can . . . make money by serving the poor as well as the rich. . . . There is a huge neglected market in the billions of poor in the developing world. Companies like Unilever and Citicorp are beginning to adapt their technologies to enter this market. Unilever can now deliver ice cream in India for just two cents a portion because it has rethought the technology of refrigeration. Citicorp can now provide financial services to people, also in India, who have only $25 to invest, again through rethinking technology. In both cases the companies make money, but the driving force is the need to serve neglected consumers. Profit often comes from progress.[170]

## Case Study: Hewlett-Packard

It is estimated that 65% of the world's population, or 4 billion people, exist on less than $2,000 per year.[171] This section of the world forms Tier 4—the largest and bottom of the four-tier pyramid that comprises the world's population—the bottom of the pyramid (BOP). They represent a huge market segment that needs the help of the developed world but also can pay their way in terms of buying essential and reasonably priced products:

> Individually, the purchasing power of Tier 4 is limited. . . . But together it adds up to trillions. [Their] general wants and needs are familiar: securing better lives for their children, getting the best price for their labor, staying healthy, and having fun.[172]

This market remains largely ignored by many companies. What is required is an innovative approach on the part of companies in terms of delivering their product to places previously thought inaccessible, at prices previously thought unprofitable:

> But to be profitable, firms cannot simply edge down market fine-tuning the products they already sell to rich customers. Instead, they must thoroughly re-engineer products to reflect the very different economics of BOP: small unit packages, low margin per unit, high volume. Big business needs to swap its usual incremental approach for an entrepreneurial mindset, because BOP markets need to be built not simply entered.[173]

Certainly, succeeding in BOP markets requires multinationals to think creatively. The biggest change though, has to come in the attitudes and practices of executives. . . . Perhaps MNCs should create the equivalent of the Peace Corps: Having young managers spend a couple of formative years in BOP markets would open their eyes to the promise and the realities of doing business there.[174]

Hindustan Lever, the Indian consumer goods company 51% owned by Unilever, knew that many Indians could not afford to buy a big bottle of shampoo. . . . So it created single-use packets (in three sizes, according to hair length) that go for a few cents—and now sells 4.5 billion of them a year.[175]

Progressive multinationals have begun to explore new ways to serve these markets. The multinational that has perhaps done the most in this area of "progressive profit," is Hewlett-Packard, which has a business unit, e-Inclusion,[176] dedicated to creating market-based solutions to problems in developing economies using IT products:

When Hewlett-Packard launched its e-Inclusion division, which concentrates on rural markets, it established a branch of its famed HP Labs in India charged with developing products and services explicitly for this market. . . . For example, 16 researchers are looking into things like speech interfaces for the Internet, solar applications, and cheap devices that can connect with the web. HP made e-Inclusion a business venture rather than a philanthropic one because it believes only systems that can sustain themselves economically can address the scale of the need—and in that scale is a business opportunity.[177]

For C. K. Prahalad (Professor at the University of Michigan Business School and "perhaps the most visible proponent of the view that the globe's poor are a huge—and hugely untapped—market")[178] the business opportunity is clear. It requires effort and commitment on the part of multinational corporations (MNCs) but there are benefits in terms of top-line growth, reduced costs, and inspired innovation.

If we stop thinking of the poor as victims or as a burden and start recognizing them as resilient and creative entrepreneurs and value-conscious consumers, a whole new world of opportunity will open up.[179]

It is simply good business strategy to be involved in large, untapped markets that offer new customers, cost-saving opportunities, and access to radical innovation. The business opportunities at the bottom of the pyramid are real, and they are open to any MNC willing to engage and learn.[180]

## Web-Based Examples and Resources

HP—e-Inclusion, http://www.hp.com/hpinfo/globalcitizenship/gcreport/socialinvest/einclu sion.html

"e-inclusion" is HP's vision of a future in which all people have access to the social and economic opportunities of the 21st century, and can use technology as a means to learn, work and thrive. Our efforts in e-inclusion seek to create new market opportunities, for ourselves and for the communities with which we engage. We do this by forging new kinds of partnerships with private and public entities to close the gap between technology-empowered and technology-excluded communities. We currently have more than 25 projects underway in approximately 20 countries on five continents. . . . Looking ahead to the next decade, many of HP's new markets and customers will come from the 90% of people currently excluded.

http://www.cra.org/Activities/grand.challenges/slides/b24b.pdf

> Initiated by Thomas Kalil (President Bill Clinton's former science and technology advisor and Assistant to the Chancellor for Science and Technology at UC Berkeley, tkalil@uclink.berkeley.edu) and presented to the Computing Research Association (CRA) on June 25, 2002.
>
> Grand Challenge: Provide affordable, useful digital services to the 4 billion people on the planet earning less that $1,500.

NextBillion.net—Development Through Enterprise, http://www.nextbillion.net/

> NextBillion.net brings together the community of business leaders, social entrepreneurs, NGOs, policy makers, and academics who want to explore the connection between development and enterprise.

Overseas Development Institute, http://www.odi.org.uk/

> ODI is Britain's leading independent think-tank on international development and humanitarian issues.

Michael Warner, "Stimulating a Step-Change in the Development Performance of Corporations," Fall, 2002, http://www.odi.org.uk/speeches/corporations2002/corporations2002.html

University of North Carolina—Base of the Pyramid Learning Laboratory, http://www.kenan-flagler.unc.edu/KI/cse/bop.cfm

> Opportunities for massive value creation, sustainable growth and human development lie at the "Base of the Pyramid" (BOP), a socio-economic designation for the 4 billion individuals that live primarily in developing countries and whose annual per capita incomes fall below $1,500 (PPP).

World Resources Institute, http://www.wri.org/

> World Resources Institute is an environmental research and policy organization that creates solutions to protect the Earth and improve people's lives.

## Questions for Discussion and Review

1. Outline the opportunity for corporations that exists in the base of the pyramid. Can you think of a company and an existing product and how it can be modified to become profitable in the developing world?

2. Have a look at HP's e-Inclusion site (http://www.hp.com/hpinfo/globalcitizenship/gcreport/socialinvest/einclusion.html) and the company's other CSR work (http://www.hp.com/hpinfo/globalcitizenship/csr/). How might HP shareholders profit from these efforts? Do these Web sites change your impression of HP?

3. Assuming a firm found a profitable niche in serving the fourth tier (the 4 billion people at the bottom of the economic pyramid), how would such a breakthrough benefit the firm in selling to the developed world at the top of the economic pyramid?

# WAGES

☑ **CSR Connection:** This issue reflects the importance of wages as a highly visible component of the organization's relationship with one of its key stakeholders, its employees.

## Issue

Jeremy Rifkin[181] outlines one of his concerns regarding capitalism: that in spite of all its efficiencies in creating innovation and opportunity,

what it's not good at is distributing the fruits, because the logic in the boardroom . . . is always cut your labor costs to improve your quarterly [numbers] and your profit margins for shareholder value.[182]

However, by reducing those labor costs—by either minimizing wage levels, outsourcing, and/or cutting labor positions within an organization—are companies also reducing the overall health of the communities within which they are based and hope to sell their products? Yet, if a firm fails to cut its costs, might that failure jeopardize the entire enterprise, harming all? Rifkin continues:

The same workers who've been let go are the same people who have consumed the goods and services. . . . They are not just a factor in the means of production. They're not only the consumers, they're the shareholders. So when you [sack] them . . . you slowly lose the purchasing power to empty inventories and long-term savings in the form of institutional pension funds to invest in the stocks and bonds of these companies.[183]

The effort to minimize the cost of production is a legitimate business strategy. But a major corporation must also come to terms with the fact that the employees whose wages they squeeze can also be the customers on whom they rely to fuel sales.

An example:[184] Nearly a century ago, Henry Ford drew no distinction between his employees and his customers. Challenging the conventional wisdom that the best way to maximize profits was to tailor your product to the wealthiest segment of society, Ford decided to market his black Model T as "America's Everyman car."[185]

For Ford, mass production went hand in hand with mass consumption. His benchmark for worker compensation was whether his own workers could afford to buy the product they were making. He offered a $5-a-day minimum wage for *all* his workers (crashing through the race barriers of the day[186])—twice the prevailing automobile industry average.

In doing so, Ford created a *virtuous circle*. Workers flocked to his factory to apply for positions. If they managed to secure one of Ford's coveted jobs, then in time they too would be able to afford one of his cars. The company flourished based on the twin pillars of a desirable product and a highly motivated employee base. "By the time production ceased for the Model T in 1927, more than 15 million cars had been sold—or half the world's output."[187]

Another example of a different corporate perspective is that adopted by Costco the warehouse membership-based retailer:

"From day one, we've run the company with the philosophy that if we pay better than average, provide a salary people can live on, have a positive environment and good benefits, we'll be able to hire better people, they'll stay longer and be more efficient," says Richard Galanti, Costco's chief financial officer.[188]

What is an acceptable wage rate to pay employees that balances the need to maintain efficient operations and also helps create a consumer base that supports sales? Different people and ideologies suggest different solutions:

- The minimum wage (determined by the government),
- The average wage for the job and industry (determined by the market), or
- A living wage (determined by nonprofits and NGOs).

An example of the discrepancies that these three different calculations can create is seen when the federal minimum wage in the United States ($5.15 per hour) is compared with the living wage in Miami-Dade County, Florida ($10.30 per hour),[189] one of the poorest and poorest-paying metropolitan areas in the United States.

## Case Study: McDonald's

**Mc.Job** \mək-'jäb\ *n* (1986): a low-paying job that requires little skill and provides little opportunity for advancement.[190]

In 2002, a summary of a report conducted by *Asian Labor Update* was covered by an online publication of the Asia Monitor Resource Center.[191] The goal of the study was to compare the purchasing power of the wages paid to McDonald's employees[192] in various Asian countries. How long would each individual need

to work to be able to buy a Big Mac sandwich at the McDonald's that employed him or her?

The responses we received show quite clearly that the target consumer group varies from country to country. Taking extreme examples, an Australian cleaner could buy three Big Macs after working for one hour, whereas a Pakistani cleaner would have to work for more than fourteen hours to buy the same burger.[193]

In Australia, where McDonald's staff work for A$10.61 (US$5.60) per hour, it costs A$3.00 (US$1.58) to purchase a Big Mac. In Pakistan, however, where the company's staff work for PR13 (US$0.22) per hour, a Big Mac costs PR185 (US$3.08). The difference between wage rates and the cost of a Big Mac produces the difference in purchase parity quoted in the report and above.

The countries covered in the report included Australia, China, Hong Kong, India, Malaysia, New Zealand, Pakistan, Philippines, South Korea, Sri Lanka, and Thailand. Significant differences were identified. Wage rates ranged from a staff member who works for IRs5.60 (US$0.11) per hour in India to the higher wages paid to McDonald's Australian employees: A$10.61 (US$5.60) per hour. In terms of the cost of burgers, Big Mac prices ranged from MR4.30 (US$1.13) in Malaysia, to NZ$3.95 (US$1.72) in New Zealand.

These differences reflect the different stages of economic development of the varied countries throughout the Asian continent; however, the differences in purchase parity—how long each worker would have to work to purchase a burger—also reflect the different perceptions of a McDonald's meal within each country. In a developed country like Australia, McDonald's food is considered fast and low-cost food. In a developing country, like India, however, McDonald's is more exotic and, therefore, relatively more expensive. For more results of the study and greater analysis, see http://www.amrc.org.hk/4202.htm

The issue of relative value is important in an age when Western consumers often judge a multinational corporation's operations in a developing country by their own Western standards rather than the standards facing the company in that developing country. The result is often very difficult for the company that believes it faces a no-win situation. For example, Nike has to manage a global network of over 700 independent supplier factories. To what degree is the company responsible for what happens within the operations of those organizations?

> The relationship is delicate. . . . NGOs have berated firms such as Nike for failing to ensure that workers are paid a "living wage." But that can be hard, even in America. . . . In developing countries, the dilemma may be even

greater: "In Vietnam, [Nike's] workers are paid more than doctors. What's the social cost if a doctor leaves his practice and goes to work for [Nike]? That's starting to happen."[194]

Another relative measure of wage levels for company employees, and an equally important indicator of the health of an organization, is the amount that is paid to corporate executives. What is an acceptable rate to pay top management? It seems that pay scales are relative and arbitrary:

> Just how much do you have to pay a guy to run an outfit with 170,000 employees that's critical to our national defense? If he's the CEO of Boeing (which actually has 167,000 employees), the answer is $4 million plus lots of incentive compensation. If he's the Commandant of the U.S. Marine Corps (which actually has 174,000 employees), the answer is $169,860. Even Boeing's chief financial officer makes 10 times that much.[195]

Ironically, a study found that

> chief executives of companies that had the largest layoffs and most underfunded pensions and that moved operations offshore to avoid U.S. taxes were rewarded with the biggest pay hikes in 2002.[196]

And what about the difference between rates for the CEO compared with those of the average worker?

> [In 1975] the average real annual compensation of the top 100 chief executives was $1.3m: 39 times the pay of the average worker. [In 2005] it is $37.5m: over 1,000 times the pay of the average worker.[197]

> The average working person's gain in pay for the 21 years from 1980 to 2001 was 74%, according to the AFL-CIO, while CEO compensation climbed 1884%.[198]

> In the past decade, companies that granted 90% of all options to CEOs and a few top

managers performed worse than those that distributed options more evenly and fairly among employees. There is no justification for increasing the compensation of CEOs from 40 times that of the average employee in the 1960s to nearly 600 times today.[199]

## Web-Based Examples and Resources

Asia Monitor Resource Center (AMRC), *Asian labor update*, http://www.amrc.org.hk/

Asia Monitor Resource Center (AMRC) is an independent non-government organization (NGO) which focuses on Asian labour concerns. The center's main goal is to support democratic and independent labour movements in Asia.

Co-op America, Resources for Consumer Action and Corporate Accountability and Creating a Sweatshop-Free Economy, http://www.coopamerica.org/programs/sweatshops/

Co-op America provides the information you need to help stop sweatshop labor and promote fair treatment of workers everywhere.

Foundation of Economic Trends, http://www.foet.org/

The Foundation on Economic Trends (FOET) was established in 1977 and is based in Washington D.C. . . . FOET examines new trends in science and technology and their impacts on the environment, the economy, culture and society. We engage in litigation, public education, coalition building and grassroots organizing activities to advance our goals.

Securities and Exchange Commission—*Executive Compensation: A Guide for Investors*, http://www.sec.gov/investor/pubs/execomp0803.htm

The federal securities laws require clear, concise and understandable disclosure about the amount and type of compensation paid to chief executive officers and other highly compensated executives of public companies.

United for a Fair Economy, http://www.faireconomy.org/

United for a Fair Economy is a national, independent, nonpartisan organization that puts a spotlight on the damaging consequences of growing economic inequality. We provide popular education resources, work with grassroots organizations, conduct research, and support creative and legislative action to build a social movement that demands a fair economy. UFE's core message is that concentrated corporate and financial power is bad for the economy, undermines democracy and can tear communities apart.

## Questions for Discussion and Review

1. What is a fair wage? What does *fair* mean? What is the lowest hourly wage for which you would be willing to work?

2. Is there a maximum amount that a CEO should earn? Is it okay to pay a CEO any amount, as long as the net benefit the CEO brings to the organization exceeds her or his compensation?

3. Is it a good idea for companies to apply a pay-scale ratio whereby the highest and lowest wage levels within an organization are kept within a certain ratio (for example, Ben & Jerry's instituted a strict policy that prevented any employee from earning more than seven times the salary of the lowest-paid worker in the company)?[200]

## NOTES

1. http://www.benettongroup.com/en/whatwesay/campaigns.htm

2. http://www.museedelapub.org/pubgb/virt/mp/benetton/pub_benetton.html

3. Ibid.

4. http://www.benettongroup.com/en/whatwesay/colors_magazine.htm

5. http://www.benettongroup.com/en/whatwesay/campaigns.htm

6. Gail Edmondson, Jack Ewing and Christina Passariello, 'Has Benetton Stopped Unraveling?' *BusinessWeek,* June 23, 2003, http://www.businessweek.com/magazine/content/03_25/b3838134_mz034.htm

7. Rissig Licha, 'How We Can Sell Brand USA Abroad,' *Miami Herald,* March 23, 2003, p5L.

8. Geraldine Bedell, 'Special Report: The Changing Face of the Brand,' *The Observer,* January 19, 2003, http://www.observer.co.uk/global/story/0,10786,877479,00.html

9. http://www.hoovers.com/, May 2005.

10. Darcy Frey, 'How Green Is BP?' *New York Times,* December 8, 2002, Section 6, p99.

11. Ibid, http://www.mindfully.org/Industry/BP-How-Green8dec02.htm

12. Ibid.

13. Hal R. Varian, 'Economic Scene: Are Bigger Vehicles Safer? It Depends on Whether You're a Passenger or a Target,' *New York Times,* December 18, 2003, pC2.

14. Amy Schatz, 'Fatal Car Crashes Start to Decline,' *Wall Street Journal,* August 11, 2004, pD1.

15. Dave Barry, 'OINK! Another Road Hog,' *Miami Herald Tropical Life,* June 23, 2004, p3. Originally published on March 21, 1999.

16. Jem Bendell, 'Have you seen my business case?' *Ethical Corporation Magazine*, November, 2002, http://www.jembendell.com/

17. 'SUV Haters of the World, Unite,' *BusinessWeek,* December 9, 2002, p10.

18. Neal E. Boudette & Karen Lundegaard, 'SUV Tax Break For Business Is Likely to End,' *Wall Street Journal,* October 7, 2004, pD6.

19. Danny Hakim, 'A Regulator Takes Aim At Hazards of SUVs,' *New York Times,* December 22, 2002, Section 3, pp 1&10.

20. Danny Hakim, 'G.M. Critical of Regulator Who Faulted SUV Safety,' *New York Times,* January 16, 2003, pC16.

21. *New York Times,* December 22, 2002, op. cit.

22. *Miami Herald Tropical Life,* June 23, 2004, op. cit.

23. Larry Armstrong & David Welch, 'Don't Tread on Me—or My SUV,' *BusinessWeek,* January 27, 2003, p38.

24. Jay Rosen, 'When Is a Car a Truck? If Uncle Sam Says So,' *New York Times,* November 26, 2002, pB9.

25.   Lorraine Woellert & David Welch, 'The Sport-Utility Critic Detroit Can't Dismiss,' *BusinessWeek*, February 17, 2003, p43.

26.   *New York Times*, January 16, 2003, op. cit.

27.   *BusinessWeek*, February 17, 2003, op. cit.

28.   The Evangelical Environmental Network and *Creation Care Magazine*, http://creationcare.org/

29.   http://www.whatwouldjesusdrive.org/

30.   Arianna Huffington, http://www.thedetroitproject.com/

31.   Alex Blyth, 'Swedish Government Considers Tax on SUVs,' *Ethical Corporation Magazine*, September 2, 2004, http://www.ethicalcorp.com/content.asp?ContentID=2665

32.   *BusinessWeek*, January 27, 2003, op. cit.

33.   *BusinessWeek*, December 9, 2002, op. cit.

34.   Alex Taylor III, 'Bill's Brand-New Ford,' *Fortune*, June 28, 2004, pp 68–76.

35.   http://fordvehicles.com/environmental/

36.   Stephen Power & Jo Wrighton, 'In Europe, SUVs May Face Taxes Amid Drive to Penalize Emissions,' *Wall Street Journal*, June 30, 2004, pA2.

37.   The two TV ads launched by the Detroit Project were released on Wednesday, January 8, 2003.

38.   Roger Martin, 'The Virtue Matrix,' *Harvard Business Review*, March 2002, Vol. 80, No. 3, pp 68–75.

39.   NikeWatch Update, December 2001, January 2002, http://www.sweatshopwatch.org/

40.   Paul Gilding, 'Making Market Magic,' ecos Corporation Web site, June 2001, http://www.ecoscorporation.com/think/stake/market_magic.htm

41.   Dan Le Batard, 'Michael Jordan's Asian Tour: Selling His Name, Not His Game,' *Miami Herald*, June 29, 2004, p1D.

42.   Nike, Inc. v. Kasky, 02–575, SUPREME COURT OF THE UNITED STATES, 123 S. Ct. 817; 154 L. Ed. 2d 767; 2003 U.S. LEXIS 556; 71 U.S.L.W. 3470; 2003 Daily Journal DAR 403, January 10, 2003, Decided.

43.   Bob Herbert, 'In America: Nike's Boot Camps,' *New York Times*, March 31, 1997, pA15.

44.   Ibid.

45.   Bob Herbert, 'In America: Nike's Pyramid Scheme,' *New York Times*, June 10, 1996, pA17.

46.   Philip H. Knight, 'Letter to the Editor: Nike Pays Good Wages to Foreign Workers,' *New York Times*, June 21, 1996, pA26.

47.   Peter Clarke, 'California Supreme Court Decision Potentially Devastating for Corporate Responsibility Reporting and SRI Funds Worldwide,' *Ethical Corporation Magazine*, October 17, 2002, http://www.ethicalcorp.com/content.asp?ContentID=242

48.   Linda Greenhouse, 'Supreme Court to Review Nike "Free Speech" Case,' *New York Times*, January 11, 2003, pp A1&A12.

49.   As a result of the case, "Nike has decided not to issue its corporate responsibility report externally for its fiscal year 2002 and will continue to limit its participation in public events and media engagement in California." Nikebiz Press Release, September 12, 2003, http://www.nike.com/nikebiz/news/pressrelease.jhtml?year=2003&month=09&letter=f

50.   *New York Times*, January 11, 2003, op. cit.

51.   Mallen Baker, 'Nike and Short-Sighted Victories in Free Speech,' *Ethical Corporation Magazine*, November 13, 2002, http://www.ethicalcorp.com/content.asp?ContentID=261

52.   Nicholas Stein, 'Labor Trade: No Way Out,' *Fortune*, January 8, 2003, http://www.fortune.com/fortune/careers/articles/0,15114,406059,00.html

53.   Nikebiz Press Release, 'Nike, Inc. and Kasky Announce Settlement of Kasky v. Nike First Amendment Case,' September 12, 2003, http://www.nike.com/nikebiz/news/pressrelease.jhtml?year=2003&month=09&letter=f

54. William McCall, 'Nike Settles Speech Lawsuit,' *Miami Herald,* September 13, 2003, pC1.

55. Elizabeth Wasserman, 'A Race for Profits,' *mbajungle.com,* March/April 2003, pp 40–41.

56. Ibid.

57. Mike France & William C. Symonds, 'Diversity Is About to Get More Elusive, Not Less,' *BusinessWeek,* July 7, 2003, pp 30–31.

58. *mbajungle.com,* March/April 2003, op. cit.

59. Michael D. Karpeles, 'Manager's Journal: Class-Action Warfare,' *Wall Street Journal,* July 6, 2004, pA16.

60. Diane Brady, 'Gender Watch: Is Your Company Up to Code?' *BusinessWeek,* July 5, 2004, p16.

61. http://www.augustadiscriminates.org/ February, 2003.

62. Carrick Mollenkamp & Betsy McKay, 'Augusta Membership Controversy Ensnares Over Two Dozen Firms,' *Wall Street Journal,* December 19, 2002, pB10.

63. Ibid.

64. 'Where Have All the Companies Gone?' *BusinessWeek,* March 10, 2003, p12.

65. 'Klan to Rally for Augusta,' *Miami Herald,* March 1, 2003, p2D.

66. Ibid.

67. Richard Sandomir, 'Sponsors to Return to Masters Next Year,' *New York Times,* August 28, 2004, pB23.

68. Martha Burk, 'Green Jacket Cronies,' *Wall Street Journal,* April 7, 2005, pA14.

69. Roger O. Crockett, 'Memo to the Supreme Court: 'Diversity Is Good Business,'' *BusinessWeek,* January 27, 2003, p96.

70. John Langone, 'Disabled but Able,' *New York Times,* April 29, 2003, pD7; a review of the book 'A Matter of Dignity: Changing the Lives of the Disabled,' by Andrew Potok, Bantam Books, 2003.

71. D. E. LeGer, 'At Goodwill, Workers Proud of Role in the U.S. War Effort,' *Miami Herald,* March 22, 2003, p1C.

72. Ibid.

73. Ibid.

74. 'Goodwill Partnership Benefits Disabled Workers,' *Miami Herald,* September 22, 2002, p1DM.

75. Ibid.

76. Poulomi Mrinal Saha, 'UK Business Sets Disability Standard,' *Ethical Corporation Magazine,* November 4, 2004, http://www.ethicalcorp.com/content.asp?ContentID=3170

77. Ibid.

78. *BizEthics Buzz,* December 2002. *BizEthics Buzz* is an online news report from *Business Ethics Magazine,* http://www.business-ethics.com/email_newsletter/sample.html

79. Ibid.

80. Lisa Roner, 'Anheuser-Busch Reports Recycling 97% of Solid Waste,' *Ethical Corporation Magazine,* June 21, 2004, http://www.ethicalcorp.com/content.asp?ContentID=2228

81. Joann Muller, 'Lean Green Machine,' *Forbes,* February 3, 2003, p44.

82. 'Ford to Issue Report on Global Climate Change,' *CSRWire,* March 31, 2005, http://www.csrwire.com/article.cgi/3689.html

83. *Forbes,* February 3, 2003, op. cit.

84. Brian Dumaine, 'Mr. Natural,' *Fortune,* October 28, 2002, pp 184–186.

85. 'ASLA to Install Green Roof on Washington, DC, Headquarters,' *CSRWire,* April 5, 2005, http://www.csrwire.com/article.cgi/3702.html

86. In April 2005, the American Society of Landscape Architects (ASLA) announced that it was replacing the 3,300 square foot roof of its Washington D.C. headquarters with a "green roof."

87. *CSRWire,* April 5, 2005, op. cit.

88.  *Forbes,* February 3, 2003, op. cit.

89.  The Fairtrade Foundation Web site, January 2003, http://www.fairtrade.org.uk/

90.  Alex Blyth, 'Oxfam Launches Fair Trade Coffee Shops,' *Ethical Corporation Magazine,* May 18, 2004, http://www.ethicalcorp.com/content.asp?ContentID=2061

91.  Katy McLaughlin, 'Is Your Grocery List Politically Correct?' *Wall Street Journal,* February 17, 2004, pp D1&D2.

92.  The Fairtrade Foundation Web site, January 2003, http://www.fairtrade.org.uk/

93.  Steve Stecklow & Erin White, 'At Some Retailers, "Fair Trade" Carries a Very High Cost,' *Wall Street Journal,* June 8, 2004, pp A1&A10.

94.  'Stuffed,' *The Economist,* July 3, 2004, p31.

95.  Poulomi Mrinal Saha, 'Ethics Still Not Influencing UK Consumers,' *Ethical Corporation Magazine,* March 15, 2005, http://www.ethicalcorp.com/content.asp?ContentID=3557

96.  By mid-2004, Starbucks had 7,500 stores open throughout the world and was continuing to expand at the rate of "two or three stores a day." Oliver Balch, 'Peter Torrebiarte, Starbucks Coffee Agronomy Company,' *Ethical Corporation Magazine,* June 24, 2004, http://www.ethicalcorp.com/content.asp?ContentID=2263

97.  Stanley Homes & Geri Smith, 'For Coffee Growers, Not Even a Whiff of Profits,' *BusinessWeek,* September 9, 2002, p110.

98.  Ibid.

99.  Ibid.

100.  Peter Asmus, '100 Best Corporate Citizens of 2003,' *Business Ethics Magazine,* Spring 2003, pp 6–10.

101.  Adam Smith, quoted in 'Economic Focus: Too Many Countries?' *The Economist,* July 17, 2004, p75.

102.  John Kay, 'Justice in Trade Is Not Simply a Moral Question,' *Financial Times* (U.S. edition), June 26, 2003, p13.

103.  Katy McLaughlin, 'Is Your Grocery List Politically Correct?' *Wall Street Journal,* February 17, 2004, pp D1&D2.

104.  Ibid.

105.  Alex Blyth, 'Oxfam Launches Fair Trade Coffee Shops,' *Ethical Corporation Magazine,* May 18, 2004, http://www.ethicalcorp.com/content.asp?ContentID=2061

106.  Lisa Roner, 'US Coffee Roasters Say Expansion of Fair Trade Depends on Consumer Demand,' *Ethical Corporation Magazine,* August 30, 2004, http://www.ethicalcorp.com/content.asp?ContentID=2623

107.  See 'Common Code for the Coffee Community' reference in Web-Based Examples and Resources.

108.  Lisa Roner, 'Starbucks Brews Up More Socially Responsible Coffee,' *Ethical Corporation Magazine,* November 2, 2004, http://www.ethicalcorp.com/content.asp?ContentID=3092

109.  Oliver Balch, 'Peter Torrebiarte, Starbucks Coffee Agronomy Company,' *Ethical Corporation Magazine,* June 24, 2004, http://www.ethicalcorp.com/content.asp?ContentID=2263

110.  Ibid.

111.  Lisa Roner, 'Coffee Alliance to Support Farmers and Conserve the Environment,' *Ethical Corporation Magazine,* September 29, 2004, http://www.ethicalcorp.com/content.asp?ContentID=2848

112.  Peter Torrebiarte, general manager of the Starbucks Coffee Agronomy Company, quoted in Oliver Balch, 'Peter Torrebiarte, Starbucks Coffee Agronomy Company,' *Ethical Corporation Magazine,* June 24, 2004, http://www.ethicalcorp.com/content.asp?ContentID=2263

113.   Alex Blyth, 'M&S to Switch All Served Coffee to Fairtrade,' *Ethical Corporation Magazine,* September 10, 2004, http://www.ethicalcorp.com/content.asp?ContentID=2715

114.   Andrew Newton, 'NGOs Bringing Bank Scrutiny Back on Track,' *Ethical Corporation Magazine,* May 2, 2004, http://www.ethicalcorp.com/content_print.asp?ContentID=1980

115.   http://www.citigroup.com/citigroup/press/2003/030604b.htm

116.   Marc Gunther, The Mosquito in the Tent,' *Fortune,* May 31, 2004, pp 158–163.

117.   Ibid.

118.   Ibid.

119.   http://www.equator-principles.com/

120.   Citigroup Web site: http://www.citigroup.com/citigroup/citizen/socialresponsibility/index.htm

121.   Alex Blyth, 'NGOs Criticize Banks' Implementation of Equator Principles,' *Ethical Corporation Magazine,* June 10, 2004, http://www.ethicalcorp.com/content_print.asp?ContentID=2188

122.   Alan Murray, 'Business: Scandals Leave Big Banks Vulnerable,' *Wall Street Journal,* April 13, 2005, pA2.

123.   Andrew Newton, 'NGOs Bringing Bank Scrutiny Back on Track,' *Ethical Corporation Magazine,* May 2, 2004, http://www.ethicalcorp.com/content_print.asp?ContentID=1980

124.   Patrick McVeigh, 'Most Valuable Players: Annual SRI Mutual Fund Review for 2002,' *Business Ethics Magazine,* Spring 2003, p18.

125.   Patrick McVeigh, '2003 Mutual Fund Review,' *Business Ethics Magazine,* Spring 2004, p18.

126.   Tania Padgett, 'Socially Responsible Funds' Popular, Although Some Express Skepticism,' *The Japan Times,* August 16, 2001, pp xx–xx.

127.   *Business Ethics Magazine,* Spring 2004, op. cit.

128.   Barbara Kiviat, 'Heart on One's Sleeve, Eye on Bottom Line,' *Miami Herald,* January 19, 2003, p3E.

129.   Paul Hawken, 'Socially Responsible Investing,' *Natural Capital Institute,* April 2005, http://www.naturalcapital.org/docs/SRI%20Report%2010–04_word.pdf

130.   *The Japan Times,* August 16, 2001, op. cit., Newsday, Inc., August 9, 2001, pA51.

131.   Dr. Jem Bendell, *Ethical Corporation Magazine,* November, 2002. http://www.jembendell.com/

132.   Bendell, op. cit., Ibid.

133.   "The Vice Fund is tiny, with assets of $6.6m. Institutions have steered clear. But it is growing fast." In 'Socially Irresponsible Investment: Virtues of Vice,' *The Economist,* November 1, 2003, pp 71–72.

134.   'Socially Irresponsible Investment: Virtues of Vice,' *The Economist,* November 1, 2003, pp 71–72.

135.   Barbara Kiviat, 'Heart on One's Sleeve, Eye on Bottom Line,' *Miami Herald,* January 19, 2003, p3E.

136.   Christopher Geczy et al., 'Investing in Socially Responsible Mutual Funds,' May 2003, http://finance.wharton.upenn.edu/~stambaug/sri.pdf

137.   Susan Scherreik, 'Greener Money,' *BusinessWeek,* February 17, 2003, p87.

138.   *The Japan Times,* August 16, 2001, op. cit., Newsday, Inc., August 9, 2001, pA51.

139.   'Microcredit Is Becoming Profitable, Which Means New Players and New Problems,' *Knowledge@Wharton,* April 20, 2005, http://knowledge.wharton.upenn.edu/article/1177.cfm

140.   Pete Engardio, 'A Way to Help Africa Help Itself,' *BusinessWeek,* July 21, 2003, p40.

141.   Ibid.

142.   http://www.yearofmicrocredit.org/

143.   Accion is one of the leading nonprofit organizations operating in the field of microlending, http://www.accion.org/

144. *Knowledge@Wharton,* April 20, 2005, op. cit.

145. Rona Fried & Marjorie Kelly, 'Getting Started in Community Investing,' *Business Ethics Magazine,* Summer 2003, pp 21–22.

146. Ibid.

147. Ibid.

148. Dennis A. Rondinelli & Ted London, 'How corporations and environmental groups cooperate: Assessing Cross-Sector Alliances and Collaborations,' *Academy of Management Executive,* Vol. 17, No. 1, 2003, p61.

149. 'Campaigners Learn Lessons of Business Advantage,' *Financial Times,* July 24, 2001, http://www.globalpolicy.org/ngos/role/globalact/business/2001/0724busi.htm

150. Michael Elliott, 'Embracing the Enemy Is Good Business,' *Time,* August 13, 2001, p29.

151. Roger Cowe, 'Analysis: Business/NGO partnerships–What's the Payback?' *Ethical Corporation Magazine,* April 16, 2004, http://www.ethicalcorp.com/content.asp?ContentID=1921

152. Greenpeace position paper, 1997, http://archive.greenpeace.org/~ozone/index.html

153. Paul Gilding, 'Making Market Magic,' ecos Corporation Web site, June 2001, http://www.ecoscorporation.com/think/stake/market_magic.htm

154. Rondinelli & London, op. cit., p65.

155. Gilding, op. cit.

156. http://www.ethicalcorp.com/content.asp?ContentID=1921

157. George Melloan, 'Global View: As NGOs Multiply, They Expand a New "Private Sector,"' *Wall Street Journal,* June 22, 2004, pA19.

158. Andrew Carnegie, quoted in 'Doing Well and Doing Good,' *The Economist,* July 31, 2004, pp 57–59.

159. John A. Byrne, 'The New Face of Philanthropy,' *BusinessWeek,* December 2, 2002, p84.

160. *The Economist,* July 31, 2004, op. cit.

161. Unless otherwise stated, all quotations and facts in this section are from John A. Byrne, 'The New Face of Philanthropy,' *BusinessWeek,* December 2, 2002, pp 82–94.

162. Michelle Conlin et al., 'The Top Givers,' *BusinessWeek,* November 29, 2004, http://www.businessweek.com/magazine/content/04_48/b3910401.htm

163. Unless otherwise stated, all quotations and facts in this section are from Michelle Conlin et al., 'The Corporate Donors,' *BusinessWeek,* December 1, 2003, pp 92–96.

164. Conlin et al., November 29, 2004, op cit., http://www.businessweek.com/magazine/content/04_48/b3910401.htm

165. *The Economist,* July 31, 2004, op. cit.

166. Robbie Shell, 'Manager's Journal: Breaking the Stereotypes of Corporate Philanthropy,' *Wall Street Journal,* November 26, 2002, pB2.

167. Charles Handy, 'What's a Business For?' *Harvard Business Review,* Vol. 80, No. 12, December 2002, p55.

168. Manuel G. Velasquez, 'Business Ethics: Concepts and Cases,' 5th Edition, Prentice Hall, 2002, p1.

169. Velasquez, op. cit., p4.

170. Charles Handy, op. cit., p55.

171. C.K. Prahalad & Allen Hammond, 'Serving the World's Poor, Profitably,' *Harvard Business Review,* September 2002, Vol. 80, No. 9, pp 48–58.

172. Cait Murphy, 'The Hunt for Globalization That Works,' *Fortune,* October 28, 2002, p164.

173. 'Face Value: Profits and Poverty,' *The Economist,* August 21, 2004, p54.

174. Prahalad & Hammond, op. cit.

175.  *Fortune,* October 28, 2002, op. cit.

176.  E-Inclusion "aims to deliver computer and Internet technology to the world's 4 billion poor people through sustainable microenterprises." *Fortune* writer David Kirkpatrick called e-Inclusion "the most visionary step I've ever seen a large tech company take." Marc Gunther, 'Can One Person Change A Major Corporation,' *Business Ethics Magazine,* Winter 2004, pp10–12.

177.  Prahalad & Hammond, op. cit.

178.  *Fortune,* October 28, 2002, op. cit.

179.  C. K. Prahalad, quoted in 'Face Value: Profits and Poverty,' *The Economist,* August 21, 2004, p54.

180.  Prahalad & Hammond, op. cit.

181.  Rifkin is president of the Foundation of Economic Trends and author of the books, 'Who Should Play God?' (1981) and 'The End of Work' (1994), in which he predicted many developments of the technological revolution and how they would affect the workplace and other aspects of society.

182.  Interview of Jeremy Rifkin by David Batstone, 'The Future of Work,' first published in *Business 2.0 Magazine,* reprinted by Right Reality Inc., February 10, 2004, http://www.business2.com/b2/

183.  Ibid.

184.  Quoted from David Batstone & David Chandler, 'Ford's Success Formula Not Followed to a T,' *Atlanta Journal-Constitution,* December 17, 2004, http://www.ajc.com/opinion/content/opinion/1204/17ford.html

185.  Lee Iacocca, 'Henry Ford,' *Time 100,* http://www.time.com/time/time100/builder/profile/ford.html

186.  'In 1913, One Ad Changed the Face of America's Middle Class,' Ford ad in *Fortune,* February 9, 2004.

187.  Iacocca, op cit.

188.  Ann Zimmerman, 'Costco's Dilemma: Be Kind to Its Workers, or Wall Street?' *Wall Street Journal,* March 26, 2004, pB1.

189.  Both figures are 2003 amounts. In 2004, "Miami Dade County ordinance requires that . . . municipal employees and workers of employers who contract with these municipalities to provide public services . . . be paid $9.25 per hour if the employer provides health insurance, or $10.59 per hour if not." Reporting a Florida International University Center for Labor Research study investigating the cost of the City of Miami implementing its living wage ordinance, *CHAIN Reaction* (e-mail newsletter), July 20, 2004, *Human Services Coalition,* Miami, FL.

190.  ". . . the new entry for 'McJob' in the 11th edition of [Merriam-Webster's] collegiate dictionary, which . . . defines the term as a dead-end occupation." Quoted in, 'Review & Outlook: Thinking Outside the Bun,' *Wall Street Journal,* November 14, 2003, pW15.

191.  *Asian Labour Update,* Issue No. 42, January–March, 2002, http://www.amrc.org.hk/4202.htm

192.  Specifically, cleaners, or the nearest equivalent worker for which the necessary data was available.

193.  *Asian Labour Update,* January–March, 2002, op. cit.

194.  *The Economist,* April 22, 2000, op. cit.

195.  Andrew Tobias, 'How Much Is Fair?' *Miami Herald,* Parade Magazine, March 2, 2003, p10.

196.  Kathy Kristof, 'Study ties biggest CEO raises to largest layoffs,' *Miami Herald,* August 30, 2003, p1C.

197.  Special Report: Meritocracy in America, 'Ever Higher Society, Ever Harder to Ascend,' *The Economist,* January 1, 2005, pp 22–23.

198.  *Miami Herald,* March 2, 2003, op. cit.

199.  Editorial, 'What We Learned in 2002,' *BusinessWeek,* December 30, 2002, p170.

200.  Kris Axtman & Ron Scherer, 'Enron Lapses and Corporate Ethics,' *Christian Science Monitor,* February 4, 2002. http://www.csmonitor.com/2002/0204/p01s01-ussc.html

# Chapter 7

## SOCIETAL ISSUES AND CASE STUDIES

## COMMUNITY

☑ **CSR Connection:** This issue reflects the importance of a strong relationship between a company and the communities within which it operates. It is central to the CSR debate.

### Issue

To what extent do business practices contribute to the community in which the organization is based and operating? Increasingly, firms are becoming more global. One consequence of this perspective is that many companies are relocating their operations offshore as part of a strategy to minimize costs. This often means that jobs are lost at home and gained by the low-cost environment overseas to which the companies relocate. From blue-collar factory jobs in China and Southeast Asia to white-collar call-center and computer-programming jobs in India, many U.S. citizens are experiencing globalization up close and personal:

By some estimates, roughly 1.3 million manufacturing jobs have moved abroad since the beginning of 1992, the bulk in the past three years to Mexico and East Asia.[1]

Forrester Research Inc. predicts that American employers will move about 3.3 million white-collar service jobs and $136 billion in wages overseas in the next 15 years.[2]

Though some of these jobs would have been lost to automation, the willingness of some companies to pursue the lowest costs stands in contrast with those companies that make a stronger commitment to the domestic communities within which they operate.

# Case Study: Fannie Mae[3]

Fannie Mae was created by the U.S. Congress in 1938 with an unusual mandate: It is a publicly traded company with a federal charter to help make home ownership more available throughout the United States.[4] The company helps implement this vision through its decade-long, $2 trillion program, American Dream Commitment,

a plan announced in 2000 to provide $2 trillion in private capital for 18 million minority and underserved Americans to own or rent a home by the end of the decade.[5]

In 2001, over 51 percent of Fannie Mae's financing went to low- and moderate-income households. . . . To aid the victims of predatory lenders, Fannie Mae allows additional flexibility in underwriting new loans for people trapped in abusive loans, if they could have initially qualified for conventional financing. In January [2002] the company committed $31 million to purchasing these types of loans.[6]

In addition to regularly ranking high on *Business Ethics Magazine's* 100 Best Corporate Citizens list (number 1 in 2004), Fannie Mae has also performed well on *Fortune's Best* Companies for Minorities, *Working Mother's* Best Companies for Working Mothers, and *The American Benefactor's* America's Most Generous Companies lists:[7]

Fannie Mae scores high in the areas of community and diversity. . . . Franklin D. Raines,[8] an Africa-American, is CEO [resigned, December 2004], and there are two women and two minorities among the company's eight senior line executives.[9]

In 2004, Fannie Mae expanded its American Dream Commitment, pledging

to help 6 million families—including 1.8 million minority families—become first-time homeowners over the next decade.[10]

Under the three-phase American Dream Commitment expansion plan, Fannie Mae will pledge significant new resources through several dozen new and enhanced mortgage initiatives to achieve the following goals:

- Expand access to homeownership for millions of first-time home buyers and help raise the minority homeownership rate to 55 percent with the ultimate goal of closing the homeownership gaps entirely;
- Make homeownership and rental housing a success for millions of families at risk of losing their homes; and,
- Expand the supply of affordable housing where it is needed most, which includes initiatives for workforce housing and supportive housing for chronically homeless.

Having met the $2 trillion American Dream Commitment goal and the company's previous Trillion Dollar Commitment launched in 1994, Fannie Mae and its partners have now provided funds for more than 28 million underserved families in 10 years.[11]

A report concerning the availability of affordable mortgages for minorities and lower-income prospective homeowners—due in part to less competition between providers in some low-income neighborhoods—indicates the important void Fannie Mae was created to fill:

African-Americans are more than twice as likely as whites to receive high-cost subprime mortgage loans. . . . People identified as Hispanic or Latino are slightly more likely than whites to pay high rates, according to an analysis by *The Wall Street Journal* of disclosures from 11 of the nation's biggest mortgage lenders.[12]

Businesses are increasingly finding it profitable to provide market-based answers to consumer segments whose needs were previously not being met.

Lower-income homeowners represent a potentially very large market to companies willing to address their specific needs and circumstances. In spite of home ownership, in general, being at an all-time high in the United States at present (69%), the corresponding rate in low-income households is only 55% and only 48% for minorities living in urban areas.[13]

There is strong evidence that high home ownership rates also help contribute to a stronger community:

One survey of consumer finances found that low-income homeowners had a net worth 12 times that of renters at the same income level. Other studies found that children of homeowners are more likely to graduate from high school and college and more likely to go on to own a home of their own. Ample research also shows that home ownership keeps communities attractive, safe and vital, generating higher property values and other economic activity.[14]

## Web-Based Examples and Resources

Consuming Industries Trade Action Coalition, http://www.citac.info/

The Consuming Industries Trade Action Coalition, or "CITAC," is committed to the development of U.S. trade policy that is consistent with the needs of America's consuming industries. We believe that the spirit of free and open competition makes our economy the most successful in the world.

Fannie Mae, http://www.fanniemae.com/

Fannie Mae is working to expand homeownership opportunities by creating products and technologies that help more people own homes. We believe that by doing so, we make a positive contribution to families, communities, and the nation.

Expanding the American Dream Commitment, http://www.fanniemae.com/initiatives/adc/index.jhtml

This past January [2004], Fannie Mae pledged to help 6 million families—including 1.8 million minority families—become first-time homeowners over the next decade. Fannie Mae's new commitment to first-time home buyers is part of the next stage of the company's American Dream Commitment, a plan announced in 2000 to provide $2 trillion in private capital for 18 million minority and underserved Americans to own or rent a home by the end of the decade.

National Congress for Community Economic Development, http://www.ncced.org/

The National Congress for Community Economic Development (NCCED) is the trade association and advocate for the community-based development industry. Founded in 1970, NCCED represents over 3,600 community development corporations (CDCs) across America. CDCs produce affordable housing and create jobs through business and commercial development activities.

NeighborWorks America, http://www.nw.org/

A national nonprofit organization created by Congress to provide financial support, technical assistance, and training for community-based revitalization efforts. Neighborhood Reinvestment Corporation, local NeighborWorks organizations and Neighborhood Housing Services of America make up the NeighborWorks system, which has successfully built healthy communities for 25 years.

Save American Manufacturing (SAM), http://www.samnow.org/

SAMNow is a continuing grassroots movement that represents the job concerns of legal American workers.

YMCA, http://www.ymca.net/

Together, the nation's more than 2,400 YMCAs are the largest not-for-profit community service organizations in America, working to meet the health and social service needs of 17.9 million men, women and children in 10,000 communities in the U.S.A.

## Questions for Discussion and Review

1. What is your position on the outsourcing-of-jobs debate? Is outsourcing good or bad? Explain using examples of corporations whose actions support your point of view.

2. Does a company like Fannie Mae deserve to be rewarded for the stance it is taking in helping build stronger communities within the United States? Or is it just identifying its niche in the market and doing what it can to make itself as successful as possible?

3. As globalization increases and the world becomes smaller and smaller, do you think the concept of a *community* will become more or less important? When a company supports a global brand and distributes products around the world, why should it feel more committed to one community over another? The idea of a company incorporated in the Bahamas, with a German CEO, a product developed in Japan, manufactured in India, and with a main market in China no longer seems an unusual concept. How does CSR fit into this picture in terms of a company's responsibility to its community?

## CORRUPTION AND BRIBERY

☑ *CSR Connection:* This issue, on both an individual and a corporate level, presents a significant CSR challenge for corporations, especially those operating internationally.

The World Bank Institute estimates bribes alone drain the equivalent of more than $1 trillion annually from the legitimate global economy of $30 trillion (based on 2001–2002 economic data). That estimate does not include the embezzlement of public funds or the diversion of assets, which might double the total cost of corruption.[15]

## Issue—Individual Corruption

To what extent do local cultural and societal practices cause conflict when judged by the values of a different society? These problems are increasing as globalization spreads and international business becomes the norm rather than the exception, leading to businesspeople coming into contact with others from many countries and societies. A 2002 survey carried out in Peru by Apoyo Opinion y Mercado and Pro Etica, a nongovernment agency with the goal of promoting ethics in Peru, found the following:

> About 70 percent of Peruvians tolerate acts of corruption, such as bribing police officers or tax evasion. . . . 63 percent said they were partially in agreement with giving "gifts or money" to speed up paperwork. Only 28 percent were totally opposed. Meanwhile, 64 percent said they tolerated bribing police officers to avoid fines. "We have reached the conclusion that corruption is a cultural act in Peru," Jose Ugaz, president of Pro Etica, told local television.[16]

The extent to which corruption permeates a society results in a real economic burden for the members of that society, as well as for the companies that operate there. Studies show that the problem is still a factor in many developing countries, in spite of anticorruption campaigns by governments in those countries:

> A study last year by . . . Transparency International, estimated that the average Mexican household pays 7% of its annual income on bribes to get public services—essentially the same level as in 2001.[17]

Motorola published its corporate guide on this and other ethical issues in 1998 aimed at helping managers stationed abroad who might face issues related to this area:

> A sample question: What do you do if you're in a country where payments are expected in business dealings? Motorola's code says no. The upshot of the ethics guide: Just because you're not at headquarters doesn't mean you throw the company's standards out the window.[18]

Ultimately, an individual can be held accountable for actions taken on behalf of the company, if those actions are illegal.

## Issue—Corporate Corruption

> At Dow Chemical Co., which has had a global-compliance program in place since 1998, regional compliance and ethics committees have been strengthened, says Thomas R. McCormick, director of Global Ethics & Compliance. "You do have certain countries that we do business in that are at higher risk because the pressure to pay bribes is higher in those countries," he says.[19]

From 1977, when the U.S. Congress passed the Foreign Corrupt Practices Act (FCPA), until the 1990s, the United States took the lead in attempting to curtail the bribery of foreign officials. This left U.S. companies operating on an uneven playing field, too often forced to choose between bribing a foreign official and placing itself in contravention of the FCPA or refusing to bribe and losing contracts. Simply put, until recently it was illegal for U.S. corporations to bribe foreign officials, but not for companies from other countries. This is changing now as other governments have also begun acting to try to curb bribery generally, through a number of international treaties and conventions. For example, in 2003, the EU took up the issue of payments by major oil companies to foreign governments in conjunction with the rights to extract oil in those countries:

> The International Monetary Fund (IMF) estimates that, in Angola alone, $1bn of oil revenue goes missing every year while three-quarters of the country's population lives in absolute poverty.[20]

Oil companies, which in the past have often been forced by some governments to sign nondisclosure agreements regarding such payments, increasingly are being forced to provide greater transparency, detailing total amounts paid so that, in theory, the governments can be held accountable for what happened to the money after it was received. In addition, the British government has announced it intends to introduce a voluntary code of conduct designed to publish the details of such payments by those companies that sign up to the agreement. Many other governments and regulating bodies are also beginning to work in this area:

> The OECD agreement [adopting tougher anticorruption laws], which took effect in 1999, has spurred tough laws in 35 countries, imposing criminal penalties on companies found guilty of bribery. Before that, the U.S. was virtually the only country with such legislation. Some, including France and Germany, even allowed companies to take tax deductions for bribes they paid.[21]

## Case Study: Legislation

The following list provides a general overview of existing legislation in this field:[22]

### The United States

The Foreign Corrupt Practices Act of 1977 (amended via the Omnibus Trade and Competitiveness Act, 1988) Department of Justice, Criminal Division, Fraud Section, http://www.usdoj.gov/criminal/fraud/fcpa.html

The Foreign Corrupt Practices Act (FCPA) prevents any person or firm in the United States from making a corrupt payment to a foreign official to obtain or keep business.

The FCPA, as amended in 1998 [states] . . . that issuers of publicly traded securities regulated by the Securities and Exchange Commission (SEC), U.S. citizens, resident aliens, and businesses organized under U.S. law . . . may not, directly or indirectly, make payments, promises or offers of anything of value to foreign officials to obtain or retain business or to secure an improper advantage.[23]

A criminal violation [of the FCPA] may result in a $2 million fine per violation. Officers, directors, or employees can face fines up to $100,000 and/or five years imprisonment. In 1994, Lockheed Corporation agreed to pay $24.8 million for violating the FCPA. The accounting provisions, further, contain criminal penalties that could result in maximum sentences of up to 10 years in prison and fines up to $1 million for individuals and $2.5 million for corporations.[24]

In March 2003, an arrest was made concerning the "largest alleged violation of the FCPA." The issue concerned bribes totaling $78 million paid by large Western oil companies ("including Mobil") to senior government officials of Kazakhstan. Monies apparently went to one bank account controlled by Mr. Nursultan Nazarbayev, the president of Kazakhstan.[25]

### Organisation for Economic Co-operation and Development (OECD)

Fighting Bribery and Corruption, http://www. oecd.org/department/0,2688,en_2649_34855_ 1_1_1_1_1,00.html

The OECD first put international corruption on its agenda in 1989 and evolved two basic objectives for its work: to fight corruption in intl. business and to help level the competitive playing field for companies. After several years spent analysing the nature of corruption in international business, the OECD Convention on Combating Bribery was signed in 1997.

The Anti-Corruption Division serves as the focal point within the OECD Secretariat to support the work of the OECD in the fight against bribery in international business through the implementation of the OECD Anti-Bribery Convention. The Division furthermore works with non-member countries in the framework of its outreach activities.

On [the OECD Bribery and Corruption] website, you will find information about the implementing mechanisms of the OECD Convention on Combating Bribery, activities with non-member states, other international anti-corruption initiatives, and co-operation with the private sector and civil society. OECD has also created the ANCORR web, an extensive reference centre about corruption and related issues.

### Organization of American States

Inter-American Convention Against Corruption (1996), http://www.oas.org/juridico/english/ Treaties/b-58.html

Designed to eliminate bribery and corruption in member countries . . . by forbidding governmental officials from demanding improper payments. . . . Unfortunately, the Inter-American Convention lacks an enforcement mechanism to ensure that its signatories fulfill their obligations.[26]

### The United Nations

Declaration against Corruption and Bribery in International Commercial Transactions (1996), http://www.un.org/documents/ga/res/51/a51r19 1.htm

On December 16, 1996, the UN General Assembly adopted a resolution

calling on member nations to take all necessary steps to eliminate corruption and obligating the U.N. to provide advice and technical support to assist countries in developing anticorruption policies.[27]

### The World Bank and International Monetary Fund

In 1996, the World Bank and the IMF instituted policies that allowed them to investigate complaints of corruption and to blacklist companies and governments that participate in bribery. . . . The World Bank has already stopped funding development projects in Nigeria, Zaire, and Kenya because of corruption. . . . The IMF also recently suspended a $220 million loan to Kenya and a $120 million loan to Cambodia "because of problems in governance which concern corruption."[28]

### The European Union

In 1995, the European Union took two important steps toward fighting corruption. First, it established a framework for countries to enforce administrative sanctions against acts of corruption. Second, it passed a Convention on the Protection of Community and Financial interests, obligating member countries to impose criminal penalties in cases of serious fraud.[29]

More recently the EU has launched the following initiatives:

- Protocol to the Convention on the Protection of the Communities' Financial Interests (EU Corruption Protocol)
- EU Corruption Convention

"but neither [initiative] has yet obtained the necessary ratifications to enter into force."[30]

### Council of Europe

Criminal Law Convention on Corruption (1999), http://conventions.coe.int/treaty/en/Treaties/Html/173.htm

covers (1) active and passive corruption of domestic or foreign officials, (2) elected representatives of domestic bodies, and (3) elected representatives and members of international courts.[31]

## Web-Based Examples and Resources

American Bar Association—Section of International Law and Practice, http://www.abanet.org/intlaw/

The American Bar Association is the largest voluntary professional membership association in the world . . . with more than 400,000 members. . . . Founded in 1933, the Section of International Law and Practice has been the leader in the development of policy in the international arena, the promotion of the rule of law and the education of international law practitioners. . . . With more than 60 substantive committees and many listserves, the Section provides specialized fora to address the significant international legal issues of our times.

Electronic Journal of Business Ethics, http://ejbo.jyu.fi/index.cgi?page=articles/0301_2

Karen Eastwood, Anna-Maija Lämsä, and Aila Säkkinen, "About Ethics and Values in Business Education–A Cross-Cultural Perspective," April 17, 2002.

Inter-American Development Bank, http://www.iadb.org/

Sponsor of the Inter-American Initiative of Social Capital, Ethics and Development, http://www.iadb.org/etica/ingles/index-i.cfm

The Inter-American Initiative of Social Capital, Ethics and Development is intended to strengthen ethical values and social capital in the countries of Latin America and the Caribbean.

Transparency International, http://www.transparency.org/

Transparency International, the only international non-governmental organization devoted to combating corruption, brings civil society, business, and governments together in a powerful global coalition.

## Questions for Discussion and Review

1. Were you aware of the FCPA? Were you also aware that you can be held personally liable for illegal actions that you take on behalf of your company, even if you were just following orders? Yet competitors in foreign countries may be able to use bribes as "just part of doing business." The result is an uneven playing field. Do you think the FCPA is unfair? Explain?

2. Why do you think corruption is more prevalent in some countries than others? What should a company do when operating in such an environment? Is it better to "Do as the Romans do" or to try to impose standards and values from home?

3. *Corruption* means different things to different people. Some people argue that campaign contributions are just another form of corruption. What is your reaction to this statement?

# COUNTRY OF ORIGIN

☑ *CSR Connection:* This issue highlights an important element of the supply chain debate within CSR.

## Issue

To what extent are consumers in the West aware of the origin of the products they buy (especially luxury products, which are discretionary and could be sacrificed without a significant decline in living standards) and the consequences of their purchase decisions? A 2002 study by Worldwatch Institute claimed that demand for many luxury goods in the West results in death and poverty in developing countries:

[The report] cites diamonds, tropical woods and the mineral coltan, used in cellular phones and other electronic products, as examples. Worldwatch claims that wars fought over these valuable materials "have killed or displaced more than 20 million people and are raising at least $12 billion a year for rebels, warlords, repressive governments, and other predatory groups around the world."[32]

One example highlighted in this report is the international trade in so-called conflict diamonds.

# Case Study: Conflict Diamonds

The United Nations' definition of conflict or "blood" diamonds:

> Conflict diamonds are diamonds that originate from areas controlled by forces or factions opposed to legitimate and internationally recognized governments, and are used to fund military action in opposition to those governments, or in contravention of the decisions of the Security Council.[33]

Definitive numbers indicating the extent of this problem throughout the diamond industry are difficult to calculate and range from De Beers' estimate of an "unquestionably small"[34] segment of the market to as much as "two per cent of the world's diamonds, mostly those extracted from Africa," according to the Agence France-Presse.[35] Many agree, however, that this illegal trade in diamonds continues to represent a significant problem both in moral and commercial terms:

> The trade in conflict and illicit rough diamonds funds and prolongs conflicts in Angola, Sierra Leone, Liberia and Democratic Republic of Congo and is also being accused of funding international terrorism.[36]

The negative publicity surrounding conflict diamonds has begun to have an impact on the collective consumer conscience and, therefore, on the industry as a whole:

> Sales of the stones have dropped 15% to 20% in Europe since 1994. Professionals in the business have been concerned about its image and competition from synthetic diamonds.[37]

Some companies have decided to take a stand on these and other CSR-related issues within their industry. The hope is that this differentiation will lead to a sustainable advantage over competitors:

> In the mid-1990s, when "conflict diamonds" first became an issue, "we felt as an industry that we blew it," [Michael J. Kowalski, Chairman and CEO of Tiffany & Co.] said. "We should have seen it coming, we should have acted sooner. . . . In 1999 . . . Tiffany helped create a "chain of custody" for diamonds as well [as its gold and silver supply chains]. As a founding member of the World Diamond Council . . . Tiffany pledged to try and eliminate the trade of diamonds in underdeveloped countries where it contributes to conflicts and exploitation, particularly of children. . . . It really is about our social license to continue to do business.[38]

Ongoing pressure has begun to result in increased progress and hope:

> More than thirty-five diamond trading and producing countries agreed . . . to launch an international certification system designed to stop "blood diamonds" from reaching world markets.[39]

The result of this agreement was the Kimberley Process, adopted in 2000. The Kimberley Process is a certification scheme that aims to track diamonds as they move along the supply chain, enabling every stone to be identified at any point:

> From January 2003, imported diamonds will require a certificate of origin and countries or traders that fail to comply will be barred from the international diamond trade.[40]

In the wake of the adoption of the Kimberley Process, a degree of momentum for reform has been established. The UN has registered its opposition to the continued trade:

> On 1 December 2000, the United Nations General Assembly adopted, unanimously, a resolution on the role of diamonds in fuelling conflict, breaking the link between the illicit transaction of rough diamonds and armed conflict, as a contribution to prevention and settlement of conflicts (A/RES/55/56).[41]

Legislation was introduced in Washington to help prevent U.S. consumers, who "purchase 65 to 70 percent of the world's diamonds,"[42] getting caught up in this trade and also bring U.S. law into alignment with that of other countries that are taking a stance on this issue. The Clean Diamond Trade Act was signed into law by President George W. Bush on April 25, 2003, and commits U.S. companies to participate in the UN-sponsored Kimberley Process, by which the country of origin certifies its diamonds:

> The [legislation] is meant to curb the trade in rough diamonds from mines controlled by antigovernment rebel groups in Sierra Leone, Angola and the Democratic Republic of Congo, who traded the stones for arms during civil conflicts that killed 3.7 million people. The smuggling of illegal diamonds also is said to be a source of funding for the al Qaeda terrorist network.[43]

At the end of June 2004, a further step was taken in trying to chart more accurately the movement of diamonds through the supply chain:

> The UK campaign group Global Witness, the ICM association of miners and diamond cutters, and Antwerp's federation of diamond dealers reached a deal in Paris last week to create a "fair-trade" mark to diamonds. . . . The quality of diamonds has long been measured by the four Cs: carat, colour, clarity and cut. The new mark will indicate that a diamond

has achieved the fifth C standard, that of cleanliness.[44]

The next step will be to ensure all the major interests throughout the industry sign up to the new certification process, as well as continue to raise public awareness about the issue:

> This new agreement is intended to strengthen the Kimberley Process . . . [which] has suffered because not all governments have enforced its requirements.[45]

The list of current participant countries that have adopted the Kimberley Process can be found at http://www.kimberleyprocess.com:8080/site/?name=participants

On July 9, 2004,

> the first case of successful industry self-regulation against trade in so-called "conflict diamonds" took place when Congo-Brazzaville was punished for failing to prove the source of its diamond exports. . . . Congo-Brazzaville was punished . . . by being expelled from the [Kimberley] Process (the first country ever to be thus censured). As a result, legal trade in its diamonds should cease. It is a test case for the industry.[46]

In September 2004, the Jewelers of America, the national association of retail jewelers, launched "a new corporate responsibility initiative,"[47] including a "Supplier Code of Conduct."[48]

## Web-Based Examples and Resources

ADiamondisForever.com, http://www.adiamondisforever.com/

Adiamondisforever.com is an information source on diamonds and is sponsored by the Diamond Trading Company, the world's leading diamond sales and marketing company. Combining promotion with education, adiamondisforever.com exists to help build interest in diamonds among consumers, as well as helping their confidence in the diamond buying process.

De Beers Group, http://www.debeersgroup.com/

De Beers produces about 45% by value of the total annual global diamond production from its mines in South Africa, and through its 50:50 partnerships with the governments of Botswana and Namibia. De Beers' gem mining operations span every category of diamond mining—open pit, underground, alluvial, coastal and under sea—while its exploration programme extends across six continents. Through its selling arm, the Diamond Trading Company (DTC) based in London, De Beers markets some two thirds of global supply, and has conducted a renowned diamond advertising and promotion campaign for over half a century.

De Beers' Value and Culture Web page can be found at http://www.debeersgroup.com/debeersweb/About+De+Beers/De+Beers+Value+and+Culture/

Diamond Trading Company's *Diamond Best Practice Principles'* http://www.debeersgroup.com/NR/rdonlyres/FAFC09A7–810C-4E97-B33B-155A45643DF4/215/BPP.pdf

Global Witness-Conflict Diamond Campaign, http://www.globalwitness.org/campaigns/diamonds/

The Conflict Diamond campaign exposes how the international diamond industry has operated for years with no rules or regulations and how this lack of corporate responsibility has wreaked havoc in some of Africa's most prolific civil wars.

Jewelers of America, http://www.jewelers.org/

Jewelers of America (JA) is the national association for the retail jeweler.

Kimberley Process, http://www.kimberleyprocess.com/

The Kimberley Process involves more than 30 governments, the European Community, the diamond industry and civil society and has been establishing minimum acceptable international standards for national certification schemes relating to trade in rough diamonds.

World Diamond Council, http://www.worlddiamondcouncil.com/

The ultimate mandate for the World Diamond Council is the development, implementation and oversight of a tracking system for the export and import of rough diamonds to prevent the exploitation of diamonds for illicit purposes such as war and inhumane acts.

Worldwatch Institute, http://www.worldwatch.org/

Founded by Lester Brown in 1974, the Worldwatch Institute offers . . . a leading source of information on the interactions among key environmental, social, and economic trends. Our work revolves around the transition to an environmentally sustainable and socially just society—and how to achieve it.

## Questions for Discussion and Review

1. Given the size of its operations, De Beers is the most important player in the diamond industry. What interest might they have in seeing the Kimberley Process either work or fail?

2. Diamonds are already very expensive. Would you be willing to pay more to ensure the integrity of the diamond you were buying? Why, or why not?

3. Regulating international trade adds costs to users, often making the producer country less competitive on the international market. On the other hand, societal benefits come from regulation. Discuss these trade-offs.

# ETHICS

☑ *CSR Connection:* This issue reflects the importance of ethics, both on a personal and business level, within the broader issue of CSR.

## Issue

To what extent do people, who are able to distinguish right from wrong, make the correct decisions, especially when there is a significant personal incentive to do otherwise?

[In 2002] Only 17 percent of Americans rate business executives' ethics as high or very high, down from 25 percent [in 2001], according to a Gallup poll sponsored by CNN and *USA TODAY*.[49]

Kim Campbell, the former prime minister of Canada, offers one possible solution to the perceived decrease in ethics within corporations—female leaders:

The qualities that are defined as masculine are also the same qualities that are defined as the qualities of leadership. There is virtually no overlap between the qualities ascribed to femininity and those to leadership. [Yet in several studies] results show that when you have a critical mass of women in an organization, you have less corruption. . . . Lest you think that all we aspire to for the world can be accomplished by male-dominated organizations, I have only to say to you: Enron, Taliban, Roman Catholic Church.[50]

Many recognize the value of instilling ethics early as a key component of a young student's education. This basic foundation then becomes a resource on which the individual can draw later in life. With the corporate scandals around the turn of this century bringing ethics to the newspaper front pages and TV headlines on a daily basis, the calls for ethics to be a core component of the curricula in business schools, which are responsible for training the next generation of business leaders, grew louder:

MBA students who say schools are doing a lot to prepare them ethically: 22%[51]

More than three out of five MBA students and grads say that American business is not "honest and ethical."[52]

Many also feel, however, that particularly at the graduate education level it is very difficult to influence the core of an individual's personality, that in a 1-semester class you cannot instill an ethical predisposition but only build on one that already exists. The characters of young adults are already formed. Can and should ethics be taught at the MBA or graduate university level?

---

## Case Study: Teaching Ethics

A recent survey of 1,100 students on 27 university campuses in the United States by a nonprofit organization, Students in Free Enterprise (SIFE, http://www.sife.org/), reveals that, although many students are concerned about the ethics of U.S. corporations, they are unable to apply the same high standards to their own personal conduct:

> Some 59% [of college students polled] admit cheating on a test (66% of men, 54% of women). And only 19% say they would report a classmate who cheated (23% of men, but 15% of women).[53]

How to marry the two? In response to greater calls for higher ethical standards within corporations, and as the producers of future business leaders, universities are now starting to teach ethics as integral elements of MBA and undergraduate business programs:

### University of Nottingham

The University of Nottingham in the UK has launched an International Center for Corporate Social Responsibility. Its MBA in corporate social responsibility began in September 2003, offering specialist modules in corporate social responsibility policies, economic crime, ethics, and corporate governance and accountability: http://www.nottingham.ac.uk/business/mba/N107.html

### Brunel University

In October 2003, Brunel School of Business and Management in the UK launched two new masters programs based around ethics and CSR:

- MSc in business, ethics, and sustainability:

[The course] will enable students to consider businesses in their wider social environment with a particular focus on various aspects of corporate social responsibility and sustainability. The course will equip students to take on a leading role in Business Ethics management/consultancy and in areas related to Environmental Management.

- MSc in business and public ethics:

[The course] has its main focus on the relationship between business and public institutions. It will enable students to take a holistic approach to the worlds of enterprise and politics, to identify and analyze social and ethical issues and to formulate integral solutions. The program will equip students for a career in the public or private sector.

These courses are supported by staff with research expertise in the relevant areas and by the Brunel Research in Enterprise, Sustainability and Ethics (http://www.brunel.ac.uk/about/acad/bbs/research/centres/brese/) and the Brunel Centre for Democratic Evaluation (http://www.brunel.ac.uk/about/acad/bbs/research/centres/bcde/).

### Erasmus University of Rotterdam[54]

In 2005, Erasmus University Rotterdam launched a series of programs "aimed at the practice of Corporate Social Responsibility," the first of which were postgraduate programs in sustainability management and sustainability auditing:

> The program we offer now provides a better theoretical base. The lectures are given by authoritative professors and guest lecturers with up to date knowledge of the sustainability practice. This ensures that the programs do not

linger in theoretical, ivory tower knowledge, but give direct handles for the daily practice.[55]

### Bainbridge Graduate Institute

Another example is the more comprehensive approach adopted by the new Bainbridge Graduate Institute near Seattle in Washington. Their MBA program focuses on ethics, sustainability, and corporate responsibility as the core around which the course is built: http://www.bgiedu.org/:

> The coursework titles . . . say it all: "Creativity and Right Livelihood," "Finance and the Triple Bottom Line," "Environmentally and Socially Responsible Management," and "Vision, Ethics, and Leadership," to name just a few.[56]

Some are concerned that the emphasis is misplaced and that stand-alone ethics classes, as one element of a wider MBA or business curriculum, are insufficient to make a significant impact, even if mandatory. "If you are serious about ethics, it means integrating it into every course and activity," says Professor Nelson Phillips, Director of the MBA program at Cambridge University's Institute of Management. This comprehensive perspective is crucial; however, at present, most courses ignore the ethical element of the subject matter they are dealing with. This is not because they are unaware of the issue but because the approach they bring to the subject does not emphasize the issue. "All management courses adopt implicit or explicit ethical positions, almost without thinking sometimes. The ethical aspect of this position is usually glossed over or trivialized," believes Professor Bob Berry of Nottingham University Business School.[57]

Opponents of mandatory curriculum provision argue that each institution should remain free to determine the academic content of its courses. They also argue that an ethical perspective, sufficiently interwoven within the program as a whole, is much more effective at producing the desired result. Robert L. Joss, the Philip H. Knight Professor and Dean, Stanford University, says that Stanford Graduate School of Business provides what it terms a "multi-layered approach to teaching ethics" within its MBA curriculum:

> First, students receive an overview of how to think about ethics during their very first week at the school. Second, we weave ethical issues throughout our regular curriculum because that's how general managers confront ethical questions—in the course of their day-to-day challenges. Third, we offer elective courses designed to address specific ethical issues such as Ethics and Global Business. . . . Fourth and finally, we try to create an atmosphere outside the classroom but within the life of the School that promotes ethical behavior.[58]

## Web-Based Examples and Resources

Aspen Institute Initiative for Social Innovation Through Business (ISIB), http://www.aspeninst .org/isib/

Mission: To increase the supply of business leaders who understand—and seek to balance—the complex relationship between business success and social and environmental progress.

Association for Integrity in Accounting (Citizen Works), http://www.citizenworks.org/ actions/aia.php

The mission of the Association for Integrity in Accounting is to provide an independent forum to present and advance positions on a wide range of critical accounting and auditing issues, standards and regulations affecting the accountability and integrity of the profession and the public interest in maintaining trust and confidence in accounting.

*Business Ethics Magazine,* http://www.business-ethics.com/

http://www.business-ethics.com/BizSchlsDropEthics.htm

It's a Heckuva Time to Be Dropping Business Ethics Courses: MBA Programs Are Downsizing Ethics Requirements at Precisely the Wrong Time.

CASEPLACE.org, http://www.caseplace.org/

CasePlace.org is a free, online service for business school faculty, students and businesses. . . . For business materials that incorporate social impact management, corporate social responsibility, and business ethics, you've come to the right place.

*Electronic Journal of Business Ethics,* http://ejbo.jyu.fi/index.cgi?page=articles/0201_1

Gilda M. Agacer, Petri Vehmanen, and Lina J. Valcarcel, "Business Ethics: Are Accounting Students Aware? A Cross-Cultural Study of Four Countries," April 17, 2002.

Ethics Resource Center (ERC), http://www.ethics.org/

The Ethics Resource Center (ERC) is a nonprofit, nonpartisan educational organization whose vision is a world where individuals and organizations act with integrity.

The mission of the Ethics Resource Center is to strengthen ethical leadership worldwide by providing leading-edge expertise and services through research, education and partnerships.

i-case: Interactive Case-studies, http://www.i-case.com/

In today's competitive business environment, managers must act as leaders, while maintaining an awareness of corporate image, company profitability, and the legal and social implications of their actions. The *i*-CASE series of online case-studies for education and training provide a thought provoking and interactive approach to examining these issues. Through video, text and interactive exercises, *i*-CASE explores the complex decisions faced by managers—business opportunities and challenges, ethical dilemmas, and social demands.

Rating Research LLC, http://www.ratingresearch.com/

Rating Research LLC (RRC) is a public rating agency that measures the critical intangible assets that constitute corporate reputation. RRC's broadly disseminated Reputation Ratings and Ethics Reputation Ratings on leading companies—and the Industry Reputation Studies that support and explain those ratings—provide interested third parties, relevant stakeholders, and the general public with greater insight into corporations' performance—both present and future.

Second Nature—Education for Sustainability, http://www.secondnature.org/

Since 1993, Second Nature has been dedicated to accelerating a process of transformation in higher education. We chose to assist colleges and universities in their quest to integrate sustainability as a core component of all education and practice, and to help expand their efforts to make human activity sustainable.

Students in Free Enterprise (SIFE), http://www.sife.org/

SIFE is a global, nonprofit organization that is literally changing the world through highly dedicated student teams on more than 1,600 university campuses in 40 countries. . . . Guided by distinguished faculty advisors and supported by businesses around the globe, SIFE Teams teach important concepts through educational outreach projects, including market economics, entrepreneurship, personal and financial success, and business ethics to better themselves, their communities and their countries.

## Questions for Discussion and Review

1. Define *ethics* and *ethical behavior.* What is the difference between *unethical* and *illegal* actions?

2. Can ethics be taught to university students? Is that a job for which universities should be held responsible?

3. What makes one person more or less ethical than another? Where does that component of an individual's character come from?

# GLOBALIZATION

☑ *CSR Connection:* This issue reflects the dramatic impact of globalization on both the global business environment and the CSR debate.

## Issue

To what extent has globalization changed the nature of the debate surrounding CSR? How has globalization made CSR more relevant and more immediate for businesses, particularly global corporations?

## Case Study: U.S. Judicial Activism

In the absence of worldwide legislation covering many of the issues to which globalization is giving rise or the absence of an effective legal system in many of the countries in which U.S. corporations operate today, U.S. courts and judges are taking it on themselves to assume jurisdiction and pronounce judgments. In doing so, U.S. courts are applying American legal concepts of rights and duties to events which took place in foreign cultures, often with different standards and expectations:

From Burma, China and Colombia to Ecuador, Nigeria and Sudan, the world's poor and exploited are coming to America. . . . They're coming to our courthouses—to seek justice from global corporations for exploitative business practices abroad.[59]

The basis for this legal long-arm reach of U.S. courts is the Alien Tort Claims Act of 1789. This legislation was originally intended to prevent pirates and assassins fleeing Europe to the safety of the shores of the young America, allowing foreigners to sue in U.S. courts for crimes that violate international law:

In 1980, a federal appeals court ruled that the law allowed foreigners to bring suit in U.S. courts over acts committed abroad. In the 1990s, human-rights lawyers began applying the law to U.S. corporations.[60]

Examples of this relatively recent interpretation in action:

Victim advocates charge . . . that Burma's military rulers forced peasants at gunpoint to help build a pipeline for Unocal Corp., torturing and killing those who resisted. The company knew and approved, they claim. Unocal denies it. . . . [Also] a Colombian labor union has brought a U.S. lawsuit against Coca-Cola Co. for allegedly hiring paramilitary units that murdered union organizers. And South Africans have sued Citigroup and other as-yet-unnamed companies for allegedly profiteering from apartheid.[61]

Rights groups and others have brought 26 cases against multinational companies under the Alien Tort Claims Act, accusing them of complicity in human rights violations.[62]

Since 1980, human-rights groups and victims of atrocities have filed about 100 lawsuits under the Alien Tort Statute. Multinational corporations have watched with concern as companies such as Exxon Mobil Corp. and Unocal Corp. have been hauled into U.S. courts for alleged collusion with repressive governments in Indonesia and Myanmar, aimed at smoothing the way for oil projects.[63]

The legal justification given for U.S. courts allowing these cases to be heard within their jurisdiction indicates the courts' attempt to react to the phenomenon of globalization. The superior court judge in Los Angeles, who removed the final barrier to the Unocal case being heard in the United States, ruled that corporations are responsible for the actions of their business partners, whether those partners are based in the same country or even whether those partners are foreign governments:

Such a decision would be reasonable, the court determined, if the jury accepted the plaintiffs' claims that Unocal knew that the military was relying on forced labor and that the company benefited, even if only indirectly, from the practice.[64]

Although none of the threatened actions have yet to come to trial, the implications are huge, both for corporate America and the foreign policy of the U.S. government. Critics and supporters of free trade argue that U.S. courts are usurping powers to which they have no right. They also argue that they are tackling issues on which they are not best placed to decide:

[Such international disputes are] rightfully a matter of U.S. foreign and trade policy. . . . U.S. judges are not in the best position to set American policy toward the government of Burma or establish acceptable global standards of conduct.[65]

Supporters, however, welcome the willingness of U.S. judges to hold corporations responsible for the sometimes horrific actions and outcomes involved in some aspects of their operations overseas from which they received financial gain:

Kenneth Roth, executive director of Human Rights Watch thinks [opposition to this judicial activism is unwarranted]. . . . The [1789 Alien Tort] statute is "absolutely a good thing. It is one of the few mechanisms available to hold abusive figures and corporations accountable."[66]

## Web-Based Examples and Resources

Domini Social Funds, http://www.domini.com/shareholder-advocacy/Current-Wo/Alien-Tort/

"Alien Tort Claims Act"

EarthRights International, http://www.earthrights.org/atca/index.shtml

Campaign "Defending the Alien Tort Claims Act."

*Ethical Corporation Magazine,* http://www.ethicalcorp.com/content.asp?ContentID=2036

Paul Tarr, "Analysis: Is Trying to Kill the Alien Tort Claims Act Digging for Fool's Gold?" May 13, 2004.

Global Policy Forum—Alien Tort Claims Act—Articles and Analysis, http://www.global policy.org/intljustice/atca/atcaindx.htm

The Alien Tort Claims Act (ATCA) of 1789 grants jurisdiction to U.S. Federal Courts over "any civil action by an alien for a tort only, committed in violation of the law of nations or a treaty of the United States." In 1980 a Paraguayan man successfully used ATCA to sue the policeman who had tortured his son to death in Paraguay. . . . An interesting development has been the recent efforts to use ATCA to sue transnational corporations for violations of international law in countries outside the U.S. If these suits are allowed to proceed, then ATCA could become a powerful tool to increase corporate accountability.

Human Rights Watch, http://www.hrw.org/campaigns/atca/

Campaign to "Defend the Alien Tort Claims Act."

International Labor Rights Fund, http://www.laborrights.org/

ILRF is an advocacy organization dedicated to achieving just and humane treatment for workers worldwide.

*John Doe v. Unocal Corp.,* Nos. 00–56603, 00–57197, Nos. 00–56628, 00–57195, UNITED STATES COURT OF APPEALS FOR THE NINTH CIRCUIT, 2002 U.S. App. LEXIS 19263; 2002 Cal. Daily Op. Service 9585; 2002 Daily Journal DAR 10794, December 3, 2001, Argued and Submitted, Pasadena, California, September 18, 2002, Filed.

Unocal—Corporate Responsibility, http://www.unocal.com/responsibility/index.htm

Our Vision: To be the world's leading energy resource and project development company—the best people, the best partner, and the best performance; To improve people's lives wherever we work.

## Questions for Discussion and Review

1. Argue for and against the grievances of foreign plaintiffs being allowed to be heard in U.S. courts, even if there is no direct impact on U.S. business or society?

2. Do U.S. corporations possess the ability or leverage to influence foreign government policy? If so, is this something they should be trying to do? Should U.S. corporations conduct business with disreputable foreign governments?

3. Are some human rights and legal principles universal?

# HUMAN RIGHTS

> ☑ *CSR Connection:* This issue reflects the potential for corporations today, given their increasing size, to be forces for either good or bad within the global business environment.

## Issue

Globalization has given multinational corporations the opportunity to expand into massive operations. Some commentators see the largest companies as possessing power beyond that of nation-states:

Of the world's 100 largest economies, 49 of them are countries and 51 are companies. General Motors has greater annual sales than the gross national products of Denmark, Thailand, Turkey, South Africa, or Saudi Arabia. Wal-Mart's economy is larger than that of Poland, Ukraine, Portugal, Israel, or Greece. Because of the size and influence of modern corporations, business ethics take on special significance.[67]

Given their increasing size, corporations have the potential to be forces for good or bad within the global business environment. The conditions within which their employees live and work—their human rights—is one area in which corporations have direct influence and for which many have been criticized.

## Case Study: Union Carbide

The accident that occurred at Union Carbide's chemical plant in Bhopal, India, on December 3, 1984, has been well documented, along with the debate over the extent of Union Carbide's culpability, both legal and moral.[68]

The purpose in presenting this case is to indicate the potential danger for companies that apply different standards of care to their operations in different countries with different rules, expectations, and needs and that are at different stages of economic development. The application of a CSR filter to an organization's strategic outlook requires companies to consider their own best interests by ensuring operating standards in any area can hold up under scrutiny by all of their key stakeholder groups.

### Bhopal: Outcome

The accident at Bhopal is widely considered to be "the worst industrial disaster in history":[69]

14,000 dead . . . more than 30,000 permanent injuries (including blindness), 20,000 temporary injuries, and 150,000 minor injuries.[70]

The principal causes of the disaster were found by Evan and Manion to be "Socio-Cultural. . . . Multiple failures of design, coupled with gross managerial negligence in allowing key safety features to be compromised."[71]

Union Carbide's actions were typical of what the authors deem the "often irresponsible actions of multi-national corporations operating in Third World countries."[72] In general, there were lax government controls of the plant and poor training and emergency preparation; however, the authors also found Union Carbide's actions to be highly negligent:

> Union Carbide Corporation's management's perception of the depreciated value of life in India resulted in negligent plant design, which did not include various fail-safe devices.[73]

### Bhopal: Penalties

The legal implications of the disaster resulted in a total of $470 million in compensation, as well as criminal charges filed against the Union Carbide management. These charges included a

> lawsuit charging [then CEO Warren Anderson] and Union Carbide with "culpable homicide" in the 1984 disaster.[74]

All penalties were upheld by the India Supreme Court, which declared Union Carbide "absolutely liable"[75] for all damages, whether accidental or caused by sabotage.

Evan and Manion concurred, concluding that the long list of "violations of basic safety procedures," which caused the accident, "were the unintended consequences of the decision to cut costs. Union Carbide had decided to drop the safety standards at the Bhopal plant well below those maintained at its nearly identical facility in Institute, West Virginia."[76]

### Union Carbide: Institutional memory?

What is perhaps most shocking about the case is that Union Carbide had not learned its lesson. Not only is it responsible for the worst industrial disaster in the world, it is also responsible for "America's worst industrial disaster." During the 1930–1932 construction of Hawk's Nest Tunnel (West Virginia), Union Carbide was found culpable in the deaths of 764 U.S. workers from silicosis (the inhalation of silicon dust). Union Carbide's management team was accused of being fully aware of the dangers of silicon dust at the time:

> The worst occupational health disaster in American history occurred [in the 1930s] when hundreds of men died and over a thousand fell ill from acute silicosis contracted during the building of Union Carbide's Hawk's Nest Tunnel through Gauley Mountain in West Virginia.[77]

## Web-Based Examples and Resources

Amnesty International USA, http://www.amnestyusa.org/business/index.do

> All companies have a direct responsibility to respect human rights in their own operations. Amnesty International believes that the business community also has a wider responsibility—moral and legal—to use its influence to promote respect for human rights.

Fair Labor Association, http://www.fairlabor.org/

> The Fair Labor Association (FLA) is a nonprofit organization combining the efforts of industry, non-governmental organizations (NGOs), colleges and universities to promote adherence to international labor standards and improve working conditions worldwide.

Global Sullivan Principles, http://www.thegsp.org

> The objectives of the Global Sullivan Principles are to support economic, social and political justice by companies where they do business; to support human rights and to encourage equal opportunity at all levels of employment, including racial and gender diversity on decision making committees and boards; to train and advance disadvantaged workers for technical, supervisory and management opportunities; and to assist with greater tolerance and understanding among peoples; thereby, helping to improve the quality of life for communities, workers and children with dignity and equality.

Greenpeace USA, http://www.greenpeaceusa.org/bhopal/

> The Dow Chemical Company, with annual sales exceeding $30 billion U.S., is the largest chemical manufacturing company in the world. Despite being one of the richest companies on the planet, Dow has done little to be a good steward of the environment. Dow's environmental track record includes the original manufacturing and distribution of now highly restricted or banned (in the United States) chemicals such as DDT, Agent Orange, Dursban (pesticide) and asbestos.[78]

International Campaign for Justice in Bhopal, http://bhopal.net/

> The International Campaign for Justice in Bhopal (ICJB) is a coalition of people's organizations, nonprofit groups and individuals who have joined forces to campaign for justice for the survivors of the Union Carbide Disaster in Bhopal.

Video—*Twenty Years Without Justice: The Bhopal Chemical Disaster,* http://bhopal.strategic
video.net

International Labor Organization Declaration on Fundamental Principles and Rights at Work, http://www.ilo.org/dyn/declaris/DECLARATIONWEB.INDEXPAGE

> Adopted in 1998, the ILO Declaration on Fundamental Principles and Rights at Work is an expression of commitment by governments, employers' and workers' organizations to uphold basic human values—values that are vital to our social and economic lives.

Responsible Care, http://www.americanchemistry.com/rc.nsf/open?OpenForm

> Making progress toward the vision of no accidents, injuries or harm to the environment, Responsible Care is good chemistry at work. Through this award-winning initiative, American Chemistry Council members and Partners demonstrate their commitment to the health and safety of employees and communities, and the environment.

Union Carbide Corporation's position, http://www.bhopal.com/

> The December 1984, Bhopal, India tragedy continues to be a source of anguish for Union Carbide employees. It was a tragic incident that killed many innocent people. The legacy of those killed and injured is a chemical industry that adheres voluntarily to strict safety and environmental standards—working diligently to see that an incident of this nature never occurs again.[79]

UN Global Compact, http://www.unglobalcompact.org/Portal/Default.asp

Through the power of collective action, the Global Compact seeks to advance responsible corporate citizenship so that business can be part of the solution to the challenges of globalisation.

Universal Declaration of Human Rights, http://www.un.org/Overview/rights.html

Adopted and proclaimed by General Assembly resolution 217 A (III) of 10 December 1948.

Voluntary Principles on Security and Human Rights, http://www.state.gov/g/drl/rls/2931.htm

Governments of the United States and the United Kingdom, companies in the extractive and energy sectors ("Companies"), and non-governmental organizations, all with an interest in human rights and corporate social responsibility, have engaged in a dialogue on security and human rights.

Witness, http://www.witness.org/

WITNESS is a human rights program that attracts the eyes of the world and inspires those who see—to act. WITNESS strengthens local activists by giving them video cameras and training in production and advocacy. WITNESS unleashes an arsenal of computers, imaging and editing software, satellite phones and email in the struggle for justice.

## Questions for Discussion and Review

1. Do a Google search of *Bhopal* and briefly investigate the background to the case. What is your evaluation of Union Carbide's conduct? Given the heavy involvement of the Indian government in owning, designing, regulating, and operating the plant, who was ultimately responsible for safety standards?

2. What duties does a company have for ensuring the human rights of its workers are upheld? What about the people who live in the communities nearby (as in Bhopal)? Is minimum adherence sufficient, and who should determine what constitutes the "minimum"?

3. Many people have heard about Bhopal and know of Union Carbide's connection to the incident. Not many people, however, know about the Hawk's Nest Tunnel incident. What is your impression of Union Carbide when you think about both events together?

## INTERNET

☑ *CSR Connection:* This issue ties in closely with the issue of globalization. Combined with the global media, the Internet is an equalizing power that allows individuals or small groups to hold corporations more accountable for their operations than ever before.

## Issue

The Internet has provided businesses with a powerful tool to expand the global reach of operations while greatly increasing efficiencies. It has also, however, increased the global exposure of businesses and their actions. The Internet provides a communications network to nonprofit organizations (NPOs), nongovernmental organizations (NGOs), and consumer activists, who use it to band together and convey their message to supporters worldwide.

## Case Study: NGO Activism

As outlined in Chapter 3, a major reason for the increased influence of NGOs and consumers within the corporate world today is the global free flow of information. The abundance of information dramatically alters the balance of power between individuals, NGOs, regulating authorities, and corporations. It is an enabling power that some feel, unless managed correctly, is in danger of spiraling out of control:

A few facts, mixed with fear, speculation and rumor, amplified and relayed swiftly worldwide by modern information technologies, have affected national and international economies, politics and even security in ways that are utterly disproportionate with the root realities. . . . These Internet- or media-borne viruses create global panics, trigger irrational behavior, blur our vision of important underlying problems, strain our infrastructure, buffet markets and undermine governments. Managed and understood, however, the forces that fuel infodemics can . . . help us reduce the number of distortional and destabilizing outbreaks of the types we have recently seen.[80]

Another powerful reason for the increased influence of NGOs today is simply the rapid growth in their numbers that took place during the last half of the 20th century. The Yearbook of International Organizations, published by the Union of International Associations, indicates the extent of this growth. In Africa in 1966, there were 4,239 registered NGOs. By 2000, this number had grown to 21,129. In the Americas, the corresponding numbers jumped from 7,471 to 27,096, and in

Europe the number of registered NGOs went from 18,212 to 73,981.[81]

Numbers for the U.S. NGO and nonprofit sectors combined, although expectedly bigger, vary, partly due to inconsistent labeling; however, the rapid growth and increased profile of the social sector is not in doubt:

Collectively, nonprofit organizations . . . have a significant impact on the [U.S.] economy, controlling more than $1 trillion in assets and earning nearly $700 billion annually.[82]

[Today there are] 1.3 million nonprofits in the U.S. . . . [The nonprofit] sector employs 1 out of every 15 Americans.[83]

The *Independent Sector*, a nonprofit-focused publication, reports,

Nonprofit employment has doubled in the last 25 years and now represents 9.5% of the U.S. work force.[84]

Howard Rheingold believes this activist trend, enhanced by technology, extends beyond organized NGOs to the spontaneous actions of individuals. By utilizing the Internet, individuals and small groups can quickly and easily band together to enact powerful change. These "Smart Mobs" are all the more powerful because of their tendency to form and disband spontaneously for single events, aligning with others who share their passion for the issue at hand. He terms this behavior a higher form of democracy, or "ad-hocracy." Rheingold focuses specifically on the power of mobile or wireless technology and text messaging, citing the overthrow of President Joseph Estrada in the Philippines in 2001, but believes the power of wireless technology in the hands of individual citizens is beyond current comprehension:

> Imagine the impact of the Rodney King video multiplied by the people power of Napster.[85]

This technology is particularly influential in areas of the world that don't yet have easy access to land telephone lines and therefore cannot access the Internet using computers, as in much of the developed world,

> especially since phones and other Net-linked mobile devices will surpass the number of online PCs next year.[86]

Thus, mobile phones open up much of the developing world to the power of the Internet and help circumvent authorities that attempt to curtail people power. In 2003, the new Chinese government of President Hu Jintao was forced to reverse policy with respect to its response to the illness SARS (severe acute respiratory syndrome) and the release of information concerning the disease. Senior party officials were fired and the government was forced to admit it had previously misled both the Chinese people and the world press. The Chinese Communist Party was held accountable by the Chinese people's ability to communicate with each other and spread information using mobile phones:

> News of the disease reached the Chinese public in Guangdong through a short-text message, sent to mobile phones in Guangzhou around noon on Feb. 8. "There is a fatal flu in Guangzhou," it read. News spread as well through Internet chat rooms favored by China's urban youth and e-mails about the virus, forwarded from person to person. The messages

were an unprecedented challenge to the state's monopoly on information.[87]

In spite of the world's ignorance of the extent of the disease's spread in China and the Chinese government's continual denials that there was even a problem, the Internet fed knowledge through to the Chinese people:

> Still, information about the virus was filtering into mobile phones and computers. While authorities had banned press reporting about the disease, text messaging was relatively uncensored.[88]

Corporations, too, should use globalization to spot consumer and activist trends originating in one area of the world before it reaches them in their area of the world:

> If you're an American firm, listen to what your European divisions and partners say. Many of tomorrow's issues, particularly in the fields of environmentalism and international human rights, get an airing in Europe before they do in the U.S. . . . Europe is becoming an "incubator" of social issues for American firms. . . . Most European companies have a broader view of who their stakeholders are; American firms often concentrate solely on their stockholders.[89]

The power of the Internet (in all its manifestations) to spread information and inform lies beyond the control of authoritarian governments, just as it lies equally beyond the control of global corporations. As consumers, nonprofits, and NGOs increasingly realize the power they have been granted to combat powers (governmental or corporate) that were previously thought to be unassailable, corporations will face much greater scrutiny and public pressure to ensure they have a genuine and effective CSR policy in place.

## Web-Based Examples and Resources

Guidestar, http://www.guidestar.org/index.jsp

Since 1994, we've focused on facilitating access to information about the operations and finances of nonprofit organizations. Our vision is to create an interactive "marketplace of information" that connects nonprofit organizations, donors, foundations, and businesses. This connection will serve as the backbone of a more effective, efficient, and well-informed nonprofit sector.

Howard Rheingold, *Smart Mobs: The Next Social Revolution,* Perseus, 2002. [book]

idealist.org, http://www.idealist.org/

Idealist.org is the online meeting place for nonprofit organizations, resources, consultants, job seekers and volunteers.

Independent Sector, http://www.independentsector.org/

Independent Sector is committed to strengthening, empowering, and partnering with nonprofit and philanthropic organizations in their work on behalf of the public good. Its membership of nonprofit organizations, foundations, and corporate philanthropy programs collectively represents tens of thousands of charitable groups serving every cause in every region of the country, as well as millions of donors and volunteers.

NGO Café, http://www.gdrc.org/ngo/

Realizing the growing importance and voice of NGOs in development in general, the NGO Café was set up on the internet as a meeting place for NGOs to discuss, debate and disseminate information on their work, strategies and results.

The basic objectives of the Café are to assist NGOs in enhancing and improving their programmes and activities; to effect a better understanding of NGOs in general; and to enable NGOs to network at local, regional and international levels.

NGO Global Network, http://www.ngo.org/

This site is the home page for our global NGO community (Non-governmental organizations associated with the United Nations). Its aim is to help promote collaborations between NGOs throughout the world, so that together we can more effectively partner with the United Nations and each other to create a more peaceful, just, equitable and sustainable world for this and future generations.

NGO Watch, http://www.ngowatch.org/

ngowatch.org is a collaborative project of the American Enterprise Institute for Public Policy Research and the Federalist Society for Law and Public Policy Studies. . . . In an effort to bring clarity and accountability to the burgeoning world of NGOs, AEI and the Federalist Society have launched ngowatch.org. This site will, without prejudice, compile factual data about non-governmental organizations. It will include analysis of relevant issues, treaties, and international organizations where NGOs are active. There will be cross-referenced information about corporations and NGOs, mission statements, and news about causes and campaigns. There will be links to NGOs and to articles and authors of interest.

NGO Worldline, http://www.sover.net/~paulven/ngo.html

A place on the Web for and about the international community of non-governmental organizations.

## Questions for Discussion and Review

1. NGOs and nonprofits, along with charities, together form the *social sector.* What important functions do these organizations perform that cannot be performed by either governmental or for-profit organizations?

2. What potential problems do you see in the rapid growth of nonprofit or nongovernmental organizations? For whom do these groups speak? To whom are they accountable? Particularly in terms of accountability, how might their legitimacy be improved?

3. What advantages and/or disadvantages are there for corporations working closely with NGOs or nonprofit organizations?

# LEGISLATION

☑ *CSR Connection:* This issue highlights the extent to which governments are responding to increased calls within their populations for greater corporate social responsibility.

## Issue

To what extent are legislatures around the world responding to increased calls for companies to be held accountable for the impact of their business operations on the societies within which they are located and operate?

---

## Case Study: Company Responsibilities Bill

In June 2002, the Company Responsibilities Bill was introduced in the UK parliament by a Labour Member of Parliament, Linda Perham. The bill was supported by a campaigning organization, CORE, which had been specifically established to push for adoption of the legislation. The summary contained within the Corporate Responsibility Bill states the purpose of the legislation:

Make provision for certain companies to produce and publish reports on environmental social and economic and financial matters; to require those companies to consult on certain proposed operations; to specify certain duties and liabilities of directors; to establish and provide for the functions of the Corporate Responsibility Board; to provide for remedies

for aggrieved persons; and for related purposes.

Corporate Responsibility Bill,
2002, UK Parliament

The legislation proposed significant responsibilities for UK companies in the area of corporate governance. There are four main principles of the CORE Bill:

1. Mandatory reporting: Companies with a turnover [sales] greater than £5m shall produce and publish reports on their economic, environmental, and social impacts.

2. Stakeholder consultation: Before embarking on major projects companies shall take

reasonable steps to consult with and respond to affected stakeholders.

3. Clearly defined directors' duties: Directors shall be required to consider the wider impacts of their business.

4. Enforcement: The creation of a Standards Board [Corporate Responsibility Board] to set standards, monitor and ensure the effective implementation of the above.[90]

Many business groups opposed the proposed legislation on the grounds that the requirements it placed on business would create yet another layer of bureaucracy and hinder efficiency:

MP Linda Perham's Private Member's Bill on Corporate Responsibility (June 2002) was both worryingly naïve and deeply concerning. If the Bill were ever to be enacted it would make the running of a business almost impossible.[91]

The UK government did not accept the proposed legislation. In response, CORE redrafted the bill (becoming the Performance of Companies and Government Departments [Reporting] Bill), which was then resubmitted by the Labour Member of Parliament, Andy King, on January 7, 2004. This legislation was also blocked by the UK government, preventing it from proceeding on January 30, 2004.

A copy of the full text of the bill can be viewed at http://www.foe.co.uk/campaigns/corporates/core/ about/bill.html

The Corporate Responsibility Coalition (CORE), http://www.foe.co.uk/campaigns/corporates/core/

Amnesty International (UK), CAFOD, Christian Aid, Friends of the Earth, New Economics Foundation and Traidcraft formed the CORE coalition . . . in response to the Government's failure to clearly set-out rules in the forthcoming Modernising Company Law Bill that would require companies to be more transparent and held accountable to a wider community of stakeholders.

## Web-Based Examples and Resources

Additional examples of CSR-related legislation:

### United States

*Sarbanes-Oxley Act, July 2002*

Goal: To better regulate corporate governance and accounting practices in the United States:

Under the law, CEOs are required to vouch for financial statements, boards must have audit committees drawn from independent directors, and companies can no longer make loans to corporate directors.[92]

*Business and Profession's Code, California*

[This] California law allows almost anyone—not just a government agency—to sue over false or misleading ads. . . . Plaintiffs suing under the statute don't have to live in California or show they were victimized. . . . Cases dismissed elsewhere are being refiled in California.[93]

Examples of the litigation in practice include the following:

- Nike (HQ Oregon) was sued by an individual activist, Marc Kasky, over the treatment of factory workers in Southeast Asia.
- KFC (Yum! Brands Inc., HQ Louisville) was sued by PETA over the way its suppliers treat the chickens they raise and sell to KFC.

### Ethics Law, September 2001, California

California fired the first shot in September 2001, when it passed legislation requiring new ethics standards. It requires arbitrators to disclose their potential conflicts of interest, such as business relationships between the parties and arbitrators' family members.[94]

### Community Reinvestment Act (CRA)

The CRA was enacted by Congress in 1977. It is implemented by a regulation, which was revised in May 1995:

The Community Reinvestment Act (CRA), enacted by Congress in 1977 (12 U.S.C. 2901) and implemented by Regulations 12 CFR parts 25, 228, 345, and 563e, is intended to encourage depository institutions to help meet the credit needs of the communities in which they operate.[95]

The Act is designed to ensure access to credit and other financial services provided by banks to all elements of the community. The legislation essentially requires banks ("depositary institutions") to do the following three things:

- Lend to medium- and low-income individuals
- Invest in community-related enterprises
- Perform community service (through such things as employee volunteer programs)

Note: The legislation covers only the banking sector and not other financial institutions or organizations such as insurance companies. For a detailed explanation of the legislation, see the following resources:

- Federal Reserve Board, http://www.federalreserve.gov/dcca/cra/
- Federal Financial Institutions Examination Council (FFIEC), http://www.ffiec.gov/cra/default.htm
- Federal Deposit Insurance Corporation (FDIC), http://www.fdic.gov/regulations/examinations/index.html
- Office of the Comptroller of the Currency (OCC), http://www.occ.treas.gov/crainfo.htm

The CRA has had real impact:

Since the CRA was enacted, banks have put more than $1.5 trillion into community development nationwide.[96]

### European Union

In May 2002, EU Members of Parliament (MPs) approved the beginning of a "social responsibility" code for firms:

> The resolution proposes the creation of an EU multi-stakeholder CSR platform as well as a requirement for companies to supply information on the social and environmental impact of their operations. It also calls for the mainstreaming of CSR in all areas of EU competence, especially in regional and social funding, since this is where companies could play a stronger role by supporting training for socially responsible restructuring.[97]

The idea will now go to the European Commission, which is under pressure to add the rules to a new directive on company law due to be unveiled later this year. If endorsed, the measure would mark the first legal step toward improving so-called corporate social responsibility (CSR) across Europe.[98]

### France and Belgium

In France, since 2002 all public companies have been required to report social and environmental information as part of the annual report.[99]

Belgium has a national kitemarking scheme so that consumers can identify companies that follow CSR principles.[100]

### UK

Minister of State at the Department of Trade and Industry (DTI) responsible for CSR, http://www.dti.gov.uk/about_dti_ministers.html

Work within the DTI on CSR can be found at http://www.dti.gov.uk/support/responsibility.htm

The UK government's full range of CSR activity can be found at http://www.societyandbusiness.gov.uk/ or http://www.csr.gov.uk/

The site illustrates examples of good business practice, gives sources of information and advice and provides a single point of entry into the full range of government activity on CSR.

http://www.csracademy.org.uk/

The CSR Academy aims to promote CSR learning through the first dedicated CSR Competency Framework. It is for companies of all sizes as well as for UK educational institutions.

## Questions for Discussion and Review

1.  The examples above show that there is a very real cost for corporations once the legislature or judiciary begin to act in a particular area. What is the argument for a company proactively implementing an effective CSR policy throughout its organization, as opposed to waiting until it is forced to change its operating practices? What is the argument for remaining reactive?

2.  What do you think about the Community Reinvestment Act (CRA)? Is this legislation the sort of activity that government should be trying to influence and control?

3.  Study the legislation posted on the CORE Web site (http://www.foe.co.uk/campaigns/corporates/core/about/bill.html). What do you think of the responsibilities it is asking UK corporations to undertake? Are they a burden to business or measures that will improve the relationship between business and society?

# LITIGATION

☑ *CSR Connection:* This issue analyzes the extent to which U.S. companies are being held accountable by U.S. courts for their actions and operations overseas.

## Issue

To what extent are global corporations, and particularly U.S.-based companies, being held accountable in U.S. courts for actions committed overseas?

Who a company chooses to do business with is not an ethical issue, right? Wrong. Companies that sold products to South Africa's former apartheid regime may find themselves liable for damages, under three lawsuits filed [in 2002] in New York and New Jersey. Among the companies being sued are Unisys, Fujitsu, Citigroup, UBS, Credit Suisse Group, IBM, and Deutsche Bank. . . . Attorney for the plaintiffs, Edward Fagan, said he may sue as many as 60 companies, including miners, car makers, drugmakers, weapons companies, banks, insurers, computer makers, and oil companies.[101]

The case is being brought under an obscure 18th-century act—the U.S. Alien Civil Torts Act—that allows citizens of foreign countries to sue any companies that do business in the United States in an American court. . . . Mr. Fagan, who is representing tens of thousands of victims of repression under apartheid, is suing the defendants collectively for more than $100bn.[102]

One of the key issues involved in this argument centers on

the extent to which the United States should compel the application of U.S. laws and regulatory standards to activities in other countries.[103]

Those who believe in the importance of free trade argue that such impositions only hurt the countries and workers they are designed to help and protect and contrive to maintain the economic dominance of the developed economies:

However protective of U.S. workers, these demands constitute harmful economic policy. They destroy the comparative advantage of the developing nations and cripple the extent to which workers in these nations can make use of their developing workplace abilities. Put starkly, these demands keep developing nations poor.[104]

Nevertheless, this is a growing phenomenon that is causing headaches for many corporations that are being accused of having applied different standards to their operations overseas, either directly or in conjunction with disreputable companies or governing regimes:

Since the early 1990s about two dozen companies have been sued for alleged complicity in abuses committed overseas—from torture in Guatemala (Del Monte) to murder in Colombia (Coke) to environmental harm in Ecuador (Texaco).[105]

As of August 2004,

twenty ACTA cases have been brought against corporations, but only five have survived a motion to dismiss and eight are still pending.[106]

---

## Case Study: Chiquita Brands

A federal judge in New Orleans, late in 2002, allowed a lawsuit by 3,000 Central American banana workers to be heard in U.S. courts. The plantation workers were suing Shell Oil, Dow Chemical, Occidental Chemical, Dole Food, Del Monte Fresh Produce, and Chiquita Brands International over the continued use of the pesticide dibromochloropropane (DBCP) in banana fields in Central America, the Caribbean, Africa, and the Philippines, although it was banned for use in most of the United States in 1977. The main medical consequence of exposure to the chemical (which was developed by Shell and Occidental in the 1940s) is sterility, as well as cancer and birth defects in children born to those who have been exposed:

[In 1961] company scientists persuaded the Department of Agriculture . . . that DBCP was safe for humans. . . . But in 1977, the Environmental Protection Agency suspended use of DBCP . . . after a third of the workers at Occidental's manufacturing plant in Lathrop, Calif., were found to be sterile. The E.P.A. made the ban permanent in 1979.[107]

The main accusation against the companies is that until "as late as 1985," they continued to ship

the pesticide to banana plantations outside the United States and allowed workers there to use it without proper education or protection, although they were well aware of the dangers for humans who were exposed to the chemical.

Unsurprisingly, perhaps, the companies have fought hard to avoid these cases being heard in U.S. courts, essentially preventing any progress. If they are judged by U.S. legal standards, the financial penalties for corporations found to be guilty are likely to be much greater than if decided by local judicial systems; however, these companies may now be beginning to regret this stance, as Latin American governments are responding to the political pressure to win redress for their constituents:

[In December 2002], after a trial in which the companies refused to take part, a Managua court ordered Shell, Dole and Dow to pay $489.4 million to 450 workers.[108]

Courts in the United States are increasingly allowing cases against multinational U.S. corporations, brought by foreign national plaintiffs, concerning operations or incidents abroad (see *Issues: Globalization*):

The result? Judicial activism has gone global. U.S. judges increasingly set the ground rules of the global economy.[109]

Chiquita as the largest employer of unionized banana workers in Latin America has been particularly affected by this issue and seems to have reacted to the unwanted attention by improving its CSR activities. The company has a dedicated corporate responsibility page on its Web site and produces its biannual *Corporate Responsibility Report* (e.g., Chiquita's 2005 report will cover operations in 2003–2004), in both English and Spanish.

Similar cases to the one outlined above, brought by other individuals, were settled locally by most of the companies involved in this case, first in 1992 and then in 1997. Additional cases remain pending, however, and the companies themselves point to the earlier settlements to indicate the end of their responsibility in the matter. In general, it is not ideal that U.S. courts are expanding their jurisdiction into areas that should remain the domain of foreign national courts:

[Such international disputes are] rightfully a matter of U.S. foreign and trade policy. U.S. judges are not in the best position to set American policy toward the government of Burma or establish acceptable global standards of conduct.[110]

Often, however, an adequate legal infrastructure in these countries that can ensure corporations are held to account for their actions overseas does not exist:

These countries have 19th century legal structures and have no system in place to deal with extremely technical class-action cases involving thousands of workers.[111]

It is also understandable that individual victims seek retribution for wrongs they feel have been committed against them and see U.S. courts as the best (and often only) way of achieving this. Perhaps the most important aspect of this legal development, however, is that increasingly corporations are being held accountable for their operations overseas. In 2005,

Shell, Dow Chemicals, Chiquita, Del Monte and Dole Food Company are facing renewed legal action by Honduran banana workers for their alleged use of [DBCP] in the 1970s and 1980s. . . . just the latest in a series of legal challenges filed by worker groups in recent years. In the Philippines, for example, Dole and others were named in a $4 billion DBCP action involving 35,000 individuals. . . . Similar legal actions have been raised in Costa Rica, Ecuador, Panama, Nicaragua and Guatemala. . . . Meanwhile, former banana workers won the right to present their case to the United Nations Human Rights Committee [in April 2005].[112]

Until now, whatever accountability that had existed was largely piecemeal and enforced through activist NGO and consumer actions (e.g., product boycotts). The legal, and therefore more official, supervision these court decisions present will hopefully ensure greater care and internal auditing before future corporate decisions are made. Besides the potential dollar damages companies face, the added negative publicity such cases generate should offer greater incentive for corporations to operate with the same degree of care and responsibility abroad that they would use at home.

## Web-Based Examples and Resources

Chiquita Brands International—Corporate Responsibility Web site, http://www.chiquita.com/

Corporate Responsibility at Chiquita is an integral part of our global business strategy. It commits us to operate in a socially responsible way everywhere we do business, fairly balancing the needs and concerns of our various stakeholders—all those who impact, are impacted by, or have a legitimate interest in the Company's actions and performance. We believe that fairly balancing the expectations of our stakeholders is essential to building a stronger and more financially successful Company.

Chiquita Brands International *Corporate Responsibility Reports,* http://www.chiquita.com/ | Corporate Responsibility | CR Reports

At Chiquita, our achievement of high standards of corporate responsibility is a source of great pride, and it has become an essential part of our culture and business strategy.

Freedom of Association, Minimum Labour Standards and Employment in Latin American Banana Operations Agreement, http://www.chiquita.com/ | Corporate Responsibility

Through this agreement, Chiquita, which is the largest employer of unionized banana workers in Latin America, reaffirmed its commitment to respect the core labor conventions of the ILO, including the convention on freedom of association.

Impact Fund, http://www.impactfund.org/

The Impact Fund is the only foundation dedicated to providing funding and technical assistance and representation for complex public interest litigation in the areas of civil and human rights, environmental justice and poverty law.

International Union of Food, Agricultural, Hotel, Restaurant, Catering, Tobacco and Allied Workers' Associations (IUF), http://www.iuf.org.uk/en/

The International Union of Food, Agricultural, Hotel, Restaurant, Catering, Tobacco and Allied Workers' Associations (IUF) is an international federation of trade unions representing workers employed in

- agriculture and plantations
- the preparation and manufacture of food and beverages
- hotels, restaurants and catering services
- all stages of tobacco processing

Rainforest Alliance's Better Banana Project, http://www.chiquita.com/ | Corporate Responsibility | Rainforest Alliance

Chiquita's commitment to the environment is also reflected in our having achieved 100% certification of our owned farms to the environmental and social standards of the Rainforest Alliances' Better Banana Project, the international standard for environmental protection and for worker health and safety in our banana farms.

Rainforest Alliance, http://www.rainforestalliance.com/

The Rainforest Alliance is a leading international conservation organization. Our mission is to protect ecosystems and the people and wildlife that live within them by implementing better business practices for biodiversity conservation and sustainability.

## Questions for Discussion and Review

1. How legitimate is it for companies to operate with different standards in different countries and cultures?

2. Why is it the responsibility of companies to decide issues such as environmental pollution levels or health and safety rules and regulations in foreign countries? If a local government has decided a certain level of activity is acceptable, why should companies increase their costs by operating to higher standards?

3. What are your thoughts regarding Chiquita's culpability in the case outlined above? What would be a suitable punishment?

# MEDIA

☑ *CSR Connection:* This issue analyzes the role of the media within globalization that allows NGOs and nonprofit organizations to spread their message and expose corporate actions that they feel are socially irresponsible.

## Issue

The expansion of global media conglomerates and the spread of TV into every corner of the world are radically changing the way we consume news and information:

Before the second world war, radio reached a mere 10% of the population, the print media no more than 20%. Now papers and TV both reach 90% of adults, and radio around 98%. The power of the media has effected a sea change in the development of public attitudes. As the raw material of politics, public opinion has become a mere reflection of the messages put out by the system, the producers of which insist unconvincingly that they follow what, in fact, they are creating. . . . Without noticing it, we are abandoning representative democracy and marching towards opinion-led democracy.[113]

The Internet extends this trend and decreases the time it takes for information to reach us. Now, when a newsworthy event occurs, we know about it almost instantly. This is important for news stations because the channel that breaks the story tends to keep hold of the viewers. And for the media today, bad news is good news is entertainment:

This obsession with speed creates problems—we report rumors, with caveats, but mistakes are made. . . . It's a complicated world. The media have a lot to say and not much time to say it. They also have to win audiences, so they sensationalize and simplify. Stalin said that every death is a tragedy; the death of a million, a mere statistic. That's how the media, albeit with different motives, work as well.[114]

The speed at which news travels today should be a point of concern for global corporations. No actions can be hidden, and if anything goes wrong, the whole world knows about it very quickly. In addition, activities around the world are viewed and judged by the standards where the news is absorbed, not where it occurred. The growth in importance of global brands in recent years leaves companies exposed to any consumer backlash against activities perceived to be unacceptable or running counter to the image a company's brand portrays.

## Case Study: CNN

"Four hostile newspapers are more to be feared than 10,000 bayonets."

—Napoleon Bonaparte[115]

The media is an essential part of the democratic society in which we live. Its role is to inform the public and also question those in power and help hold them accountable to those they are supposed to serve; however, in an age of information overload and advertising revenue driven by viewer numbers, what information to present to the public and how to present it becomes central to the integrity of the industry. The temptation to condense in order to capture people's attention soon leads to the need to entertain to keep them watching.

Today the news of the world is conveyed in 30-minute segments, squeezed between the sports and personal finance programs. *CNN Headline News,* without blushing, manages to fit the day's major news from around the world into "The Global Minute"! Twenty-four-hour news today is a CNN world of voyeurism and reality TV, where your difficulties are everyone else's fascinating tidbits:

Fear of embarrassment at the hands of NGOs and the media has given business ethics an even bigger push. Companies have learnt the hard way that they live in a CNN world, in which bad behavior in one country can be seized on by local campaigners and beamed on the evening television news to customers back home.[116]

CNN, launched in June 1980, came to prominence in the living rooms of the world and North America in particular during the first Gulf War.

Their willingness to push the envelope in what is expected of their frontline reporters enabled them to carry on presenting after the competition had evacuated to safety:

CNN had been a failing venture until the 1991 Gulf War, when it provided the only television coverage from inside Baghdad. That exclusive was possible only because every other network had pulled its correspondents to protect their lives. Tom Johnson, CNN's president at the time, wanted to do the same, but [Ted] Turner told him: "I will take on myself the responsibility for anybody who is killed. I'll take it off of you if it's on your conscience." No one was killed, but Mr. Turner's roll of the dice with other men's lives is no less jarring.[117]

The role CNN plays in conveying information to the public is now a legitimate consideration for the U.S. government when selecting military bombing targets during a war. This is particularly so when the targets are located in civilian or urban areas. As in all aspects of society today, rapidly developing technology allows more things to be done in a much shorter time frame. In a war, the information field commanders receive has multiplied exponentially, as has the speed in which they must decide what to do. When the wrong decision or a mistake is made, CNN is there to tell the world:

When missiles do go awry, as happened when the United States accidentally struck the Chinese Embassy in Belgrade in May 1999 . . . there is alarm worldwide.[118]

The "CNN Test" is the test military commanders must consider when choosing potential targets for bombing during warfare today. This issue was the focus of a number of news items in the lead up to the second Iraq war (March, 2003):[119]

> Military commanders have long had legal advisers. But more than ever, attorneys are in the teams that choose the strategies, the targets and even the weapons to be used. . . . And legal issues aren't the only factors [to consider]. . . . Commanders must also worry about "the CNN test." Is the target worth all the loss of innocent life—and the inevitable outcry?[120]

Public opinion greatly influences a country's foreign policy (which, after all, is made by politicians who need to be reelected). And the media today plays a central role in shaping that public opinion. People react much more strongly to pictures that they see than to words that they read. With words, they have to use their own imagination, which requires effort; pictures are spoon-fed to the public via TV. And, when the pictures are riveting, they're played over and over again until they become ingrained in the public conscience. From Vietnam to Somalia to the World Trade Center towers in New York, TV footage personalizes the story, introduces emotions, and removes the larger context within which foreign policy decisions must be made:

> [The WTO protests in Seattle in 1999] revealed a new face of globalization: the rising influence of civil society in international relations. . . . Now, international crises are measured on the CNN scale, but the media always focus on extraordinary events, distorting reality.[121]

## Web-Based Examples and Resources

10 × 10, http://tenbyten.org/10x10.html

> 10 × 10™ (ten by ten) is an interactive exploration of the words and pictures that define the time. . . . Every hour, 10x10 collects the 100 words and pictures that matter most on a global scale, and presents them as a single image, taken to encapsulate that moment in time. Over the course of days, months, and years, 10x10 leaves a trail of these hourly statements which, stitched together side by side, form a continuous patchwork tapestry of human life.

Accuracy in Media, http://www.aim.org/

> Accuracy In Media is a nonprofit, grassroots citizens watchdog of the news media that critiques botched and bungled news stories and sets the record straight on important issues that have received slanted coverage.

BBC World, http://www.bbcworld.com/

> BBC World is the BBC's commercially funded international 24-hour news and information channel broadcasting around the world from its base at BBC Television Centre in London. . . . Viewers who wish to keep ahead of global news events, but not just the headlines—turn to BBC World for the story behind the headlines—the why's and how's of the event as well. BBC World keeps its viewers not just informed, but well informed, with in-depth analysis and cutting edge interviews—the story from all sides.

CNN, http://www.cnn.com/, http://www.timewarner.com/

Turner Broadcasting, http://www.timewarner.com/corp/businesses/detail/turner_broadcasting/
   index.html

   CNN is the original 24-hour cable television news service. In 2003, CNN/U.S. delivered
   its highest audience levels in a decade, maintaining a 20-percent-plus advantage vs. its two
   closest competitors in total unique viewers and all key demographics.

Independent Media Center, http://www.indymedia.org/

   The Independent Media Center is a network of collectively run media outlets for the creation of radical, accurate, and passionate tellings of the truth. We work out of a love and
   inspiration for people who continue to work for a better world, despite corporate media's
   distortions and unwillingness to cover the efforts to free humanity.

Komarow, Steven, "U.S. Attorneys Dispatched to Advise Military," *USA TODAY,* March 10,
   2003, http://www.usatoday.com/news/world/iraq/2003–03–10-jags_x.htm

Laity, Mark, "The Media: Part of the Problem or Part of the Solution?" *Kent Bulletin
   Magazine,* The University of Kent at Canterbury, No. 42, Spring 2004, pp 8–10, http://
   www.kent.ac.uk/alumni/pdf/kent42.pdf

mediachannel.org, http://www.mediachannel.org/

   MediaChannel is a media issues supersite, featuring criticism, breaking news, and investigative reporting from hundreds of organizations worldwide. As the media watch the
   world, we watch the media.

Rocard, Michel, "Entente *Cordiale?" Kent Bulletin Magazine,* The University of Kent
   at Canterbury, No. 35, Autumn 2000, pp 10–11, http://www.kent.ac.uk/alumni/pdf/kent
   35.pdf

## Questions for Discussion and Review

1. Do the media today report the news or distort the news? Do we watch *news* or *entertainment*? What do you think CNN's role, or the BBC's, should be? What about
   Aljazeera[122]? Is news reporting objective or culturally biased?

2. Should the armed services have to answer to CNN or any other news organization?
   Isn't that the responsibility of the civilian planners and politicians that shape
   the strategies that the armed services implement? Should the media's powers
   be restricted during wartime? Have embedded journalists helped the reporting
   of war or just upped the entertainment level closer to Hollywood special-effects
   levels?

3. Is collateral damage or friendly fire an acceptable cost of war? Is it acceptable for
   innocent lives to be sacrificed in the name of national security?

# PATENTS[123]

> ☑ *CSR Connection:* This issue reflects the criticism faced by some companies that seek to own the sole rights to a technology or a process that they have invented, for a limited period of time.

## Issue

Who should own intellectual property when the greater public interest is at stake?

In 1910, [the Diamond Match Company] obtained a patent for the first nonpoisonous match. That product was so critical to the public's health that President Taft made a plea to the company to voluntarily surrender its patent rights. Despite the enormous money-making potential of the idea, Diamond Match did so. It even sent employees to other matchmaking factories to show them the process.[124]

At what point does a need to encourage corporations to invest in the research and development necessary to stimulate new discoveries by allowing them to profit from their inventions become an abuse of an unfair monopoly position?

The research-based pharmaceutical industry . . . currently spends upwards of $33 billion annually on R&D, investing a far greater percentage of sales (17.7%) in research and development than any other industrial sector, including electronics (6%), telecommunications (5.1%) and aerospace (3.7%).[125]

When failures are figured in, it costs an average of $800 million to develop a single marketable medicine, according to researchers at Tufts University.[126]

Amazingly:

Only one in every 5,000 products screened is ultimately approved as a new medicine; the others drop out because of concerns about safety, efficacy or profitability. And only three in 10 of the drugs that are approved and marketed ultimately produce revenues that recoup their R&D costs.[127]

Is it acceptable for pharmaceutical companies to oppose cheaper generic alternatives of their medication in countries where the majority of people who require that medication cannot afford to pay the full retail price? How about opposing the export of generic drugs to countries that do not have the capability to produce those drugs themselves—regulation the EU aims to introduce?[128] Is it acceptable for a company to patent the DNA of a naturally occurring plant or food (that some argue should be available for all to benefit from), simply because they were the first to make the patent application? Does that answer change if that process or piece of knowledge has existed in local folklore or customs for many generations? The rewards for commercial success lead corporations to push for whatever they can get:

> Battling against "unfair" intellectual property rights on plant varieties is a mainstay in [Rural Advancement Foundation International's] workload. Recently, the group forced a private research institute in Australia to drop two patents on cowpeas because RAFI discovered that the germ plasma originated from a public trust gene bank. The discovery led to the reversal of the patents and the investigation of a subsequent 147 similar patents.[129]

## Case Study: Generic Drugs

At the World Trade Organization (WTO) meeting in Doha, Qatar, in November 2001, member states agreed that

> patent protection—though imperative to the development of new, life-prolonging drugs— "should not prevent member [states] from taking measures to protect public health." In other words, when weighing public health against property rights, public health should always be a bit heavier.[130]

Initially poor countries would be allowed to manufacture generic drugs, under certain emergency circumstances, as long as they only produced and distributed them domestically. This agreement, however, was effectively meaningless because most countries lack the necessary technology and expertise to manufacture the drugs. The WTO member states gave themselves a deadline of 12 months to reach a further detailed agreement outlining the production and sale (including exports) of generic drugs to the poorest countries of the world. This had not occurred by December 2002, and the blame for that failure was placed largely on the U.S. government and the U.S. pharmaceutical industry:[131]

> The United States was the lone holdout on an agreement that would have permitted companies in the developing world to copy patented drugs and sell them at low prices to the poorest nations of Africa and Asia.[132]

After a further 9 months of negotiation and debate (and some say stalling by the pharmaceutical industry[133]), an agreement was finally reached

by the WTO in Geneva in August 2003. The U.S. pharmaceutical companies have legitimate concerns regarding the smuggling of generic drugs from developing countries back into developed ones, particularly Europe and North America. There are also worries that developing countries will invoke the "emergency circumstances" rule too leniently, allowing generic producers to generate profits at the expense of U.S. pharmaceutical companies. Both of these issues affect the profit-related incentives companies need to continue developing ground-breaking medicines. However,

> Concerns over smuggling are understandable, but they pale in comparison to the concerns of Third World inhabitants who suffer from deadly diseases.[134]

> Diplomats also were anxious to counter critics who say the WTO . . . puts corporate profits in rich countries ahead of the suffering and death in poor ones. . . . The average AIDS patient in the United States takes a combination of drugs that costs about $14,000 per patient each year. . . . Generic drugs would cost a fraction of that figure.[135]

Needless to say, the U.S. pharmaceutical industry paints a different picture of its role in the process and heralds the Geneva agreement as a success. Pfizer, which played a prominent role in the negotiations, posted this statement on its Web site:

> There are now more than 28 million people infected with HIV/AIDS in Sub-Saharan Africa,

a region that includes some of the poorest countries in the world. That total constitutes more than 70 percent of all those living with HIV/AIDS worldwide. Globally, an estimated 3 million people died from AIDS in 2001—a staggering 8,000 each day.

Pfizer has stepped forward in partnership with governments and non-governmental organizations to develop a series of initiatives to address the HIV/AIDS crisis in the U.S. and abroad. Pfizer's strategy is to partner with effective organizations already in place to offer results-oriented programs that will have a significant impact in preventing the spread of the disease and easing the health burdens of those who have been infected by the virus. This comprehensive, team-based approach combines the distribution of critical medicines with training, education, mentoring and the building of sound medical infrastructures.[136]

Although all the major pharmaceutical companies have reduced the prices of their AIDS drugs, many still face pressure to reduce their prices further. In April 2003, GlaxoSmithKline announced the fifth cut in its prices since 1997 to a total of as much as 47% of the price charged in the United States and Europe, for some drugs:

> The discounts are available to the world's poorest countries and all of sub-Saharan Africa—a total of 63 countries . . . and now many, such as Glaxo, sell them there at no profit.[137]

In poor places like Guatemala, the price difference between branded and generics are crucial. A cocktail of AIDS-fighting brand drugs that cost $10,000 a year in 2000 now costs $700 because of generic competition. [Médecins Sans Frontières, MSF] says that the generic equivalent is $400, and [it] can get generics from India for $300.[138]

Nevertheless, critics of the U.S. pharmaceuticals are still pushing for further concessions. They complain that there are still too many restrictions preventing the timely manufacture and purchase of sufficient quantities of generic drug alternatives at reasonable prices:

> Even with all these savings, in a country where the average worker earns under $100 a month . . . only 1,500 of the 67,000 HIV-positive patients in Guatemala are being treated.[139]

The criticism is being heeded by interested parties such as the Pharmaceutical Shareowners Group (PSG), a grouping of institutional investors with significant pharmaceutical holdings who argue that the public perception of the industry is vital to maintaining the "social contract" necessary for continued acceptance and success.[140]

## Web-Based Examples and Resources

Access to Essential Medicines Campaign, http://www.accessmed-msf.org/

MSF is campaigning internationally for greater access to essential medicines.

Doctors Without Borders (Médecins Sans Frontières, MSF), http://www.msf.org/

Médecins Sans Frontières (MSF) is an international humanitarian aid organisation that provides emergency medical assistance to populations in danger in more than 80 countries.

Drugs for Neglected Diseases Initiative, http://www.dndi.org/

In 2003, seven organisations from around the world joined forces to establish DNDi: five public sector institutions—the Oswaldo Cruz Foundation from Brazil, the Indian Council for Medical Research, the Kenya Medical Research Institute, the Ministry of Health of

Malaysia and France's Pasteur Institute; one humanitarian organisation, Médecins sans Frontières (MSF); and one international research organisation, the UNDP/World Bank/ WHO's Special Programme for Research and Training in Tropical Diseases (TDR), which acts as a permanent observer to the initiative.

European Patent Office, http://www.european-patent-office.org/index.en.php

The mission of the EPO—the patent granting authority for Europe—is to support innovation, competitiveness and economic growth for the benefit of the citizens of Europe.

Generic Pharmaceutical Association, http://www.gphaonline.org/

America's Generic Pharmaceutical Association helps make American health care more affordable and more widely available.

Global Business Coalition on HIV/AIDS (GBC), http://www.businessfightsaids.org/

The Global Business Coalition on HIV/AIDS (GBC) is a rapidly-expanding alliance of international businesses dedicated to combating the AIDS epidemic through the business sector's unique skills and expertise.

Heineken's HIV/AIDS Policy, http://www.smartwork.org/resources/heineken.shtml

An example of one corporation's attempts to fight AIDS amongst its African workforce.

International Intellectual Property Alliance, http://www.iipa.com/

The International Intellectual Property Alliance (IIPA) is a private sector coalition formed in 1984 to represent the U.S. copyright-based industries in bilateral and multilateral efforts to improve international protection of copyrighted materials.

Pfizer, http://www.pfizer.com/

Pfizer Inc discovers, develops, manufactures, and markets leading prescription medicines for humans and animals and many of the world's best-known consumer brands. Our innovative, value-added products improve the quality of life of people around the world and help them enjoy longer, healthier, and more productive lives. The company has three business segments: health care, animal health and consumer health care. Our products are available in more than 150 countries.

PharmAccess International (PAI), http://www.pharmaccess.org/

PharmAccess International is a small, flexible, not-for-profit organization active in the health sector, with a focus on HIV/AIDS therapy in resource-poor countries. . . . PAI combines the experience of treatment in the developed world with knowledge about the feasibility to accomplish (cost-) effective treatment in developing world settings. Collaboration, pragmatism and adaptation to local circumstances are our guiding principles.

Pharmaceutical Research and Manufacturers of America, http://www.phrma.org/

The Pharmaceutical Research and Manufacturers of America (PhRMA) represents the country's leading research-based pharmaceutical and biotechnology companies, which are devoted to inventing medicines that allow patients to live longer, healthier, and more productive lives. The industry invested an estimated $33.2 billion in 2003 in discovering and developing new medicines. PhRMA companies are leading the way in the search for new cures.

Pharmaceutical Shareowners Group (PSG), http://www.pharmashareownersgroup.org/

The Pharmaceutical Shareowners Group (PSG) is an international grouping of long-term institutional investors who have a significant exposure to the pharmaceutical sector.

Rural Advancement Foundation International (RAFI), http://www.rafiusa.org/

RAFI-USA is dedicated to community, equity and diversity in agriculture. While focusing on North Carolina and the southeastern United States, we also work nationally and internationally. RAFI-USA is playing a leadership role in responding to major agricultural trends and creating a movement among farm, environmental and consumer groups to:

- Promote sustainable agriculture
- Strengthen family farms and rural communities
- Protect the diversity of plants, animals and people
- Ensure responsible use of new technologies.

World Intellectual Property Organization, http://www.wipo.int/

The World Intellectual Property Organization (WIPO) is an international organization dedicated to promoting the use and protection of works of the human spirit. These works—intellectual property—are expanding the bounds of science and technology and enriching the world of the arts. Through its work, WIPO plays an important role in enhancing the quality and enjoyment of life, as well as creating real wealth for nations.

## Questions for Discussion and Review

1. Is it acceptable for pharmaceutical companies to oppose cheaper generic alternatives of their medication in countries where the majority of people who require that medication cannot afford to pay for it? In general, is it acceptable that the same drugs cost vastly different amounts in different countries—even within the developed world?

2. Is it acceptable for a company to patent the DNA of a naturally occurring plant or food (that some argue should be available for the benefit of all) simply because they were the first to make the patent application? Does that answer change if that process or piece of knowledge has existed in local folklore or customs for many generations?

3. Look at Heineken's HIV/AIDS policy (detailed at http://www.smartwork.org/resources/heineken.shtml and summarized at http://www.smartwork.org/resources/policies.shtml). What benefits do you see for the firm? Do you think other firms would benefit by following Heineken's example?

# PATRIOTISM

☑ *CSR Connection:* This issue analyzes the possibility of negative stakeholder reaction to corporate actions that might be perceived as unpatriotic.

## Issue

Businesses rely on the societies within which they operate and could not exist or prosper in isolation. They need the infrastructure that society provides, its source of employees, not to mention its consumer base. Paying corporate taxes should represent one aspect of a minimum commitment to the societies on which corporations depend; however, increasingly corporations seek to reduce their tax contribution as a painless way of inflating earnings. This is being done by exploiting tax code loopholes and incorporating organizations offshore.

### Exploiting Tax Code Loopholes

With the help of a network of industries that together conspired against the Internal Revenue Service (IRS) in the United States—investment banks (which introduced the opportunity), lawyers (who signed off on the legality of the plans), and accountants (who failed to properly audit these activities)—some companies have been able to vastly reduce their tax liabilities by exploiting existing loopholes in the tax code. The tax-avoidance industry

> mushroomed in the 1990s bull market, fueled by the rise of stock option compensation and an aggressive push by accountants and investment bankers to develop and peddle such strategies.[141]

Some companies were guiltier than others. Enron was one of the most guilty—as executives became too close to the professions advising and auditing the company—and was able to "achieve $2 billion in tax and accounting benefits" over 6 years:

> The transactions were generally structured in two ways: to duplicate losses, thus doubling its tax deduction, or to get a tax benefit by acquiring an asset but making little or no outlay. . . . Enron relied on a small group of lawyers, accountants and banks, which were paid more than $87 million in fees. . . . The various maneuvers let the Houston company escape federal income taxes from 1996 through 1999. It paid just $63 million in 2000 and 2001.[142]

However, culpability is shared by those companies that were coming up with these tax avoidance schemes and approaching companies with them:

A host of prominent U.S. companies, including Whirlpool Corp., Clear Channel Communications Inc. and Tenet Healthcare Corp., used a KPMG LLP tax shelter that the Internal Revenue Service subsequently classified as abusive. . . . The IRS says the shelter shaved a total of at least $1.7 billion off the tax bills of more than two dozen companies.[143]

One of the problems is the complexity of the tax code and the lack of resources the IRS has to check up on companies:

Unlike the reams of information collected by the SEC, the IRS gets scant data in a tax return. The returns offer few clues as to what might be illegitimate. The proliferation of tax rules, which now number more than 50,000 also means that accountants are able to create tax-avoidance devices that are assumed to be legal unless expressly forbidden in the code.[144]

### *Incorporating Organizations Offshore*

Some companies seek to reincorporate their organizations offshore, irrespective of where the majority of daily operations actually take place or the majority of employees are based. Figures show that the move can be very profitable for the company involved:

[Recently] corporations have been aggressively taking advantage of a variety of loopholes and complicated tax dodges—including moving their headquarters overseas—to lower their tax bills. That's a big reason why corporate income taxes have steadily fallen from over 12% of federal revenues in 1997 to less than 10% [today].[145]

More than 60% of U.S. corporations didn't owe any federal taxes for 1996 through 2000, years when the U.S. economy boomed and corporate profits soared. . . . By 2003, [corporate tax receipts as a percentage of the federal budget] had fallen to just 7.4% of overall federal receipts, the lowest rate since 1983, and the second-lowest rate since 1934.[146]

The average tax rate for public U.S. companies was 12% in 2002, down from 15% in 1999 and 18% in 1995.[147]

Tax avoidance by corporations in offshore tax havens could cost the U.S. Treasury $4 billion in lost taxes over the next 10 years if Congress does not act, according to an estimate by the Congress' Joint Committee on Taxation.[148]

The combination of these two tactics is having a significant impact on the amount of corporate taxes companies are paying:

Using tax credits stemming from a section of the tax code meant to encourage production of fuel from nonconventional sources, last year Marriott recorded a net tax benefit from [coal treatment machinery the company had invested in to receive tax benefits] of $74 million. It expects a similar savings in 2003—in all, more than double its initial $60 million investment. That bonus was the biggest factor in driving the company's effective tax rate down to 6.8%, from 36.1% in 2001, as Marriott clearly disclosed to shareholders. That tax boon accounted for more than a quarter of last year's $277 million in earnings.[149]

To what extent will consumers view either or both of these actions as unpatriotic? Companies are deliberately pushing the limits of the law in order to minimize the contribution they make to government revenue in the form of corporate taxation. As a consequence, the percentage burden of total taxation revenue contributed by individuals is rising. Some general statistics:

> In 1940, companies and individuals each paid about half the federal income tax collected; now the companies pay 13.7% and individuals 86.3%.[150]

> Aggressive use of corporate tax shelters cost states as much as $12.4 billion in 2001. That's more than a third of the total taxes that states were able to collect from corporations that year.[151]

> Tax traitors prospered [in 2001] to the tune of $2.7 billion, the amount awarded in federal government contracts to U.S. companies that evaded paying U.S. corporate income taxes by incorporating overseas. The tally by the General Accounting Office was made at the request of Congressmen Jim Turner (D-Texas) and Henry Waxman (D-California).[152]

Patriotism is an unavoidable aspect of American life, a factor that has only increased since September 11, 2001. Although the number of American cars being bought may be decreasing, the Dow Jones Patriotism Index[153] shows that other patriotic indicators (flag ownership, patriotic town names, visits to national monuments, etc.) are all way up. The degree to which a firm's actions are considered loyal or patriotic by the society in which it is based, and on which it relies, is an issue that should not be ignored.

## Case Study: Tyco

By fiscal 2001, Tyco was saving over $600 million a year in income taxes thanks to one of the most aggressive efforts ever by a multi-national to avoid paying U.S. taxes. Before Tyco moved to Bermuda in 1997, 35% of its income was going to pay taxes. By the end of the Kozlowski era, that had been sliced to 18.5%.[154]

Moving offshore (Tyco relocated to Bermuda through a reverse merger with ADT Ltd. in 1997) places all non-U.S. income beyond the reach of taxes levied by the U.S. government.

By setting up financial subsidiaries abroad in tax havens (Tyco's subsidiary in Luxembourg was named Tyco International Group, TIG), companies are able to avoid taxes in other ways. In Tyco's case, TIG would borrow money (billions of dollars)

from Tyco and then reloan the money straight back to its parent company:

> The interest that Tyco's U.S. units pay on these loans is not taxed in Luxembourg and is tax-deductible in the U.S.—thus cutting Tyco's U.S. tax liabilities. By 2001, Tyco had $16.7 billion in such intracompany loans outstanding.[155]

Subsidiaries such as these (Tyco had over 100 entities set up in tax havens such as the Cayman Islands, Barbados, and Jersey) assist in protecting the company from several different tax obligations. These moves were part of the reason that

> Tyco was able to report in 2001 that while 65% of its revenues came from the U.S., only 29% of its income did.[156]

This trend has now become large enough to register on political radar screens. Politicians are increasingly annoyed at the lack of patriotism displayed by companies and would like to penalize those that ignore their pleas to remain incorporated within the United States:

> [In 2002] the [California] State Treasurer's office ceased making investments in or doing business with U.S. companies that locate offshore to avoid paying taxes. The federal Homeland Security Act, by contrast, includes a provision. . . . that allows companies incorporated offshore to bid on contracts with the new agency.[157]

[In 2002] California state Treasurer Phil Angelides announced that the state's two big pension funds, Calpers and TIAA-CREF, would stop investing in U.S. corporations that relocate offshore to avoid taxes.[158]

There is a lot at stake for these companies, were there ever to be a public backlash on this issue:

Ten of the biggest companies that have relocated offshore for tax advantages, or plan to do so, had nearly $1.1 billion in federal contracts in the 2001 fiscal year. A total of $763 million was for defense and homeland-security projects. Contract values:[159]

| *Offshore Companies With Federal Contracts* | | *2001 Contracts (in millions)* | |
|---|---|---|---|
| *Company, Product* | *Moved to Bermuda* | *Total Federal* | *Defense/Home Security* |
| Foster Wheeler, Clinton, N.J. Engineering, environmental, and construction | Reincorporated May 25, 2001 | $286.3 | $248.8 |
| Accenture Consulting, offshoot of Arthur Andersen, Chicago | Incorporated July 2001 | $281.9 | $144.8 |
| Tyco, Exeter, N.H. Electronics, security, health, and engineering | Reincorporated March 1997 | $224.2 | $182.5 |
| Monday, Offshoot of PricewaterhouseCoopers, New York | Incorporated March 27 [no year given] | $220.8 | $129.1 |
| Ingersoll-Rand, Woodcliff Lake, N.J. Industrial equipment, construction, and security | Reincorporated December 31, 2001 | $40.3 | $39.2 |
| APW, Waukesha, Wis. Electronics and technology | Reincorporated July 2000 | $7.1 | $4.9 |
| Cooper Industries, Houston, Electric equipment, tools, and hardware | Reincorporated May 21 [no year given] | $6.4 | $6.0 |

*(Continued)*

(Continued)

| Company, Product | Moved to Bermuda | Total Federal | Defense/Home Security |
|---|---|---|---|
| Stanley Works, New Britain, Conn. Toolmaker | Voted to reincorporate in Bermuda May 9 [no year given]; disputed, new vote authorized | $5.7 | $5.3 |
| Fruit of the Loom, Bowling Green, Ky. Apparel | Reincorporated March 4, 1999 | $2.4 | $2.4 |
| Weatherford, Houston, Drilling, oil and gas technology and services | Reincorporated June 26 [no year given] | $0.2 | $0.2 |

Source: William M. Welch, *USATODAY*.com, July 30, 2002. From House Ways & Means Committee; Office of Rep. Richard Neal; Federal Procurement Data Center.

Legislation has been proposed in Congress and several states, including California, Massachusetts, and Pennsylvania, to prevent legislatures from giving government contracts to U.S. companies that relocate overseas. It's already the law in North Carolina for businesses that relocate after 2001.

Some companies, however, are still unwilling to pass up the potential dollar savings such a move promises:

Shareholders in scandal-hit conglomerate Tyco have voted to keep their company registered in Bermuda, resisting a move to bring it back to the U.S. . . . The company, whose shares plummeted 71% last year, is one of a handful which have come under the microscope for reincorporating abroad to save on U.S. taxes—a practice decried by many as unfair and even unpatriotic. . . . Major pension funds and other institutions holding Tyco shares wanted the company back onshore, because they said that would mean greater accountability on the part of its senior executives.[160]

Others are beginning to change their attitude as the feared "un-American" label is beginning to attach itself to those companies that push too aggressively to avoid paying taxes:[161]

Tax evasion is wrong and share holder rights are important. Indeed, those are principles that should be applied to all U.S. corporations, whether they choose to make their official homes in Hamilton or Houston.[162]

Whether remaining incorporated in the United States is in the economy's best interests, however, is a difficult assessment to make:

Someone owes Stanley Works an apology. Last year, Connecticut politicians and the AFL-CIO shamed the tool and hardware company out of reincorporating in Bermuda so it could save $30 million in corporate income taxes. Attorney General Richard Blumenthal and GOP Congresswoman Nancy Johnson will no doubt now want to take some responsibility for the company's decision this week to lay off 1,000 workers and close nine facilities.[163]

Nevertheless, legislation has also been proposed in Congress to force companies to declare their headquarters in the same country as the majority of their shareholders.[164]

In general, in Congress there has been a sharp populist reaction against the thought of companies making this move in order to avoid paying taxes. Legislators are making a stand where they can. In June 2004, a potential $10-billion government contract linked to homeland security was voted down in Congress because the company it was awarded to, Accenture, is headquartered in Bermuda:

> The 35–17 vote reflects the bipartisan resentment in Congress toward companies whose parents locate offshore to limit their U.S. tax liability.[165]

Eventually the contract passed Congress and was awarded to Accenture,[166] but the difficulties faced and negative publicity received by the company indicate the growing consequences facing companies that make decisions such as these in areas that are sensitive to shifting public concern.

## Web-Based Examples and Resources

AFL-CIO, http://www.aflcio.org/corporateamerica/ns08022002.cfm

> Stanley Works Surrenders—Cancels Reincorporation to Bermuda Under Pressure

Calpers, http://www.calpers.ca.gov/

> The California Public Employees' Retirement System (CalPERS) provides retirement and health benefit services to more than 1.3 million members and nearly 2,500 employers. Our membership consists of active, inactive and retired members from the State, school districts and local public agencies.

"Come Home To America" campaign, http://www.calpers-governance.org/tyco/default.asp

> American corporations like Tyco, Ingersoll-Rand, McDermott, Nabors Industries and Cooper Industries operate from the U.S., but have established mailing addresses in offshore havens to avoid taxes. That's a bad move for shareholders.
>     Major institutional investors including public pension funds, union funds, state treasurers and others want these companies to Come Home to America.

Citizens for Tax Justice, http://www.ctj.org/

> Citizens for Tax Justice is a nonpartisan, nonprofit research and advocacy organization dedicated to fair taxation at the federal, state, and local levels.

Flag Manufacturers Association of America, http://www.associationheadquarters.com/Newsroom/PressReleases/6_8_03.htm

> Representing an industry annually manufacturing more than 100 million flags of all types and sizes, top United States flag manufacturers have joined together to educate and promote the quality, variety, and proper use of flags manufactured in the United States.

Howtobuyamerican.com, http://www.howtobuyamerican.com/

> Supporting American-Made Products and Services from American-Owned Companies.

National Museum of Patriotism, http://www.museumofpatriotism.org/

The National Museum of Patriotism is a nonprofit organization dedicated to promoting the history of patriotism.

Socialfunds.com, http://www.socialfunds.com/news/article.cgi/1093.html

William Baue, "Back in the U.S.A.," April 15, 2003.

A combination of investors, activists, and congresspeople are working to make sure U.S. companies keep paying their share of taxes.

Stanley Works, http://www.stanleyworks.com/

Whose life has not been touched in some way by a product bearing the Stanley® name? . . . Stanley touches more people on a daily basis than you probably ever imagined.

Tax Justice Network, http://www.taxjustice.net/

The global Tax Justice Network arose out of meetings at the European Social Forum in Florence, late 2002, and at the World Social Forum in Porto Alegre, early 2003. It is a response to harmful trends in global taxation, which threaten states' ability to tax the wealthy beneficiaries of globalisation.

Tyco International Ltd., http://www.tyco.com/

A global company in over 100 countries with 267,000 employees worldwide. We manufacture, distribute and service products and systems for a broad spectrum of markets.

## Questions for Discussion and Review

1. Do you think it is unpatriotic for an organization to attempt to minimize its business costs? Does that opinion change if that strategy involves reincorporating overseas, when the majority of operations and employees are based in the United States? Is it unpatriotic or smart to incorporate overseas to avoid taxes, considering that Congress supports multibillion dollar contracts for firms like Accenture that move overseas?

2. Is *patriotism* an issue that falls within the CSR perspective of a company? Is this something that U.S. companies should worry about more than companies from other countries?

3. What does it mean to be an *American company* in an age of global megabrands and globalization?

# SCIENCE AND TECHNOLOGY

☑ *CSR Connection:* This issue discusses some of the many issues of ethics and social responsibility that creep into science and technological development.

# Issue

To what extent do new scientific and technological developments create moral and ethical dilemmas as new frontiers are crossed? To what extent are scientists responsible for the inventions they create?

Scientists celebrate the freedom to pursue truth without regard for social consequences. In the words of Robert Oppenheimer, the physicist who led America's crash program to build an atomic bomb: "If you are a scientist, you believe that it is good to find out how the world works; that it is good to find out what the realities are, that it is good to turn over to mankind at large the greatest possible power to control the world and to deal with it according to its lights and values." Oppenheimer justified his efforts on these grounds, figuring that political judgments about the bomb's use were for others to make.[167]

As research and development continually pushes science and technology to break new ground, the business opportunities to exploit these developments expand in tandem. To what extent are companies operating in these fields constrained by the morals and ethics of the societies within which they are based?

---

## Case Study: Cloning

There appears to be a general consensus within the mainstream scientific community that the cloning of humans for reproductive purposes is morally unacceptable. The process is currently illegal in "two dozen countries"[168] and the condemnation and derision that greeted the announcement by the company Clonaid of the first human cloned baby (named Eve and born December 26, 2002) showed this opposition to be holding fast:

> "It's very difficult to identify the kinds of problems you might have with a cloned human baby," said Glenn McGee, Ph.D., associate director for education at the University of Pennsylvania School of Medicine's Center for Bioethics. "That's why no respectable scientist would ever attempt this experiment."[169]

There is no doubt, however, that the pursuit of science led to the development of the technology that enabled this experiment to happen in the first place. It is also true that, for some, the technology developed to clone humans is acceptable under certain circumstances, whereas others think the

whole idea is completely unacceptable. Is it acceptable, for example, to clone a human and allow that creation to live long enough only for stem cells to be extracted, from which, undeniably, there is great potential for medical and regenerative benefits to be derived at some point in the future? Or is human life so precious that to play God, only to then destroy the potential life created, is morally reprehensible?

The fierce debate surrounding this distinction held up legislation on this issue in Congress in 2002. This delay resulted in the legal vacuum that existed at the time the cloned baby was announced, which meant that the United States had "no specific law forbidding the creation of human clones."[170] The announcement that a clone had been created, however, led those against the idea in principle to redouble their efforts and block those who see the technology as potentially bringing relief to sufferers of Alzheimer's or Parkinson's diseases (along with many other diseases) and their families.

In February 2003, the U.S. House of Representatives voted "to ban all human-cloning experiments, whether for baby-making or to create cells that might be used to treat disease."[171] The Senate, however, is less willing to condemn the whole industry, recognizing the potential medical benefit for the treatment of many diseases such as Parkinson's and Alzheimer's. President George Bush, in announcing his thoughts on the subject in August 2001, struggled to find a compromise:

> Research on embryonic stem cells raises profound ethical questions, because extracting the stem cell destroys the embryo, and thus destroys its potential for life. . . . As the discoveries of modern science create tremendous hope, they also lay vast ethical mine fields.[172]

In the end, he announced that government money could not be used to fund the development of the stem cell lines that are necessary for such research; however, if scientists could obtain these stem cell lines already created from elsewhere, federal money could be used to conduct the necessary research:

> Embryonic stem cell research offers both great promise and great peril. So I have decided we must proceed with great care. As a result of private research, more than 60 genetically diverse stem cell lines already exist. They were created from embryos that have already been destroyed, and they have the ability to regenerate themselves indefinitely, creating ongoing opportunities for research. I have concluded that we should allow federal funds to be used for research on these existing stem cell lines, where the life and death decision has already been made. This allows us to explore the promise and potential of stem cell research without crossing a fundamental moral line, by providing taxpayer funding that would sanction or encourage further destruction of human embryos that have at least the potential for life.[173]

President Bush's convoluted stance has since come under repeated calls for change. These calls increased following the death in June 2004 of former President Ronald Reagan, who suffered from Alzheimer's disease.[174]

At the global level, the UN tried to negotiate a treaty that would satisfy two competing camps on the issue. One camp, led by the United States, sought an outright ban on any kind of human cloning. The second camp, led by many European nations, sought to ban cloning for reproductive purposes but permit it for scientific research. In the end, the intransigence of both sides resulted in a compromise that is likely to solve little:

> In a victory for advocates of stem cell research, U.N. diplomats gave up trying to craft a treaty to outlaw human cloning. . . . Member nations had been split between two treaty proposals for a year. In the end, both sides realized they would not get enough support for a treaty to achieve worldwide ratification.[175]

The two sides will reconvene in February 2005 to negotiate a compromise, an "ambiguous, nonbinding declaration."[176]

Are scientists responsible for the technology that they create, or is it the people that use or abuse that technology who are to blame?

> Science needs to respect the dignity of the human person, for good purposes, therapeutic purposes, not to manipulate. . . . Just because a person or a group is religious doesn't mean that they have a good ethical foundation.[177]

## Web-Based Examples and Resources

Association for Science in the Public Interest, http://www.public-science.org/

> The Association for Science in the Public Interest (ASIPI) is a professional society dedicated to fostering the participation of scientists in public processes, the conduct of community research and the promotion of scientific work that supports the public good.

Christopher Reeve Paralysis Foundation, http://www.christopherreeve.org/

> The Christopher Reeve Paralysis Foundation (CRPF) is committed to funding research that develops treatments and cures for paralysis caused by spinal cord injury and other central nervous system disorders. The Foundation also vigorously works to improve the quality of life for people living with disabilities through its grants program, paralysis resource center and advocacy efforts.

Coalition for the Advancement of Medical Research, http://www.stemcellfunding.org/fastaction/

> The Coalition for the Advancement of Medical Research (CAMR) is comprised of nationally-recognized patient organizations, universities, scientific societies, foundations, and individuals with life-threatening illnesses and disorders, advocating for the advancement of breakthrough research and technologies in regenerative medicine— including stem cell research and somatic cell nuclear transfer—in order to cure disease and alleviate suffering.

National Institutes of Health—Stem Cell Information, http://stemcells.nih.gov/index.asp

President George Bush, "Remarks by the President on Stem Cell Research," August 9, 2001, http://www.whitehouse.gov/news/releases/2001/08/20010809–2.html

Stem Cell Research Foundation, http://www.stemcellresearchfoundation.org/

> It is the goal of the Stem Cell Research Foundation (SCRF) to help . . . support innovative basic and clinical research in the emerging and critical area of stem cell therapy. Since 2000, SCRF has awarded more than $1.2 million in research grants. SCRF is currently supporting a total of 9 research grants. SCRF is a program of the American Cell Therapy Research Foundation, a federally recognized 501(c)(3) nonprofit, tax-exempt organization.

## Questions for Discussion and Review

1. Are scientists responsible for the technology that they create? Or is it others, often politicians, who decide how the technology should be used and who should be held responsible?

2. Read President Bush's remarks on stem cell research at http://www.whitehouse.gov/news/releases/2001/08/20010809–2.html. Then read this *BBC News* online article shortly before President Reagan's death at http://news.bbc.co.uk/2/hi/americas/3700015.stm. What are your thoughts about the fine line the president drew to justify the spending of federal money on stem cell research? Did he get it right? To what extent should issues such as faith and ethics play a role in such decisions?

3. As technology plays an increasingly prominent role in our lives, how can government legislation keep up with the pace of change? Even now, with a subject as relatively unimportant as e-mail spam, for example, it seems that as soon as one law is made, then a way to circumvent it is already in place. Performance-enhancing drugs in sport are another example. Can government adequately police science and technology as it develops at a faster and faster speed? How?

## SEX

> ☑ *CSR Connection:* This issue highlights the difficult line companies walk between tactics that they know help sell products and actions that threaten to lose the support of some stakeholders.

### Issue

To what extent is it acceptable, in an age of shifting morals and the increasing acceptance of sex and violence in entertainment, to use sex to sell to consumers? Does this definition of *acceptable* shift when the consumers are underage children and teenagers?

We all know that "sex sells." . . . But, amazingly, corporate responsibility has nothing specific to say about it. . . . However wonderful sex can be, in the wrong hands (as it were), it leads to serious social problems. . . . And even if you think that consenting adults are fair game for the sexual predators of the advertising industry, you can't ignore the increasing horror with which many parents observe in-your-face sexuality's sashay from the parents' bedroom to the kids' playroom—and what this trend is doing to their children's identities.[178]

Deciding where to draw the line is becoming increasingly difficult, as what is acceptable is redefined with each new generation. When does a company's tactics move from representing progressiveness to having crossed the line?

---

## Case Study: Abercrombie & Fitch

This topic is particularly sensitive where children, teenagers, or "tweens" form the main segment of the target market. Abercrombie & Fitch (A&F), which had already been accused of racism in its store staffing practices,[179] nevertheless continued to push the envelope:

The 2003 Christmas shopping season may be only a few weeks old, but it's already pretty clear who the big loser is: Abercrombie & Fitch. In November, in the face of a boycott led by the National Coalition for the Protection of Children & Families, the company recalled its racy catalog, the *A&F Quarterly,* which bears more resemblance to *Playboy* than to the *Wilson Quarterly*. . . . The company also faces a class-action lawsuit filed by former Clinton

Justice Department civil rights hand Bill Lann Lee, which claims the all-American retailer discriminates against nonwhite job applicants.[180]

The result of the ensuing commotion caused by the magazine was the forced recall of the 2003 *Christmas Field Guide* catalog (which included the label "Group Sex" on the cover[181]) and the declaration by A&F that they would no longer produce the controversial quarterly magazine.[182] A large part of the reason for the about-face was an awareness campaign and boycott of stores orchestrated by a coalition of several organizations promoting family values (see *Web-Based Examples and Resources* below).[183] The most high-profile component of the campaign was a full page advertisement in both *USATODAY* and the *Wall Street*

*Journal,* taken out in the name of "The Campaign for Corporate Responsibility," appealing to investors to divest any shareholdings they had in the company:

> Some corporations dump toxic chemicals into our rivers. Others spit poisonous toxins into the air. Then there's Abercrombie and Fitch . . . actively flooding today's youth market with an overdose of sex and self-gratification, all in the name of shareholder profit. It's high time they were called to account for their cultural pollution.[184]

Was the publication and resulting negative publicity worth it for the company? Possibly, yes. The company certainly got as much free publicity as they could have hoped for—publicity, due to its edginess, that may well have helped lagging sales within its target consumer group.[185] The sort of people who advocated against the company are not the sort of people who are likely to shop at the store:

> Protests and boycotts have done little to dampen the retailer's in-your-face marketing. It seems company honchos believe any kind of publicity—good or bad—is positive because it gets people talking about you. And maybe that's the point. Maybe that's one way of attracting the famously fickle youth market. Whatever draws a parent's ire may be exactly what a teenager wants to wear.[186]

As long as the company remains racy (within the bounds of legality)—and still manages to appeal to and reflect the desires of its target audience—there is a chance they will continue to conclude that "sex *still* sells."[187]

## Web-Based Examples and Resources

Abercrombie & Fitch, http://www.abercrombie.com/

> Abercrombie & Fitch Co. is a leading specialty retailer encompassing three concepts— Abercrombie & Fitch, abercrombie, and Hollister Co. The company focuses on providing high-quality merchandise that compliments the casual classic American lifestyle. . . . Abercrombie & Fitch, which targets ages 18 through college, went public in October 1996 and spun-off from The Limited in May 1998. abercrombie kids (ages 7–14) was introduced in 1997. The latest concept, Hollister Co. was introduced in July 2000, and targets 14–18 year olds.

American Decency Association, http://www.americandecency.org/abercrombie.htm

> Since February 2000, the American Decency Association has campaigned against Abercrombie & Fitch because of their use of pornography to appeal to the prurient interests of youth. Abercrombie & Fitch's *Spring Quarterly 2004* was a pleasant surprise as the catalog did not include images of nudity. Many ministries shared the concern regarding Abercrombie and Fitch and ultimately our united efforts did make a difference. Even despite favorable news in recent months, we continue to encourage concerned individuals to avoid shopping at their stores.

Citizens for Community Values, http://www.victimsofpornography.org/

> Recognizing that pornography is affecting our families and friends . . . is the key to changing lives.

Focus on the Family, http://www.family.org/

> Focus on the Family began in 1977 in response to Dr. James Dobson's increasing concern for the American family.

National Coalition for the Protection of Children & Families' boycott against A&F, http://www.nationalcoalition.org/

> The National Coalition launched a public awareness campaign November 10 [2003] aimed at exposing A&F's irresponsible promotion of risky sexual behaviors to teens in its "mag-alog." The National Coalition asserts that Abercrombie & Fitch is selling a moral philosophy of sexuality that not only doesn't work but also is actually harming America's youth."

## Questions for Discussion and Review

1. Does sex *still* sell? Is that okay?

2. View Abercrombie & Fitch's Web site. What is your impression of Abercrombie & Fitch? Was your opinion altered by the protests over their advertising campaigns? Are you offended by the company's marketing at all? Were you bothered by the actions of groups who were protesting against the company?

3. What about the accusations of racism in the company's staffing policies? Does Abercrombie seek to present an image of purity and perfection in its models and PR literature that does not reflect the diversity of U.S. society today? Does this hurt the company?

# UNIVERSITIES AND CSR

> ☑ *CSR Connection:* This issue emphasizes the point that any organization, whether for-profit or nonprofit, has an interest in striving to meet its key stakeholder groups' needs and concerns.

## Issue

CSR and stakeholder theory are concepts that can be applied to any organization, for-profit or nonprofit. It is important for all organizations that seek to remain legitimate over the long term to remain transparent and accountable to as many of their stakeholder groups as possible.

The West Coconut Grove case study below details one example of how the University of Miami (UM) is seeking to implement a CSR policy by contributing to the local community within which it is based. UM's Institute for Urban and Social Economy (INUSE) drives this project:

> [INUSE] has demonstrated how the university, through interdisciplinary interaction, can be a good and benevolent neighbor by focusing its resources on small-scale goals that add

up to larger changes. From legal and business aid clinics to urban design strategies to plans for the School of Medicine to facilitate better access to health and human services, the University of Miami is positioned to be a catalyst for positive change.[188]

---

## Case Study: West Coconut Grove

### The Living Traditions of Coconut Grove

Our mission is to foster an interdisciplinary program of research, education and outreach that supports the people, places and processes essential for creating and sustaining family-centered communities.[189]

> —Dr. Samina Quraeshi (Henry R. Luce Professor in Family and Community, University of Miami)

The Living Traditions of Coconut Grove is a project that seeks to combine the academic advantage for hundreds of students and faculty provided by a practical, interdisciplinary program with an ongoing real-life application that benefits those in need and seeks to revitalize an important, yet neglected, part of the local community:

West Coconut Grove is Miami's founding neighborhood, boasting the sixth generation of descendents of the first Bahamian settlers. For decades, this community has fought to retain its identity amidst the external pressures of encroaching development and the internal assaults of continuing poverty and social ills such as drug abuse. Without intervention and long-term goals for improvement, succumbing to these pressures is the most likely scenario for this important and unique Miami neighborhood's future.[190]

The project is driven by UM, but the goal is to empower the local community to implement change themselves, a "university-community collaborative" (http://www.cgcollaborative.org/). The university sees itself as the driver and technical advisor (utilizing skills, energy, and expertise from across a number of different departments), but the alliances forged and strategic partnerships formed are to be put to use in the community.

The project brings together many departments from within UM (spearheaded by the Architecture Department), together with the City of Miami, Miami-Dade County, and the Department of Housing and Urban Development, all working in partnership with the residents of West Coconut Grove. As well as revitalizing and renovating the local community through design innovation, the project also sets out to document the history of the area and the lives of the people living there. Legal advice from the law department is available, and projects also include the construction of affordable housing, which is then reintegrated back into the community.

The collaborative's first of three affordable homes, designed by students from the Architectural School, was completed and presented to its new owner in March 2005.

The project is funded by grants from the John S. and James L. Knight Foundation and the Henry R. Luce Foundation. Already successful, the project continues.

---

## Web-Based Examples and Resources

Coconut Grove Collaborative, http://www.cgcollaborative.org/

The mission of the Coconut Grove Collaborative is to work together to improve housing, business and quality of life in Coconut Grove, to protect, preserve and promote a prosperous community that will retain its residents, attract other families, businesses and individuals, and serve as a pleasant place to live, visit and invest.

Henry R. Luce Foundation, http://www.hluce.org/

The late Henry R. Luce, co-founder and editor-in-chief of Time Inc., established the Henry Luce Foundation in 1936. . . . The work of the Luce Foundation reflects the interests of four generations of the Luce family. These include the interdisciplinary exploration of higher education; increased understanding between Asia and the United States; the study of religion and theology; scholarship in American art; opportunities for women in science and engineering; and environmental and public policy programs.

John S. and James L. Knight Foundation, http://www.knightfdn.org/

John S. and James L. Knight Foundation, improving journalism worldwide and investing in the vitality of 26 US communities.

Living Traditions of Coconut Grove Exhibition, http://www.miami.edu/UMH/CDA/UMH_ Main/1,1770,2593–1;15221–3,00.html

An interdisciplinary initiative at the University of Miami has transcended campus boundaries. West Coconut Grove has, since 1999, provided a "community building" opportunity for students and faculty from UM's schools of Architecture, Arts & Sciences, Communication, Law, Medicine, and the Departments of History and Art to work toward creating a vision for the future, and improving the environment for residents of this neglected area through several projects that address a range of uses, from design, health and child welfare to legal and business.

University of Miami, http://www.miami.edu/

Today, the University of Miami is one of the largest, most comprehensive private research universities in the southeastern United States with a well-earned reputation for academic excellence. More than 15,000 undergraduate and graduate students from every state and more than 114 nations around the world call UM home during the academic semesters.

## Questions for Discussion and Review

1. Should a nonprofit organization, such as a university, be concerned with CSR? What are the benefits? Is there any downside?

2. Identify the stakeholders of a university. Why should a university strive to meet the needs and concerns of each of these stakeholder groups? Is the obligation any different for a public university than for a private university?

3. Investigate the CSR policies of your own university. Does it have some kind of CSR mission statement, perhaps labeled "Community Relations"?

## NOTES

1. Clare Ansberry, 'Laid-Off Factory Workers Find Jobs Are Drying Up for Good,' *Wall Street Journal*, July 21, 2003, pp A1&A8.

2. 'Outsourcing Abroad,' *Wall Street Journal*, July 14, 2003, pA2.

3. The Fannie Mae case was selected because of the organization's unusual setup as a publicly traded company with a federal charter to help make home ownership more available throughout the United States. In spite of the accusations of financial and accounting irregularities in 2004–2005 that flared between Fannie Mae, the Office of Federal Housing Enterprise Oversight (OFHEO), and the Securities and Exchange Commission (SEC), which caused the resignation of Fannie Mae's CEO and CFO, as well as proposals for the tighter regulation of both Fannie Mae and Freddie Mac, the specific mandate of the organization with respect to its community and increasing home-ownership rates among lower income households presents a relevant and important CSR perspective.

4. "Under the Federal Housing Enterprises Financial Safety and Soundness Act of 1992, HUD [Department of Housing and Urban Development] was given the authority to set explicit goals for Fannie [Mae] and Freddie [Mac] to promote affordable housing for moderate to very low income families and to provide financing for homebuyers and renters in underserved areas." James E. Murray, 'Fannie and Freddie Grow Up,' *Wall Street Journal*, March 25, 2005, pA8.

5. http://www.fanniemae.com/initiatives/adc/index.jhtml?p=Initiatives&s=Expanding+the+American+Dream+Commitment

6. 'Business Ethics Names 100 Best Corporate Citizens for 2002,' *Business Ethics Magazine*, 2002, http://www.business-ethics.com/2002_100_best_corporate_citizens.htm

7. Ibid.

8. Franklin Raines was the first African American man to lead a Fortune 500 company. 'Spotlight on Diversity,' *mbajungle.com*, March/April 2003.

9. *Business Ethics Magazine*, 2002, op. cit.

10. http://www.fanniemae.com/initiatives/adc/index.jhtml

11. http://www.fanniemae.com/initiatives/adc/expansion.jhtml?p=Initiatives&s=Expanding+the+American+Dream+Commitment

12. James R. Hagerty & Joseph T. Hallinan, 'Blacks Are Much More Likely to Get Subprime Mortgages,' *Wall Street Journal*, April 11, 2005, pA2.

13. Kenneth D. Wade, 'The Joy of Buying the First House,' *Miami Herald*, November 20, 2004, Op-ed. page.

14. Ibid.

15. Bernadette Hearne, 'Analysis: The World Bank and Action on Corporate Corruption,' *Ethical Corporation Magazine*, May 20, 2004, http://www.ethicalcorp.com/content_print.asp?ContentID=2079

16. 'Corruption a Cultural Act for Peruvians,' *Miami Herald*, December 4, 2002, p10A.

17. David Luhnow & Jose De Cordoba, 'A Tale of Bribes and Romance Roils Mexican Politics,' *Wall Street Journal*, June 23, 2004, pp A1&A10.

18. Heesun Wee, 'Corporate Ethics: Right Makes Might,' *BusinessWeek*, April 11, 2002, http://www.businessweek.com/bwdaily/dnflash/apr2002/nf20020411_6350.htm

19. Kris Maher, 'Global Companies Face Reality of Instituting Ethics Programs,' *Wall Street Journal*, November 9, 2004, pB8.

20. Patrick Bartlett, 'EU Investigates Oil Giants,' BBC News, June 12, 2003, http://news.bbc.co.uk/1/hi/business/2984006.stm

21. Carol Matlack et al., 'Cracking Down on Corporate Bribery,' *BusinessWeek* online, December 6, 2004, http://www.businessweek.com/magazine/content/04_49/b3911066_mz054.htm?c=bwinsiderdec3&n=link11&t=email

22. John W. Brooks, 'Fighting International Corruption,' *International Law News*, Vol. 31 No. 3, Summer 2002.

23. Brooks, op. cit., p1.

24. Brooks, op. cit., p16.

25. Joshua Chaffin, 'The Kazakh Connection: How Money Buys Access to the Politicians and Power-Brokers in Washington,' *Financial Times* (U.S. edition), June 26, 2003, p11.

26. Brooks, op. cit., p17.

27. Ibid.

28. Ibid.

29. Ibid.

30. Ibid.

31. Brooks, op. cit., p18.

32. 'News: Summary for December 2002,' *Ethical Corporation Magazine,* December 24, 2002, http://www.ethicalcorp.com/NewsTemplate.asp?IDNum=477

33. http://www.un.org/peace/africa/Diamond.html

34. http://www.debeersgroup.com/

35. Alex Blyth, 'Agreement Reached on "Fair-Trade" Mark for Diamonds,' *Ethical Corporation Magazine,* June 30, 2004, http://www.ethicalcorp.com/content.asp?ContentID=2295

36. Global Witness: Conflict Diamond Campaign, http://www.globalwitness.org/campaigns/diamonds/

37. 'Diamonds to Get "Ethical" Label,' *BBC News, Business,* June 23, 2004, http://newswww.bbc.net.uk/1/low/business/3834677.stm

38. 'Tiffany & Co.: A Case Study in Diamonds and Social Responsibility,' *Knowledge @ Wharton,* November 2004, http://knowledge.wharton.upenn.edu/article/1074.cfm

39. Ethical Corporation Magazine, December 24, 2002, op. cit.

40. Ibid.

41. http://www.un.org/peace/africa/Diamond.html

42. Tosin Sulaiman, 'Law Targets "Blood Diamonds,"' Miami Herald, May 8, 2003, p2A.

43. Ibid.

44. *Ethical Corporation Magazine,* June 30, 2004, op. cit.

45. Ibid.

46. 'Special Report: The Diamond Cartel. The Cartel Isn't Forever,' *The Economist,* July 17, 2004, pp 60–62.

47. http://www.jewelers.org:8080/3.consumers/ethics/index.shtml

48. Lisa Roner, 'Jewelers of America Launch Corporate Responsibility Initiative,' *Ethical Corporation Magazine,* September 23, 2004, http://www.ethicalcorp.com/content.asp?ContentID=2820

49. 'The Leaders Who Run Toward Crises,' *New York Times,* December 22, 2002, Section 3, p12.

50. 'Why Women Should Rule the World,' *Fortune,* October 28, 2002, p160.

51. 'Business Ethics Classes: To Require or Not?' *Business Ethics Magazine,* Summer 2003, p20.

52. Survey of MBAs by The Committee of 200 in *Worthwhile Magazine,* http://www.worthwhilemag.com/entry/2004/10/06/winning_the_war_for_talent.php, and reported in *the Wag* e-newsletter, October 13, 2004.

53. 'You Mean Cheating Is Wrong?' *BusinessWeek,* December 9, 2002, p8.

54. http://www.few.eur.nl/few/eurac/

55. 'Start of Educational Programs Aimed at the Practice of Corporate Social Responsibility,' *CSR Wire,* April 28, 2005, http://www.csrwire.com/article.cgi/3840.html

56. 'An Island of Ethics: The New Bainbridge Graduate Institute,' *Business Ethics Magazine,* Fall 2003, p5.

57. 'Seeing the Good Side of Business,' *The Times,* October 3, 2002, MBA insert, p7.

58. The Association to Advance Collegiate Schools of Business (AACSB), *eNewsline,* 'Dean's Corner,' February 17, 2003, http://www.aacsb.edu/publications/enewsline/

59. Elliot Schrage, 'A Long Way to Find Justice,' *Washington Post* in *Daily Yomiuri,* July 17, 2002, p20.

60. Paul Magnusson, 'Making a Federal Case out of Overseas Abuses,' *BusinessWeek,* November 25, 2002, p78.

61. Ibid.

62. Juan Forero, 'Rights Groups Overseas Fight U.S. Concerns in U.S. Courts,' *New York Times* June 26, 2003, pA3.

63. Robert S. Greenberger & Pui-Wing Tam, 'Court Backs U.S. Firms in Human-Rights Suits,' *Wall Street Journal,* June 30, 2004, pA3. Note: The Unocal case, which had advanced the furthest in U.S.

courts at the time, announced in December 2004, on the eve of having its case heard on appeal, that it would settle for an undisclosed sum. See: Lisa Roner, 'Unocal Settles Landmark Human Rights Suits,' *Ethical Corporation Magazine,* December 20, 2004, http://www.ethicalcorp.com/content.asp? ContentID=3312

64. *Washington Post* in *Daily Yomiuri,* July 17, 2002, op. cit.

65. Ibid.

66. Cait Murphy, 'Is This the Next Tort Trap?' *Fortune,* June 23, 2003, p30.

67. O. Lee Reed et al., 'The Legal & Regulatory Environment of Business,' 12th Edition, McGraw-Hill, 2002, p133.

68. A Google search of *Bhopal* in May 2005 resulted in 1,240,000 results.

69. William M. Evan & Mark Manion, 'Minding the Machines: Preventing Technological Disasters,' Pearson Education, 2002, p289.

70. Evan & Manion, op. cit., p7.

71. Evan & Manion, op. cit., p18, Fig. 1–1.

72. Evan & Manion, op. cit., p289.

73. Evan & Manion, op. cit., p7.

74. Ibid.

75. Ibid.

76. Evan & Manion, op. cit., p8.

77. Martin Cherniack, M.D., 'The Hawk's Nest Incident: America's Worst Industrial Disaster,' Yale University Press, March 1989, http://yalepress.yale.edu/YupBooks/viewbook.asp?isbn=0300044852

78. On February 6, 2001, Union Carbide merged with a subsidiary of the Dow Chemical Company and became a wholly owned subsidiary of the company. Dow purchased all of the shares of Union Carbide stock, but Union Carbide continues to exist as a separate legal entity with its own assets and liabilities.

79. In November 1994, Union Carbide Corporation sold its 50.9% interest in Union Carbide India Limited to McLeod Russel (India) Ltd. of Calcutta.

80. David J. Rothkopf, 'When the Buzz Bites Back,' *Washington Post* in *Daily Yomiuri,* May 14, 2003, pp 19&23.

81. Paul Gilding, 'Making Market Magic,' *Ecos Corporation,* June 2001, http://www.ecoscorporation.com/think/stake/market_magic.htm

82. Gail A. Lasprogata & Marya N. Cotton, 'Contemplating "Enterprise": The Business and Legal Challenges of Social Entrepreneurship,' *American Business Law Journal,* Vol. 41, 2003, pp 67–113.

83. Wilder Center for Communities, June 2003, http://www.wilder.org

84. George Melloan, 'Global View: As NGOs Multiply, They Expand a New "Private Sector,"' *Wall Street Journal,* June 22, 2004, pA19.

85. Howard Rheingold, quoted by Robert D. Hof, 'Coming on the Net: People Power,' *BusinessWeek,* November 18, 2002, p18.

86. Robert D. Hof, 'Coming on the Net: People Power,' review of the book, 'Smart Mobs: The Next Social Revolution,' by Howard Rheingold, *BusinessWeek,* November 18, 2002, p18.

87. John Pomfret, 'Outbreak Provided Opening for New President of China,' *Washington Post* in *Daily Yomiuri,* May 14, 2003, p7.

88. Ibid.

89. Michael Elliott, 'Embracing the Enemy Is Good Business,' *Time,* August 13, 2001, p29.

90. http://www.foe.co.uk/campaigns/corporates/core/about/index.html

91. Ruth Lea, 'Corporate Social Responsibility: IoD Member Opinion Survey,' The Institute of Directors, UK, November, 2002, p14.

92. 'Will Overseas Boards Play by American Rules?' *BusinessWeek,* December 16, 2002, p36.

93. Michael Arndt, 'A Golden State for Lawsuits,' *BusinessWeek,* July 21, 2003, p8.

94. 'Revenge of the Investor,' *BusinessWeek*, December 16, 2002, p122.

95. FFIEC Web site, June 2003, http://www.ffiec.gov/cra/about.htm

96. Tom Bearden, 'Community Investment,' *The Online NewsHour,* December 20, 2004, http://www.pbs.org/newshour/bb/economy/july-dec04/community_12-20.html

97. http://www.iese.edu/

98. 'Euro MPs Approve "Social Responsibility" Code for Firms,' Ananova, http://www.ananova.com/business/story/sm_598700.html?menu=business.latestheadlines

99. Deborah Doane, 'Mandated Risk Reporting Begins in UK,' *Business Ethics Magazine,* Spring 2005, p13.

100. Will Hutton, 'Capitalism Must Put Its House in Order,' *The Guardian,* November 24, 2002, http://observer.guardian.co.uk/business/ethics/story/0,12651,846563,00.html

101. *BizEthics Buzz,* December 2002. *BizEthics Buzz* is an online news report from *Business Ethics Magazine,* http://www.business-ethics.com/email_newsletter/sample.html

102. David Usborne, 'Household names face apartheid profiteering charges,' *The Independent* in *Daily Yomiuri,* May 25, 2003, p14.

103. George L. Priest, 'Supreme Wisdom,' *Wall Street Journal,* June 18, 2004, pA10.

104. Ibid.

105. Cait Murphy, 'Is This the Next Tort Trap?' *Fortune,* June 23, 2003, p30.

106. Lisa Roner, 'Unocal Prepares to Test Supreme Court's ACTA Ruling,' *Ethical Corporation Magazine,* August 4, 2004, http://www.ethicalcorp.com/content.asp?ContentID=2490. Note: The Unocal case, which had advanced the farthest in U.S. courts at the time, announced in December 2004, on the eve of having its case heard on appeal, that it would settle for an undisclosed sum. See: Lisa Roner, 'Unocal Settles Landmark Human Rights Suits,' *Ethical Corporation Magazine,* December 20, 2004, http://www.ethicalcorp.com/content.asp?ContentID=3312

107. David Gonzalez with Samuel Loewenberg, 'Banana Workers Get Day in Court,' *New York Times,* January 18, 2003, pp B1&B3.

108. Ibid.

109. Elliot Schrage, 'A Long Way to Find Justice,' *Washington Post* in *Daily Yomiuri,* July 17, 2002, p20.

110. Ibid.

111. *New York Times,* January 18, 2003, op. cit.

112. Oliver Balch, 'Honduran Banana Workers Sue Multinationals Over Dangerous Pesticide Use,' *Ethical Corporation Magazine,* April 19, 2005, http://www.ethicalcorp.com/content.asp?ContentID =3643

113. Michel Rocard, 'Entente *cordiale?' Kent Bulletin,* The University of Kent at Canterbury, No. 35, Autumn 2000, pp 10–11, http://www.kent.ac.uk/alumni/pdf/kent35.pdf

114. Mark Laity, 'The Media: Part of the Problem or Part of the Solution?' *Kent Bulletin,* The University of Kent at Canterbury, No. 42, Spring 2004, pp 8-10, http://www.kent.ac.uk/alumni/pdf/kent42.pdf

115. Quoted in Mark Laity, Ibid.

116. 'Business ethics: Doing well by doing good,' *The Economist,* April 22, 2000, pp 65–68.

117. Noah Oppenheim, 'Bookshelf: From Network to Nowhere,' *Wall Street Journal,* October 21, 2004, pD8.

118. Steven Komarow, 'U.S. Attorneys Dispatched to Advise Military,' *USA Today,* March 10, 2003, http://www.usatoday.com/news/world/iraq/2003-03-10-jags_x.htm

119. National Public Radio, March 15, 2003.

120. *USA Today,* March 10, 2003, op. cit.

121. Shunji Yanai, former Japanese ambassador to the U.S., quoted in 'Diplomacy Under Scrutiny,' *Daily Yomiuri,* May 23, 2003, p13.

122. http://english.aljazeera.net/

123. A short history of the evolution of patents and related legislation can be found at http://www.thepfizerjournal.com/default.asp?a=article&j=tpj30&t=How%20Patents%20Arose

124. Kris Axtman & Ron Scherer, 'Enron lapses and corporate ethics,' *Christian Science Monitor,* February 4, 2002, http://www.csmonitor.com/2002/0204/p01s01-ussc.html

125. Henry I. Miller, 'Bookshelf: Fighting Disease Is Only Half the Battle,' *Wall Street Journal,* August 25, 2004, pD10.

126. Matthew Herper, 'Pfizer Wins One for Sane Patents,' *Forbes.com,* February 17, 2004, http://www.forbes.com/2004/02/17/cx_mh_0217pfe.html

127. *Wall Street Journal,* August 25, 2004, op. cit.

128. Rikki Stancich, 'EU Generic Drugs Exports Plan Raises Health-Risk and Market Concerns' *Ethical Corporation Magazine,* November 2, 2004, http://www.ethicalcorp.com/content.asp?Content ID=3091

129. Paul Gilding, 'Making Market Magic,' *Ecos Corporation Newsletter,* June 2001, p6, http://www.ecoscorporation.com/think/stake/market_magic.htm

130. Editorial, 'For the World's Poor,' *Miami Herald,* August 11, 2003, p6B.

131. Ibid. The United States is "home to 70 percent of all pharmaceutical research."

132. Ibid.

133. An agreement was delayed for 2 days by final haggling from the pharmaceutical industry, during which time African delegations noted "that 8,480 more people had died in Africa of HIV/AIDS and other diseases." Naomi Koppel, 'Poor Countries Can Now Buy Generic Drugs,' *Miami Herald,* August 31, 2003, p13A.

134. *Miami Herald,* August 11, 2003, op. cit.

135. Naomi Koppel, 'Poor Countries Can Now Buy Generic Drugs,' Miami Herald, August 31, 2003, p13A.

136. http://www.pfizer.com/subsites/philanthropy/caring/global.health.hiv.html

137. 'Firm Drops Drug Prices for AIDS in Poor Lands,' *Miami Herald,* April 29, 2003, p14A.

138. John Dorschner, 'Stage Is Set for a Struggle Over Generics,' Miami Herald, November 9, 2004, pp 1E&2E.

139. Ibid.

140. Sarah Boseley, 'Investors Urge Drug Firms to Do More for World's Poor,' *The Guardian,* September 20, 2004, p6.

141. Nanette Byrnes et al., 'Hacking Away—At Tax Shelters,' *BusinessWeek,* February 24, 2003, p41.

142. Deborah Solomon, 'Enron Cut Tax Bill by $2 Billion in Working Around IRS Rules,' *Wall Street Journal,* February 14, 2003, pA3.

143. 'One KPMG Tax Shelter Shaved $1.7 Billion Off Taxes for 29 Firms,' *Wall Street Journal,* June 16, 2004, pp A1&A8.

144. *BusinessWeek,* February 24, 2003, op. cit.

145. Editorial, 'What's Missing From the Dividend Debate,' *BusinessWeek,* January 13, 2003, p142.

146. John D. McKinnon, 'Many Companies Avoided Taxes Even as Profits Soared in Boom,' *Wall Street Journal,* April 6, 2004, pp A1&A8.

147. Justin Lahart, 'Corporate Tax Burden Shows Sharp Decline,' *Wall Street Journal,* April 13, 2004, pp C1&C3.

148. William M. Welch, *USATODAY.com,* July 30, 2002, http://usatoday.com/

149. Nanette Byrnes & Louis Lavelle, 'Special Report: The Corporate Tax Game—How Blue-Chip Companies Are Paying Less and Less of the Nation's Tax Bill,' *BusinessWeek,* March 31, 2003, pp 79–87.

150. Ibid.

151. 'Dodging the Taxman,' *BusinessWeek,* July 28, 2003, p12.

152. *Business Ethics Magazine,* Fall 2002, p8.

153. June Kronholz, 'The State of Patriotism,' *Wall Street Journal,* July 2, 2004, pp W1&W4.

154. *BusinessWeek,* December 23, 2002, pp 68–69.

155. *BusinessWeek,* December 23, 2002, op. cit.

156. Ibid.

157. Alexandra Starr, 'Welcome to the Republic of California,' *BusinessWeek,* December 16, 2002, p132.

158. William M. Welch, *USATODAY.com,* July 30, 2002, http://usatoday.com/

159. *USAtoday.com,* July 30, 2002, op. cit.

160. 'Tyco Votes to Stay Offshore,' *BBC News,* March 6, 2003, http://news.bbc.co.uk/1/hi/business/2827683.stm

161. *BusinessWeek,* December 23, 2002, op. cit.

162. Andrew Hill, 'Patriotism Is No Cure for Fraud,' *FT.com,* March 5, 2003, 20:00.

163. Editorial, 'Sorry, Stanley,' *Wall Street Journal,* May 9, 2003, pA10.

164. National Public Radio, March 6, 2003.

165. David Rogers, 'Accenture's Contract Draws Fire As House Panel Clears a Budget,' *Wall Street Journal,* June 10, 2004, pA4.

166. 'House Reverses Bar on Security Project for Accenture,' Wall Street Journal, June 17, 2004, pA4.

167. Gregg Bloche, 'Rogue Science on Trial,' *Los Angeles Times* in *Daily Yomiuri,* May 12, 2003, p13.

168. Linda Greenhouse, 'FDA. Exploring Human Cloning Claim,' *New York Times,* December 30, 2002, pA9.

169. Fred Tasker, 'Simple Science Belies Danger and Complexity,' *Miami Herald,* December 28, 2002, p13A.

170. Larry Lebowitz, 'Debate Over Ban May Return to Congress,' *Miami Herald,* December 28, 2002, p13A.

171. Sheryl Gay Stolberg, 'House Votes to Ban All Human Cloning,' New York Times, February 28, 2003, pA20.

172. 'Remarks by the President on Stem Cell Research,' August 9, 2001, http://www.whitehouse.gov/news/releases/2001/08/20010809-2.html

173. Ibid.

174. 'Senators Ask Bush to Ease Restrictions on Stem Cell Research: Reagan's Death Elevates Issue,' *CNN.com,* June 8, 2004.

175. Associated Press, 'UN Won't Pursue Ban on Cloning of Humans,' *Miami Herald,* November 19, 2004, p31A.

176. Ibid.

177. Elinor J. Brecher & Carol Rosenberg, 'Ethicist: This Ought to Horrify,' *Miami Herald,* December 28, 2002, p13A.

178. Steve Hilton, 'Will Sexual Marketing Be the Next Consumer Backlash?' *Ethical Corporation Magazine,* April 12, 2004, http://www.ethicalcorp.com/content.asp?ContentID=1900

179. Federal lawsuit filed in California's Northern District on June 17, 2003. Shelly Branch, 'Maybe Sex Doesn't Sell, A&F Is Discovering,' *Wall Street Journal,* December 12, 2003, pp B1&B2. The three discrimination lawsuits were eventually settled with A&F agreeing to pay ". . . $40 million dollars to Latino, African American, Asian American and women applicants and employees who charged the company with discrimination"; *CSRWire.com,* November 17, 2004, http://www.csrwire.com/article.cgi/3244.html. The settlement resulted in a drop in third-quarter profits for A&F in 2004; Stephanie Kang, 'Abercrombie Profit Falls After Charge For Settling Suits,' *Wall Street Journal,* November 10, 2004, pB3.

180. Daniel Gross, 'Abercrombie & Fitch's Blue Christmas,' *MSN.com, Moneyline.* Posted Monday, December 8, 2003, at 11.53 AM PT, http://slate.msn.com/id/2092175/

181. David Carr & Tracie Rozhon, 'Abercrombie & Fitch to End Its Racy Magazine,' *New York Times,* December 10, 2003, pp C1&C8.

182. 'Abercrombie to Kill Catalog After Protests Over Racy Content,' *Wall Street Journal,* December 10, 2003, pB4.

183. The decision was also partly reached, no doubt, by the rapid decline in the company's share price in the days prior to the announcement: "After put-putting along in the $28–$31 range since the summer, its stock price promptly fell off a cliff, dropping from a November high on the 13th of $29.82 to a low of $24.37 the day before the announcement—with a precipitous one-day slide of $2.61 on Dec. 4." Editorial, 'A Clothier Gets a Dressing Down,' *Wall Street Journal,* December 12, 2003, pW15.

184.  Full-page advertisement in *Wall Street Journal,* December 10, 2003, pB7D.

185.  "Abercrombie has been wrestling with a sales slump, and last week it posted a 13% decline in same-store sales in November." 'Abercrombie to Kill Catalog After Protests Over Racy Content,' *Wall Street Journal,* December 10, 2003, pB4.

186.  Ana Veciana-Suarez, 'There's a Crack in Abercrombie's Mirror (and Logic),' *Miami Herald,* August 3, 2003, pp 1K&2K.

187.  For example, see Cassell Bryan-Low & David Pringle, 'Sex Cells,' *Wall Street Journal,* May 12, 2005, pB1.

188.  'The Living Traditions of Coconut Grove,' University of Miami School of Architecture and INUSE, 2002, p5.

189.  'The Living Traditions of Coconut Grove,' University of Miami School of Architecture and INUSE, 2002, p7.

190.  'The Island District West Coconut Grove,' University of Miami, Vol. 1, No. 1, Fall 2002, p1.

# Chapter 8

# SPECIAL CASES OF CSR

This chapter, "Special Cases of CSR," is divided into four categories: Companies Doing CSR Well; Companies Criticized for Their CSR Efforts; Companies Trying to Do CSR Well; and Companies Persevering Against All the Odds. Each section contains examples of corporations succeeding, ignoring, attempting, and persevering with regard to CSR-related issues within their industries. Our intent in this section, however, is not to label companies either good or bad CSR companies. Instead, we offer these further examples of good or bad corporate behavior by firms facing specific circumstances. Our motive is to reinforce further the purpose behind this book: to structure an overarching framework for the study of CSR and provide Internet-based references as starting points for further investigation.

In lieu of discussion questions for each case below, consider the following:

1. Do you agree with the action taken?

2. With the benefit of hindsight, what would you have done differently?

3. What benefits or harm to stakeholders resulted in each situation?

At the end of each example is a general Internet reference. Given the specific nature of much of the content cited, the URL is intended as a jumping-off point for further Web-based investigation.

## COMPANIES DOING CSR WELL

This section includes examples of companies successfully dealing with various issues from a CSR perspective. By definition, adopting a CSR stance in today's business environment involves being both proactive and innovative. The cases listed below suggest a large degree of seemingly genuine intent, demonstrating that these firms recognize the value to their organizations of acting from a CSR perspective.

## Bank of America

Bank of America, in its first year as the title sponsor of the PGA Tour event, the Colonial (May 22–25, 2003, http://www.pgatour.com/tournaments/r021/index.html) at Fort Worth, Texas, invited Annika Sörenstam, the best player on the LPGA Tour, to compete. Before that time, no female player had played in a PGA Tour event since 1945:

> No one has won more golf tournaments than Sörenstam over the last two seasons, [Tiger] Woods included. Last year alone, she shattered the LPGA Tour scoring record and won 13 times around the world, the most by anyone in nearly 40 years. . . . The last time a female played a PGA Tour event, Babe Zaharias qualified for the 1945 Los Angeles Open and made the 36-hole cut before a 79 knocked her out of the final round. . . . The Colonial National Invitation Tournament made its debut the following year. . . . No course has hosted a PGA Tour event longer than Colonial.[1]

With the controversy surrounding Augusta National Golf Club (host of the U.S. Masters) and its refusal to include women as club members in mind (see *Issues: Diversity—Discrimination* in Chapter 6), Bank of America was making a significant statement:

> [*Golf World*] magazine cited unnamed sources as saying Bank of America, in its first year as the title sponsor, wants Sörenstam to play.[2]

Interestingly, as soon as this story emerged, other golf tournaments (the B.C. Open in New York State and the Chrysler Classic in Tucson, Arizona) quickly tried to jump on the bandwagon by also offering Sörenstam exemption invitations.

Sörenstam accepted the Colonial's invitation to play Wednesday, February 12, 2003.

- http://www.bankofamerica.com/

## Coca-Cola

Advertising aimed directly at children has become a controversial business tactic:

> For five decades, Coca-Cola has prohibited its marketers from aiming soft-drink ads at young kids. Now the company says it won't market any drinks—including water or juices—directly to children under 12. The change comes amid a torrent of criticism when it comes to the kinds of food and drinks that children consume.[3]

In addition, although arguing that it is a lack of exercise, rather than a sharp increase in calories, that has contributed most toward the rise in obesity within developed countries in general, Coke is prepared to assume some responsibility in promoting healthier living by its consumers:

> [Coke Chairman and CEO, E. Neville] Isdell added during the speech that the food industry hasn't gotten enough credit for steps it has taken to provide consumers with healthier options and smaller portion sizes. . . . "Healthier consumers are going to be good for us," he said. "They will grow older, healthier, wealthier and, hopefully, therefore able to buy more from us."[4]

- http://www.coca-cola.com/

## Fast-Food Industry

Under pressure from a combination of stricter regulation (particularly in Europe) and growing consumer concerns and demand for better quality food, the fast-food industry is increasingly turning to research conducted by scientists for help in ensuring the well-being of animals that are slaughtered for fast food:

McDonald's, Burger King, KFC and Wendy's have all underwritten research and recently hired what are called "animal welfare specialists" to help them devise new standards aimed at ensuring more humane treatment of the animals destined for their kitchens. Industry trade groups are promoting the new rules and conducting audits of livestock producers to assure they are being followed, though some groups express concern about higher costs and other complications.[5]

Developmental areas include reduction in the use of antibiotics (for sick animals) and growth-promoting antibiotics (for healthy animals), increased living space (particularly for pregnant animals), improving other environmental issues (like inside lighting for hens), culling techniques, and a reduction in other artificial means of promoting production (e.g., McDonald's "has also told its eggs suppliers to stop the practice of withholding food and water to induce hens to lay larger eggs").

- http://www.mcdonalds.com/

## Heineken

Heineken is operating in Africa because it is profitable for the company to do so; however, the continent presents many operational challenges, one of which is AIDS among the workforce:

According to a report by the World Economic Forum, two-thirds of 1,620 companies operating in Africa expect AIDS to affect their profits over the next five years, but only 12% have an AIDS policy. A U.N. survey found that just 21 of 100 large multinationals have AIDS programs.[6]

Heineken is trying to fight the disease and protect its workers (thereby protecting the company's investment in personnel and training):

The $9 billion (sales) Dutch giant has guaranteed anti-retroviral drug coverage not only to its staff of 6,000 in Africa but also to their immediate dependents.[7]

The company's reaction to the disease has been termed "extraordinary" and is recognized as a leading effort among multinationals working in Africa:

Over the past year Heineken has been treating employees in Rwanda and neighboring Burundi, where one in eight people is infected with HIV. The company is rolling out the program in four other countries—the two Congos, Nigeria and Ghana. . . . In all, Heineken—which had net profits of $1.2 billion in its latest fiscal year—expects to spend $2 million a year treating workers in Africa.[8]

The bottom-line return for Heineken makes good business sense, as it does for other companies operating in Africa (such as the mining company Anglo American Plc.) that have introduced similar programs for employees:

[Anglo America] expects to treat 3,000 people [in 2004], up from 223 in 2003. In a report delivered to the International AIDS Conference held in Bangkok in July [2004], the company said the treatment costs were "offset by the sharp decline in mortality—from 30% to 3.4% in the first year—and in absenteeism due to illness."[9]

- http://www.heinekeninternational.com/

## IKEA

The issue of how companies interact with their many stakeholder groups is a key component of any CSR-oriented strategic perspective:

Furniture retailer IKEA's experiences illustrate the importance of monitoring external opinion. In the early 1980s, the company was included in Greenpeace's campaign against furniture retailers that use wood from ancient forests. . . . [In response] IKEA soon adopted a best practice approach to stakeholder monitoring and consultation. IKEA worked closely with Greenpeace to align its activities with the NGO's objectives, working in partnership with the organisation to improve its environmental performance. IKEA now receives international praise for its environmental practices, which include only using wood certified by the Forest Stewardship Council and recycling 75 percent of its stores' waste. As revenues have steadily grown, IKEA believes its approach to environmental management has contributed to consumer loyalty.[10]

- http://www.ikea.com/

## Johnson & Johnson

The crisis surrounding Tylenol in 1982 is regarded as the model example of crisis management and product recall:

When seven people died after ingesting cyanide-laced Tylenol capsules, maker Johnson & Johnson immediately alerted customers nationwide, via the media, not to consume Tylenol products. Along with stopping production and advertising of Tylenol, Johnson & Johnson recalled all Tylenol capsules—which totaled about 31 million bottles valued at more than $100 million. Though it must have been tempting to disclaim a link between Tylenol and the seven deaths, Johnson & Johnson worked with consumers, the media and officials from the outset. After the scare was resolved, Johnson & Johnson immediately worked to ensure the integrity of the Tylenol brand name—and it was successful. Tylenol remains a leading over-the-counter pain medication in the United States.[11]

- http://www.jnj.com/

## Mattress Giant

In April 2002, the attorney general of Florida, Bob Butterworth, issued investigative subpoenas to Mattress Giant Corporation after accusing the company of misleading customers about the price of its beds. . . . According to Florida officials, Mattress Giant failed to consistently honor mattress prices given in advertisements from October 2001 to April 2002.[12]

By way of settling the case, Mattress Giant agreed

to donate 500 beds to homeless shelters . . . in Broward, Miami-Dade and Palm Beach counties.[13]

The company admitted no wrongdoing and also managed to settle the case in a way that was satisfactory to Florida officials and contributed to the communities in which it is located. The company managed to turn a potentially damaging situation (in terms of public perception of the company and its product) into a positive situation, in which it was giving back to the local community.

- http://www.mattressgiant.com/

## Microsoft (Bill Gates)

Bill Gates, discussing a $70 million grant his foundation (the Bill & Melinda Gates Foundation) had just made to the University of Washington, in an area in which the foundation doesn't normally operate, said that:

Our foundation, in general, does not fund basic biology research activities. And this grant does not represent a new direction for our global health program. If my dad [who sits on the university's board of regents] wasn't involved in this campaign, if the university weren't part of this community, this wouldn't have made our list of things to do.[14]

Business cannot do everything. Certainly, they cannot stray too far from their obligation to their stakeholders to remain profitable. CSR is not about a company pursuing the favorite charitable interests of the CEO. CSR is about ensuring the company strives to meet the needs and address the concerns of key stakeholders. If the company's stakeholders are content, then the company is much more likely to be successful over the long term. Although this is a personal donation by Bill Gates, it benefits a key constituent of Microsoft and is therefore consistent with a strategic CSR strategy.

- http://www.microsoft.com/

## Newman's Own

All profits, after taxes, generated from the sale of Newman's Own products are given away to charities:

In 1982, Newman's Own began with Mr. Newman's famous Oil & Vinegar Salad Dressing. Newman's Own now offers an expanded line of salad dressings, pasta sauces, salsas, popcorn, lemonade and steak sauce. The company's products have achieved a stellar place on supermarket shelves with a range of distinctive, high-quality foods.

Newman attributes the extraordinary success of his food company to two policies, from which he never deviates. First, he insists on top-quality products without the addition of artificial ingredients or preservatives. Second, he gives away all profits, after taxes, from the sale of the products to educational and charitable organizations, both in the United States and foreign countries where his products are sold. Newman's Own is now distributed in all major retail grocery chains in the United States. Since its inception, Newman's Own has also increased its international distribution to include Canada, Australia, Iceland, England, Germany, France, Israel and Japan. Thousands of charities have received donations from Paul Newman as a result of the sale of Newman's Own products worldwide. Over $125 million has been donated since 1982.[15]

- http://www.newmansown.com/

## Nike[16]

Nike is progressive in terms of institutionalizing CSR within the organization. It was among the first major companies to reach several CSR milestones:

- Vice president, corporate responsibility—first appointed January 1998.
- Corporate Responsibility Committee—established September 2001.
- *Corporate Responsibility Report*—first published October 2001.
- First apparel company to publicly disclose its complete global supplier base (the company names and locations of over 700 supplier factories), first published April 2005.

One of the reasons for this innovative CSR outlook is Nike's negative experience with NGO critics during the 1990s. Ideally, a company would be able to look ahead and integrate CSR within the organization as a preventative measure rather than react to the external environment after significant damage has been done; however, once it understood the dangers of standing still, Nike was able to react to the changing environment quickly (relative to other companies within and outside its industry) and continues to act progressively in terms of CSR, which has stood the company in good stead ever since. Nike will never satisfy all its critics, but today it consults and communicates with a significant proportion of its stakeholders throughout all areas of operations.

- http://www.nikebiz.com/

## Pepsi

In order to predict and then maximize the potential of market opportunities as they arise, it is important that a company reflects the market in which it seeks to operate. The 2000 Census highlighted the cultural diversity within the United States, a trend that will only increase. Companies wishing to maximize market share looking forward need to ensure that cultural diversity is well represented within their organization. Pepsi has a track record of innovation in this respect:

1949: Pepsi signs a 12-month advertising contract with *Ebony* magazine, the first time a major company signs such a contract with a minority publication.[17]

1986: Pepsi runs the first Spanish-language TV commercial on a major network.[18]

2004: Pepsi ranks number 7 in *Fortune* magazine's "50 Best Companies for Minorities." "Five of PepsiCo's 13 top officers are minorities—the highest percentage on our list."[19]

2005: DiversityInc ranked Pepsi fourth on its annual list of the best companies for diversity. In additional rankings, Pepsi took the top spot for the best workplace for African Americans and Latinos.[20]

The company is able to draw a direct bottom-line benefit from its efforts to create a more diverse working environment:

In 2003, Pepsi attributed one percentage point of its 7.4% revenue growth, or about $250 million, to new products inspired by diversity efforts.[21]

- http://www.pepsi.com/

## Procter & Gamble[22]

In order to appeal to the "fastest-growing U.S. demographic group," Procter & Gamble launched its first national prime-time advertisement in Spanish during the 2003 Grammy Awards program aired on a Sunday evening on CBS. The ad is also due to be shown during other national programs, such as coverage of the Latin Grammys. The advertisement, for Crest toothpaste, is in Spanish, with an English tag line:

White teeth and fresh breath . . . in any language.

Native Spanish-speaking consumers represent an important and growing market segment for many consumer product companies in the United States. By offering an advertisement in Spanish during programs many of these consumers will watch, P&G is appealing to them in a way that is more likely to be well received.

CSR represents an organization's ability to incorporate as many stakeholder needs as possible within the firm's perspective. Recognizing and reflecting the growing diversity of the population is an important component of this perspective.

- http://www.pg.com/

## Prudential Insurance

Prudential's willingness to think progressively on an issue that could have created much negative publicity ended up with them being the torchbearer for a practice that quickly became the industry standard: viatical settlements:

An example of [a socially responsible corporate] practice is Prudential Insurance's introduction, in 1990, of viatical settlements—contracts that allow people with AIDS to tap the death benefits in their life insurance policies to pay for medical and related expenses. The move generated so much goodwill that competing insurers soon offered viatical settlements as well. Very quickly, corporate behavior that had seemed radical became business as usual throughout the insurance industry.[23]

The term *viatical* originated from

the Latin word viaticum (making provisions for a journey), and were specifically those policies belonging to people expected to have less than 24 months to live. . . . The business has continued to grow: Policies with a total face value of around $10 billion were bought and sold [in 2004], according to the Viatical and Life Settlement Association of America.[24]

- http://www.prudential.com/

## September 11, 2002

On the first anniversary of the September 11 terrorist attacks, there was a large degree of media coverage planned to commemorate the day. There was great difficulty, however, attracting advertisers willing to finance these programs by airing their commercials at the same time:

Anxious to avoid the appearance of cashing in on a day of nationwide mourning, many major advertisers and media outlets have decided to keep ads off the airwaves on September 11.[25]

Thus, in spite of the lost opportunity for businesses to target a large and attentive audience,

media companies lost an estimated $300 million last year in the aftermath of last year's terrorist attacks. . . . A year later, with September 11 remaining a sensitive date in the national conscience, many media owners feel a little red ink is preferable to risking a public rapping for putting business ahead of propriety. . . . "You don't want to be coming out of fairly serious programming and going into something that could be interpreted as commercially taking advantage of that day. Why take the chance?"[26]

- http://www.september11news.com/

## Sony PlayStation

A TV ad campaign for Sony's PlayStation II that aired in January 2003 had the following slogan:

Live in your World.

Play in Ours.

The slogan was probably aimed at preventing the criticism video games receive due to the negative effects they are alleged to have on the people, particularly children, who play them. Of obvious concern is the rise in teenage violence that has been linked to increasingly violent video games. The National Institute on Media and the Family released a report in December 2002, the "MediaWise Video Game Report Card," that they claimed supported this position.[27] The report card provides a snapshot of the interactive gaming industry with a focus on issues related to child welfare.

Encouraging participants to separate their real and fantasy worlds represents an attempt by Sony to remind players that the games should be kept in perspective. The company also probably wanted to head off any accusation that it is selling games irresponsibly.

- http://www.sony.com/

## Southwest Airlines

Southwest Airlines is described as "the world's most admired and most profitable airline."[28] The company is an example of the benefits of treating employees as real members of the team:

An exemplar [of service to employees] is Southwest Airlines, the Dallas-based airline whose . . . employees are 83 percent unionized, and which is known to be employee-centered and non-hierarchical. What's striking about this firm is its no-layoff policy. In the wake of the September 11 terrorist attack when the industry faced significant losses, many airlines cut schedules and reduced workforces by up to 20 percent.[29]

Southwest is the only major carrier to remain profitable in every quarter since September 11 [2001]. While its six biggest rivals have grounded 240 aircraft and laid off more than 70,000 workers, Southwest—which has never laid off a soul in its 31 years—has kept all of its 375 planes and 35,000 people flying. . . . Although its stock has dropped 25% since the attacks, Southwest is still worth more than all the other biggies combined.[30]

The company has sought to raise morale post September 11, when the rest of the industry was mired in doom and gloom:

When the federal government offered cash grants to prop up the industry, Parker included this money in the company's profit-sharing formula for employees, even though he wasn't required to.[31]

* http://www.southwest.com/

## Starbucks[32]

Starbucks was another organization that moved quickly to integrate CSR operationally within the organization as a whole. Before CSR became a widely recognized term, Starbucks had initiated the following policy components:

* Comprehensive CSR homepage, with social responsibility "listed as a guiding principle of the company's mission."

* Senior CSR officer (VP for corporate social responsibility) and the *CSR Annual Report.*

* Adopted early the "fair-trade" and "conservation" approach to its coffee buying and offers four categories of sustainable coffees: fair trade, organic, farm direct, and conservation. Each category plays a specific role in supporting different aspects of sustainable coffee-farming practices.

* http://www.starbucks.com/

## COMPANIES CRITICIZED FOR THEIR CSR EFFORTS

This section includes examples of companies that have made disastrous decisions for their organizations, the justification for which is hard to imagine, viewing the resulting outcomes from an objective perspective. Hindsight is always twenty-twenty, but it also appears that if these organizations had been approaching each of these issues from a CSR perspective, a more favorable outcome might have resulted.

## American Airlines

In an effort to avoid American Airlines (AA, the world's largest airline) falling into bankruptcy, the management of the company negotiated a deal in 2003 with the relevant labor unions for employees. The deal involved the employees voting to accept $1.62 billion worth of annual concessions. The day after the vote result (in favor of the concessions) was announced, it emerged that AA's CEO and Chairman, Donald J. Carty, had neglected to tell the union leadership that although he was asking the employees to make sacrifices, the company was also ensuring executive retention bonuses and pension plans for top management were to be fully protected in the event that the company filed for Chapter 11 bankruptcy. This was protection regular employees and members of the regular pension plan, already approximately $3.4 billion underfunded, would not receive.[33] Worse was the fact that the news only emerged when AA filed its annual, year-end 10-K. The company had requested a 2-week filing extension from the SEC, giving the impression that the delay had been requested so that information would become public only after the union votes had been counted.

In spite of the fact that what AA executives had done was standard in an industry in turmoil and necessary to retain its qualified managers[34]—and that Carty was already the lowest paid CEO among the six largest airline companies[35]—the fallout was widespread. Under the headline, "What Was Don Carty Thinking?" *BusinessWeek* summed up the whole affair with the quote:

> "This has probably been the most badly handled transaction in my 30 years in the industry," says airline expert Mo Garfinkle of GCW Consulting. . . . The price of Carty's bungling is likely to be his job.[36]

Donald J. Carty resigned as CEO and chairman of American Airlines on Thursday, April 24, 2003.[37] The consequences of the crisis spread throughout the board:

> Bonuses for the company's top seven executives were later cancelled, but $41 million in pension funding for 45 executives was left in place.[38]

To add insult to injury, it was later announced that the board of directors had decided that Carty would not receive a severance package from the airline.[39]

- http://www.aa.com/

## Bridgestone/Firestone

In 2001, Ford Motor Company and Bridgestone/Firestone Tire Company broke off a 100-year corporate relationship over a growing controversy concerning a number of automobile accidents (including many fatalities) involving Ford Explorer SUVs that were fitted with Firestone tires:

Accidents involving Firestone-equipped Explorers have accounted for most of the at least 174 deaths and more than 700 injuries that prompted Firestone to recall its 15-in. S.U.V. tires. . . . Ford faces hundreds of lawsuits that seek damages totaling more than $590 million.[40]

In many of the accidents, the tread on the tires had separated and/or the SUVs had rolled over, and both companies blamed the other's product for the problem. Ford stated that Explorers running on Goodyear tires had a much better safety record than those running on Firestone tires, whereas Firestone countered with the statement that their tires on other SUVs worked just fine:

One conclusion stands out amid all the examples of mutually assured destruction: while neither Ford Explorers nor Firestone tires may be unusually dangerous in their own right, the combination of the two has sometimes proved lethal.[41]

The controversy resulted in a massive recall initially by Firestone of 6.5 million tires (August 2000) and then a further 13 million Firestone tires by Ford (May 2001). The corporate bickering and fallout painted both companies in a bad light and damaged both brands:

Nowhere is the damage more evident, however, than in Bridgestone's financial statement. The company reported an 80 percent decline in net earnings in the year 2000, citing the recall as the primary factor. Bridgestone/Firestone established a reserve of $388 million to cover recall expenses, in addition to $463 million set aside to cover related legal expenses. The value of the company's stock fell by $10 billion in one month alone.[42]

- http://www.bridgestone-firestone.com/

## Defense Contractors

To what extent should businesses be allowed to profit from a country's need or suffering? President Franklin D. Roosevelt set the tone in the United States in the buildup to the Second World War:

Our present emergency and a common sense of decency make it imperative that no new group of war millionaires shall come into being in this nation as a result of the struggles abroad. The American people will not relish the idea of any American citizen growing rich and fat in an emergency of blood and slaughter and human suffering.[43]

However, today Roosevelt's pleas would fall on deaf ears:

While the average [U.S.] army private in Iraq earns about $20,000 a year, the average CEO among the 37 largest publicly traded defense contractors made 577 times more money in 2002, $11.3 million. . . . [Because of the Iraq War, by May 1, 2003] twelve soldiers will never see 20. At least 13 weapons executives took home more than $20 million in compensation since 2000.[44]

According to a new report from United for a Fair Economy, "More Bucks for the Bang: CEO Pay at Top Defense Contractors,"[45] median CEO pay at the 37 largest defense contractors rose 79 percent from 2001 to 2002, while overall CEO pay climbed only 6 percent.[46]

- http://www.govexec.com/top200/02top/s3chart1.htm

## ExxonMobil

Unlike BP and later Shell, who have "been willing to confront the unpleasant truth that not only their business practices but also their core products are probable causes of global warming," ExxonMobil "ran ads trying to discredit global-warming science."[47] ExxonMobil remained a member of the Global Climate Coalition (a business coalition of companies that seeks to represent business interests in the environmental debate, http://www.globalclimate.org/) well after BP and Shell had left. The company

still tries to sow public skepticism toward global warming theories and has reportedly worked behind the scenes to remove a prominent scientist from the United Nations climate change panel and still refuses to pay $5 billion in punitive damages ordered by an Alaska court after the 1989 Valdez oil spill.[48]

A recent campaign sponsored by Greenpeace, Friends of the Earth, and people and planet (http://www.stopesso.com/) targeting Esso (ExxonMobil operates under the Esso brand in some countries) is beginning to hurt the company. The campaign states three main reasons to boycott the company:

Esso denies the reality of global warming; Esso is not investing in alternatives; and Esso is sabotaging global action—Esso has done more than any other company to undermine the Kyoto Protocol, the only international treaty to stop global warming.[49]

The anti-Esso campaign Web site quotes the company's CEO as having said:

We do not now have sufficient scientific understanding of climate change to make reasonable predictions and/or justify drastic measures. . . . Some reports in the media link climate change to extreme weather and harm to human health. Yet experts see no such pattern.[50]

The campaign was later expanded in the UK to target an alleged "support for war in Iraq and environmental crimes, by Esso and its Texan parent company, ExxonMobil Corporation."[51]

- http://www.exxonmobil.com/

## Ford

In the 1960s, Ford's position within the U.S. market was facing increasing competition from overseas, particularly from Japanese car companies. Japanese cars were smaller and more fuel-efficient than the cars Detroit was producing at the time. One of the prongs of the company's campaign to claw back market share was the introduction of the Pinto car:

The Pinto was to be a low-cost subcompact that would weigh less than 2,000 pounds, cost less than $2,000, and be brought to market in 2 years instead of the normal 4.[52]

The Pinto was a top priority for Ford, but it was also brought to market on a much quicker schedule than the company was used to. Much of the normal process was streamlined to meet the tighter deadlines. The design and styling of the car was one area in which this caused problems, especially regarding the positioning of the gas tank at the rear of the vehicle behind the rear axle, which rendered it more vulnerable in accidents involving rear-end collisions:

> When an early model of the Pinto was crash-tested, it was found that, when struck from the rear at 20 miles per hour or more, the gas tank would sometimes rupture and gas would spray out and into the passenger compartment. In a real accident, stray sparks might explosively ignite the spraying gasoline and possibly burn any trapped occupants.[53]

In spite of the potential danger, Ford managers decided to proceed with the car. The design specifications met all legal and regulatory requirements imposed by the government at the time (for example, "government regulations required that a gas tank only remain intact in a rear-end collision of less than 20 miles per hour").[54] It was felt that the Pinto was as safe as other cars on the market at the time. The managers also conducted a cost-benefit analysis to see the financial implications of redesigning the car:

> The study showed that modifying the gas tank of the 12.5 million autos that would eventually be built would cost about $11 a unit for $137 million. However, statistical data showed that the modification would prevent the loss of about 180 burn deaths, 180 serious burn injuries, and 2,100 burned vehicles. At the time, the government officially valued a human life at $200,000, insurance companies valued a serious burn injury at $67,000, and the average residual value on subcompacts was $700. So, in monetary terms, the modification would have the benefit of preventing losses with a total value of only $49.15 million: [(180 deaths × $200,000) + (180 injuries × $67,000) + (2,100 vehicles × $700) = $49.15 million].
>
> Thus, a modification that would ultimately cost customers $137 million (because the costs of the modification would be added to the price of the car) would result in the prevention of customer losses valued at only $49.15 million. It was not right, the study argued, to spend $137 million of society's money to provide a benefit society valued at only $49.15 million.
>
> Ford subsequently went ahead with production of the unmodified Pinto. It is estimated that in the decade that followed at least 60 persons died in fiery accidents involving Pintos and that at least twice that many suffered severe burns over large areas of their bodies, many requiring years of painful skin grafts. Ford eventually phased out the Pinto model.[55]

- http://www.ford.com/

## Genetically Modified (GM) Labeling

Transparency in food labeling was the goal of an Oregon initiative (Measure 27) slated for the elections of November 5, 2002. If passed, the initiative "would require food companies to clearly label any product sold or produced in the state that contains GM ingredients."[56] The campaigners, officially, were not taking a stance for or against GM foods but just arguing that consumers had a right to know exactly what is contained within the food they are buying.

The food and biotech industries fought the initiative, out of concern that "such labeling could cause consumers to reject genetically modified food."[57]

That's shortsighted. The food industry would be better off educating the public about the safety and benefits of genetic modification. Their fear of a labeling law only means they have done a lousy job so far. . . . By blocking grassroots attempts to put advisory labels on food, the food and biotech industries look as if they have something to hide.[58]

The tactic, however, may well have paid off in the short term. The initiative was soundly defeated, with only 27% of voters supporting the move and 73% rejecting it:

Around the world, 19 countries require such labeling, and the European Union has banned the sale of any newly engineered products since 1988. . . . In U.S., such labeling isn't required. About a dozen varieties of soybeans, corn and tomatoes genetically altered to resist pests, frost and weed killers have been approved for human consumption and are common ingredients in processed food.[59]

- http://www.monsanto.com/

## Hewlett-Packard

The print cartridge industry is big business:

Research firm InfoTrends/CAP Ventures expects Americans to go through 86.5 million laser-toner cartridges and 604 million inkjet cartridges [in 2005].[60]

Hewlett-Packard controls a large slice of this market, in which customers usually spend significantly more on ink and toner than they do on the printers themselves. This results in a market that HP is keen to protect:

At HP, inkjet supplies carry 35% profit margins and generated $2.2 billion in operating profits last year—over 70% of the company's total.[61]

There is danger, however, for HP in relying on the printer cartridge market for such a large percentage of the company's annual profits. Customers are beginning to realize the significant price premium they are paying for these environmentally unfriendly products. They are also discovering the innovative ways that companies are beginning to employ to compete with HP in this market. HP needs to be aware of the evolving business landscape driven by stakeholder concerns:

Buyers and legislators are beginning to revolt, distressed at the cost and environmental impact of zillions of discarded ink cartridges. The European Parliament passed a bill late last year that could force manufacturers such as HP and Lexmark to eliminate by 2006 chips in their ink cartridges that sometimes hinder customers from refilling and reusing the cartridges.[62]

In the past five years, the share of the global ink-jet-cartridge market held by remanufactured cartridges has risen to 17% from 14%, says imaging-industry tracker Lyra Research. Lyra expects that to rise to 24% by 2008.[63]

- http://www.hp.com/

# McDonald's

In choosing to contest a libel trial against two private citizens (activists) in the UK who had been leafleting stores complaining of the nutritional content of McDonald's menus, as well as the ethical nature of the company's operating practices, McDonald's opened themselves up to all sorts of trouble. At the same time, the company was providing the activists with much more publicity than they could ever have hoped to get had they simply ignored them. The trial, infamously known as the "McLibel Trial" (which McDonald's spent millions of pounds prosecuting and in which the two defendants represented themselves), provided NGOs and activists around the world endless ammunition with which to attack McDonald's:

> The McLibel Trial is the infamous British court case between McDonald's and a postman and a gardener from London (Helen Steel and Dave Morris). It ran for two and a half years and become the longest ever English trial. . . . The [June 1997] verdict was devastating for McDonald's. The judge ruled that they "exploit children" with their advertising, produce "misleading" advertising, are "culpably responsible" for cruelty to animals, are "antipathetic" to unionization and pay their workers low wages. But Helen and Dave failed to prove all the points and so the Judge ruled that they *had* libelled McDonald's and should pay 60,000 pounds damages. They refused and McDonald's knew better than to pursue it.[64]

In February 2005, the European Court of Human Rights ruled that the two activists did not receive a fair trial and that the British government should provide compensation:

> The British government was ordered to pay 35,000 euros in damages to the two and 47,000 euros in costs, and to offer the pair a retrial.[65]

- http://www.mcdonalds.com/

# Video Game Industry

TV video games are growing rapidly, both in terms of sales and the influence they have on those who play them (large numbers of whom are children):

> In less than a decade, the video game industry has become a major player in entertainment. Video games racked up $10.3 billion in sales of software and hardware in 2002, a 10-percent gain over 2001. . . . By comparison, movie-theater box-office receipts totaled $9.3 billion last year, according to Exhibitor Relations, a market research firm in Los Angeles.[66]

Many people would like to see the industry move to control the content of many of the more violent games on the market and, in particular, limit the access of children to these games; however, the video game industry has fought strongly to block any attempt to legislate in this area (e.g., making it a criminal offense to sell violent games to underage children). The industry claims a First Amendment defense and cries "censorship" every time there is a danger of tightening restrictions.

Of concern are games such as *Grand Theft Auto: Vice City,* a particularly violent game in which players can hijack cars, shoot, and kill:

In one scene, the player can have cyber sex with a prostitute and then kill her—by bashing her head with a baseball bat—to earn extra points. . . . In December [2002], the National Institute on Media and the Family gave the overall video game industry a failing grade because of the increasing level of violence in many games.[67]

The Lion & Lamb Project,[68] a grassroots organization dedicated to discouraging violence in children's lives, states,

Video games are now a prime form of entertainment among America's youth. An estimated 70 percent of children ages 2 to 18 have access to video games at home, with a third playing games in their bedrooms, according to recent surveys.[69]

Although these games still sell well within the industry's current target market segment of younger males, a progressive company might seek to limit the extremes of some of the violence portrayed. This would reduce the negative publicity generated by people opposed to the industry. At the same time, the large growth potential within the video game market rests with female game players, who might respond better to a different content emphasis.

- http://www.gamespot.com/gamespot/features/video/hov/ (The History of Video Games)

## COMPANIES TRYING TO DO CSR WELL

This section includes examples of companies that have attempted, with seemingly genuine intent, to implement CSR-related policies and ideas; however, due to issues of timing, misinterpretation of stakeholder concerns, or issues beyond their control, their efforts were either ignored or resulted in less than the intended outcome. This section shows that, even with a CSR perspective integrated throughout the organization, it is impossible to avoid all negative outcomes within a firm's sphere of operations.

### Berkshire Hathaway

There is a danger to a brand in pursuing philanthropic interests unconnected to a corporation's core operations or, worse, pursuing the CEO's favorite projects or interests. Such philanthropy risks alienating or upsetting the very shareholders on whose behalf the donation is being made.

An instructive example is the controversy created by Berkshire Hathaway's previously celebrated philanthropy program when it became known that a significant amount of money (controlled by Warren Buffett) was being given to the Buffett Foundation. The money was being used

to finance trials of the abortion pill RU-486; it has purchased suction machines used for abortions around the world; and it has funded the deployment of the controversial sterilization pellet Quinicrine in Third World countries.[70]

Whatever an individual's stance concerning abortion,

those concerned with good corporate governance should applaud [the decision to end the program of charitable giving]. As Milton Friedman noted long ago, charitable contributions are a dubious corporate enterprise. Their only legitimacy resides in an attempt to enhance the business of a company. In Berkshire Hathaway's case, there was the rub. . . . The program offered as many opportunities for threatening profits as for enhancing charitable self-expression.[71]

- http://www.berkshirehathaway.com/

## Cadbury

In May 2003, Cadbury (the UK chocolate company) launched a nationwide campaign, "Cadbury Get Active":

The campaign will focus on getting young people more active by providing funding to support teacher training and resources in schools.[72]

By collecting the special tokens printed on "over 160 million chocolate bars," children could win a share of £8.8 million of sports equipment for their schools and also get the chance to meet and compete with one of Britain's most popular athletes (Paula Radcliffe), who was endorsing the company's campaign. The company was also providing support for teachers teaching sport in UK schools.

The campaign, however, which had also been endorsed by the UK Sports Minister, Richard Caborn, drew controversy and criticism from some observers, including the UK's Food Commission ("UK's leading independent watchdog on food issues," http://www.food comm.org.uk/), because of the amount of chocolate children will need to consume in order to receive the incentives being dangled before them:

To get enough wrappers for a volleyball net, children would have to buy £2,000 worth of bars and scoff 1.25 million calories.[73]

The BBC reported that, in order to receive a cricket set, the children at a school would need to buy and consume 2,730 chocolate bars, at a cost of over £1,000, containing 500,000 calories.[74]

The company plans to print tokens on 160 million chocolate bars for the duration of the campaign. The Food Commission calculated this would have the following impact:

Using these figures, we calculated that to earn a single netball, worth about £5, primary school children would need to spend just under £40 on chocolate, consume over a kilogram of fat, and over 20,000 calories.

To earn the most expensive item Cadbury's has to offer (a set of posts for a volleyball net) secondary school children would need to eat 5,440 chocolate bars containing over 33kg of fat and nearly one-and-a-quarter million calories. That's over 900 chocolate bars for each member of the volleyball team![75]

If children consumed all the promotional chocolate bars, they would eat nearly two million kilos of fat and more than 36 billion calories.[76]

- http://www.cadbury.co.uk/

## Kraft

On July 1, 2003, Kraft Foods announced what it called a global initiative to help address the rise in obesity. The company pledged to improve nutrition and reduce serving sizes, eliminate more controversial marketing techniques such as targeting schools, improve product labeling, and help promote better diet and fitness regimes for its customers. The company said that all this was an attempt to help combat the growing incidence of obesity in the United States:

> "The rise in obesity is a complex public health challenge of global proportions," said Betsy D. Holden, Co-CEO of Kraft Foods. "Just as obesity has many causes, it can be solved only if all sectors of society do their part to help. Kraft is committed to product choices and marketing practices that will help encourage healthy lifestyles and make it easier to eat and live better."[77]

The world's press interpreted Kraft's move in a different light, however, as shown by some of the headlines the story's coverage generated, such as the *Guardian's* story the next day: "Lawsuits Frighten Kraft Into Fighting Flab."

> Kraft Foods, the world's biggest maker of processed foods, said yesterday that it would shrink its ready-made meals and snacks to help combat the obesity epidemic. It also wants to stave off the threat of lawsuits by overweight people. Fee-hungry lawyers who have become rich on tobacco lawsuits have begun to salivate over the U.S. food industry. Kraft, controlled by Altria, which also owns the cigarette maker Philip Morris, is sensitive to the threat.[78]

Litigation against McDonald's brought by overweight plaintiffs—as well as the stated commitment of activist lawyer and George Washington University professor John Banzhaf to find a way to effectively sue the junk-food industry—have startled companies within the industry into action:

> The lawsuits argue that greasy, calorie-laden hamburgers and French fries are just as much a public health crisis as tobacco. In fact, Banzhaf and his coterie of legal followers are employing many of the same tactics that led to multibillion-dollar judgments against Big Tobacco.[79]

From the public's point of view, the company is attempting to do too little too late, and for all the wrong reasons. The same actions 5 or 10 years ago would have been hailed as farsighted and progressive. Introduced today, so soon after the rise in threat to their industry, the same action smacks of short-term, self-interested thinking that generates only negative coverage read by a cynical general public.

The cynical perspective was strengthened a year later as the company appeared to backtrack somewhat from its earlier pronouncements:

> Now, however, rather than limiting servings per package, Kraft will keep larger bags and boxes in circulation and provide nutritional information for the entire package rather than

just one serving. . . . Kraft's change in tactics is not surprising. Many consumers would probably be surprised by how little they would eat if all of their munchies were limited to a single serving.[80]

- http://www.kraft.com/

## Malden Mills

Aaron Feuerstein, CEO of Malden Mills (founded in 1906, family owned), was an excellent man to work for:

Here was a CEO with a unionized plant that was strike-free, a boss who saw his workers as a key to his company's success.[81]

In 1995, a fire destroyed Malden Mills' textile plant in Lawrence, an economically depressed town in northeastern Massachusetts. With an insurance settlement of close to $300 million in hand, Feuerstein could have, for example, moved operations to a country with a lower wage base, or he could have retired. Instead, he rebuilt in Lawrence and continued to pay his employees while the new plant was under construction.[82]

He met the payroll for idle workers as the company rebuilt, and he was idolized throughout the media. . . . The national attention to Feuerstein's act brought more than the adulation of business ethics professors—it brought increased demand for his product, Polartec, the lightweight fleece the catalogue industry loves to sell.[83]

In addition to full pay, Feuerstein also continued all his employees on full medical benefits and guaranteed them a job when the factory was ready to restart production:

Rebuilding in Lawrence would cost over $300 million while keeping 1,400 laid-off workers on full salaries for a period of up to 3 months would cost an additional $20 million. "I have a responsibility to the worker, both blue-collar and white collar," Feuerstein later said. "I have an equal responsibility to the community. It would have been unconscionable to put 3,000 people on the streets [two weeks before Christmas] and deliver a death blow to the cities of Lawrence and Methuen. Maybe on paper our company is [now] worth less to Wall Street, but I can tell you it's [really] worth more."[84]

But the increased demand for Polartec his actions generated wasn't enough to offset the debt he had built up waiting for the plant to be rebuilt: $100 million.[85] This situation was compounded by the downturn in the market, as well as cheaper fleece alternatives flooding the market. Malden Mills filed for bankruptcy protection in November 2001.

CSR is an important component of a company's strategic and operating perspective; however, alone it is not enough. It certainly does not replace the need for an effective business model, and no company, whatever the motivation, can or should spend money that it does not have indefinitely.

- http://www.polartec.com/

## Monsanto

Monsanto had pitched genetically modified food as a large part of the solution to Third World poverty and starvation. By adapting foods to grow in severe conditions, crops could be produced in many more places than is currently possible:

> In the second half of the 1990s Monsanto dramatically failed to walk the talk on sustainability as it launched genetically modified crops onto the market and it was met with a global campaign that coined the powerful term "Frankenfood." Ongoing fallout has included the breakup of the company, serious damage to the whole life-sciences sector, threats to the U.S.-style industrialized food system and the rapid growth of a vibrant organic farming industry.[86]

However, in spite of the company's PR battle failures, perhaps the war is being won:

> The planting of genetically modified crops increased in 2002 despite lingering concern in some countries about their safety and environmental effects.[87]

> [In 2005], roughly 75% of U.S. processed foods . . . contain some genetically modified, or GM, ingredients. . . . More than 80% of the soy and 40% of the corn raised in [the U.S.] is a GM variety. Global plantings of biotech crops . . . grew to about 200 million acres [in 2004], about two-thirds of it in the U.S.[88]

- http://www.monsanto.com/

## Nestlé

S. Prakash Sethi highlighted the controversy surrounding the distribution of infant formula throughout LDCs (less developed countries) as a good example of the problems faced by corporations when consumer expectations exceed existing legal obligations.[89] In the late 1960s, debate around this issue began to surface, culminating in 1974 with the publication of a pamphlet by Mike Muller titled, *The Baby Killer.* Nestlé, inadvertently feeding the fire, sued the public action group that produced the pamphlet:

> Thus, between 1974 and mid-1976 when the case was decided, the issue received considerable international media coverage.[90]

The ultimate result was to permanently connect in the public's mind the controversy with Nestlé, although at the time there were a number of businesses involved. As awareness about the issue spread, the reaction of the various corporations was continually called into question, and the problem ballooned:

> Some public interest groups launched a campaign to boycott Nestlé products in the United States. At the LDC level, the government of Papua New Guinea passed a law declaring baby bottles, nipples, and pacifiers health hazards and their sale restricted through prescription only. The objective was to discourage indiscriminate promotion, sale, and consumption of infant food formulas.[91]

In an attempt to appease consumer criticism, the International Council of Infant Food Industries (ICIFI),[92] a corporation-led industry forum, was established and a code of practice introduced; however, it was criticized as being too weak from an early stage, and those companies committed to improving the situation withdrew and introduced their own, more restrictive, policy practices.

Nestlé's response to the problem continues today in the form of a page on its company Web site (http://www.nestle.com/Our_Responsibility/Infant_Formula/Charter/The+Charter.htm) dedicated to promoting its "responsible" promotion today of its infant formula in developing countries. It also provides a link to another site (http://www.babymilk.nestle.com/) dedicated to the "facts." The controversy, however, and opposition to Nestlé as an organization continues. The company is involved in a claim for compensation that it is making against the Ethiopian government (and therefore the Ethiopian people, too) for $6 million. As a result, it finds itself the target of a campaign waged by Oxfam in the UK who, although not dismissing the legality of the claim, find it morally reprehensible that the company can be claiming that amount of money from a country that is so poor and has 11 million people facing famine.

Oxfam has organized a Web site (http://www.maketradefair.com/) where people can register their opposition to the company's stance. Oxfam is using this public backing to make sure their criticism of Nestlé is heard loud and clear and claim to have had some success. Oxfam states that "nearly 50,000" e-mails were sent to the Web site and that "after just a week Nestlé retreated,"[93] backing off from the figure of $6 million (to offer a lower figure of $1.5 million) and also stating that any money received will be reinvested within Ethiopia (a commitment Oxfam claims had not previously been made by the company).[94]

- http://www.nestle.com/

## PETA

Although not a company, PETA is still an organization that should strive to remain transparent and accountable to as many of its stakeholders as possible. Any organization that fails to meet consistently the needs and goals of a significant proportion of its stakeholders is unlikely to remain viable over the long term.

> People for the Ethical Treatment of Animals (PETA) is the largest animal rights group in the world. We have more than 700,000 members around the globe. . . . We work to help people understand that the things they do every day either help or hurt animals—animals in our lives, like the dogs and cats who live with us, and animals we never see, like cows, chickens, and pigs killed for food. PETA believes that animals are not ours to eat, wear, experiment on, or use for entertainment.[95]

Not many people would argue with most of PETA's goals. Many, however, take issue with the extent to which the organization takes its point of view (elevating the rights of animals to a status that is equal, or sometimes above, those of humans) and also the method by which it attempts to convey its message and achieve its goals (direct, often violent, action). Accusations have also been made that, while trying to improve its own public face, PETA finances other much more radical operations:

The FBI lists the group and its counterpart, the Animal Liberation Front [ALF], as domestic terrorists. The government has said the two groups are responsible for more than 600 cases of ecoterrorism around the country, such as spray-painting buildings, breaking windows, and burning fur farms.[96]

The organization is a relatively powerful fund-raising operation, gathering $13 million in direct donations and fundraisers in the fiscal year 2000. Some of the donations the organization has made with these funds have raised eyebrows:

Notwithstanding claims by PETA leader Ingrid Newkirk that her organization is not violent, her defense of ALF is not merely rhetorical: It included $45,000 for the legal defense of an ALF arsonist accused (and ultimately convicted) of torching a Michigan State research lab.[97]

[One accuser] cites a $1,500 contribution PETA made in April 2001 to the North American Earth Liberation Front, a violent activists group that has taken responsibility for setting fire to buildings and businesses. Most recently, the group claimed responsibility for burning Ford vehicles at a large dealership in Pennsylvania.[98]

- http://www.peta.org/

## Shell

Greenpeace's influence in persuading consumers to buy a product it approves of (see Greenfreeze in *Issues: NGO and Corporate Cooperation*, Chapter 6) is mirrored by its willingness to prevent sales of any product or corporation whose actions it deems to be detrimental to the environment and wider society:

When Greenpeace called for a lightening boycott of Shell in June 1995 over the company's decision to dump the Brent Spar oil platform at the bottom of the Atlantic, sales plummeted by 70% in some countries, prompting a dramatic change of heart within days.[99]

As part of its protest, Greenpeace activists occupied the oil platform prior to it being sunk:

The Greenpeace occupation was only part of that protest. Many people in Britain and elsewhere in Europe boycotted Shell products. It was a campaign during which the company said lost it millions of dollars. And one Shell station in Germany was firebombed.[100]

Undoubtedly, dumping the platform at sea was the cheapest and technically easiest option for Shell. Dismantling it close to land (Greenpeace's favored alternative) "will cost Shell £43m in total, compared to the £4.5m cost of dumping."[101] But, the decision to sink the platform was arguably also the best ecological solution, due to the potential for contamination of the shoreline and cost of transporting and dispensing of the toxic materials it contained.

Greenpeace also made a serious miscalculation regarding the amount of toxic material it accused Shell of leaving on the platform and had to publicly apologize for its mistake later. Nevertheless, public perception carried the day, and Shell, because it failed to consult with relevant interested parties in advance, lost the PR war to Greenpeace:

In July 1998 all the governments of the north east Atlantic region agreed to ban future dumping of steel-built oil installations.[102]

At about the same time, Shell was being criticized for its operations in Nigeria. In particular, links were made by NGOs between the company and perceived human rights abuses by the Nigerian government:

In 1995 the oil giant was hit by a double whammy of attacks over plans to sink the old Brent Spar oil rig in the North Sea and over its alleged complicity in the execution of Ogoniland indigenous leaders by Nigeria's military regime. Shell suffered painful sales losses in Germany, and a barrage of criticism forced a far-reaching company transition towards sustainability.[103]

However, when a multinational corporation is operating in a country, and their presence is a benefit to the local population, "What other choices does a company have?" In Shell's case, supporters of the company argue:

"How export proceeds, revenue collections, oil royalties, and earnings are allocated [is] a decision of the Nigerian government," not of Royal Dutch/Shell. Critics wrongly conflated the two.[104]

- http://www.shell.com/

## University of Nottingham

Although not a company, the University of Nottingham in the UK is still an organization that should strive to remain transparent and accountable to as many of its stakeholders as possible. Any organization that fails to meet consistently the needs and goals of a significant proportion of its stakeholders is unlikely to remain viable over the long term.

In 2002, the university launched an International Center for Corporate Social Responsibility, and its MBA in corporate social responsibility began in September 2003. The MBA course offers specialist modules in corporate social responsibility policies, economic crime, ethics, and corporate governance and accountability:

http://www.nottingham.ac.uk/public-affairs/press-releases/index.phtml?menu=press releasesarchive&code=NOT-103/02&create_date=23-jan-2004

The university quickly ran into trouble, however, when it became known that the center was launched with a £3.8 million donation from British American Tobacco (BAT), the international tobacco group with the second largest global market share:

http://www.lshtm.ac.uk/news/2002/tobaccoindustry.html

http://www.christian-aid.org.uk/news/media/pressrel/020211p.htm

http://www.nottingham.ac.uk/

## Wal-Mart

In July 2003, Wal-Mart, "the largest private employer in the United States,"[105]announced it would extend its antidiscrimination policy to include gay and lesbian employees. At the time of Wal-Mart's announcement, this was not a legal requirement; but many commentators in the field have expressed the opinion that, given shifting social opinion in this area to one of greater tolerance, such a requirement might not be far off. In order not to be caught as the case that results in a Supreme Court decision changing the law, many organizations are altering their antidiscrimination policies in anticipation of such a change:

> Nine out of the 10 largest Fortune 500 companies have rules prohibiting discrimination against gay workers, according to the Human Rights Campaign, a Washington-based gay-rights organization that monitors discrimination laws. Exxon-Mobil Corp. is the exception.[106]

> During the last decade, many of America's leading corporations have come to a similar conclusion. More than 300 of America's 500 most successful companies prohibit discrimination against lesbians and gays. In the top 10, Exxon remains the last company to hold out against equal rights. However, 27% of shareholders voted at its annual general meeting last May for a broader non-discrimination policy. It has become the next public target for gay rights groups, and may soon be forced to change.[107]

Wal-Mart executives said that the move was in response to communication they had received from gay employees asking for the antidiscrimination policy to be expanded to include them, although there was also considerable pressure from gay-rights groups.

Although Wal-Mart has acted progressively in this instance, however, it is still a target for other discrimination-related issues. Previously, Wal-Mart "has been sued by the U.S. government 16 times for allegedly violating anti-discrimination laws."[108] The company has been a particular target for women's rights organizations that claim the company has long held a discriminatory attitude toward women. Wal-Mart has now been sued by campaigners seeking a class action lawsuit and

> back pay and punitive damages for all women who worked at Wal-Mart since December 1998. . . . Feminists charge that Wal-Mart discriminates against women in both pay and promotion and encourages a corporate culture that seeks to keep women in their place. . . . Last September, the National Organization for Women named Wal-Mart its "National Merchant of Shame" over labor issues.[109]

- http://www.walmart.com/

# COMPANIES PERSEVERING AGAINST ALL THE ODDS

This section includes examples of companies that have recognized that either their company or their industry has passed through its CSR threshold.[110] Belatedly, these companies are attempting to change the perception of their industry, company, or product in the minds of consumers. In large part, the attempts listed here represent significant efforts to reorient a

CSR perspective. Cynics would question the degree to which such conversions are genuine, however, and many suspect that the perception of each industry, company, or product is so thoroughly ingrained within the social conscience as to represent an almost impossible task.

## British American Tobacco

The tobacco industry has long since passed through its CSR threshold. The consequences of a failure to recognize the danger to their industry before it happened have been well documented:

> The Tobacco Project serves as the liaison to the NAAG [National Association of Attorneys General] Tobacco Committee and settling states on the implementation and enforcement of the Tobacco Master Settlement Agreement (MSA). . . . In 1998, the Attorneys General of 46 states signed the MSA with the four largest tobacco companies in the United States to settle state suits to recover costs associated with treating smoking-related illnesses. According to the Agreement, the tobacco industry is projected to pay the settling states in excess of $200 billion over the next 25 years. (Four states—Florida, Minnesota, Texas and Mississippi settled their tobacco cases separately from the MSA states.)[111]

In response to the increased litigation and negative attention on the industry, the tobacco companies have become increasingly open about the dangers of their product and have made very public moves to alter the public conception of their company and the products they produce:

> BAT managed to confound some of its severest critics by releasing the first social and environmental report from the tobacco industry—one that more stringently followed the emerging standards than any other. The company managed to strongly challenge the notion that there can never be a socially responsible tobacco company by displaying serious intent. . . . And the inclusion of the company in the Dow Jones Sustainability Index was the icing on the cake.[112]

- http://www.bat.com/

## McDonald's[113]

Litigation in the United States has increased concern regarding obesity within the fast-food industry:

> The Centers for Disease Control and Prevention regards fat as a leading health problem, estimating that 15 percent of children and 65 percent of all adults are overweight. A recent spate of lawsuits has food companies and restaurants fearing they may be blamed for it.[114]

Calls from outside the industry demand innovations (such as improved food labeling) and have suggested all restaurants consider listing nutrition and calorie contents next to different menu items. Combined with the diet-fueled food crazes that appeared around the same time as growing concerns regarding obesity, consumers are demanding greater participation in setting a more responsible food agenda. Even the Cookie Monster from *Sesame Street* is being forced to undergo a "health makeover":

Has the health craze gone too far when even Cookie Monster is blasting carbs and white sugar? . . . There's even a new song—*A Cookie Is a Sometimes Food,* where Cookie Monster learns there are "anytime" foods and "sometimes" foods.[115]

To avoid the class action lawsuits faced by the tobacco industry, many companies are attempting to reduce their level of culpability. Among the fast-food companies, McDonald's has taken the lead in instigating "a broad-based campaign to position itself as a corporate leader in the fight against obesity."[116] The ultimate goal is "to alter the widely held view that McDonald's sells junk food and only junk food."[117] Aspects of the company's plans include getting rid of the super-size meal option, using white meat in chicken nuggets, promoting salads over burgers, and offering healthier alternatives for children, such as apple slices instead of fries and milk-based drinks instead of sodas. As part of the company's "Go Active!" campaign, exercise recommendations will be advertised within stores, and children will be

encouraged to take at least 10,000 steps a day—recorded by a McDonald's pedometer. . . . The company's Ronald McDonald House Charities arm said it plans to commit $80 million over the next five years to "the health and well-being of children."[118]

In March 2005, McDonald's broadened its campaign to include a wider offering of healthy foods (fruit salads) and the launch of an advertising campaign "featuring tennis stars Venus and Serena Williams to promote physical fitness."[119]

The reaction from critics:

John Banzhaf III, professor of public interest law at George Washington University, in Washington, and a consultant to a movement to hold the fast-food industry legally responsible for the nation's obesity epidemic [said] "I'd say all of this is PR."[120]

The campaign also coincided with the release of a documentary by Morgan Spurlock, who aimed to record the health implications of a month spent eating only McDonald's food:

Supervised by three doctors and a nutritionist . . . Mr. Spurlock, a fit, active New Yorker, happily set out to ruin his health and succeeded beyond his wildest expectations. There was some weight gain—18 pounds by the end of the experiment—and also mood swings, loss of sex drive and nearly catastrophic liver damage. His general practitioner . . . worries that his patient may succumb to liver failure before the 30 days are up.[121]

Is the company wasting its time?

"If I want to eat healthy, I'll eat at home," said Chuck Horton, 33, as he lunched at a crowded McDonald's in Garrisonville, Va. "I come to McDonald's for one reason: the fries. . . . I think this healthy-eating thing has gone too far."[122]

As Chris Burke, a member of the fourth grade at Galloway School in Atlanta, notes,

"[When we watch TV] my Dad and I always wonder why McDonald's sponsors the Olympics. . . . Which Olympic athletes eat at McDonald's?"[123]

It is also true, however, that McDonald's is successful and wouldn't be so unless it was doing something right:

By 2003, McDonald's had 31,100 outlets in 119 countries, fed 47 million people every day, and had sales of $17.1 billion. . . . Today, of course, McDonald's gets blamed for all sorts of ills: obesity, poorly paying McJobs, factory farms, a global dumbing-down of food, American hegemony. . . . [Ray Kroc, creator of the McDonald's empire, however] never tired of seeing another pair of Golden Arches go up, and he never felt the need to apologize for it, either. "We provide food that customers love, day after day after day. People just want more of it," Kroc said. As every salesman knows, you can't go wrong giving people what they want.[124]

- http://www.mcdonalds.com/

## NBC

In March 2002, NBC was forced to abandon its brief, 3-month experiment to bring liquor advertising back to TV. NBC knew their move would be controversial but thought they had addressed as many constituent concerns as possible by adopting a progressive set of guidelines that allowed liquor companies to advertise in a similar way to beer and wine companies but also required them to

run four months of so-called social responsibility ads on subjects like designated drivers before they could run commercials for brands of liquor.[125]

The guidelines also placed strict limits on content and required that the ads run only at night.

The move, however, brought a great deal of protest from politicians and groups such as the American Medical Association, and NBC remained isolated on the issue with none of the other broadcast networks adopting the idea.

The NBC retreat is indicative of the sensitivities that still exist as advertisers and media companies try to determine where the line of public accountability is—and not step over it, or at least not without considerable preparation and explanation. Even as four-letter words begin to be heard on the shows watched by tens of millions of broadcast network viewers, the NBC about-face indicates that there are still some advertising frontiers that will be extremely hard to cross.[126]

- http://www.nbc.com/

## Philip Morris Companies

In addition to hostile litigation, the tobacco industry in the United States faces a rapidly declining domestic market for its product:

Only 22.1% of the U.S. adult population are smokers and cigarette consumption is sliding by 2% to 3% annually.[127]

In response to this increasingly challenging business environment, Philip Morris, the world's biggest cigarette maker, released a 20-page antitobacco brochure in mid-November 2002. Quotes included the following:

Smokers are far more likely to develop serious diseases, like lung cancer, than nonsmokers.[128]

The company's stated goal for voluntarily releasing the document was to raise awareness, but in the light of recent punitive damage awards against the tobacco companies in highly publicized suits filed by victims of smoking, many observers felt this was an attempt by the tobacco industry to try and make it harder for smokers to file such suits in the future.

CEO of R.J. Reynolds Tobacco Holdings Inc., Andrew Schindler, explained in the *Wall Street Journal* why his company would not be following the lead of Philip Morris and BAT:

People don't like pharmaceutical companies, and they make products that help people. We make cigarettes. People are never going to like us.[129]

Philip Morris, in particular, has made a belated effort to publicize their opponents' arguments. The company has also launched all of the above information on its relatively progressive Web site (http://philipmorrisusa.com/) with the following under the "Health Issues" section: "Cigarette Smoking and Disease," "Addiction," "Quitting Smoking," "Low Tar Cigarettes," "Secondhand Smoke," and "Surgeon General Reports":

We agree with the overwhelming medical and scientific consensus that cigarette smoking causes lung cancer, heart disease, emphysema and other serious diseases in smokers. Smokers are far more likely to develop serious diseases, like lung cancer, than non-smokers. There is no "safe" cigarette.[130]

- http://www.philipmorris.com/

## NOTES

1. 1620 Golf Web Wire Services, February 11, 2003, http://www.golfweb.com/u/ce/multi/0,1977,6182652,00.html
2. 'PGA Event for Sörenstam?' *Miami Herald,* February 11, 2003, p2D.
3. Cox, 'Coke Won't Pitch to Kids,' *Miami Herald,* July 19, 2003, p3C.
4. Chad Terhune, 'Coke CEO Admits Obesity Is Big Issue,' *Wall Street Journal,* June 18, 2004, pB3.
5. David Barboza, 'Animal Welfare's Unexpected Allies,' *New York Times,* June 25, 2003, pp C1&2.
6. Catherine Arnst, 'Why Business Should Make AIDS Its Business,' *BusinessWeek,* August 2, 2004, p78.
7. Silvia Sansoni, 'Keeping Alive,' *Forbes,* February 3, 2003, pp 64–66.
8. Ibid.
9. *BusinessWeek,* August 2, 2004, op. cit.
10. Judy Larkin, 'Managing Reputation Risk,' *Ethical Corporate Magazine* Web site, April 25, 2003, http://www.ethicalcorp.com/content.asp?ContentID=530
11. Xenophon Strategies Case Study, 'Bridgestone/Firestone Tire Recall: A Case-study,' 2001 [unpublished manuscript].
12. 'Mattress Giant Settles Case,' *Miami Herald,* October 31, 2002, p3C.
13. Ibid.
14. Interview with Bill Gates, 'Biology and Bill Gates,' *BusinessWeek,* May 5, 2003, pp 76–77.

15. http://www.newmansown.com/3a_history.html

16. http://www.nikeresponsibility.com/

17. 'Spotlight on Diversity,' *mbajungle.com,* March/April 2003.

18. Ibid.

19. Jonathan Hickman, '50 Best Companies for Minorities: The List,' *Fortune,* June 28, 2004, p140.

20. Chad Terhune, 'Pepsi, Vowing Diversity Isn't Just Image Polish, Seeks Inclusive Culture,' *Wall Street Journal,* April 19, 2005, pB1.

21. Ibid.

22. Christina Hoag, 'Crest to Air Ad in Spanish During Grammys,' *Miami Herald,* February 22, 2003, p1A.

23. Roger Martin, 'The Virtue Matrix,' *Harvard Business Review,* March 2002, Vol. 80, No. 3, pp 68–75.

24. Karen Richardson, 'Viaticals May Draw More Insurers,' *Wall Street Journal,* May 18, 2005, pC3.

25. 'Not Many Ads Will Be Seen on September 11,' *Miami Herald,* September 1, 2002, Business & Money, p1.

26. Ibid.

27. http://www.mediafamily.org/research/report_vgrc_2002–2.shtml

28. Wendy Zellner & Michael Arndt, 'Holding Steady: As Rivals Sputter, Can Southwest Stay on Top?' *BusinessWeek,* February 3, 2003, pp66–68.

29. 'Business Ethics Names 100 Best Corporate Citizens for 2002,' http://www.business-ethics.com/2002_100_best_corporate_citizens.htm

30. *BusinessWeek,* February 3, 2003, op. cit.

31. *BusinessWeek,* February 3, 2003, op. cit.

32. All quotations in this section are from http://www.starbucks.com/aboutus/csr.asp

33. Scott McCartney, 'Unions Weigh Options at American,' *Wall Street Journal,* April 21, 2003, pA3.

34. Ibid.

35. Howard Discus, 'American Airlines: Carty Apologizes Again, but Union Still Plans Revote,' *Sacramento Business Journal,* April 22, 2003, http://sacramento.bizjournals.com/sacramento/stories/2003/04/21/daily15.html

36. Wendy Zellner, 'What Was Don Carty Thinking?' *BusinessWeek,* May 5, 2003, p32.

37. 'AMR Announces New Leadership,' AMR Press Release, April 24, 2003.

38. 'Carty Gets No Severance,' *Miami Herald,* June 14, 2003, p3L.

39. Ibid.

40. John Greenwald, 'Inside the Ford/Firestone Fight,' *Time Online Edition,* May 29, 2001.

41. Xenophon Strategies Case Study, 'Bridgestone/Firestone Tire Recall: A Case-study,' 2001 [unpublished manuscript].

42. Ibid.

43. Derrick Z. Jackson, 'Who Won the War? Defense CEOs,' *Miami Herald,* May 1, 2003, p7B.

44. Ibid.

45. http://www.faireconomy.org/press/2003/BucksforBang.pdf

46. 'CEOs at Defense Contractors Earn 45% More,' United for a Fair Economy Press Release, April 28, 2003, http://www.faireconomy.org/press/2003/MoreBucksForBang_pr.html

47. Darcy Frey, 'How Green Is BP?' *New York Times,* December 8, 2002, Section 6, p99.

48. Ibid.

49. http://www.greenpeace.org.uk/climate/climatecriminals/esso/case.cfm

50. Ibid.

51. Ian Herbert, 'Greenpeace Raids Hit Esso Stations in Anti-War Action,' *The Independent,* February 25, 2003, p11.

52. Manuel G. Velasquez, 'Business Ethics: Concepts and Cases,' 5th edition, Prentice Hall, 2002, pp 73–75.

53.   Ibid.

54.   Ibid.

55.   Ibid.

56.   Julie Forster, 'GM Foods: Why Fight Labeling?' *BusinessWeek,* November 11, 2002, p44.

57.   Ibid.

58.   Ibid.

59.   'Oregon Rejects GM Food Labeling Initiative,' *Food & Drink Weekly,* November 11, 2002, http://www.findarticles.com/p/articles/mi_m0EUY/is_43_8/ai_94461771

60.   Pui-Wing Tam, 'Cartridges for a Cause,' *Wall Street Journal,* May 6, 2005, pB1.

61.   Ben Elgin, 'Can HP's Printer Biz Keep Printing Money?' *BusinessWeek,* July 14, 2003, pp 68–70.

62.   Ibid.

63.   *Wall Street Journal,* May 6, 2005, op. cit.

64.   The McLibel Trial, McSpotlight, April, 2003, http://www.mcspotlight.org/case/

65.   Heather Timmons, 'Court Faults Britain's Handling of Libel Case,' *New York Times,* February 16, 2005, pC8.

66.   Beatrice E. Garcia, 'Sex, Violence, and Video,' *Miami Herald,* February 2, 2003, pp 1E&8E.

67.   Ibid.

68.   http://www.lionlamb.org/media_violence_video_games.htm

69.   http://www.lionlamb.org/violence_vid_games_facts.htm

70.   Thomas Strobhar, 'Giving Until It Hurts,' *Wall Street Journal,* August 1, 2003, pW15.

71.   Ibid.

72.   Cadbury, UK Web site, May 2, 2003.

73.   'Chocolate Offer: Will It Get Kids Fit or Fat?' *BBC News,* April 29, 2003, http://news.bbc.co.uk/1/hi/talking_point/2984599.stm

74.   *BBC World,* April 29, 2003, op. cit.

75.   Food Commission Web site, May 2, 2003, http://www.foodcomm.org.uk/

76.   'Chocolate for Footballs Scheme Criticized,' *BBC News*, April 29, 2003, http://news.bbc.co.uk/1/hi/uk/2984069.stm

77.   'Kraft Foods Announces Global Initiatives to Help Address Rise in Obesity,' Kraft Foods press release, July 1, 2003, http://www.kraft.com/newsroom/07012003.html

78.   David Teather, 'Lawsuits Frighten Kraft Into Fighting Flab,' *The Guardian,* July 2, 2003, http://www.guardian.co.uk/international/story/0,3604,989069,00.html

79.   Elaine Walker, 'Battle of the Bulge,' *Miami Herald,* July 3, 2003, p1C.

80.   Tom & David Gardner, 'Motley Fool: Kraft Rethinks Portions,' *Miami Herald,* June 20, 2004, p3E.

81.   Marianne Jennings, 'Seek Corporate Balance,' *Miami Herald,* September 1, 2002, p11L.

82.   Roger Martin, 'The Virtue Matrix,' *Harvard Business Review,* March 2002, Vol. 80, No. 3, pp. 68–75.

83.   *Miami Herald,* September 1, 2002, op. cit.

84.   Velasquez, op. cit., pp 122–123.

85.   Mitchell Pacelle, 'Can Mr. Feuerstein Save His Business One Last Time?' *Wall Street Journal,* May 9, 2003, pp A1&A6.

86.   Paul Gilding, 'Making Market Magic,' ecos Corporation Web site, June 2001, http://www.ecoscorporation.com/think/stake/market_magic.htm

87.   Andrew Pollack, 'Planting of Modified Crops Rose in 2002,' *New York Times,* January 16, 2003, pC6.

88.   'Genetically Modified Food Items Are Common, but Little Noticed,' *Wall Street Journal,* March 24, 2005, pD4.

89.   S. Prakash Sethi, 'A Conceptual Framework for Environmental Analysis of Social Issues and Evaluation of Business Response Patterns,' *Academy of Management Review,* Vol. 4, No. 1, 1979, pp 63–74.

90. Ibid.

91. Ibid.

92. The ICIFI has since been replaced by the Association of Infant Food Manufacturers (IFM).

93. http://www.maketradefair.com/

94. Ibid.

95. PETA's Web site, http://www.peta.org/, February 2003.

96. Emily Gersema, 'PETA Denies Accusation of Supporting Violence,' *Miami Herald,* February 16, 2003, p26A.

97. 'Review and Outlook: Fair or Fowl?' *Wall Street Journal,* July 16, 2004, pW11.

98. *Miami Herald,* February 16, 2003, op. cit.

99. Guardian Special Report, 2002, 'Power to the People,' *The Guardian,* December 20, 2002, http://www.guardian.co.uk/famine/story/0,12128,863479,00.html

100. *BBC News,* 'Brent Spar's Long Saga,' November 25, 1998, http://news.bbc.co.uk/1/hi/sci/tech/218527.stm; and *BBC News,* 'Brent Spar Gets Chop,' November 25, 1998, http://news.bbc.co.uk/1/hi/world/europe/221508.stm.

101. Ibid.

102. Ibid.

103. Gilding, op. cit.

104. Jagdish Bhagwati, 'In Defense of Globalization,' Oxford University Press, 2004. Quoted in Bruce Bartlett, 'Bookshelf: The Shipping News,' *Wall Street Journal,* June 24, 2004, pD10.

105. Maxine Clayton, 'Wal-Mart to Protect Gay Workers,' *Miami Herald,* July 3, 2003, p1C.

106. Ibid.

107. Suzanne Goldenberg & David Teather, 'Wal-Mart Wakes Up to Gay Rights,' *The Guardian,* July 3, 2003, http://www.guardian.co.uk/international/story/0,,989828,00.html

108. *Miami Herald*, July 3, 2003, op. cit.

109. Sally Pipes, 'Women Work, Shop at Wal-Mart,' *Miami Herald*, June 6, 2003, p7B.

110. For a detailed explanation of the concept of the CSR threshold see Chapter 4.

111. http://www.naag.org/issues/issue-tobacco.php

112. Mallen Baker, 'Analysis: 2002—A Year in Corporate Social Responsibility,' *Ethical Corporation*, December 27, 2002, http://www.ethicalcorp.com/NewsTemplate.asp?IDNum=469

113. This example is subtly different from the situation facing Cadbury and Kraft in the *Companies Trying to Do CSR Right* section above. Although all three companies are trying to react to the same situation (the rising level of obesity and threat of lawsuits because of the perceived contribution they have made to the problem), the fast-food industry in general, and McDonald's in particular, is seen by some as being synonymous with unhealthy food. Because of this more direct connection within consumer minds, the task facing the company in trying to alter this perception is likely to be much more difficult.

114. Emily Gersema, 'Coming Soon to Menus: Fat Facts?' *Miami Herald*, October 24, 2003, p3C.

115. Chelsea J. Carter, 'He's Going to Health in a Handbasket,' *Miami Herald*, April 10, 2005, p15M.

116. Richard Gibson, 'McDonald's Seeks Ways to Pitch Healthy Living,' *Wall Street Journal*, May 27, 2004, pD7.

117. Steven Gray, 'McDonald's Touts Its New Formula to Battle Obesity,' *Wall Street Journal*, April 16, 2004, pA11.

118. *Wall Street Journal*, May 27, 2004, op. cit.

119. Madlen Read, 'McDonald's to Promote Active, Healthy Lifestyle,' *Miami Herald*, March 9, 2005, p3C.

120. *Wall Street Journal*, April 16, 2004, op. cit.

121. A.O. Scott, 'When All Those Big Macs Bite Back,' *New York Times*, May 7, 2004, pB18.

122. Dave Carpenter, 'A New McHealthier Menu,' *Miami Herald*, April 16, 2004, p3C.

123. Betsy Morris, 'The Littlest Skeptics,' *Fortune*, June 29, 2004, p104.

124. Michael Arndt, 'The Creator of McWorld,' *BusinessWeek*, July 5, 2004, p18.

125. Stuart Elliott, 'Facing Outcry, NBC Ends Plan to Run Liquor Ads,' *New York Times*, March 21, 2002, Section C, p1.

126. Ibid.

127. Vanessa O'Connell, 'New Tactics at Philip Morris Help Stem Tide of Lawsuits,' *Wall Street Journal*, May 11, 2005, pA1.

128. 'What's the Marlboro Man's Game?' *BusinessWeek*, December 2, 2002, p50.

129. 'The Year's Toughest Talk,' *mbajungle.com*, December 2002/January 2003, p68.

130. http://philipmorrisusa.com/health_issues/cigarette_smoking_and_disease.asp

# Part III

# APPENDIXES

*Strategic Corporate Social Responsibility* is a sourcebook of information about CSR as practiced today. Beyond companies and concepts, Part III offers a variety of information sources focused on the specific subject of CSR: a directory of CSR-focused organizations with Web site references; online CSR news and information sources; and a more traditional bibliography of published sources (books and journal articles) about CSR. Part III, as a result, strengthens the book's claim to be part of any professional or business library.

These appendixes are an additional resource beyond the case study references and URLs provided throughout the book. In such a rapidly evolving field, however, it is foolhardy to attempt to present exhaustive accounts. None of the lists below is presented as complete but instead intended as additional assistance to help the eager reader delve further into this complex subject.

Part III is organized as follows:

– Directory of CSR-Related Organizations and Internet Links

– Directory of Online CSR Information Sources and Publications

– CSR Bibliography
  • Books
  • Journal Articles

# Appendix A

## DIRECTORY OF CSR-RELATED
## ORGANIZATIONS AND INTERNET LINKS

African Institute of Corporate Citizenship, http://www.aiccafrica.org/

> The African Institute of Corporate Citizenship (AICC) is a non-governmental organisation committed to promoting responsible growth and competitiveness in Africa by changing the way companies do business in Africa.

Aspen Institute Business and Society Program (formerly Aspen ISIB), http://www.aspeninstitute.org/isib/

> The Business and Society Program is an independently funded policy program at the Aspen Institute, dedicated to increasing the supply of business leaders who understand and seek to balance the complex relationship between business success and social and environmental progress.

Association of Independent Corporate Sustainability and Responsibility Research, http://www.csrr-qs.org/

> A new European standard (CSRR-QS 1.0) has been drawn up with the objective of promoting confidence in those Groups performing Corporate Sustainability and Responsibility Research (CSRR). CSRR-QS 1.0 is the first quality standard conceived and worked out at sector level in the field of CSR and SRI research and analysis. The project was initiated, supported and funded by the European Commission, Employment and Social Affairs DG.

As You Sow Foundation, http://www.asyousow.org/

> As You Sow is a non-profit organization dedicated to promoting corporate social responsibility.

Beyond Grey Pinstripes, http://www.beyondgreypinstripes.org/

Beyond Grey Pinstripes highlights the most innovative MBA programs and faculty infusing environmental and social impact management into the business school curriculum.

Business Alliance for Local Living Economies (BALLE)

Building Economies for the Common Good, http://www.livingeconomies.org/BALLE/

BALLE Mission: To create, strengthen and connect local business networks dedicated to building strong Local Living Economies.

BALLE Vision: We envision a sustainable global economy as a network of Local Living Economies. Living economies sustain community life and natural life as well as long-term economic viability.

Business for Social Responsibility (BSR), http://www.bsr.org/

Business for Social Responsibility (BSR) is a global nonprofit organization that helps member companies achieve commercial success in ways that respect ethical values, people, communities and the environment. BSR member companies have nearly $2 trillion in combined annual revenues and employ more than six million workers around the world.

Business in the Community, http://www.bitc.org.uk/

Business in the Community is a unique movement of companies across the UK committed to continually improving their positive impact on society, with a core membership of 700 companies, including 80% of the FTSE 100.

Business Roundtable Institute for Corporate Ethics, http://www.businessroundtable.org/also at: http://www.darden.edu/corporate-ethics/

This Institute is a bold investment that will bring together the best educators in the field of ethics, active business leaders and business school students to forge a new and lasting link between ethical behavior and business practices.

Canadian Business for Social Responsibility (CBSR), http://www.cbsr.ca/

Founded in 1995, CBSR is a non-profit, business-led, national membership organization of Canadian companies that have made a commitment to operate in a socially, environmentally and financially responsible manner, recognizing the interests of their stakeholders, including investors, customers, employees, business partners, local communities, the environment and society at large.

Caux Round Table, http://www.cauxroundtable.org/

The Caux Round Table (CRT) is a group of senior business leaders from Europe, Japan and North America who are committed to the promotion of principled business leadership. The CRT believes that business has a crucial role in identifying and promoting sustainable and equitable solutions to key global issues affecting the physical, social and economic environments.

Centre for Business Relationships, Accountability, Sustainability and Society (BRASS), http://www.brass.cf.ac.uk/

The ESRC Centre for Business Relationships, Accountability, Sustainability and Society exists to understand and promote the key issues of sustainability, accountability and social responsiveness, through research into key business relationships.

Center for Corporate Change, http://www.vailleadership.org/programs/index.htm

The Center for Corporate Change, a component of the Vail Leadership Institute, was established out of a concern for the state of corporate ethics. It is based on the premise that business is not a game but an integral component of our nation's democratic capitalistic society.

Center for Corporate Citizenship at Boston College, http://www.bcccc.net/

The Center for Corporate Citizenship is a leading resource on corporate citizenship, providing research, executive education, consultation and convenings on citizenship topics. Our mission is to establish corporate citizenship as a business essential, with the goal that all companies act as economic and social assets by integrating social interests with other core business objectives.

Center for Corporate Citizenship (U.S. Chamber of Commerce), http://www.uschamber.com/ccc/

The Center for Corporate Citizenship is a business service organization of the U.S. Chamber of Commerce. It exists to enable and facilitate corporate civic and humanitarian initiatives particularly in terms of civic engagement, economic development, economic security, and disaster management/economic recovery.

Centre for Corporate Social Responsibility, http://www.centreforcsr.org.sg/

The Centre for CSR, an independent not-for-profit organisation, was set up on 17th April 2003 by a group of like-minded and civic-conscious individuals and seeks to raise the awareness of the community at large about the importance of Corporate Social Responsibility (CSR). . . . The Centre for CSR aims to be a national platform for the discussion and understanding of CSR and to be a leading Centre for CSR globally and more particularly in the Asia Pacific.

Center for Economic and Social Justice, http://www.cesj.org/

The Center for Economic and Social Justice (CESJ), established in 1984, promotes a free enterprise approach to global economic justice through expanded capital ownership. CESJ is a non-profit, non-partisan, ecumenical, all-volunteer organization with an educational and research mission.

Center for Ethical Leadership, Seattle, http://www.ethicalleadership.org/

The Center motivates people to practice ethical leadership, inspires institutions to create cultures of integrity and gathers the community to animate cultural change, all for the common good.

Center for Public Integrity, http://www.publicintegrity.org/

The mission of the Center for Public Integrity is to provide the American people with the findings of our investigations and analyses of public service, government accountability and ethics related issues.

CEOs for Cities, http://www.ceosforcities.org/

CEOs for Cities is a national bipartisan alliance of mayors, corporate executives, university presidents and other nonprofit leaders. Its mission is to advance the economic competitiveness of cities. Its national meetings and research products underscore the organization's basic tenet, which is that urban economies are strengthened when public and private sectors come together to collaborate on economic development policy-making and practice.

CERES Network for Change, Coalition for Environmentally Responsible Economies, http://www.ceres.org/

Today, it is often difficult for corporations, activists and socially responsible investors to have honest, meaningful dialogue on corporations' environmental and social practices. CERES provides an innovative forum for this kind of exchange and a unique opportunity for real accountability and real results.

Community Business Limited, http://www.communitybusiness.org.hk/

Community Business is committed to working with companies on corporate social responsibility in Hong Kong.

Conversations with Disbelievers, http://www.conversations-with-disbelievers.net/

Welcome to the Conversations with Disbelievers website which for the first time brings together much of the available quantitative evidence that addressing social challenges can help businesses improve their financial bottom lines. . . . The website is designed to be used by business managers, nonprofit leaders, consultants and public policy makers alike to provide practical guidance on how best to use the available evidence in encouraging businesses to address social objectives.

Corporate Citizenship Unit, http://users.wbs.warwick.ac.uk/group/ccu/

The Corporate Citizenship Unit (CCU) aims to become a globally recognised centre of excellence in the area of research and teaching in corporate citizenship by bringing together diverse people from business, government, and civil society organisations to examine changes in the relationship between corporations, states and communities.

Corporate Culture, http://www.communicatingforgood.co.uk/

This website is the definitive online resource of customer-led CSR communications.

Corporate Responsibility, http://www.corporateresponsibility.nl/

This website is designed to function as a platform for the dissemination of information on the subject of Corporate [Social] Responsibility.

Corporate Social Responsibility Forum (part of the Prince of Wales Business Leaders Forum), http://www.csrforum.com/

The Prince of Wales Business Leaders Forum is an international charity which was founded in 1990 to promote socially responsible business practices that benefit business and society, and which help to achieve socially, economically and environmentally sustainable development. The Forum works at the very highest levels in 60 of the world's leading multinational companies, and is active in some 30 emerging and transition economies.

Corporate Social Responsibility Forum, http://www.csrforum.com/

The International Business Leaders Forum is an international educational charity set up in 1990 to promote responsible business practices internationally that benefit business and society, and which help to achieve social, economic and environmentally sustainable development, particularly in new and emerging market economies.

Council for Ethics in Economics, http://www.businessethics.org/

The Council for Ethics in Economics is a worldwide association of leaders in business, education, and other professions working together to strengthen the ethical fabric of business and economic life. The Council identifies and responds to issues important for ethical economic practices and assists in the resolution of these issues.

CSR Academy, http://www.csracademy.org.uk/

The CSR Academy aims to promote CSR learning through the first dedicated CSR Competency Framework. It is for companies of all sizes as well as for UK educational institutions.

CSR Australia, http://www.csra.com.au/

Founded in 2003 Corporate Social Responsibility Australia Inc. is a national not for profit membership based Incorporated Association whose mission is to help business achieve profitability, competitiveness and sustainable growth through the continuous improvement of skills, knowledge and ethical behaviour and by applying the principles of Corporate Social Responsibility.

CSR Europe, http://www.csreurope.org/

CSR Europe is the business-to-business network for Corporate Social Responsibility in Europe. We are a membership-based organization. Our mission is to help companies achieve profitability, sustainable growth and human progress by placing Corporate Social Responsibility (CSR) in the mainstream of business practice.

CSR Meetup Groups, http://csr.meetup.com/

Meet other local people interested in implementing or learning about corporate, values-based decision making.

CSR Watch, http://www.csrwatch.com/

Your eye on the anti-business movement.

EMPRESA, http://www.empresa.org/

EMPRESA is an American alliance of CSR-based business organizations that promotes corporate social responsibility (CSR) throughout the Americas.

Equal Exchange, http://www.equalexchange.com/

Equal Exchange was founded in 1986 to create a new approach to trade, one that includes informed consumers, honest and fair trade relationships and cooperative principles. As a worker-owned co-op, we have accomplished this by offering consumers fairly traded gourmet coffee direct from small-scale farmer co-ops in Latin America, Africa and Asia.

EU Multi-Stakeholder Forum on CSR, http://forum.europa.eu.int/irc/empl/csr_eu_multi_ stakeholder_forum/info/data/en/csr%20ems%20forum.htm

The European Multi-Stakeholder Forum on Corporate Social Responsibility (CSR EMS Forum), chaired by the Commission, brings together European representative organisations of employers, business networks, trade unions and NGOs, to promote innovation, convergence, and transparency in existing CSR practices and tools. The Forum's mandate was approved at the launch on 16th October 2002.

CSR Final Report, http://europa.eu.int/comm/enterprise/csr/documents.htm

European Academy of Business in Society, http://www.eabis.org/

The European Academy of Business in Society (EABIS) is a unique alliance of academic institutions, companies and other stakeholders committed to integrating business in society into the heart of business theory and practice in Europe.

http://www.csrcampaign.org/

The European Business Campaign on Corporate Social Responsibility has set itself the goal of mobilising 500,000 business people and partners to integrate CSR into their core business by 2005.

European Business Ethics Network, http://www.eben.org/

The European Business Ethics Network, EBEN, is the only International network dedicated wholly to the promotion of business ethics in European private industry, public sector, voluntary organizations, and academia.

European Union's CSR Website, http://europa.eu.int/comm/employment_social/ soc-dial/csr/csr_index.htm

Useful CSR Internet Links: http://europa.eu.int/comm/employment_social/soc-dial/csr/ csr_links.htm

Foundation for Global Community—Business and Sustainability, http://www.globalcommunity .org/business/index.shtml

The Foundation for Global Community's Business and Sustainability Group (BSG) focuses on educating local companies about the principles of sustainable development and promoting a broader measurement of business success, namely the 'Triple Bottom Line.'

Global Exchange, http://www.globalexchange.org/

Global Exchange is a human rights organization dedicated to promoting environmental, political, and social justice around the world. Since our founding in 1988, we have been striving to increase global awareness among the US public while building international partnerships around the world.

Global Reporting Initiative (GRI), http://www.globalreporting.org/

Recognized by the recent UN World Summit on Sustainable Development, the Global Reporting Initiative (GRI) is an independent global institution which is developing a generally accepted framework for sustainability reporting. The aim of the GRI Guidelines is to enable companies and other organizations to prepare comparable "triple bottom line" reports on their economic, environmental and social performance.

Global Sullivan Principles of Social Responsibility, http://globalsullivanprinciples.org/

The objectives of the Global Sullivan Principles are to support economic, social and political justice by companies where they do business; to support human rights and to encourage equal opportunity at all levels of employment, including racial and gender diversity on decision making committees and boards; to train and advance disadvantaged workers for technical, supervisory and management opportunities; and to assist with greater tolerance and understanding among peoples; thereby, helping to improve the quality of life for communities, workers and children with dignity and equality.

Group of 77 at the United Nations[1], http://www.g77.0rg/

As the largest Third World coalition in the United Nations, the Group of 77 provides the means for the developing world to articulate and promote its collective economic interests and enhance its joint negotiating capacity on all major international economic issues in the United Nations system, and promote economic and technical cooperation among developing countries.

Heartland Institute, http://www.thoughtleadergathering.com/

Founded in 1995 by Craig and Patricia Neal, Heartland Institute creates Essential Conversations among individuals and within organizations to help bring about the systemic change needed in these extraordinary times. . . . Our programs are anchored in the belief that essential conversations among leaders will transform our organizations and the world.

ILO Tripartite Declaration of Principles Concerning MNEs and Social Policy, http://www
.ilo.org/public/english/standards/norm/sources/mne.htm

Institute for Global Ethics, http://www.globalethics.org/

Mission: To promote ethical behavior in individuals, institutions, and nations through research, public discourse, and practical action.

Interfaith Center on Corporate Responsibility, http://www.iccr.org/

For thirty years the Interfaith Center on Corporate Responsibility (ICCR) has been a leader of the corporate social responsibility movement. ICCR's membership is an association of 275 faith-based institutional investors, including national denominations, religious communities, pension funds, endowments, hospital corporations, economic development funds and publishing companies. ICCR and its members press companies to be socially and environmentally responsible.

International Association for Business and Society (IABS), http://www.iabs.net/

IABS is a learned society devoted to research and teaching about the relationships between business, government and society.

International Business Ethics Institute, http://www.business-ethics.org/

Fostering global business practices to promote equitable economic development, resource sustainability and just forms of government.

International Business Leaders Forum, http://www.iblf.org/, http://www.iblf.org/csr/csrwe bassist.nsf/content/f1.html

The IBLF is an international educational charity set up in 1990 to promote responsible business practices internationally that benefit business and society, and which help to achieve social, economic and environmentally sustainable development, particularly in new and emerging market economies.

International Centre for Business Performance and Corporate Responsibility, http://mubs .mdx.ac.uk/Research/Research_Centres/icbpcr/

The Centre is located at Middlesex University's Business School, and aims to be an internationally-renowned 'Centre of Excellence' in the promotion of corporate responsibility and its relationship to business performance in both financial and non-financial dimensions.

International Centre for Corporate Social Responsibility, http://www.nottingham.ac.uk/ business/ICCSR/

The ICCSR engages in mainstream teaching and research in the broad area of corporate social responsibility.

International Institute for Sustainable Development, http://www.iisd.org/

The International Institute for Sustainable Development contributes to sustainable development by advancing policy recommendations on international trade and investment, economic policy, climate change, measurement and indicators, and natural resources management.

Japan for Sustainability, http://www.japanfs.org/en/business/reports.html

Here are links to environmental / sustainability reports of Japanese companies. The reports disclose their policies, strategies and performance in environmental, social and/or sustainability management.

LifeWorth, http://www.lifeworth.com/

As more of us work on corporate responsibility, sustainable business and responsible investment, we are forming a new profession and a new social movement. . . . We support this new movement and profession by bringing together people and organizations with common values.

Net Impact, http://www.net-impact.org/

Net Impact is a powerful and influential network of over 10,000 MBA students and professionals committed to using the power of business to create a better world. Through education, career resources, events, and access to an international network, Net Impact helps members to utilize their business skills for positive social change.

New Academy of Business, http://www.new-academy.ac.uk/

The New Academy of Business was founded in 1995 by Anita Roddick to provide entrepreneurs, managers and organisational leaders with the insights and capacities necessary to respond progressively to the emerging challenges of sustainability and organisational responsibility.

Nordic Partnership, http://www.nordicpartnership.org/

The Nordic Partnership is an NGO-business network founded in 2001 by the World Wide Fund for Nature (WWF), Danish media centre Monday Morning and key corporate players operating in the Nordic region. . . . Using a partnership approach, the members of the Nordic Partnership work together to find new ways of making sustainable initiatives more attractive and rewarding to business. By doing this, we aim to provide fresh perspectives, challenges and recommendations to the 'rules of the game' that relate to sustainable development.

Organization for Economic Co-operation and Development (OECD), http://www.oecd.org/
department/0,2688,en_2649_33765_1_1_1_1_1,00.html

The emergence of private initiatives for corporate responsibility–including the development of codes of conduct, management systems for improving compliance with these codes and non-financial reporting standards—has been an important trend in international business over the last 25 years. The Investment Committee's work in this area is part of its broader efforts to support implementation of the OECD Guidelines for Multinational Enterprises and to enhance the contribution of international investments to sustainable development.

Procott, http://www.procott.org/

> A procott (flipside of boycott) is a movement educating and organizing around conscious consumer efforts to support the production and purchase of earth/justice-friendly goods and services.

Project Sigma, http://www.projectsigma.com/

> Project SIGMA aims to provide clear, practical advice to organisations to help them make a meaningful contribution to sustainable development.

Public Citizen, http://www.citizen.org/

> Public Citizen is a national, nonprofit consumer advocacy organization founded by Ralph Nader in 1971 to represent consumer interests in Congress, the executive branch and the courts.
>
> We fight for openness and democratic accountability in government, for the right of consumers to seek redress in the courts; for clean, safe and sustainable energy sources; for social and economic justice in trade policies; for strong health, safety and environmental protections; and for safe, effective and affordable prescription drugs and health care.

Social Venture Network, http://www.svn.org/

> Founded in 1987 by some of the nation's most visionary leaders in socially responsible entrepreneurship and investment, Social Venture Network (SVN) is a nonprofit network committed to building a just and sustainable world through business.

Society for Business Ethics, http://www.societyforbusinessethics.org/

> The Society for Business Ethics (SBE) is an international organization of scholars engaged in the academic study of business ethics and others with interest in the field.

Spirit in Business, http://www.spiritinbusiness.org/

> Mission: To connect leaders in a global community of inquiry, learning and action, to release the creative power of individuals and organizations for the benefit of the whole.

Sustainable Business Institute, http://www.sustainablebusiness.org/

> The Sustainable Business Institute (SBI) is a non-profit, non-partisan organization dedicated to bringing about increased understanding of, and commitment to, the concept of sustainability within business and communities worldwide.

Sustainability Education Center, http://www.sustainabilityed.org/

> The Sustainability Education Center (SEC) was created in 1995 in response to the growing need for educational materials and professional development focused on sustainability.

Tomorrow's Company, http://www.tomorrowscompany.com/

Tomorrow's Company represents a practical future of sustainable success which makes sense to shareholders and to society. The Centre for Tomorrow's Company is a think-tank and catalyst, researching and stimulating the development of a new agenda for business. Our purpose is to create, with business, a future for business which makes equal sense to staff, shareholders and society.

UN Global Compact Principles, http://www.unglobalcompact.org/

Through the power of collective action, the Global Compact seeks to advance responsible corporate citizenship so that business can be part of the solution to the challenges of globalisation.

UN Millennium Development Goals, http://www.un.org/millenniumgoals/

By the year 2015, all 191 United Nation Member States have pledged to meet these goals.

Win-Win Partners, http://winwinpartner.com/

Win-Win Partners are companies and organizations achieving competitive advantage through community investment.

World Business Council for Sustainable Development, http://www.wbcsd.org/

The World Business Council for Sustainable Development (WBCSD) is a coalition of 160 international companies united by a shared commitment to sustainable development via the three pillars of economic growth, ecological balance and social progress.

World Resources Institute, http://www.wri.org/

World Resources Institute is an independent nonprofit organization with a staff of more than 100 scientists, economists, policy experts, business analysts, statistical analysts, map-makers, and communicators working to protect the Earth and improve people's lives.

## NOTE

1. "The G77 (the descendent of the former nonaligned countries) accounts for nearly 80 percent of the world's population," Noam Chomsky, 'The Crimes of "Intcom,"' *Foreign Policy*, September/October 2002, pp 34–35.

# APPENDIX B

## DIRECTORY OF ONLINE CSR INFORMATION SOURCES AND PUBLICATIONS

*Brooklyn Bridge Newsletter*—TBLI Group, http://www.tbli.org/index-newsletter.html

> *Brooklyn Bridge* publishes a digital Newsletter on SRI/CSR every month.

Business and Human Rights Resource Center, http://www.business-humanrights.org/

> The Business & Human Rights Resource Centre is an independent, international, non-profit organisation, in a collaborative partnership with Amnesty International sections and leading academic institutions. Our online library covers over 1800 companies, over 160 countries, over 150 topics.

*Business and Society,* http://www.sagepub.com/journalManuscript.aspx?pid=131

> *Business & Society* publishes the most outstanding scholarship on social issues and ethics, and their impact and influence on organizations. In this fast-growing, ever-changing, and always challenging field of study, *Business & Society* is the only peer-reviewed scholarly journal devoted entirely to research, discussion, and analysis on the relationship between business and society.

*Business Ethics Magazine,* http://www.business-ethics.com/index.html

> The mission of *Business Ethics* is to promote ethical business practices, to serve that growing community of professionals striving to work and invest in responsible ways.

*Business Ethics Magazine's* Corporate Social Responsibility Report, 100 Best Corporate Citizens, http://www.business-ethics.com/whats_new/100best_2005.html

*Business Ethics Quarterly,* http://www.societyforbusinessethics.org/beq.htm

> *Business Ethics Quarterly* (BEQ) is the journal of the Society for Business Ethics. BEQ publishes scholarly articles and book reviews on all aspects of ethics in business, especially those that raise conceptual, methodological, practical, or theoretical issues.

*Chronicle of Philanthropy,* http://philanthropy.com/

*The Chronicle of Philanthropy* is the newspaper of the nonprofit world. It is the No. 1 news source, in print and online, for charity leaders, fund raisers, grant makers, and other people involved in the philanthropic enterprise.

Common Dreams News Center, http://www.commondreams.org/

Breaking news and views for the progressive community.

CSR Online Survey, http://www.csr-survey.org/

How companies communicate CSR to customers and shareholders, is vital. It says as much about their brand as do their products and services. It will affect not only their reputation in the City, but also with their customers. The aim of this survey was to look at how well—or badly—Britain's top companies are communicating their CSR activities.

*CSR Wire*—Corporate Social Responsibility Newswire Service, http://www.csrwire.com/

*CSRwire* seeks to promote the growth of corporate responsibility and sustainability through solutions-based information and positive examples of corporate practices.

*CSR Wire*—CSR Directory, http://www.csrwire.com/directory/

*CSRwire* and the SRI World Group technical team have developed this searchable, online version of the CSR Directory as a free service to the CSR community.

*Electronic Journal of Business Ethics and Organization Studies,* http://ejbo.jyu.fi/index.cgi?page=cover

*Electronic Journal of Business Ethics and Organization Studies,* the aim of which is to promote research and practise of business and organization ethics.

*Ethical Corporation Magazine,* http://www.ethicalcorp.com/

*Ethical Corporation Magazine* is an independent business publication for corporate responsibility, producing 12 issues per year.

*Ethical Performance,* http://www.ethicalperformance.com/

*Ethical Performance* is a monthly newsletter for professionals with a corporate social responsibility or socially responsible investment brief. It is the only independent business newsletter to cover trends in

- social reporting
- corporate governance
- ethical codes of practice
- socially responsible investment
- risk and reputation management
- supply chain monitoring.

*Ethics in Economics Quarterly*, http://www.businessethics.org/ethicsq.htm

The quarterly publication of the Council for Ethics in Economics.

*ETHICOMP Journal,* http://www.ccsr.cse.dmu.ac.uk/journal/

The *ETHICOMP Journal* aims to further the work of the conference series—recognised as one of the premier international events on computer ethics and social responsibility attended by delegates from all over the world.

EurActiv.com (Corporate Social Responsibility page), http://www.euractiv.com/Section? idNum=3750340

EurActiv.com is now the leading online media on European Union policies.

*Faith in Business* quarterly, http://www.fibq.org/

*Faith in Business* is a quarterly journal relating Christian faith and values to the business world.

Global Corruption Report, http://www.globalcorruptionreport.org/

*The Global Corruption Report . . .* is the new publication of Transparency International (TI), the leading global anti-corruption NGO. It provides an overview of the state of corruption around the globe.

Greenbiz.com, http://www.greenbiz.com/

The nonprofit, nonpartisan GreenBiz.com works to harness the power of technology to bring environmental information, resources, and tools to the mainstream business community.

*GreenMoney Journal,* http://www.greenmoneyjournal.com/

The *GreenMoney Journal* encourages and promotes the awareness of socially & environmentally responsible business, investing and consumer resources in publications & online.

*Journal of Business Ethics,* http://www.kluweronline.com/issn/0167–4544

The *Journal of Business Ethics* publishes original articles from a wide variety of methodological and disciplinary perspectives concerning ethical issues related to business.

*Journal of Corporate Citizenship,* http://www.greenleaf-publishing.com/jcc/jcchome.htm

The *Journal of Corporate Citizenship* (JCC) aims to publish the best ideas integrating the theory and practice of corporate citizenship in a format that is readable, accessible, engaging, interesting and useful for readers in business, consultancy, government, NGOs and academia.

mallenbaker.net, http://www.mallenbaker.net/csr/

This site is part of the personal site of Mallen Baker—Development Director for Business in the Community. It is an expression of my own interest and concern in how companies respond to the agenda for corporate citizenship—the growing need to manage issues that affect their business reputation—and to respond to the growing needs and concerns of a range of different stakeholders.

New Academy Review, http://www.new-academy-review.com/

*The International Journal of Corporate Social Responsibility, Sustainability, Leadership and Ethics.*

Nonprofit Management Educational Resources, http://www.uwex.edu/li/index.html

The Learner Resource Center provides you with a number of resources on the web that could provide you with assistance in a variety of nonprofit management and leadership issues.

*NonProfit Times,* http://www.nptimes.com/

The leading business publication for nonprofit management.

NPT Top 100

The leading in-depth study of America's Top 100 Nonprofits.

OneWorld.net, http://www.oneworld.net/

The OneWorld network and portal brings you the latest news, action, campaigns and organisations in human rights and global issues across five continents and in 11 different languages, published across its international site, regional editions, and thematic channels.

Simon Zadek, http://www.zadek.net/

This site is a resource area for people concerned with improving the social, environmental and economic performance of business.

Socialfunds.com, http://www.socialfunds.com/

SocialFunds.com features over 10,000 pages of information on SRI mutual funds, community investments, corporate research, shareowner actions, and daily social investment news.

Socially Responsible Investing (SRI) Compass, http://www.sricompass.org/

The SRI Compass is the first European online resource featuring all existing green and ethical retail funds and indices in Europe. The SRI Compass is the result of a joint initiative by CSR Europe and the SiRi Group with the support of Euronext.

Spirit in Business, http://www.spiritinbusiness.org/

Spirit in Business is for business people who care.
Spirit in Business is about an economy that works for everyone.

*Stanford Social Innovation Review*, http://www.ssireview.com/?stanford

Discover powerful insights from leading executives and world-class faculty. *Stanford Social Innovation Review* presents the best ideas in nonprofit management, philanthropy and corporate citizenship. Find out what works and what doesn't. And how to strengthen your social impact.

SustainableBusiness.com, http://www.sustainablebusiness.com/

Vision: A world where human activities live in harmony with earth's carrying capacity.

*Worthwhile Magazine,* http://www.worthwhilemag.com/

The editorial mission of *Worthwhile* is to put purpose and passion on the same plane as profit. *Worthwhile* offers a roadmap for business success that is more personally fulfilling and socially responsible. We live by the motto that it is impossible to have a meaningful life without meaningful work.

# APPENDIX C

## CSR BIBLIOGRAPHY

The following publications present key concepts within the field of CSR, which helped formulate the ideas presented in *Strategic Corporate Social Responsibility*. The list is by no means intended to be complete but provided here as a complementary addendum to the end-notes and other references throughout.

## Books

Aaronson, Susan, and Reeves, James, 'Corporate Responsibility in the Global Village: The Role of Public Policy,' National Policy Association, 2002, http://www.npa1.0rg/midas//npa-showprod.asp?Style=&Category=14&Product=618

Ackerman, R. W., and Bauer, R. A., 'Corporate Social Responsiveness,' Reston, 1976.

Anderson, Jerry W., 'Corporate Social Responsibility: Guidelines for Top Management,' Quorum Books, 1989.

Andriof, Jörg, Waddock, Sandra, Husted, Bryan, and Sutherland-Rahman, Sandra, 'Unfolding Stakeholder Thinking: Theory, Responsibility and Engagement,' Greenleaf Publishing, 2002.

Arena, Christine, 'Cause for Success: 10 Companies That Put Profit Second and Came in First,' New World Library, 2004, http://www.causeforsuccess.com/

Backman, J., ed., 'Social Responsibility and Accountability,' New York University Press, 1975.

Bakan, Joel, 'The Corporation: The Pathological Pursuit of Profit and Power,' Free Press, 2004.

Barnard, C. I., 'The Functions of the Executive,' Harvard University Press, 1938.

Barrett, Richard, 'Liberating the Corporate Soul: Building a Visionary Organization,' Butterworth-Heinemann, 1998.

Batstone, David, 'Saving the Corporate Soul & (Who Knows?) Maybe Your Own,' Jossey-Bass, 2003.

Batten, Jonathan A., 'Social Responsibility: Corporate Governance Issues,' Elsevier Science & Technology Books, 2003.

Benioff, Marc, and Southwick, Karen, 'Compassionate Capitalism: How Corporations Can Make Doing Good an Integral Part of Doing Well,' Career Press, Inc., 2004.

Berle, Adolf A., and Means, Gardiner C., 'The Modern Corporation and Private Property,' Harcourt, Brace & World, 1968.

Bornstein, David, 'How to Change the World: Social Entrepreneurs and the Power of New Ideas,' Oxford University Press, 2003.

Borowitz, Andy, 'Who Moved My Soap? The CEO's Guide to Surviving in Prison,' Simon & Schuster, 2003.

Bowen, H. R., 'Social Responsibilities of the Businessman,' Harper & Row, 1953.

Brown, Halina Szejnwald, 'Corporate Environmentalism in a Global Economy: Societal Values in International Technology Transfer,' Quorum Books, 1993.

Brown, Lester R., 'Eco-Economy: Building an Economy for the Earth,' W.W. Norton & Co., 2002.

Buono, Anthony F., 'Corporate Policy, Values, and Social Responsibility,' Praeger, 1985.

Carroll, A. B. ed., 'Managing Corporate Social Responsibility,' Little, Brown, 1977.

Carroll, A. B., 'Business and Society: Managing Corporate Social Performance,' Little, Brown, 1981.

Carroll, Archie B., and Buchholtz, Ann K., 'Business and Society: Ethics and Stakeholder Management,' South-Western College, 2002.

Chamberlain, Neil W., 'The Limits of Corporate Responsibility,' Basic Books, 1973.

Clark, J. M., 'Social Control of Business,' McGraw-Hill, 1939.

Cohan, Peter S., 'Value Leadership: The 7 Principles That Drive Corporate Value in Any Economy,' Jossey-Bass, 2003.

Collins-Chobanian, Shari, ed., 'Ethical Challenges to Business As Usual,' Pearson Prentice Hall, 2005.

Committee for Economic Development, 'Social Responsibilities of Business Corporations,' CED, 1971.

Davis, K., and Blomstrom, R. L., 'Business and Its Environment,' McGraw-Hill, 1966.

Doh, Jonathan P., and Teegen, Hildy, 'Globalization and NGOs: Transforming Business, Government, and Society,' Praeger, 2003.

Drucker, Peter F., 'Concept of the Corporation,' John Day, 1946. Republished in 1993 by Transaction Publishers.

Drucker, P. F., 'The Practice of Management,' Harper & Row, 1954.

Dunning, John H., 'Making Globalization Good: The Moral Challenges of Global Capitalism,' Oxford University Press, 2003.

Eells, R., 'Corporate Giving in a Free Society,' New York, 1956.

Eells, R., and Walton, C., 'Conceptual Foundations of Business,' 3rd ed., Irwin, 1974.

Estes, Ralph, 'Tyranny of the Bottom Line: Why Corporations Make Good People Do Bad Things,' Berrett-Koehler Publishers, 1996.

Etzioni, Amitai, 'The Spirit of Community: Rights, Responsibilities, and the Communitarian Agenda,' Crown, 1993.

Evan, William M., and Manion, Mark, 'Minding the Machines: Preventing Technological Disasters,' Prentice Hall, 2002.

Farmer, Richard N., 'Corporate Social Responsibility,' Science Research Associates, 1973. Re-published in 1985 by Lexington Books.

Frederick, William Crittenden, 'Values, Nature, and Culture in the American Corporation,' Oxford University Press, 1995.

Freeman, R. Edward, 'Strategic Management: A Stakeholder Approach,' Pitman, 1984.

French, Peter A., 'Collective and Corporate Responsibility,' Columbia University Press, 1984.

Friedman, Milton, 'Capitalism and Freedom,' University of Chicago Press, 1962.

Grayson, David, and Hodges, Adrian, 'Corporate Social Opportunity! Seven Steps to Make Corporate Social Responsibility Work for Your Business,' Greenleaf Publishing, 2004.

Greider, William, 'The Soul of Capitalism: Opening Paths to a Moral Economy,' Simon & Schuster, 2003.

Gunderson, Nels L., 'Corporate Social Responsibility: A Survey of the Literature,' Vance Bibliographies, 1986.

Harvard Business Review, 'Harvard Business Review on Corporate Responsibility (HARVARD BUSINESS REVIEW PAPERBACK SERIES),' Harvard Business School Press, 2003.

Heald, M., 'Management's Responsibility to Society: The Growth of an Idea,' 1957.

Heald, M., 'The Social Responsibilities of Business: Company and Community, 1900–1960,' Case Western Reserve University Press, 1970.

Himmelstein, Jerome L., 'Looking Good and Doing Good: Corporate Philanthropy and Corporate Power,' Indiana University Press, 1997.

Hollender, Jeffrey, 'What Matters Most: Business, Social Responsibility, and the End of the Era of Greed,' Basic Books, 2004.

Hollender, Jeffrey, and Fenichell, Stephen, 'What Matters Most: How a Small Group of Pioneers Is Teaching Social Responsibility to Big Business, and Why Big Business Is Listening,' Basic Books, 2004.

Holliday, Charles, Schmidheiny, Stephan, and Watts, Philip, 'Walking the Talk: The Business Case for Sustainable Development,' Greenleaf Publishing, 2002.

Hopkins, Michael J. D., 'The Planetary Bargain: Corporate Social Responsibility Comes of Age,' MacMillan Press, 1999.

Hopkins, Michael J. D., 'The Planetary Bargain: Corporate Social Responsibility Matters,' Earthscan, 2003.

Human Resources Network, 'The Handbook of Corporate Social Responsibility: Profiles of Involvement,' Chilton Book Co., 1975.

Jacoby, Neil H., 'Corporate Power and Social Responsibility: A Blueprint for the Future,' Macmillan, 1973.

John, Steve, and Thomson, Stuart, 'New Activism and the Corporate Response,' Palgrave Macmillan, 2003.

Johnson, H. L., 'Business in Contemporary Society: Framework and Issues,' Wadsworth, 1971.

Karake, Zeinab A., 'Organizational Downsizing, Discrimination and Corporate Social Responsibility,' Quorum, 1999.

Kotler, Philip, and Lee, Nancy, 'Corporate Social Responsibility: Doing the Most Good for Your Company and Your Cause,' J. Wiley, 2004.

Kreps, T. J., 'Measurement of the Social Performance of Business,' U.S. Government Printing Office, 1940.

Labatt, Sonia, 'Industry, the Environment and Corporate Social Responsibility: A Selected and Annotated Bibliography,' Council of Planning Librarians, 1990.

Laszlo, Christopher, 'The Sustainable Company: How to Create Lasting Value Through Social and Environmental Performance,' Island Press, 2003.

Litvin, Daniel B., 'Empires of Profit: Commerce, Conquest and Corporate Responsibility,' Texere, 2003.

Manne, H. G., and Wallich, H. C., 'The Modern Corporation and Social Responsibility,' American Enterprise Institute for Public Policy Research, 1972.

Martin, Roger L., 'The Responsibility Virus: How Control Freaks, Shrinking Violets—and the Rest of Us—Can Harness the Power of True Partnership,' Basic Books, 2002.

Maurasse, David, 'A Future for Everyone: Innovative Social Responsibility and Community Partnerships,' Routledge, 2004.

McDonough, William, and Braungart, Michael, 'Cradle to Cradle,' North Point Press, 2002.

McGuire, J. W., 'Business and Society,' McGraw-Hill, 1963.

McIntosh, Malcolm, 'Raising a Ladder to the Moon: The Complexities of Corporate Social and Environmental Responsibility,' Palgrave Macmillan, 2003.

Micklethwait, John, and Wooldridge, Adrian, 'The Company: A Short History of a Revolutionary Idea,' Modern Library, 2003.

Mitchell, Lawrence E., 'Corporate Irresponsibility: America's Newest Export,' Yale University Press, 2001.

Monks, Robert A. G., 'Power and Accountability,' HarperBusiness, 1991.

Nolan, Stuart, 'Patterns of Corporate Philanthropy: Executive Hypocrisy,' Capital Research Center, 1993.

Nourick, Shari, 'Corporate Social Responsibility: Partners for Progress,' Organisation for Economic Co-operation and Development, 2001.

OECD, 'Corporate Responsibility: Private Initiatives and Public Goals,' Organisation for Economic Co-operation and Development, 2001.

OECD, 'Foreign Direct Investment, Development and Corporate Responsibility,' Organisation for Economic Co-operation and Development, 1999.

Paine, Lynn Sharp, 'Value Shift: Why Companies Must Merge Social and Financial Imperatives to Achieve Superior Performance,' McGraw-Hill, 2003.

Pava, Moses L., 'Corporate Responsibility and Financial Performance: The Paradox of Social Cost,' Quorum Books, 1995.

Post, James E., Lawrence, Anne T., and Weber, James, 'Business & Society: Corporate Strategy, Public Policy, and Ethics,' McGraw-Hill; 10th ed., 2002.

Prahalad, C. K., 'The Fortune at the Bottom of the Pyramid: Eradicating Poverty Through Profits,' Wharton School Publishing, 2004.

Preston, L. E., and Post, J. E., 'Private Management and Public Policy: The Principle of Public Responsibility,' Prentice Hall, 1975.

Rees, Stuart, and Wright, Shelley, 'Human Rights, Corporate Responsibility: A Dialogue,' Pluto Press, 2000.

Reynolds, David B., 'Taking the High Road: Communities Organize for Economic Change,' M.E. Sharpe Inc., 2002.

Riahi-Belkaoui, Ahmed, 'The Role of Corporate Reputation for Multinational Firms: Accounting, Organizational, and Market Considerations,' Quorum Books, 2001.

Roome, Nigel J., 'Sustainability Strategies for Industry: The Future of Corporate Practice,' Island Press, 1998.

Rosenberg, Hilary, 'A Traitor to His Class: Robert A.G. Monks and the Battle to Change Corporate America,' J. Wiley, 1999.

Rothman, Howard, and Scott, Mary, 'Companies With a Conscience: Intimate Portraits of Twelve Firms That Make a Difference,' 3rd ed., Myers Templeton, 2004, http://www .companieswithaconscience.com/

Schwartz, Peter, and Gibb, Blair, 'When Good Companies Do Bad Things: Responsibility and Risk in an Age of Globalization,' J. Wiley, 1999.

Selekman, B., 'A Moral Philosophy for Business,' McGraw-Hill, 1959.

Simon, John G., 'The Ethical Investor: Universities and Corporate Responsibility,' Yale University Press, 1972.

Sims, Ronald R., 'Ethics and Corporate Social Responsibility: Why Giants Fall,' Praeger, 2003.

Stack, Jack, and Burlingham, Bo, 'A Stake in the Outcome: Building a Culture of Ownership for the Long-Term Success of Your Business,' Currency/Doubleday, 2002.

Steger, Ulrich, 'The Business of Sustainability: Building Industry Cases for Corporate Sustainability,' Palgrave Macmillan, 2004.

Steiner, G. A., 'Business and Society,' Random House, 1971.

Sullivan, Thomas F. P., 'The Greening of American Business: Making Bottom-line Sense of Environmental Responsibility,' Government Institutes, 1992.

Tichy, Noel M., McGill, Andrew R., and St. Clair, Lynda, 'Corporate Global Citizenship: Doing Business in the Public Eye,' New Lexington Press, 1997.

Velasquez, Manuel G., 'Business Ethics: Concepts and Cases,' 5th ed., Prentice Hall, 2002, http://cwx.prenhall.com/velasquez/

Waddock, Sandra A., 'Leading Corporate Citizens: Vision, Values, Value-added,' McGraw-Hill, 2002.

Walton, C. C., 'Corporate Social Responsibilities,' Wadsworth, 1967.

Wartick, Steven Leslie, 'International Business and Society,' Blackwell Business, 1998.

Whitman, Marina V. N., 'New World, New Rules: The Changing Role of the American Corporation,' Harvard Business School Publishing, 1999.

Wilson, Ian, 'The New Rules of Corporate Conduct: Rewriting the Social Charter,' Quorum, 2000.

## Journal Articles

Abbott, W. F., and Monsen, R. J., 'On the Measurement of Corporate Social Responsibility: Self-reported Disclosures as a Method of Measuring Corporate Social Involvement,' *Academy of Management Journal,* 22, 501–515, 1979.

Ackerman, R. W., 'How Companies Respond to Social Demands,' *Harvard Business Review,* 51 (4), 88–98, 1973.

Agle, Bradley R., Mitchell, Ronald K., and Sonnenfeld, Jeffrey A., 'Who Matters to CEOs? An Investigation of Stakeholder Attributes and Salience, Corporate Performance, and CEO Values,' *Academy Of Management Journal,* 42 (5), 507–525, October 1999.

Auppede, K. E., Carroll, A. B., and Hatfield, J. D., 'An Empirical Investigation of the Relationship Between Corporate Social Responsibility and Profitability,' *Academy of Management Journal,* 28, 446–463, 1985.

Bagnoli, Mark, and Watts, Susan G., 'Selling to Socially Responsible Consumers: Competition and the Private Provision of Public Goods,' *Journal of Economics & Management Strategy,* 12 (3), 419, 2003.

Bansal, Pratima, and Roth, Kendall, 'Why Companies Go Green: A Model of Ecological Responsiveness,' *Academy Of Management Journal,* 43 (4), 717–736, 2000.

Bansal, Pratima, and Bogner, William C., 'Deciding on ISO 14001: Economics, Institutions, and Context,' *Long Range Planning,* 35 (3), 269, 2002.

Beadle, Roy, and Ridderbeekx, Ronald, 'CSR Communication in a Controversial Sector,' *Strategic Communication Management,* 5 (5), 20, 2001.

Beliveau, Barbara, Cottrill, Melville, and O'Neill, Hugh M., 'Predicting Corporate Social Responsiveness: A Model Drawn From Three Perspectives,' *Journal of Business Ethics,* 13 (9), 731, 1994.

Blumenthal, Dannielle, and Bergstrom, Alan J., 'Brand Councils That Care: Towards the Convergence of Branding and Corporate Social Responsibility,' *Journal of Brand Management,* 10 (4/5), 327, 2003.

Boiral, Olivier, 'The Certification of Corporate Conduct: Issues and Prospects,' *International Labour Review,* 142 (3), 317–340, 2003.

Bowman, E. H., and Haire, M., 'A Strategic Posture Toward Corporate Social Responsibility,' *California Management Review,* 18, 49–58, 1975.

Brammer, Stephen, and Millington, Andrew, 'Stakeholder Pressure, Organizational Size, and the Allocation of Departmental Responsibility for the Management of Corporate Charitable Giving,' *Business and Society,* 43 (3), 268–295, 2004.

Burke, Lee, and Logsdon, Jeanne M., 'How Corporate Social Responsibility Pays Off,' *Long Range Planning,* 29 (4), 495, 1996.

Carroll, Archie B., 'A Three-Dimensional Conceptual Model of Corporate Performance,' *Academy of Management Review,* 4 (4), 497–505, 1979.

Carroll, A. B., 'Corporate Social Responsibility: Will Industry Respond to Cutbacks in Social Program Funding?' *Vital Speeches of the Day,* 49, 604–608, July 15, 1983.

Carroll, Archie B., 'The Pyramid of Corporate Social Responsibility: Toward the Moral Management of Organizational Stakeholders,' *Business Horizons,* 34 (4), 39, 1991.

Carroll, A. B., 'Social Issues in Management Research: Experts' Views, Analysis and Commentary,' *Business and Society,* 33, 5–29, 1994.

Carroll, Archie B., 'Corporate Social Responsibility: Evolution of a Definitional Construct,' *Business and Society,* 38 (3), 268–295, 1999.

Carter, Craig R., and Jennings, Marianne M., 'The Role of Purchasing in Corporate Social Responsibility: A Structural Equation Analysis,' *Journal of Business Logistics,* 25 (1), 145, 2004.

Cochran, P. L., and Wood, R. A., 'Corporate Social Responsibility and Financial Performance,' *Academy of Management Journal,* 27, 42–56, 1984.

Dalton, D. R., and Cosier, R. A., 'The Four Faces of Social Responsibility,' *Business Horizons,* 19–27, May/June 1982.

Davis, Keith, 'Can Business Afford to Ignore Social Responsibilities?' *California Management Review,* 2 (3), 70–76, 1960.

Davis, K., 'Understanding the Social Responsibility Puzzle: What Does the Businessman Owe to Society?' *Business Horizons,* 10, 45–50, 1967.

Davis, K., 'The Case for and Against Business Assumption of Social Responsibilities,' *Academy of Management Journal,* 1, 312–322, 1973.

Dawkins, Jenny, and Lewis, Stewart, 'CSR in Stakeholder Expectations: And Their Implication for Company Strategy,' *Journal of Business Ethics,* 44 (2/3), 185–193, 2003.

Donaldson, Thomas, and Dunfee, T. W., 'Towards a Unified Conception of Business Ethics: Integrative Social Contracts Theory,' *Academy of Management Review,* 19, 252–284, 1994.

Donaldson, Thomas, and Preston, L. E., 'The Stakeholder Theory of the Corporation: Concepts, Evidence, and Implications,' *Academy of Management Review,* 20, 65–91, 1995.

Drucker, P. F., 'The New Meaning of Corporate Social Responsibility,' *California Management Review,* 26, 53–63, 1984.

Editorial, 'The Next Stage for CSR: Economic Democracy,' *Business Ethics Magazine,* http://www.business-ethics.com/thenext.htm

Eilbert, H., and Parket, I. R., 'The Current Status of Corporate Social Responsibility,' *Business Horizons,* 16, 5–14, August 1973.

Epstein, E. M., 'The Corporate Social Policy Process: Beyond Business Ethics, Corporate Social Responsibility, and Corporate Social Responsiveness,' *California Management Review,* 29, 99–114, 1987.

Fitch, H. G., 'Achieving Corporate Social Responsibility,' *Academy of Management Review,* 1, 38–46, 1976.

Frederick, W. C., 'The Growing Concern Over Business Responsibility,' *California Management Review,* 2, 54–61, 1960.

Frederick, William C., 'Moving to CSR4: What to Pack for the Trip,' *Business and Society,* 37 (1), March 1998.

Friedman, Milton, 'The Social Responsibility of Business Is to Increase Its Profits,' *New York Times Magazine,* September 13, 1970.

Greening, Daniel W., and Gray, Barbara, 'Testing a Model of Organizational Response to Social and Political Issues,' *Academy Of Management Journal,* 37 (3), 467, 1994.

Handy, Charles, 'What's a Business For?' *Harvard Business Review,* 80 (12), 49–55, 2002.

Heath, Joseph, and Norman, Wayne, 'Stakeholder Theory, Corporate Governance and Public Management: What Can the History of State-Run Enterprises Teach Us in the Post-Enron Era?' *Journal Of Business Ethics,* 53 (3), 247, 2004.

Hemphill, Thomas A., 'Corporate Citizenship: The Case for a New Corporate Governance Model,' *Business And Society Review,* 109 (3), 339–361, 2004.

Hess, David, Rogovsky, Nikolai, and Dunfee, Thomas W., 'The Next Wave of Corporate Community Involvement: Corporate Social Initiatives,' *California Management Review,* 44 (2), 110, 2002.

Holmes, S. L., 'Executive Perceptions of Corporate Social Responsibility,' *Business Horizons,* 19, 34–40, 1976.

Jackson, C., and Bundgard, T., 'Achieving Quality in Social Reporting: The Role of Surveys in Stakeholder Consultation,' *Business Ethics: A European Review,* 11 (3), 253, 2002.

Jones, T. M., 'Corporate Social Responsibility Revisited, Redefined,' *California Management Review,* 59–67, Spring 1980.

Lantos, Geoffrey P., 'The Boundaries of Strategic Corporate Social Responsibility,' *Journal of Consumer Marketing,* 18 (7), 595–630, 2001.

Lewis, Stewart, 'Reputation and Corporate Responsibility,' *Journal of Communication Management,* 7 (4), 356, 2003.

Lichtenstein, Donald R., Drumwright, Minette E., and Braig, Bridgette M., 'The Effect of Corporate Social Responsibility on Customer Donations to Corporate-Supported Nonprofits,' *Journal of Marketing,* 68 (4), 16–32, 2004.

Maignan, Isabelle, and Ferrell, O. C., 'Corporate Social Responsibility and Marketing: An Integrative Framework,' *Journal of the Academy of Marketing Science,* 32 (1), 3, 2004.

Maignan, Isabelle, Ferrell, O. C., Hult, G., and Tomas H., 'Corporate Citizenship: Cultural Antecedents and Business Benefits,' *Journal of the Academy of Marketing Science,* 27 (4), 455–469, 1999.

Margolis, Joshua D., and Walsh, James P., 'Misery Loves Companies: Rethinking Social Initiatives by Business,' *Administrative Science Quarterly,* 48 (2), 268, 2003.

Martin, Roger, 'The Virtue Matrix,' *Harvard Business Review,* 80 (3), 68–75, 2002.

McWilliams, Abigail, 'Corporate Social Responsibility: A Theory of the Firm Perspective,' *Academy of Management Review,* 26 (1), 117–128, 2001.

Middlemiss, Nigel, 'Communicating CSR to the Financial Community,' *Strategic Communication Management,* 8 (1), 22, December 2003/January 2004.

Mitchell, Ronald K., Agle, Bradley R., and Wood, Donna J., 'Toward a Theory of Stakeholder Identification and Salience: Defining the Principle of Who and What Really Counts,' *Academy of Management Review,* 22 (4), 853–886, 1997.

Moldoveanu, Mihnea, and Sharp Paine, Lynn, 'Case-study: Royal Dutch/Shell in Nigeria' *Harvard Business School,* Ref. No.: 9–399–126 (rev. April 20, 2000), 1999.

Murphy, Elizabeth, 'Best Corporate Citizens Have Better Financial Performance,' *Strategic Finance,* 83 (7), 20, 2002.

Murray, Keith B., and Vogel, Christine M., 'Using a Hierarchy-of-Effects Approach to Gauge the Effectiveness of Corporate Social Responsibility to Generate Goodwill Toward the Firm: Financial Versus Non-financial Impacts,' *Journal of Business Research,* 38 (2), 141, 1997.

Ostas, Daniel, T., and Loeb, Stephen E., 'Teaching Corporate Social Responsibility in Business Law and Business Ethics Classrooms,' *Journal of Legal Studies Education,* 20, 61–88, 2003.

Porter, Michael E., and Kramer, Mark R., 'The Competitive Advantage of Corporate Philanthropy,' *Harvard Business Review,* 80 (12), 57–68, 2002.

Prahalad, C. K., and Hammond, Allen, 'Serving the World's Poor, Profitably,' *Harvard Business Review,* 80 (9), 48–58, 2002.

Ramasamy, Bala, and Ting, Hung Woan, 'A Comparative Analysis of Corporate Social Responsibility Awareness,' *Journal of Corporate Citizenship,* 109, Spring 2004.

Roberts, Robin W., 'Determinants of Corporate Social Responsibility Disclosure: An Application of Stakeholder Theory,' *Accounting, Organizations and Society,* 17 (6), 595, 1992.

Samuelson, P. A., 'Love That Corporation,' *Mountain Bell Magazine,* Spring 1971.

Sarbutts, Nigel, 'Can SMEs "Do" CSR? A Practitioner's View of the Ways Small- and Medium-Sized Enterprises Are Able to Manage Reputation Through Corporate Social Responsibility,' *Journal of Communication Management,* 7 (4), 340, 2003.

Sethi, S. P., 'Dimensions of Corporate Social Performance: An Analytic Framework,' *California Management Review,* 58–64, Spring 1975.

Sethi, S. Prakash, 'A Conceptual Framework for Environmental Analysis of Social Issues and Evaluation of Business Response Patterns,' *Academy of Management Review,* 4 (1), 63–74, 1979.

Sharfman, Mark, 'Changing Institutional Roles: The Evolution of Corporate Philanthropy, 1883–1953,' *Business and Society,* 33 (3), 236, 1994.

Smith, N. Craig, 'Corporate Social Responsibility: Whether or How?' *California Management Review,* 45 (4), 52, 2003.

Stovall, O. Scott, Neill, John D., and Perkins, David, 'Corporate Governance, Internal Decision Making, and the Invisible Hand,' *Journal of Business Ethics,* 51 (2), 221–227, 2004.

Strand, R., 'A Systems Paradigm of Organizational Adaptations to the Social Environment,' *Academy of Management Review,* 8, 90–96, 1983.

Swanson, D. L., 'Addressing a Theoretical Problem by Reorienting the Corporate Social Performance Model,' *Academy of Management Review,* 20, 43–64, 1995.

Tuzzolino, E, and Armandi, B. R., 'A Need-hierarchy Framework for Assessing Corporate Social Responsibility,' *Academy of Management Review,* 6, 21–28, 1981.

Wartick, S. L., and Cochran, P. L., 'The Evolution of the Corporate Social Performance Model,' *Academy of Management Review,* 10, 758–769, 1985.

Windsor, Duane, 'The Future of Corporate Social Responsibility,' *International Journal of Organizational Analysis,* 9 (3), 225–256, 2001.

Wood, D. J., 'Corporate Social Performance Revisited,' *Academy of Management Review,* 16, 691–718, 1991.

Zenisek, T. J., 'Corporate Social Responsibility: A Conceptualization Based on Organizational Literature,' *Academy of Management Review,* 4, 359–368, 1979.

# INDEX

# ABOUT THE AUTHORS

**William B. Werther Jr.** is the Codirector of the Center for Nonprofit Management at the University of Miami. He is a Fellow and former Chair of the International Society for Productivity and Quality Research, a Fellow in the World Academy of Productivity Science, and former Chair for the Managerial Consultation Division of the Academy of Management. His teaching and research focus on strategy and its human resource and corporate social responsibility implications.

With 30 years of experience among nonprofit, government, and business organizations, *Fortune,* the *Wall Street Journal,* the *Washington Post,* and the *Nightly Business Report* (PBS) have sought his expertise. Public sector involvement includes work for the White House Conference on Productivity, the U.S. House of Representatives, NASA, and the Arizona State Senate. Private sector work includes Anheuser-Busch, Bell Canada, Citicorp, Fiat, IBM, State Farm, UPS, and scores of others.

He is an award-winning teacher and author of *Third Sector Management* (Georgetown University Press, 2001) and *Human Resources and Personnel Management* (McGraw-Hill, 1996, now in its fifth edition), in addition to more than 90 articles. He earned a PhD (University of Florida, 1971) in Economics and Business Administration (Phi Beta Kappa). Prior to joining the faculty at the University of Miami in 1985, he was a Professor of Management at Arizona State University for 14 years. Additionally, he teaches at the Universidade do Porto (Portugal), where he serves as Visiting Professor each spring.

**David Chandler** (MBA, University of Miami and MSc, East Asian Business, University of Sheffield, UK) is the Associate Director of the Center for Nonprofit Management at the University of Miami.

Since graduating with an undergraduate degree in American Studies: Politics and Government in 1991 (University of Kent, UK), he has divided his time between the United States, the UK, and Japan (he speaks Japanese), working in the fields of politics, education, and business.

He has a track record of execution and unique achievement in overcoming barriers in a variety of cultural, business, and political environments at the highest levels. His accomplishments in recent years include winning the 2004 *Miami Herald* Student Business Plan Contest; inventing the Japanese translation of the world's best-selling word game *Scrabble;*

publishing an award-winning book about the Japan Exchange and Teaching (JET) Program (the world's largest exchange program), in its second edition in Japan and also translated into Japanese (http://www.jetprogram.com/); securing a one-on-one meeting with Junichiro Koizumi, the Japanese prime minister, who wrote the forewords to the Japanese editions of his book; and acting as Japan agent for Chris Moon, internationally renowned motivational speaker and anti–land mine campaigner, who ran the Olympic torch into the Opening Ceremony stadium for the 1998 Winter Olympic Games.